Language and Globalization

Series Editors: **Sue Wright**, University of Portsmouth, UK and **Helen Kelly-Holmes**, University of Limerick, Ireland.

In the context of current political and social developments, where the national group is not so clearly defined and delineated, the state language not so clearly dominant in every domain, and cross-border flows and transfers affect more than a small elite, new patterns of language use will develop. The series aims to provide a framework for reporting on and analysing the linguistic outcomes of globalization and localization.

Titles include:

David Block
MULTILINGUAL IDENTITIES IN A GLOBAL CITY
London Stories

Jenny Carl and Patrick Stevenson (*editors*)
LANGUAGE, DISCOURSE AND IDENTITY IN CENTRAL EUROPE
The German Language in a Multilingual Space

Diarmait Mac Giolla Chríóst
LANGUAGE AND THE CITY

Julian Edge (*editor*)
(RE)LOCATING TESOL IN AN AGE OF EMPIRE

Aleksandra Galasińska and Michał Krzyżanowski (*editors*)
DISCOURSE AND TRANSFORMATION IN CENTRAL AND EASTERN EUROPE

Roxy Harris
NEW ETHNICITIES AND LANGUAGE USE

Jane Jackson
INTERCULTURAL JOURNEYS
From Study to Residence Abroad

Clare Mar-Molinero and Patrick Stevenson (*editors*)
LANGUAGE IDEOLOGIES, POLICIES AND PRACTICES
Language and the Future of Europe

Clare Mar-Molinero and Miranda Stewart (*editors*)
GLOBALIZATION AND LANGUAGE IN THE SPANISH-SPEAKING WORLD
Macro and Micro Perspectives

Ulrike Hanna Meinhof and Dariusz Galasinski
THE LANGUAGE OF BELONGING

Richard C. M. Mole (*editor*)
DISCURSIVE CONSTRUCTIONS OF IDENTITY IN EUROPEAN POLITICS

Leigh Oakes and Jane Warren
LANGUAGE, CITIZENSHIP AND IDENTITY IN QUEBEC

Colin Williams
LINGUISTIC MINORITIES IN DEMOCRATIC CONTEXT

Forthcoming titles:

John Edwards
CHALLENGES IN THE SOCIAL LIFE OF LANGUAGE

Helen Kelly-Holmes and Gerlinde Mautner
LANGUAGE AND THE MARKET

Mario Saraceni
THE RELOCATION OF ENGLISH

Christina Slade and Martina Mollering
FROM MIGRANT TO CITIZEN
Testing Language, Testing Culture

Language and Globalization
Series Standing Order ISBN   978–1–4039–9731–9 Hardback
                                        978–1–4039–9732–6 Paperback
                                        (*outside North America only*)

You can receive future titles in this series as they are published by placing a standing order. Please contact your bookseller or, in case of difficulty, write to us at the address below with your name and address, the title of the series and the ISBN quoted above.

Customer Services Department, Macmillan Distribution Ltd, Houndmills, Basingstoke, Hampshire RG21 6XS, England

Intercultural Journeys

From Study to Residence Abroad

Jane Jackson
The Chinese University of Hong Kong, Hong Kong

palgrave
macmillan

First published 2010 by
PALGRAVE MACMILLAN

Palgrave Macmillan in the UK is an imprint of Macmillan Publishers Limited, registered in England, company number 785998, of Houndmills, Basingstoke, Hampshire RG21 6XS.

Palgrave Macmillan in the US is a division of St Martin's Press LLC, 175 Fifth Avenue, New York, NY 10010.

Palgrave Macmillan is the global academic imprint of the above companies and has companies and representatives throughout the world.

Palgrave® and Macmillan® are registered trademarks in the United States, the United Kingdom, Europe and other countries

ISBN 978–0–230–52721–8   hardback

This book is printed on paper suitable for recycling and made from fully managed and sustained forest sources. Logging, pulping and manufacturing processes are expected to conform to the environmental regulations of the country of origin.

A catalogue record for this book is available from the British Library.

A catalog record for this book is available from the Library of Congress.

10 9 8 7 6 5 4 3 2 1
19 18 17 16 15 14 13 12 11 10

Printed and bound in Great Britain by
CPI Antony Rowe, Chippenham and Eastbourne

*For the Special English Stream explorers and other students
who cross languages and cultures on stays abroad*

Contents

List of Tables

Preface

Introduction

With the advent of accelerating globalization, cultural sensitivity and proficiency in more than one language are assuming higher levels of importance in higher education. Universities around the world are grappling with the question: How can they prepare their graduates for today's complex, interconnected world? In response, many institutions are developing study abroad programs to offer their students the opportunity to experience another culture and language firsthand. Many assume that this will automatically lead to enhanced intercultural understanding and greater proficiency in the host language. But is this the case?

What does it mean to be an "intercultural speaker" or "mediator" and how can one develop a deeper level of intercultural awareness and sensitivity? Why do some individuals return from study abroad with a broader, more intercultural, global identity while others reject the host environment and cling more tightly to their homeland and localized identity? Why do some enhance their second language (L2) proficiency while others do not? What can account for these different developmental trajectories?

These are some of the questions I have been asking myself in the last decade or so. Before I began researching study abroad in 2000, I would hear tales of Hong Kong exchange students who returned home with negative images of the host culture and a seemingly higher level of ethnocentricism. By contrast, others would beam with excitement when recounting their sojourn experiences and newfound love of travel. With enhanced self-confidence, these individuals would seek out opportunities to interact across cultures and use their L2 both at home and abroad. The contrast was startling.

Intercultural Journeys: From Study to Residence Abroad focuses on the actual experiences of advanced L2 students who traveled from their home environment to a foreign land as part of a faculty-led, short-term study abroad program.[1] This book explores the linkage between intercultural awareness and sensitivity, language development, and identity reconstruction in young adult L2 learners.

Overview of the book

The book comprises eight chapters. In Chapters 1 and 2, my aim is to provide theoretical background to my investigation of the language and cultural development of advanced L2 students. The remaining chapters focus on case studies of selected participants; their stories have implications for international education both at home and abroad.

In Chapter 1 I discuss the impact of globalization on institutions of higher education and the spread of English as an international language. Internationalization policies have led to increased opportunities for intercultural contact on home campuses and the proliferation of a great variety of study abroad programs. I explain how these developments have elevated the importance of intercultural communicative competence and intercultural sensitivity in both domestic and global contexts. Since short-term study abroad programs, in particular, have increased dramatically in recent years, it is important to understand what actually happens on programs of this nature. Can they propel participants to a higher level of intercultural sensitivity and L2 proficiency? What elements cultivate a more open, ethnorelative mindset? What factors appear to facilitate the development of intercultural communicative competence? Interculturality? Global citizenship?

In Chapter 2 I explore theoretical perspectives of interculturalists, L2 educators, and identity theorists in an effort to explain the complex connection between language, culture, and identity. I delve into the constructs of "interculturality" and "intercultural speaker" (e.g., Alred and Byram, 2002; Alred, Byram, and Fleming, 2003; Byram, 2003, 2008; P. M. Ryan, 2003, 2006) and link them to the notions of intercultural communicative competence (e.g., Byram, 1997; Fantini, 2007), intercultural sensitivity (Bennett and Bennett, 2004a; Bhawuk and Brislin, 1992), and sociopragmatic awareness (Rose and Kasper, 2001). I discuss several models of intercultural (communicative/communication/global) competence, including Byram's (1997) model of intercultural communicative competence, Chen and Starosta's (2008) model of intercultural communication competence, Deardorff's (2004) process model of intercultural competence, Hunter's (2004) model of global competence, and Bennett's (1993) Developmental Model of Intercultural Sensitivity (DMIS) in conjunction with poststructuralist notions of identity (re)construction (e.g., Block, 2007; Norton, 2000; Pavlenko and Lantolf, 2000). I then review recent studies that investigate the development of intercultural sensitivity/interculturality in study abroad students.

Chapter 3 outlines my investigation of the language, identity, and intercultural expansion of Hong Kong university students who took part in a short-term study abroad program in England. After explaining the home institution's internationalization policy, I describe the aims and components of the Special English Stream (SES), including unique presojourn, sojourn, and postsojourn elements. I then explain how I carried out my ethnographic investigation of the 2005 cohort, which made use of the Intercultural Development Inventory (IDI), a psychometric instrument which measures intercultural sensitivity as conceptualized in the DMIS (Hammer and Bennett, 2002; Hammer, Bennett, and Wiseman, 2003). After providing the profile of the full group, I explain why I decided to focus on four of the participants in this book. The selected young people, all of whom had an advanced proficiency in English, experienced different trajectories. Their stories offer insight into internal and external factors that may lead to differing outcomes. Why did some more fully embrace interculturality? Why did some develop more sociopragmatic awareness, intercultural communicative competence, and a global identity? What can we learn from their journeys?

Chapters 4 to 6 examine the developmental trajectories of the four case participants: Nora, Mimi, Lana, and Jade (pseudonyms). In Chapter 4, I compare and contrast their presojourn language ability and usage, self-identity, and (inter)cultural sensitivity. Throughout, I link their oral and written narratives and my field notes with their IDI scores (on entry into the SES and after the intensive presojourn preparation).

In Chapters 5 and 6 I focus on the young women's sojourn and reentry experiences. During their five-week stay in England, we see how they respond to the new environment and increased contact across cultures in English. In the process, we become familiar with each woman's level of self-awareness and reaction to cultural difference. After returning to Hong Kong, they offer further insight into the impact of the sojourn on their self-identity and language and (inter)cultural development. Chapter 5 focuses on Nora and Mimi, who began their journeys with the lowest levels of intercultural sensitivity among the four case participants. Chapter 6 explores the trajectories of Lana and Jade, who acquired higher levels of intercultural competence.

In Chapter 7 I summarize the key findings of my study and revisit the theoretical constructs and models that were discussed in Chapters 1 and 2. In particular, I challenge the rather naïve linkage between L2 development and intercultural sensitivity put forward by Bennett, Bennett, and Allen (2003). I also discuss the potential impact of inflated perceptions of intercultural sensitivity, a phenomenon that I observed in my participants.

Chapter 8 links theory with praxis. It focuses on the practical implications of my findings for the development of intercultural communicative competence and ethnorelativism in L2 students and others who cross cultures, both at home and abroad. In particular, I suggest ways to improve practices in the design, delivery, and evaluation of intercultural communication/L2 courses and study abroad programs for language learners. I emphasize the merits of experiential learning and systematic, critical reflection to promote interculturality and intercultural communicative competence in L2 speakers.

Each year that I investigate the learning of study abroad students, I learn more. While this book cannot resolve all issues related to interculturality, it does raise awareness of multiple factors that can result in different developmental pathways to intercultural communicative competence. I hope it will stimulate further interest and research and, ultimately, bring about enhanced international education for L2 students around the globe.

Acknowledgments

This study was generously supported by a direct grant from the Chinese University of Hong Kong (Ref. 2010288). I wish to express deep gratitude to the Special English Stream (SES) students who shared their experiences, thoughts, and feelings with me as they crossed languages and cultures. This study would not have been possible without their cooperation and candor. They remain anonymous for reasons of confidentiality. Thanks are also due to the research assistants who conducted/transcribed interviews or processed survey data: Chan Wai Nga (Gloria), Chan Ying Shan (Erica), Law She Kay (Lourdes), Liu Ka Ying (Queenie), Man Ming Yu (Laura), Pan Ping (Cathy), and Wong Kin Hung (Karen). I am also grateful to the series editors, Sue Wright and Helen Kelly-Holmes, and the anonymous reviewers who provided very thoughtful comments on an earlier draft of this book. Finally, I wish to thank Jill Bell, Priyanka Gibbons, and the production team at Palgrave Macmillan and MPS Limited (a Macmillan Company).

1
Globalization, Internationalization, and Study Abroad

Introduction

This chapter explores the relationship between globalization and the internationalization of higher education. I begin by defining what is meant by globalization, hybridity, and glocalization before discussing the rise of English as a global language and the emergence of global, hybrid identities. I then raise awareness about the multiple, complex effects of globalization on higher education policies and practice. I explore the wide range of internationalization strategies that institutions are employing to meet these growing challenges – both on home campuses and abroad. I explain how this has led to the proliferation of diverse study abroad programs and the spread of English as an international language of education in many parts of the world.

Intensification of globalization

Globalization is not new. The exchange of ideas, goods, and people has long been a feature of human history; however, what is different today is the dramatic increase in the speed and volume of this contact due to advances in information and communication technologies. The world is experiencing an unprecedented intensification of economic, cultural, political, and social interconnectedness (Held, McGrew, Goldblatt, and Perraton 1999). This trend is the subject of passionate debate as scholars put forward different conceptualizations and conflicting understandings of its consequences.

For Scholte (2000: 16), globalization entails "a process of removing government-imposed restrictions on movements between countries in order to create an 'open', 'borderless' world economy." Along the same lines, Rogers and Hart (2002: 12), characterize this phenomenon as "the degree to which the same set of economic rules applies everywhere in an increasingly interdependent world." Knight and de Wit (1997: 6) offer a broader conceptualization, defining globalization as "the flow of technology, economy, knowledge, people, values, [and] ideas ... across borders," while Appadurai (1990) simply depicts it as "a dense and fluid network of global flows." What binds many of these definitions together is the notion of "interconnectedness" and the compression of time and space.

For this book, I am adopting Inda and Rosaldo's (2006: 9) portrayal of globalization. Acknowledging the cultural dimension of this movement, these social scientists characterize it as "spatial-temporal processes, operating on a global scale that rapidly cut across national boundaries, drawing more and more of the world into webs of interconnection, integrating and stretching cultures and communities across space and time, and compressing our spatial and temporal horizons." This definition aptly captures the growing interdependence of societies and cultures that is giving rise to both challenges and opportunities, as Stephen Ryan (2006: 26) explains: "Globalization can be viewed as either an opportunity to be embraced, allowing people to break free from the stifling restrictions of nationality and tradition, or it can be construed as a threat, removing the security of familiar local networks and imposing an unwanted external uniformity." Whatever one's conception, positive or negative, globalization remains "the most powerful force shaping the world in the present and foreseeable future" (Lindahl, 2006: 8).

Glocalization, localization, and hybridity

In today's interdependent world, globalization is now intrinsically linked to localization, as Dissanayake (2006: 556) explains: "One of the defining features of the modern world is the increasingly complex and multifaceted interaction of localism and globalism. Clearly, this process has been going on for centuries, but its velocity has risen dramatically during the past half century." Owing to this "intensification of worldwide social relations," Giddens (1990: 64) maintains that "local happenings are shaped by events occurring many miles away and vice versa." In effect, globalization has led to profound changes in the economic, social, cultural, and political dimensions of communities on all continents. Underscoring the pervasive complexity of this process, McGrew (1992: 65) argues that "patterns of human interaction, interconnectedness and awareness are reconstituting the world as a single social space"; this is bringing about globalism – "subjectively internalized changes" in the way we view our everyday life (Cohen and Kennedy, 2000).

Some fear this "compression of the world" (Robertson, 1992), is leading to "standardization across cultures" and "greater levels of sameness" (McCabe, 2001: 140). For critics, this implies "the hegemony of the capitalist system" and "the domination of the rich nations over the poor" (Olson, Green, and Hill, 2006: vi). Hence, while many herald the acceleration of globalization, others condemn it as a modern form of colonialism (McCabe, 2001; Scharito and Webb, 2003).

Though negative connotations may summon fears of cultural homogenization, this is not an inevitable outcome. Knight and de Wit (1997: 6) insist that "globalization affects each country in a different way due to a nation's individual history, traditions, culture, and priorities." This localized response can lead to cultural hybridity, a phenomenon which Rowe and Schelling (1991: 231) define as "the ways in which forms become separated from existing practices and recombine with new forms in new practices." Through this dynamic, global process, diverse "cultural forms and practices intermingle and traverse across social boundaries" (Lam, 2006: 217) and are gradually combined into what Nederveen Pieterse (1994) refers to as a "global mélange" of cultures. For Kraidy (2005: 148), hybridity is the "cultural logic" of globalization, ensuring that "traces of other cultures exist in every culture." This process of glocalization is a byproduct of intercultural contact and communication and is forever changing cultural landscapes around the world. New practices continually emerge due to "a communicative confrontation between specific cultural forms of differently structured societies" (Baraldi, 2006: 54). What ensues is a dynamic, hybrid environment, providing further evidence that the impact of globalization is "neither fixed nor certain" (Dixon, 2006: 320).

World Englishes – the spread of a global language(s)

The reach of globalization extends well beyond the realm of trade, tourism, and commerce; it infiltrates the cultural fabric of societies and alters linguistic codes. Canagarajah (2005: 195–6) observes that globalizing forces have made "the borders of the nation state porous and reinserted the importance of the English language for all communities." Stephen Ryan (2006: 28) further argues that "globalization could not happen without its own language, and that language is unquestionably English."

The dominance of English on the world stage has never been greater: "English is not only a language of wider communication in the modern world, it is far more than that – it is, in a singularly powerful sense, *the* 'global language' of commerce, trade, culture, and research in the contemporary world" (Reagan and Schreffler, 2005: 116). With the emergence of the "knowledge society" or "knowledge economy", English has become the de facto lingua franca for scientific communication, business negotiations, diplomacy, academic conferences, and international education in many nations on all continents. In transforming English language learning and use into commodities for a global marketplace, the linguistic and cultural capital of English (Bourdieu, 1986, 1991) has evolved and grown exponentially in recent decades. As Lam (2006: 228) observes, "glocalized spaces of cultural and economic exchange are redefining the forms of cultural capital – embodied ways of knowing and reasoning, schemes of perception and appreciation (Bourdieu, 1986) – that some young people are developing."

The response to the spread of English is not uniform, however. In some quarters the language is considered a homogenizing, Western vehicle of power and privilege and is met with resistance and suspicion. In other regions, instead of rejecting English outright, local cultures are fashioning their own, hybrid form of the language (Kachru and Smith, 2008). Drawing on Pennycook's (2000) notion of postcolonial performativity, Lin and Martin (2005: 5) maintain that English today is "neither a Western monolithic entity nor necessarily an imposed reality"; in their view, "local peoples are capable of penetrating English with their own intentions and social styles." Consequently, the rise and dominance of the language internationally has not led to the adoption of a single form (e.g., British English). Globalization has brought about "a new society, in which English is shared among many groups of non-native speakers rather than dominated by the British or Americans" (Warschauer, 2000: 512) or what Kachru (1985) refers to as "the inner circle."[1] In many parts of the world, including Asia, there is a growing belief that "the English language belongs to all those who use it," as McConnell (2000: 145) explains:

> Many Asians insist that English belongs to all its speakers. They reject the idea that the standard varieties such as British, American, Canadian, or Australian are the only correct models. In their opinion, English must reflect the reality of their world. In this way, English fits into the pattern of multilingual societies like Singapore or the Philippines. These New Englishes are helping Asians to forget the unpleasant associations of English as the language of colonial oppression and cultural imperialism.

With increasing intercultural contact, new hybrid codes are continuing to emerge, reflecting local influences and character as well as the dominance of global forces. Kachru, Kachru, and Nelson (2006: xvii) draw our attention to "the expanding fusions and hybridizations of linguistic forms and the unprecedented variations in global functions of world Englishes." These scholars explain that "the colonial and post-colonial eras opened challenging new doors for contacts with a great variety of distinct linguistic structures and cultures associated with Asian, African, and Native American languages" (ibid.: xvii). In Singapore and India, for example, nativized, colloquial versions of English have emerged, providing new forms of insider identity. Accordingly, non-native bilingual speakers of English may now seek to be recognized as "competent, authoritative users of their own variety as opposed to imperfect or deficient speakers of British or American standard English" (Ferguson, 2008: 146). This "decentring" of the native speaker has profound implications for the learning and teaching of English in non-English-speaking countries, a development that is explored further in this chapter.

Englishization and code usage

The spread of English has greatly influenced linguistic behavior in many parts of the globe. For example, we are witnessing an increase in both code-switching[2] and code-mixing[3] among bilingual or emerging bilingual speakers in localities where English and other language(s) are used (Coulmas, 2005; Myers-Scotton, 2006; Swann, Deumert, Lillis, and Mesthrie, 2004; Trudgill, 2003). Further, as noted by McArthur (1998), English has become the most widely used language in the world for both code-mixing and code-switching styles of communication.

Kachru (2005), for example, observes that many South Asians routinely mix English with their mother tongue in both oral and written discourse (e.g., in informal conversations, newspapers). This practice may be motivated by multiple factors (e.g., sociolinguistic, psycholinguistic, literary, situational, pragmatic/instrumental, identity). "It is not necessarily for lack of competency that speakers switch from one language to another, and the choices they make are not fortuitous. Rather, just like socially motivated choices of varieties of one language, choices across language boundaries are imbued with social meaning" (Coulmas, 2005: 109). Kachru (2005: 114) agrees, adding that "the social value attached to the knowledge of English" in many situations may be even more important than instrumental motives.

When English is deemed "an indicator of status, modernization, mobility and 'outward-looking' attitude," South Asians (and other L2 speakers) may seek to enhance their social positioning by incorporating this international language into their discourse (Kachru, 2005: 114). Code-mixing then functions as "an index of social identity" (Myers-Scotton, 2006: 406) and prestige. In Hong Kong and Nigeria, for example, the desire for an elevated social status can motivate educated elites to use a mixture of English and the vernacular. Further, Trudgill (2003: 23) posits that code-mixing may serve as a strategy to project a dual identity: "that of a modern, sophisticated, educated person *and* that of a loyal, local patriot."

Interestingly, sociolinguists have discovered differences in the way that "non-English-speaking" communities and individuals respond to the mixing of the vernacular with English. Some are very receptive while others strongly resist this trend, especially in certain domains (e.g., at home). Consequently, both linguistic and social restrictions may influence code choices and attitudes (Coulmas, 2005; Myers-Scotton, 2006). In some social contexts or situations, for instance, speakers may switch less frequently to English or even shun code-mixing completely to maintain in-group ties and avoid being outgrouped. Conversely, "[s]peakers may attempt to use codes to renegotiate and perhaps resist the established identities, group loyalties, and power relations" (Canagarajah, 1999: 73). The relationship between code choice, identity, and culture is dynamic, complex, and context-dependent.

English as an international language (EIL)

Globalization necessitates a re-examination of long-held beliefs about language, language teaching, and learning, as well as language attitudes and motivation. With the trend toward world Englishes and a shift in ownership of the language, we are now witnessing the displacement of "native speaker" norms in the formal instruction of English in many non-English-speaking communities. Teaching English as a foreign language (TEFL) has traditionally focused on native-speaker models of a particular variety of the language (e.g., British or American English)[4] but this is gradually being replaced by the teaching of English as an international language[5] (EIL) (Alptekin, 2002; Brown, 2006; McKay, 2002, 2004; McKay and Bokhorst-Heng, 2008).

From Stephen Ryan's (2006: 24) perspective, "a language functioning on the global scale of present-day English alters our sense of ownership of the language; the distinctions between the learner and the user become blurred, and this in turn obscures the boundaries between the learner of a language and any target language community." This displacement of the native speaker is bringing about significant changes in the ways in which non-native speakers perceive the language and themselves, as Lamb (2004: 5) explains: "In the minds of learners, English may not be associated with particular geographical or cultural communities but with a spreading international culture incorporating (inter alia) business, technological innovation, consumer values, democracy, world travel, and the multifarious icons of fashion, sport and music."

Yashima (2009), for example, discovered that Japanese university students associate English with "the world around Japan" rather than a particular English-speaking country; this "international posture" can serve as a motivating force to learn the language. Since it is now common for nonnative speakers to communicate in English with other nonnative speakers who have a different first language (L1), EIL learners may prefer to speak a localized variety of English rather than a "native-speaker, standard" form of the language (e.g., Received Pronunciation). This phenomenon is evident in a growing number of postcolonial contexts (e.g., Singapore, Ghana, Hong Kong, Liberia, Indonesia). "[A]s English loses its association with particular Anglophone cultures and is instead identified with the powerful forces of globalization," Lamb (2004: 3) observes that "individuals may aspire towards a 'bicultural' identity which incorporates an English-speaking globally involved version of themselves in addition to their local L1-speaking self." It is to this notion of identity reconstruction that I now turn.

New global, hybrid identities

Globalization is now recognized as a significant impetus for change in ways of conceptualizing the world and one's place in it. As Kim (2008: 36) explains, due to this "web of interdependence," individuals are developing "an outlook on humanity that is not locked in a provincial interest of one's ascribed group membership, but one in which the individual sees himself or herself to be a part of a larger whole that includes other groups, as well." Stephen Ryan (2006: 31) further argues that, due to global forces, "an analysis of linguistic and cultural identity that is solely dependent on notions of nationality or ethnicity surely belongs in another era." Rizvi, Engel, Nandyala, Rutkowski, and

Sparks (2005: 12) also draw our attention to the linkage between globalization and novel forms of identity:

> Under the conditions of globalization ... discrete national cultural formations can no longer be taken for granted, as there is now an ever-increasing level of cultural interactions across national and ethnic communities. With the sheer scale, intensity, speed and volume of global cultural communication, the traditional link between territory and social identity has been broken, as people can more readily choose to detach identities from particular times, places, and traditions.

Increasingly, contemporary identity theorists feel compelled to take a fresh look at the multifaceted, evolving relationship between globalization and identity formation and change.

Critics warn that globalization is leading to "homogenizing tendencies" (McCabe, 2001), including "the loss of national identity and culture" (Olson et al., 2006: vi). Others disagree. "Some homogenisation of taste does appear to be a concomitant of globalisation, but there is little evidence that globalisation is eradicating identities and local practices" (Ferguson, 2008: 144). In certain communities, for instance, Rizvi (2007) observes that we are actually witnessing the "resurgence of localized cultural identities" as well as "the development of globalized cultural practices." In some localities, global forces are "opening a space for new identities and contesting established values and norms" (Stromquist and Monkman, 2000: 110). Ferguson (2008: 144) concurs, noting that globalization "makes possible new identities, adding an additional layer to what is already available." Increased border crossings and intercultural contact, in Hall's (1992) view, have had a "pluralizing" effect on identity (re)construction, resulting in a plethora of hyphenated identities which are now less "fixed or unified." For S. Ryan (2006: 31), globalization offers "opportunities to develop a social identity as a full-fledged member of a global community," extending oneself beyond the local.

Globalization, from Lam's (2006: 218) perspective, is "creating greater fluidity and multiplicity in the identity formation of young people" as they have greater access to other cultures through the media and Internet than previous generations. She explains that "learning takes place within this globalized context in the form of intercultural practices wherein young people draw upon and reshape diverse cultural materials, develop multisite and multilayered identifications, and navigate the overlapping and dividing lines among cultures, ethnicities, languages, and nations" (ibid.: p. 228). This is giving rise to an appreciation of "intercultural capital" and the creation of multiple, "cosmopolitan identities."

Whatever one's stance, it is impossible to deny that increased contact between diverse cultures, whether through face-to-face interaction or hypermedia, is transforming how we define ourselves. Novel, hybrid identities are emerging, giving rise to a range of conflicting emotions and affiliations. At times, people may experience pangs of insecurity, fear, and disequilibrium, while, at others, they may take steps to embrace a broader, more inclusive global self.

English as an emblem of a global identity

The unique status of English as a global language plays a key role in identity reconstruction. Recognizing the conflicting nature and pressures of globalization, Kramsch (1999: 131) argues that "the global spread of English challenges learners of English to develop both a global and a local voice." Other applied linguists (e.g., Arnett, 2002; Lamb, 2004; Pavlenko and Norton, 2007; S. Ryan, 2006, 2009) observe that this global language can link EIL learners with a dynamic, "imagined community" of world citizens. Young people in non-English-speaking countries may develop global hybrid identities that fuse "local and global values" and "override other social identities, such as nationality and ethnicity" (Arnett, 2002: 33). As their "global self" becomes an integral part of their identity, they may deepen their investment in mastering English, the language which functions as an emblem of their international persona.

This phenomenon is in line with a poststructuralist orientation, which regards identities as "socially constructed, self-conscious, ongoing narratives that individuals perform, interpret and project in dress, bodily movements, actions and language" (Block, 2007: 27). Basically, as people come face to face with the effects of globalization (e.g., unequal power relations, English as a lingua franca, increased intercultural contact in their home environment and beyond), they are pressed to negotiate new subject positionings in diverse discursive contexts. This fluid, dynamic sense of "multiple selves" contrasts sharply with structuralists' interpretation of identity as fixed and constant. Describing identity as "a complex and multilayered construct," Block (2007: 27) maintains that individuals are not only "shaped by their sociohistories," they also "shape their sociohistories as life goes on." The notions of power and agency, limitations and affordances are addressed further in Chapter 2.

The impact of globalization on the internationalization of higher education

"Economic, political, and societal forces," according to Altbach and Knight (2007: 290), are also "pushing 21st century higher education toward greater international involvement." In particular, accelerating globalization has led to increased investment in knowledge industries (e.g., higher education, scientific training) to meet the demand for highly educated individuals who can interrelate effectively with people from different cultures and succeed in the competitive, global marketplace (Dolby, 2007; Pang, 2006; Turner and Robson, 2008).

With increasing global interdependency and new challenges facing graduates, institutions of higher education around the world are reassessing their mission and responsibilities. Most feel obliged to address the following questions: How can we best prepare our students to become global citizens and professionals in today's diverse world? How might we help them become internationally knowledgeable and interculturally competent? What can we do to provide students with a transformative international education? What action should we take to help faculty enhance their intercultural competence? How can we attract students and faculty from other countries to our campus?

The policy-based response of many is internationalization, which Kälvermark and van der Wende (1997: 19) define as "any systematic sustained effort aimed at making higher education more responsive to the requirements and challenges related to the globalization of societies, economy and labor markets." More specifically, it entails "the process of integrating an international, intercultural or global dimension into the purpose, functions or delivery of post-secondary education" (Knight, 2004: 11). Different from globalization, internationalization is "more oriented toward bilateral and/or multilateral processes involving knowledge of specific countries, which leads to the development of business, educational, social, and cultural relationships" (McCabe, 2001: 141). For the purposes of this book, globalization and internationalization are considered dynamically linked concepts, whereby the former serves as "the catalyst" and the latter is "a response in a proactive way" (Knight, 1999).

As a by-product of the social, cultural, political, academic, and economic challenges posed by globalization (Knight and de Wit, 1999; Taylor, 2004), institutions of higher education are taking steps to attract international students to their home campus. Some are motivated by the desire or need to generate additional revenue. Others wish to attract talent from abroad and stress the benefits for local students who will gain more exposure to other cultures and languages. Many institutions are also undergoing restructuring to embed an international dimension into their teaching and research. At minimum, on a pragmatic level, they recognize that students and faculty must be better equipped to contribute to their nation's effectiveness and competitiveness on the international stage. Increasingly, institutions also acknowledge the importance of mindful intercultural communication to promote peace, stability, and cooperation in the world. This is heightening awareness of the need for enhanced intercultural understanding and skills to stimulate personal and professional development and responsible global citizenship.

Internationalization through global learning outcomes and assessment

As institutions turn their attention to the preparation of globally competent students (and faculty), increasing numbers are recognizing the importance of defining what this actually means. International educators and administrators in diverse localities are now grappling with the following issues: What knowledge, attitudes, and skills do students need in order to be globally and interculturally competent? What experiences, at home and abroad (both inside and outside the classroom) promote this kind of learning? How can faculty enhance their own global literacy?[6] How can they incorporate innovative, effective internationalization strategies into their curricula? How should intercultural and global competences be assessed?

The posing of these questions is a significant step forward. All too often institutions have been preoccupied with increasing student participation in internationalization activities (e.g., study abroad) without "delineating and documenting the desired outcomes of these activities for students" (Olson, Green, and Hill, 2005: 9). The same can be said for faculty exchange programs, where the focus has often been on the number who take part rather than on what they've actually gained from the experience. Moreover, until recently, many institutions overlooked ways in which returning students and faculty can share their new understandings with those who remain on their home campus.

It is imperative that institutions formulate comprehensive, integrative policies to guide, unify, and sustain their internationalization efforts both on home soil and abroad. When devising these plans, Knight (2003: 17) maintains that policy-makers must consider the following questions: "Is internationalization a vehicle for increased understanding and appreciation of cultural diversity and fusion or is it an agent of cultural homogenization? How do the curriculum, teaching/learning process, research, extra-curricular activities and academic mobility contribute to intercultural understanding and cultural hybridization/homogenization?" Rizvi (2007) further argues that a curriculum approach must provide students with "skills of inquiry and analysis rather than a set of facts about globalization." This necessitates a comprehensive, integrative, strategic approach in the planning, implementation, and evaluation of internationalization efforts. Hence, van der Wende (1994) calls for internationalization strategies to affect the following three levels of education: micro (teaching and learning processes in classroom settings); medio (curriculum design and development, including factors that determine teaching and learning content/ methods); and macro (decision making related to institutional policies and practices).

Owing to local culture, history, politics, priorities, and resources, institutions of higher education are adopting a very diverse range of aims and strategies. The Working Group on Assessing International Learning, sponsored by the American Council on Education, has developed a list of international learning outcomes that is providing direction for the formulation of goals and international education assessment initiatives in North America and beyond. (For further information about this project, see www.acenet.edu/programs/international.) In response to increasing demands for greater accountability, the American-based Forum on Education Abroad has published *A Guide to Outcomes Assessment in Education Abroad* (Bolen, 2007); this edited collection promotes the systematic documentation of learning outcomes in study abroad. As part of their Quality Improvement Program, the Forum has also developed *Standards of Good Practice for Education Abroad*, including a code of ethics (see www.fea.org). Similar efforts are underway in Europe where the "Bologna process"[7] is leading to sweeping reforms in international education in European institutions of higher education (e.g., the setting of specific learning outcomes, internal and external quality assurance, international accreditation processes) (Verlag, 2006).

To help students develop "an imagination that is both self-reflexive and critical" (Rizvi, 2007), an expanding number of institutions of higher education are incorporating critical thinking skills into the learning experience. As institutions play a strategic role in the formation of citizens and future professionals, Schoorman (1999) advocates the adoption of critical pedagogy to achieve these learning outcomes. This can help prepare students to work and gain citizenship in a global community while simultaneously promoting diverse cultural traditions in teaching and learning. Gacel-Ávila (2005: 125) observes that this approach fosters "students' awareness of a global perspective on human problems" and helps them "to recognize and respect cultural differences."

For Olson et al. (2005: iv), internationalization requires "a strategy that integrates attention to *inputs* (institutional goals, strategies, and activities) with attention to *outputs* (outcomes and measures of student learning)." This approach provides a crucial, but often overlooked, link between an institution's internationalization initiatives and the attitudes, knowledge, and skills that students are expected to develop. As critical engagement, innovation, and self-reflexivity are pedagogically important, assessment practices must be put in place that reward these elements of student learning.

In some institutions, internationalization efforts focus on their home campus; others offer study abroad programs or exchanges abroad, or both. In some cases, strategies and activities at home and abroad are connected and fully integrated, while in others, they remain separate domains (e.g., Anderson, 2005; Cushner and Karim, 2004; Green and Olson, 2003; Naidoo, 2006; Pang, 2006; Teichler, 2004). The following sections offer insight into the growing range of options available today.

Internationalization at Home (IaH)

The term "Internationalization at Home" (IaH) refers to "the embedding of international/intercultural perspectives into local educational settings" (Turner and Robson, 2008: 15) in order to raise the global awareness and intercultural understanding of faculty and "non-mobile" students. Through a variety of measures, IaH initiatives aim to prepare individuals for life in an interconnected world whereby contact with people from other cultures (e.g., face-to-face, e-mail) is increasingly the norm (Beelen, 2007; Dunstan, 2003; Nilsson, 2003; Paige, 2003; Rizvi, 2006; Teekens, 2003, 2007). In recognition of its importance in the field of international education, in 2003 a special issue of the *Journal of Studies in International Education*, edited by Bengt Nilsson and Matthias Otten, focused on IaH initiatives. Linking theory with practice, contributors discuss institutional policies and provide descriptive case studies of IaH initiatives (e.g., internationalized curricula, intercultural learning both in and outside the classroom).

On an institutional level, strategic plans are being developed and implemented to weave an IaH dimension into curricula and organizational practices. Leaders in higher education (e.g., presidents, vice presidents, deans, provosts, directors) are being called on to maximize the global learning of their students, including those who remain on their home campus throughout their studies. The European Association for International Education (EAIE) has a special interest group devoted to IaH and an increasing number of European universities (e.g., in Scandinavia, the Netherlands) have designated IaH a key element in their internationalization policies. In the United States, NAFSA: Association of International Educators created a clearinghouse to promote the sharing of best internationalization efforts at institutions of higher education, including policy-level initiatives (www.nafsa.org/statelevel). Through the Senator Paul Simon Award for Campus Internationalization, NAFSA annually recognizes selected US institutions that demonstrate "overall excellence in internationalization efforts as evidenced in practices, structures, philosophies, and policies" (www.nafsa.org/about.sec/leadership_recognition/senator_simon_award).

For academic faculty, IaH may consist of departmental discussions about what constitutes global learning in a particular discipline, mentoring programs on global education, and workshops, retreats, or lectures that focus on intercultural communication or ways to enhance the design, delivery, and evaluation of international curricula (O'Donovan and Mikelonis, 2005; Olson et al., 2006). The integration of a global perspective into curricula and modes of assessment can be a very dynamic, creative process. At the University of Minnesota, for example, multidisciplinary teams employ a "transformational model"[8] through a series of workshops and retreats with faculty. Their aim is to build an international dimension into the scope and sequence of on-campus courses. Similar efforts are underway in Canada at Malaspina University-College, where week-long "Internationalizing the curriculum" workshops are held annually to facilitate the sharing of internationalization findings and practices among faculty (Wilkie, 2007).

IaH may promote deep collaboration between scholars and faculty members from diverse backgrounds (e.g., team teaching, curriculum design and development). Through research or education grants, faculty may be encouraged to take part in applied, collaborative international research, or international assessment projects. To stimulate IaH initiatives among faculty, some institutions are formally recognizing innovative global practice (Olson et al., 2006). As well as the professional development of faculty, IaH may include the orientation, mentoring, and integration of foreign teaching assistants into campus life.

For students, IaH usually consists of courses and programs that have an international, intercultural, global, or comparative dimension (e.g., a "globalized" curriculum, L2 education, area, regional, or cultural studies), work placements or projects at international organizations, and the integration of local and international students both in and outside class. Relevant extracurricular activities include international student clubs and organizations and/or international and intercultural events on campus. Students may be actively encouraged to take part in local cultural and ethnic community organizations through internships, placements, course projects, and applied research. In some courses, participation in these international activities may be credit-bearing. Instructional technology may also facilitate IaH learning and intercultural contact (e.g., lectures may be delivered by virtual visiting professors, students may use their L2 to collaborate on projects with counterparts at a foreign university, the World Wide Web may connect students with foreign libraries and access databases). The possibilities for virtual intercultural contact are changing the landscape of IaH as university students on their home campus are "traveling" to other lands through the Internet.

Owing to globalizing forces and the dominance of English on the world stage, many institutions with a less widely spoken language are offering English language training and English-medium courses on their home campus. These initiatives are driven by a range of goals (e.g., to raise their profile on the world stage, to attract international students and secure more funding through tuition revenue, to create a more diverse, international environment at home, to provide local students with enhanced opportunities for contact with other languages and cultures).

This trend cuts across disciplinary boundaries. Nowadays, it is possible to study a wide variety of subjects in English in a growing number of non-English-speaking countries, including Finland (e.g., business administration), India (e.g., applied information technology), Sweden (e.g., engineering), China (e.g., medicine), Russia (e.g., engineering), South Africa (e.g., law and management), United Arab Emirates (e.g., liberal arts), and Mexico (Teaching English as Foreign Language Training). It is even possible to do a full-degree in this international language in many non-English-speaking countries. For example, Finland now has more than 100 bachelor's programs in English; the Netherlands offers

940 undergraduate and postgraduate degree programs, Germany has 350, and Sweden offers 450 master's degree programs (Altbach, 2008; Forrest, 2008; West, 2008). Further, universities in Asia and Latin America have established degree programs in English to attract international students.

Supporters of this development stress the economic and intellectual benefits for host nations, including increased access to scientific knowledge and enhanced opportunities for global networking. This is not the full picture, however. As Knight (2007: 59) observes, critics lament the "commercialization and commodification" of education programs whereby English-medium teaching is driven by financial imperatives. Further, the spread of English, as noted earlier, is considered by some to be a threat to local identities and character. As Altbach (2008: 59) explains, "Not only is English the dominant language, but its relationship with the controlling trends in international science and scholarship is a powerful combination of forces contributing to decreasing diversity of themes and methodologies." The role of English as the leading language of internationalization remains contentious in some quarters.

Internationalization abroad/cross-border education/transnational education

Internationalization abroad activities, which are sometimes referred to as cross-border education or transnational education,[9] involve the movement of people, education courses, programs, education providers, and projects, whether these activities are through virtual or physical movement, or through exchange agreements, government or privately subsidized programs, commercial for-profit initiatives, nonprofit ventures, or a combination of agreements (Knight, 2003; McBurnie and Ziguras, 2006). In recent years there has been an unprecedented growth in distance and e-learning education that crosses national boundaries. This dimension "encompasses a wide range of aspects of international activity at policy, managerial, and practice levels" (Turner and Robson, 2008: 15). For Rauhvargers (2001: 28), transnational education includes "all types of higher education study programmes or educational services (including distance education) in which the learners are located in a country different from the one in which the awarding institution is based."

The internationalization of faculty

For faculty, academic mobility may involve educators going abroad for professional development or international exchange. The Fulbright

Teacher Exchange Program, for instance, provides opportunities for American faculty to teach in another country for six weeks, a semester, or a full academic year. The Fulbright-Hays Faculty Research Abroad Fellowship offers support for American faculty who conduct research in modern foreign languages and area studies in order to enhance their competency in the language and their knowledge of the host culture. In Europe, the European Community Action Scheme for the Mobility of University Students (the ERASMUS program)[10] facilitates the mobility and exchange of faculty in 31 European countries. Increasingly, nations and individual institutions of higher education across the globe have their own exchange agreements with foreign counterparts to facilitate international exchange and cooperation.

Each year, the Council on International Educational Exchange (CIEE) offers intensive faculty development seminars to encourage participants to incorporate an international dimension or global perspective into their course design, research, or administration when they return to their home campus. CIEE seminars have been hosted in a wide range of countries including the United Arab Emirates and Oman, Mongolia, Ghana, and Turkey. These educational site visits raise awareness about such diverse global issues as conflict management; development amid the HIV/AIDS pandemic; language policy and planning; contemporary educational reform and the role of women in Islamic countries; and interfaith dialogue.

In institutions of higher education, funding may facilitate collaborative, international research, global/intercultural curriculum development projects, or international assessment projects on foreign soil. These initiatives provide the opportunity for academics to establish ties with scholars from another country, exposing both parties to new ideas and practices. Faculty may also participate in development projects in a range of disciplines and countries (e.g., teacher education in Vietnam, L2 programs in China, curriculum development in Bangladesh, technological training in Egypt, health care in Botswana, international business/trade in Cambodia).

Program mobility

Program mobility may consist of academic courses delivered abroad without students having to leave their home country. Offshore programs such as twinning arrangements and satellite campuses are becoming popular. With a branch model, an offshore campus may be set up in another country, often with some form of foreign investment

(Naidoo, 2006; Verbik, 2007). In 2005, the Observatory on Borderless Higher Education identified nearly 100 offshore campuses, including joint ventures whereby the hosting institution is a partner and uses the name of the foreign institution (McBurnie and Ziguras, 2006). In many cases the mother institution is a top-tier university in its home country. In a twinning arrangement, an institution delivers a degree program on foreign soil that is similar to the one offered on the home campus or is slightly modified (Kritz, 2006; Schuerholz-Lehr, 2007). Program partnerships, in which universities, polytechnics or vocational training colleges in two or more countries collaborate on a specific academic program, are being developed in many regions of the world. Distance education, in which all or most of a program is delivered on foreign soil via the Internet or by videoconferencing, has also grown in popularity.

Brand name American universities such as MIT (Massachusetts Institute of Technology), Stanford, and NYU (New York University) offer on-site dual-degree and joint research opportunities in Singapore (Rubin, 2008). NYIT (New York Institute of Technology) has branch campuses in Bahrain, Jordan, the United Arab Emirates, Brazil, Canada, and China. Qatar has become an education hub in the Arabian Gulf by hosting branch campuses of five well-known American institutions: Carnegie Mellon University, Georgetown University's School of Foreign Service, Virginia Commonwealth University, Texas A&M University, and Weill Cornell Medical College (Dessoff, 2007; Lewin, 2008). Further, Boston's Suffolk University has branch campuses in Spain and Senegal, to name a few.

Institutions in other nations are also branching out. For example, Australia's Monash University offers full-degree programs in Malaysia and South Africa. In partnership with Xi'an Jiaotong University, the University of Liverpool in the UK has recently opened a new campus in Suzhou, China, while England's University of Nottingham has a branch in Malaysia. In 2002, Queen's University in Ontario, Canada opened the country's first international law program abroad. Canadian and European lecturers and senior legal advisors jointly teach at the University's International Study Centre in East Sussex, England (Wilkie, 2007). Malaysia's University College of Technology and Innovation has overseas campuses in Pakistan, Sri Lanka, India, and Australia. In the United Arab Emirates, Dubai has created the "Knowledge Village"; education providers include institutions from the UK, India, Australia, Belgium, and Ireland.

Branch campuses can help mother institutions cultivate international relationships, enhance their standing on the world stage, and generate additional revenue through tuition and agreements with hosting countries; however, their proliferation is not without critics. International educators (e.g., Dessoff, 2007; Lewin, 2008; McBurnie and Ziguras, 2006; Rauhvargers, 2001) are raising troubling questions about quality assurance, academic integrity, and the appropriateness of transplanted curricula. In response, the UNESCO/Council of Europe Working Party devised a Code of Good Practice for the Provision of Transnational Education in European countries (see www.eaie.org).

In the case of branch campuses, concern is also being voiced about the global education of students and faculty who remain on home soil instead of venturing abroad to further their education. McBurnie and Ziguras (2006: 37) caution that "it cannot be assumed that an international branch campus automatically provides its graduates with an international outlook." For this reason, they advocate that all institutions "be creatively committed to promoting student and staff mobility, an internationalized curriculum and strategies for internationalization at home, wherever home may be" (ibid.: 37).

Student mobility

An area of significant growth in international education is student mobility whereby the participants go abroad for educational purposes, that is, to study, teach, do research, or participate in apprenticeships. Initiatives in this domain take diverse forms: direct exchange programs between institutions in different countries, field schools (e.g., anthropology, environmental engineering, art and design, architecture, cultural studies), internships or service learning[11] in a foreign country (e.g., in business, health sciences), volunteering/working abroad, study abroad (with multiple variations, including duration), international research, and collaborative development projects with students/institutions abroad.

To complicate matters, the terms used for these various options may differ. As noted by Peterson, Engle, Kenney, Kreutzer, Nolting, and Ogden (2007: 163), "Semantic ambiguity has long plagued the education abroad profession." In an effort to standardize terms and facilitate comparisons of international education and study abroad programs and research, in 2006 the Forum on Education Abroad established a task force to develop a glossary (see www.forumea.org; Peterson et al., 2007). The primary audience is American education abroad professionals and faculty as well as receiving institutions who host American students on study abroad programs. Some effort is made to contrast terms and definitions with those employed in the UK and other countries. The study abroad definitions and terms used in the remainder of this book are generally consistent with the Forum on Education Abroad's glossary.

In 2007 there were 3 million students enrolled in higher education outside their home countries (OECD, 2007) and UNESCO estimates that this number will rise to almost 8 million by 2025 (Davis, 2003). While some join "year abroad" programs, many more are now taking part in short-term sojourns or internships, ranging from four to seven weeks or micro-sojourns lasting three weeks or less (Chieffo and Griffiths, 2003; Edwards, Hoffa, and Kanach, 2005; Spencer and Tuma, 2008). The amount of presojourn preparation, ongoing sojourn support, and reentry debriefing provided ranges from none at all to the integration of credit-bearing components into the undergraduate curriculum in the home institution.

There are many other variations in these study abroad programs, including housing options (e.g., homestays; residence in a dormitory; living alone; sharing an apartment with host nationals, students from one's own country, or a mix of international students from other countries). Some programs may be faculty-led, whereby an instructor or professor from the home institution accompanies a cohort abroad, an option that is becoming increasingly common for American students. For example, an American business professor may travel to the host culture with a group of students and teach in an international management or marketing program alongside host nationals. Students may also venture abroad to enhance their foreign language proficiency and/or understanding of another culture. They may travel on their own or with peers and join an intensive foreign language immersion program at a language institute attached to a university or a commercial language center.

In addition to short-term sojourns, institutions are establishing exchange agreements with foreign counterparts, providing more opportunities for students to go abroad on their own for a semester or academic year. Sojourners may then join host nationals and other international students in classes. While some exchange students take courses in a L2 (e.g., the language of the host country), others may continue to study in their L1 (e.g., medicine in English). For example, as noted previously, due to globalization and internationalization, a growing number of non-English-speaking countries are offering international students exposure to local (and global) course content in English-medium courses.

Conclusions

The trend of global interdependence presents opportunities as well as challenges for communities, institutions, and individual citizens on all continents. Today's ever-changing world increasingly demands global competency, effective intercultural communication skills, and linguistic ability in English, the global language of the twenty-first century. Globalizing forces have accelerated the pace of internationalization in institutions of higher education both at home and on foreign soil. This has brought about a dramatic increase in the number and diversity of study abroad programs, including short-term sojourns. Chapter 2 delves into potential outcomes of internationalization and the need for institutions to define what is meant by global competence and intercultural communicative competence.

2
Intercultural and Global Competencies

Introduction

In this chapter I examine key theoretical concepts related to culture and the development of intercultural and global competencies, paying particular attention to L2 speakers. After defining the multifarious concept of culture, I explore the relationship between interculturality, intercultural contact, and the constructs of "the intercultural speaker" and "intercultural mediator." I then review current theoretical models that address the following questions: What are the attributes and behaviors of an interculturally competent communicator? What does it mean to be globally competent? What roles do intercultural sensitivity and host language proficiency play in the development of intercultural communicative competence? I conclude by reviewing empirical studies that center on the developmental trajectories of L2 sojourners.

Culture and agency

Culture has been defined in numerous ways by scholars from a variety of disciplines. Among intercultural communication theorists, it has traditionally been thought to encompass the learned and shared values, beliefs, and behaviors of a human group (Gudykunst, 2004; Lustig and Koester, 2006). Kroeber and Kluckhohn (1952: 181) offer the following definition, drawing on more than 150 interpretations of this construct:

> Culture consists of patterns, explicit and implicit, of and for behavior acquired and transmitted by symbols, constituting the distinctive achievements of human groups, including their embodiments

in artifacts; the essential core of culture consists of traditional (i.e., historically derived and selected) ideas and especially their attached values; culture systems may, on the one hand, be considered as products of action, on the other as conditioning elements of further action.

This set of collective meanings and understandings (e.g., learned ways of thinking, expressing emotions) is believed to provide a common frame of reference to help members of a culture adapt to their environment, make sense of their world, coordinate their activities, and construct cultural identities. For example, behavioral expectations and scripts (e.g., "cultural knowledge" about norms of politeness, greeting rituals) help people function in their social, cognitive, and physical environs. This view of culture as "accumulated, shared knowledge" is in accord with the following definition that was formulated by Seelye (1997: 23), an applied linguist, who sought to capture the relationship between language and culture. He defines culture as:

> the systematic, rather arbitrary, more or less coherent, group-invented and group-shared creed from the past that defines the shape of "reality," and assigns the sense and worth of things; it is modified by each generation and in response to adaptive pressures; it provides the code that tells people how to behave predictably and acceptably, the cipher that allows them to derive meaning from language and other symbols, the map that supplies the behavioral options for satisfying human needs.

Challenging traditional notions of culture as "unproblematically shared," Moon (2008: 17) vigorously argues that individual voices are neither recognized nor validated in this orientation, as "differences within national boundaries, ethnic groups, genders, and races are obscured." From this critical theorist's perspective, the "contested nature of 'culture' often gets lost in homogenizing views of 'culture as nationality' where dominant cultural voices are often the only ones heard, where the 'preferred' reading of 'culture' is the only reading" (ibid.: 16). Kramsch (2002: 277) concurs, noting that "hegemonic" definitions of culture fail to fully capture its "fluid, changing, and conflictual" nature. Giroux (1992: 26) also maintains that culture involves "lived antagonistic relations within a complex of socio-political institutions and social forms that limit as well as enable human action." Along similar lines, Sehlaoui (2001: 43) prefers to define culture as "a dynamic process within a given social context in which individuals are in a constant struggle for representation and the need to have an authentic voice." For García Canclini (2006: 126),

> [t]he cultural encompasses the whole of the processes through which we represent and imaginatively intuit the social. We conceive of and negotiate our relationships with others, that is, the differences; we order their dispersion and their incommensurability through a delimitation that fluctuates between the order that makes functioning in society (local and global) possible and the actors that open it up to the possible.

While every member of a human group acquires a segment of the collective understandings of a culture, Kashima (2000) cautions that no single individual in the group has a complete grasp of all of this knowledge. Moreover, as Chiu and Hong (2006: 18–19) assert, people are not mere "passive recipients of cultural influence." Rather, they are "active agents who strive to adapt to their physical environment" in order to "live a productive and a harmonious life with other members in their group." For these social psychologists, culture is "both a product [of collaborative action] and a signature of human agency" (ibid.: 19). Instead of simply embracing messages from a culture, in the course of daily life people both "reproduce" and "refine" culture (Chiu and Hong, 2006). This perspective recognizes diversity within cultures (e.g., differences in values, practices, preferred identities, strength of membership affiliations) and the element of change.

In this age of accelerating globalization, traditional, homogenizing notions of culture which lock people into categories (e.g., ethnic labels, national cultures) are outmoded and inappropriate. Increased intercultural contact, multiple discourses, and the evolution of hybrid, fluid identities, compel us to acknowledge the dynamic and conflictual nature of culture today. These global developments and new insights have significant implications for intercultural communication theories and practice.

What is interculturality? What does it mean to be interculturally literate?

My understanding of interculturality, of being intercultural, draws on many disciplines, including social psychology, L2 education, intercultural communication, speech communication, anthropology, sociology, and linguistics. Educators and theorists in these fields have offered their own unique ideas about what it means to be intercultural.

Framing interculturality as "an aspiration rather than a reality," Schmelkes (2006: 3) maintains that this construct "assumes that between cultural groups there are relations based upon respect and equality." More specifically, this position "rejects asymmetries; that is, inequalities between cultures measured by power that benefit one cultural group above another or others." Correspondingly, Leclercq (2003: 9) defines interculturality as "the set of processes through which relations between different cultures are constructed," whereby "[t]he aim is to enable groups and individuals who belong to such cultures within a single society or geopolitical entity to forge links based on equity and mutual respect."

How might this ideal be achieved in practice? What steps can be taken to foster what Heyward (2002: 10) refers to as intercultural literacy – "the understandings, competencies, attitudes, language proficiencies, participation and identities necessary for successful cross-cultural engagement"? For Alred, Byram, and Fleming (2006), L2 specialists, becoming intercultural (or "interculturally literate") entails the following process:

- Questioning the conventions and values we have unquestioningly acquired as if they were natural
- Experiencing the Otherness of Others of different social groups, moving from one of the many in-groups to which we belong to one of the many out-groups that contrast with them
- Reflecting on the relationships among groups and the experience of those relationships
- Analyzing our intercultural experience and acting upon the analysis (p. 1)

Interculturality, from Alred et al.'s (2006: 2) standpoint, "challenges us to be willing to become involved with Otherness, to take up others' perspectives by reconstructing their perspectives for ourselves, and understanding them from within … it does not imply abandoning our own perspectives but rather becoming more conscious of them." This is in accord with Bredella's (2003: 228) observation that "an indispensable feature of the intercultural experience is that we refrain from imposing our categories and values on others but instead learn to reconstruct their frame of reference and see them as they see themselves."

This orientation emphasizes differences between in-groups (people who identify and associate with each other due to religious, ethnic, social, or cultural bonds) and out-groups (people who are regarded as outsiders by in-group members). If one is to respond to intercultural experiences in a sensitive, respectful manner, these scholars maintain that an awareness of Self and Other is imperative. Moreover, those who cross cultures must actively engage in critical reflection and analysis. As Alred, Byram, and Fleming (2003: 4) explain being intercultural involves "both the awareness of experiencing otherness and the ability to analyse the experience and act upon the insights into self and other which the analysis brings."

Interculturality and the intergroup contact theory

Does intercultural contact necessarily lead to enhanced appreciation and respect for other cultures? Will it reduce prejudice? Will contact across cultures automatically generate greater intercultural under-standing and friendship? Do stays abroad facilitate the development of a more inclusive, intercultural mindset? Expanding on the work of Williams (1947), Allport (1954), a cross-cultural psychologist, developed the intergroup contact theory, which has relevance for this discussion of interculturality. He speculated that face-to-face contact between different groups of people may reduce intergroup prejudice provided that the following key conditions are met: equal group status within the situation, common goals, intergroup cooperation rather than compe-tition, and the support or encouragement of higher authorities. In a meta-analysis of more than 500 tests of this hypothesis, Pettigrew and Tropp (2000) found that when Allport's (1954) situational conditions prevailed, greater intergroup contact was typically associated with less intergroup prejudice, although this was not guaranteed. What happens if these optimal conditions are not realized?

When the quality of intercultural contact is unsatisfactory, Allen, Dristas, and Mills (2007), Bateman (2002), Stroebe, Lenkert, and Jonas (1988), and Isabelli-García (2006) maintain that study and residence abroad may not lead to greater understanding and appreciation of the host culture. In fact, student sojourners may return home with heightened negative stereotypes of their hosts (Stangor, Jonas, Stroebe, and Hewstone, 1996), "a strengthened sense of national identity" (Block, 2007), and a higher degree of ethnocentrism (Jackson, 2008). If sojourners perceive their hosts to be disrespectful of their in-group and mindless of their preferred identity, it can have detrimental effects on sojourner attitudes, adjustment, and willingness to engage. Negative experiences or unmet expectations may result in elevated levels of stress, homesickness, a heightened sense of identification with one's in-group, and rejection of host nationals. This, in turn, limits the potential for the development of intercultural communicative competence, a construct that will be explored further in this chapter.

As Smith, Bond, and Kağitçibaşi (2006: 245) warn, "a major determinant of successful acculturation[1] is inevitably the degree and quality of contact with the majority group. ... [H]aving contact with persons from other groups does not guarantee improved relations with them." This notion is echoed by Alred et al. (2003) and other interculturalists (e.g., P. M. Ryan, 2006), who observe that intercultural contact alone is not sufficient to bring about interculturality; in fact, negative encounters may actually impede personal expansion. In their review of intergroup contact studies, Pettigrew and Tropp (2000) found that members of minority and majority groups may view and respond to intergroup encounters differently. Consequently, these psychologists called for researchers to pay close attention to "the subjective nature" of intergroup contact to gain a more comprehensive understanding of factors that inhibit positive intercultural relations. This is crucial, as negative sentiments (e.g., perceptions of discrimination and rudeness) may discourage further intercultural contact and the development of interculturality.

"Languaging," identity expansion, and the process of becoming intercultural

How do L2 sojourners perceive and experience contact with host nationals? What characteristics or attributes are associated with those who seize opportunities to use their L2 skills in the host culture? Do those who excel in the academic arena necessarily thrive in the host culture or are different skills, attributes, and mindsets required for successful intercultural adjustment and engagement?

Drawing a distinction between formal ("skill-acquisition") and informal language learning, Phipps and Gonzalez (2004) use the term "languaging" to account for the process involved when learners use language "to make sense of and shape the world" around them (e.g., the host culture). For these linguists, "[l]anguaging is a life skill. It is inextricably interwoven with social experience – living in society – and it develops and changes constantly as that experience evolves and changes" (ibid.: 2–3). L2 students have "an opportunity to enter the languaging of others, to understand the complexity of the experience of others to enrich their own" (ibid.: 3). As tourists or sojourners in a foreign land, language learners face new challenges when they try to express themselves through the host language in daily life. Phipps (2006) portrays learners in these situations as "agents" in charge of their own learning. Her notion of "languagers" is in line with poststructuralist perceptions of language learning, agency, and identity expansion:

> "Languagers", for us, are those people, we may even term them "agents" or "language activists", who engage with the world-in-action, who move in the world in a way that allows the risk of stepping out of one's habitual ways of speaking and attempt to develop different, more relational ways of interacting with the people and phenomena that one encounters in everyday life. "Languagers" use the ways in which they perceive the world to develop new dispositions for peptic action in another language and they are engaged in developing these dispositions so that they become habitual, durable. Languaging, then, is an act of dwelling.
>
> (Phipps, 2006: 12)

In her depiction of "language activists," Phipps (2006) cites traits that interculturalists (e.g., Chen and Starosta, 2008; Kim, 2001, 2005, 2008) associate with successful adjustment, adaptation, and relationship-building in new cultural settings, namely, risk-taking, willingness to try new things, the appropriation of new behaviors, openness, and resilience. She hypothesizes that those who are willing to "step outside" familiar "ways of speaking" and explore new "more relational ways of interacting" may, over time, become at ease in social settings in the host culture.

Bourdieu (1977, 1991) explains that when people enter "new" fields (e.g., cultural scenes in the host environment), they bring with them a "set of dispositions" or habitus.[2] These behaviors (e.g., communication styles) and worldviews may not be a comfortable fit within the new field. Using academic language in a formal L2 classroom differs considerably from the informal discourse situations that typify daily life in the host culture. Moreover, not all language learners react to face-to-face intercultural contact in the same way. Some may find the environment inhospitable and limit their use of the host language; others may find their hosts welcoming and fully embrace the opportunity to explore and grow. In an earlier investigation of study abroad, I discovered significant differences in the way that L2 sojourners respond to life in the host environment:

> In the host culture some L2 sojourners ("social actors") may decide to learn and use their L2 only to a certain extent (e.g., to express their basic needs and wants), avoiding new ways of being in the world.

Some may resist the language of the host community, believing that it positions them unfavourably or disrespects their first language. By contrast, others may embrace the new linguistic community, interact more frequently across cultures, and experience identity expansion.

(Jackson, 2008: 36)

What may happen in language learners who are receptive to interculturality and identity expansion? What might their journey be like? "The process of becoming intercultural," from Phyllis Ryan's (2006: 21) experience, "creates a heightened sense of self constantly being challenged through contact with different cultures ... Learning about oneself involves the change from a monocultural to an intercultural frame of reference." Her description of "an intercultural person" offers further insight into the adaptive, transformative nature of those who are open to intercultural contact and personal expansion:

> The intercultural person has a style of self-consciousness that is capable of negotiating ever new formations of reality while being capable of negotiating the conflicts and tensions inherent in cross-cultural contacts. This person undergoes personal transitions that are always in a state of flux with continual dissolution and reformation of identity and growth. It is the adaptive nature that distinguishes them from other human beings.
>
> (Ryan, 2006: 21)

This conception of identity reconstruction is in accord with poststructuralist notions of the Self as socially constructed, fluid, fragmented, and multiple (Giroux, 1992; Guilherme, 2002; Kim, 2008).

The intercultural speaker

The term "intercultural speaker" is used by Byram (1995) to denote foreign language/culture learners who successfully communicate across languages and cultures to establish intercultural relationships. These individuals "operate their linguistic competence and their sociolinguistic awareness ... in order to manage interaction across cultural boundaries, to anticipate misunderstandings caused by difference in values, meanings and beliefs, and ... to cope with the affective as well as cognitive demands of engagement with otherness" (ibid.: 25).

Intercultural speakers are competent, flexible communicators (Byram and Zarate, 1997; Kramsch, 1993, 1998) who "engage with complexity and multiple identities" and "avoid stereotyping which accompanies perceiving someone through a single identity" (Byram, Gribkova, and Starkey, 2002: 5). For Guilherme (2004: 298), *critical* intercultural speakers are able to "negotiate between their own cultural, social and political identifications and representations with those of the other," and in the process, become aware of "the multiple, ambivalent, resourceful, and elastic nature of cultural identities in an intercultural encounter" (ibid.: 125). The term "intercultural speaker" is still widely used today, although some scholars have expressed a preference for the term "intercultural mediator" to emphasize "the individual's potential for social action rather than the competencies acquired as a consequence of teaching" (Alred and Byram, 2002: 341).

The Self–Other dichotomy

Byram's work on interculturality has had a marked influence on the teaching of foreign languages in Europe and beyond, although it has received criticism of late. Block (2007: 119), for example, claims that Byram's theory "essentializes cultures as metaphorical spaces, divided by 'borders' that individuals can occupy. In doing so, it also does not take on board the emerging diversity and complexity of societies around the world due to social changes wrought by advanced technology or the influx of migrants, or both." Critics argue that this Self–Other dichotomy limits one's understanding of the multiple factors and personal attributes that can impact on the communication between individuals – aspects that go beyond the scope of behaviors and traits associated with particular cultures. An overemphasis on difference, they maintain, can result in greater objectification of the Other (e.g., Dahlen, 1997; Dervin, 2006; Kramsch, 2002). For this reason, Holliday (2005: 37) argues that "we all need to understand and digest the normal complexity of the lives of those who are different from us – and how cultural stereotyping of the foreign Other is *not* useful and hides the essences of who people really are."

Further, this notion of interculturality, in Block's (2007: 119) view, "carries with it certain assumptions about conversation breakdowns taking place when interlocutors come from different sociocultural and linguistic backgrounds." He argues that interculturalists attribute these "misunderstandings" to "a lack of intercultural competence on the part of the non-local interlocutor" (ibid.: 119). While it is important to avoid simplistic, dualistic thinking, his criticism does not fully reflect the work of Byram and other L2 educators/interculturalists who acknowledge individual variations within and across cultures and advocate openness to multiple interpretations of "critical incidents" across cultures. Cultural differences (e.g., norms of politeness) *do* exist and those who cross cultures need to bear this in mind when they enter another cultural milieu. It is also important to be sensitive to individual differences and avoid making snap judgments in encounters with "the Other", "no matter whether this 'Other' is different from a national, ethnic, social, regional, professional or institutional point of view" (Sercu, 2002: 62). Failing to concede the existence of cultural differences will not lead to respect and understanding between people who have been socialized to view the world differently. What then are the characteristics and behaviors of an interculturally competent communicator?

What is intercultural competence? Intercultural communicative competence?

Many definitions of intercultural (communicative/communication) competence have been developed in the last few decades by speech communication specialists/interculturalists and L2 educators who have a particular interest in the cultural dimension of language learning and use. Interculturalists have long criticized applied linguists for largely ignoring the cultural component in language education curricula/research; conversely, L2 educators have rebuked interculturalists for overlooking or downplaying the language component in their discussions of intercultural communication. Much can be learned by examining the work of theorists and practitioners in both areas of specialization. In today's complex, globalizing world, whenever possible, an interdisciplinary approach is imperative to integrate and build on the strengths of different modes of research and understandings.

How do speech communication specialists/interculturalists view intercultural competence? "Interculturally competent persons," according to Chen and Starosta (2006: 357), "know how to elicit a desired response in interactions and to fulfill their own communication goals by respecting and affirming the worldview and cultural identities of the interactants." For these interculturalists, intercultural communication competence is "the ability to acknowledge, respect, tolerate, and integrate cultural differences that qualifies one for enlightened global citizenship" (ibid.: 357). In Jandt's (2007: 48) view, "[g]ood intercultural communicators have personality strength (with a strong sense of self and are socially relaxed), communication skills (verbal and nonverbal), psychological adjustment (ability to adapt to new situations), and cultural awareness (understanding of how people of different cultures think and act)." With reference to sojourners and immigrants, Taylor (1994: 154) defines intercultural competence as "an adaptive capacity based on an inclusive and integrative world view which allows participants to effectively accommodate the demands of living in a host culture."

Byram (1997), a L2 education specialist, makes a distinction between intercultural competence and intercultural communicative competence. For him, the former refers to the skills and ability that individuals employ to interact in their native language with people from another culture. By contrast, the latter enables individuals to interact successfully across cultures while using a second language. Intercultural communicative competence focuses on "establishing and maintaining relationships" instead of merely communicating messages or exchanging information (Byram, 1997: 3). This involves "accomplishing a negotiation between people based on both culture-specific and culture-general features that is on the whole respectful of and favourable to each" (Guilherme, 2004: 297).

For Fantini (2007: 9), an L2 educator, intercultural communicative competence is "a complex of abilities needed to perform *effectively* and *appropriately* when interacting with others who are linguistically and culturally different from oneself." Implicit in this definition are individual traits and characteristics (e.g., personality); the domains of relationships, communication and collaboration; the dimensions of knowledge, attitude, skills, and awareness; proficiency in the host language; and a developmental process. In Fantini's (2007) definition, the construct "effective" relates to one's perception of one's performance in intercultural encounters, drawing on an "etic" or outsider's view of the host/L2 culture. By contrast, the notion of "appropriacy" is linked to how one's behavior is perceived by one's hosts (i.e., an "emic" or insider's understanding of what is acceptable in the host/L2 culture). This conceptualization of intercultural communicative competence acknowledges the importance of Self and Other as it incorporates the "views of both sojourners and hosts regarding outcomes" (ibid.: 9).

In Dervin and Dirba's (2006: 257) view, L2 speakers possess intercultural competence "when they are able/willing to communicate effectively with others, accept their position as 'strangers' when meeting others, and realize that all individuals, including themselves, are multicultural and complex (sex, age, religion, status in society, etc.)." For Sercu (2005: 2), an interculturally competent individual possesses the following traits and skills:

[T]he willingness to engage with the foreign culture, self-awareness and the ability to look upon oneself from the outside, the ability to see the world through the others' eyes, the ability to cope with uncertainty, the ability to act as a cultural mediator, the ability to evaluate others' points of view, the ability to consciously use culture learning skills and to read the cultural context, and the understanding that individuals cannot be reduced to their collective identities.

In a survey of 23 leading intercultural communication experts (including Michael Byram, Janet Bennett, and Guo-Ming Chen), Deardorff (2004: 181) aimed to achieve a common understanding of intercultural competence as "a student outcome of internationalization efforts at institutions of higher education." The top three elements that her informants associated with this construct were "awareness, valuing, and understanding of cultural differences; experiencing other cultures; and self-awareness of one's own culture" (ibid.: 247). After reviewing nine definitions in the literature on intercultural communication, they considered the following one derived from Byram's (1997) work as most relevant to their institution's internationalization strategies: "Knowledge of others, knowledge of self; skills to interpret and relate; skills to discover and/or to interact; valuing others' values, beliefs, and behaviors; and relativitizing one's self. Linguistic competence plays a key role" (Byram, 1997: 34). Interestingly, although the majority of the experts surveyed were not language educators, they appeared to recognize the importance of language in intercultural encounters as they gave the highest rating to a definition that included this element. Drawing on their input, Deardorff (2004: 194) concluded her study by formulating the following broad definition of intercultural competence: "the ability to communicate effectively and appropriately in intercultural situations based on one's intercultural knowledge, skills and attitudes." The language dimension was not made explicit.

Models of intercultural (communicative/communication) competence

Building on their own definition of intercultural (communicative/communication) competence, numerous interculturalists, L2 educators, and international educators have devised models to explicate their understandings of these constructs. I now turn my attention to several models that have particular relevance for my investigation of L2 sojourners. The first one was developed by an L2 educator; the others are the work of speech communication specialists/interculturalists or international educators.

Byram's model of intercultural communicative competence

Byram's (1997) model of intercultural communicative competence is one of the most widely accepted, especially in Europe where it has had a profound impact on the integration of culture into L2 teaching. As O'Dowd (2003: 120) explains, this conceptual framework is viewed by many as "a representative model of what elements the process of inter-cultural learning should aim to develop in learners."

In the first part of this "prescriptive, ideal model," Byram (1997: 48) cites the following *linguistic* elements as characteristic of an intercultural speaker:

- *Linguistic competence*: the ability to apply knowledge of the rules of a standard version of the language to produce and interpret spoken and written language.
- *Sociolinguistic competence*: the ability to give to the language pro-duced by an interlocutor – whether native speaker or not – meanings which are taken for granted by the interlocutor or which are negoti-ated and made explicit with the interlocutor.
- *Discourse competence*: the ability to use, discover and negotiate strate-gies for the production and interpretation of monologue or dialogue texts which follow the conventions of the culture of an interlocutor or are negotiated as intercultural texts for particular purposes.

The second part of this theory identifies five components or *savoirs* that are linked to the *cultural* dimension of the intercultural speaker's competence. The first two are considered prerequisites for successful intercultural/interlingual communication:

- Intercultural attitudes (*savoir être*) – curiosity and openness, readi-ness to suspend disbelief about others cultures and belief about one's own intercultural attitudes.
- Knowledge (*saviors*) – of social groups and their products and prac-tices in one's own and interlocutor's country.

Finally, the next three components feature the skills deemed necessary for successful communication across cultures and languages:

- Skills of interpreting and relating (*savoir comprendre*): ability to interpret a document or event from another culture, to explain it and relate it to documents or events from one's own.

- Skills of discovery and interaction (*savoir apprendre/faire*): ability to acquire new knowledge of a culture and to operate this knowledge in real-time communication.

- Critical cultural awareness (*savoir s'engager*): an ability to evaluate critically and on the basis of explicit criteria, perspectives, practices and products in one's own and other cultures and countries.

(Byram et al., 2002: 12–13)

What are the implications of this model for L2 teaching? How can language teachers integrate a cultural component into their language teaching? Byram et al. (2002: 6) offer the following advice:

[D]eveloping the intercultural dimension in language teaching involves recognizing that the aims are: to give learners intercultural competence as well as linguistic competence; to prepare them for interaction with people of other cultures; to enable them to understand and accept people from other cultures as individuals with other distinctive perspectives, values and behaviours; and to help them to see that such interaction is an enriching experience.

In addition to L2 teaching, this general model has implications for the assessment of intercultural communicative competence, as Byram et al. (2002: 26) explain: "The role of assessment is therefore to encourage learners' awareness of their own abilities in intercultural competence, and to help them realize that these abilities are acquired in many different circumstances inside and outside the classroom."

Chen and Starosta's model of intercultural communication competence

Chen and Starosta (2008), speech communication specialists, have developed and refined their own model of intercultural communication competence, which emphasizes a "transformational process of symmetrical interdependence." Their conceptual framework entails three "equally important," interrelated dimensions that work together to create "a holistic picture of intercultural communication competence": (1) affective or intercultural sensitivity, (2) cognitive or intercultural awareness, and (3) behavioral or intercultural adroitness. This model does not, however, deal explicitly with communication across cultures in a L2.

Intercultural communication competence, in Chen and Starosta's (2008: 223) view, "demands positive emotion that enables individuals to be sensitive enough to acknowledge and respect cultural differences." This affective process is linked to the following personal elements or characteristics: "self-concept, open-mindedness, nonjudgmental attitudes, and social relaxation" (ibid.: 223). Similar to Byram (1997), these scholars have found that people who are competent intercultural communicators possess higher levels of self-awareness (e.g., knowledge of one's own personal identities/cultures) and cultural awareness (e.g., understanding of how cultures differ). To be competent intercultural communicators, Chen and Starosta (2008: 227) maintain that individuals must also enhance their intercultural adroitness ("message skills, knowledge regarding appropriate self-disclosure, behavioral flexibility, interaction management, and social skills"). These skills and actions, in their view, are vital for world citizens to act effectively in intercultural encounters and "achieve the goal of multicultural interdependence and interconnectedness in the global village" (ibid.: 227).

Recognizing "the complex multicultural dynamics" of "our current global society," Chen and Starosta (2008: 227) recommend that measures of intercultural communication competence take into account the multiple perspectives and identities that are now a common feature within communities and cultures:

> The trends of technology development, globalization of the economy, widespread population migration, development of multiculturalism, and the demise of the nation-state in favor of sub- and supranational identifications have shrunk and multiculturalized the world, and traditional perceptions of *self* and *other* must be redefined. The global context of human communication and the need to pursue a state of multicultural coexistence require that we abolish the boundaries separating *me* and *you*, *us* and *them*, and develop a theory of communication competence that takes into account individuals' multiple identities.

Challenging traditional notions of Self and Other, their recommendation is in line with Moon (2008) and other critical theorists (e.g., Block, 2007; Dervin, 2006; Kramsch, 2002) who rally against homogenizing, static perspectives of culture that fail to recognize diversity within groups.

The process model of intercultural competence

Based on the input of 23 leading interculturalists, Deardorff (2004: 194) devised a graphic representation of intercultural competence that depicts movement from "the individual level of attitudes/personal attributes to the interactive cultural level in regard to the outcomes." It draws attention to the internal shift in frame of reference that is critical for effective and appropriate behavior in intercultural encounters. A strength of her process model is that it acknowledges the *ongoing* complexity of the development of intercultural competence and the importance of reflection in the life-long journey toward interculturality.

Similar to Chen and Starosta's (2008) and Byram's (1997, 2006) models, Deardorff's (2004) conceptual framework accentuates the vital role that attitude plays in intercultural learning. Significantly, the intercultural experts she surveyed stress that "the attitudes of openness, respect (valuing all cultures), curiosity and discovery (tolerating ambiguity)" are necessary for one to become interculturally competent (Deardorff, 2004: 193). Further, in accord with Byram's (1997) *savoirs*, her model recognizes that intercultural competence necessitates knowledge and understanding of "one's own cultural norms and sensitivity to those of other cultures" (Deardorff, 2008: 37).

Deardorff's process model (2004, 2006, 2008) identifies key internal outcomes that may occur as a result of "an informed frame of reference shift," namely, adaptability, an ethnorelative perspective, empathy, and a flexible mindset. Her graphic also specifies desired external outcomes that can be assessed (e.g., "behaving and communicating appropriately and effectively" in intercultural situations). In Deardorff's (2008: 42) words, her model provides "a holistic framework for intercultural competence development and assessment." This linkage between input and outcomes is consistent with the recommendations of international education experts (e.g., Olson et al., 2005) and the tenets of outcome-based assessment that were discussed in Chapter 1.

Deardorff's (2004, 2006, 2008) process model is intended to offer direction for the preparation of "global-ready graduates." The emphasis on reflection and awareness of Self and Other, however, does not sufficiently address the intercultural learning of L2 speakers. Testing this model with this population is essential to determine its usefulness for them and perhaps discover linguistic or non-linguistic dimensions that could be incorporated into the model.

What is global competence? Global citizenry?

Owing to the impact of globalization, more international educators and theorists are now focusing attention on what it means to be globally competent. Similar to intercultural competence, there are many definitions of global competence (sometimes referred to as "transnational competence" or "global citizenry"). Lambert (1996) defines a globally competent person as an individual who has knowledge of current events, the capacity to empathize with others, the ability to maintain a positive attitude, L2 competence, and the ability to value foreign ways of doing things. For Olson and Kroeger (2001), a globally competent individual has sufficient substantive knowledge (e.g., understanding of cultures, languages, global events and concerns), perceptual understanding (e.g., open-mindedness, sophisticated cognitive processing, resistance to stereotyping), and intercultural communication skills (e.g., adaptability, empathy, cross-cultural awareness, intercultural mediation) to interact successfully in a globally interconnected world. These international educators argue that "anything less than a global intercultural education places our students at a severe disadvantage as they go forth into our globally interdependent and interculturally complex world" (ibid.: 135).

The Stanley Foundation (2003), an American organization which supports research on global education, defines global competency as "an appreciation of complexity, conflict management, the inevitability of change, and the interconnectedness between and among humans and their environment." This body emphasizes that "globally competent citizens know they have an impact on the world and that the world influences them. They recognize their ability and responsibility to make choices that affect the future."

For Donatelli, Yngve, Miller, and Ellis (2005: 134), global competence signifies "the desired pedagogical outcome of education abroad programs; that is, successful 'internationalization', or the capacity to become a functioning 'global citizen' in the modern world." These international educators cite the following as common traits of global competence:

- General knowledge of one's own culture, history, and people;
- General knowledge of cultures, histories, and peoples other than one's own;
- Fluency in a world language other than one's native tongue;
- Cross-cultural empathy;
- Openness and cognitive flexibility;

- Tolerance for ambiguity, perceptual acuity, and attentiveness to non-verbal messages; and
- Awareness of issues facing the global community.

(Ibid.: 134)

Employing a methodology similar to that of Deardorff (2004), Hunter (2004) surveyed senior international educators, transnational corporation human resource managers, and United Nations officials to determine their perception of the knowledge, skills, attitudes, and experiences necessary to become globally competent. For these individuals, a globally competent person is someone who is "able to identify cultural differences to compete globally, collaborate across cultures, and effectively participate in both social and business settings in other countries" (Deardorff and Hunter, 2006: 77). Global competence entails "having an open mind while actively seeking to understand cultural norms and expectations of others, leveraging this gained knowledge to interact, communicate and work effectively outside one's environment" (Hunter, 2004: 74).

Based on the input of these experts, Hunter (2004) developed the global competence model to provide a framework for international educators to prepare "global-ready graduates." Central to his model is the conviction that if one is to achieve global competency, one must recognize that one's own worldview is not universal. Similar to Deardorff's (2006) process model, it emphasizes that "[a]ttitudes of openness, curiosity, and respect are key starting points upon which to build the requisite knowledge and skills" (Deardorff and Hunter, 2006: 79). Accordingly, both models have relevance for investigations of the intercultural development of study abroad students.

The Developmental Model of Intercultural Sensitivity

This review would be incomplete without an examination of the Developmental Model of Intercultural Sensitivity (DMIS), which is widely used in the field of intercultural communication today. Phenomenological in nature, this theoretical framework was developed by M. J. Bennett (1993) to explain the observed and reported experiences of individuals in intercultural encounters. It centers on the constructs of ethnocentricism and ethnorelativism (Bennett 1997, 2004; Bennett and Bennett, 2004a; Landis, Bennett and Bennett, 2004). In the former, "the worldview of one's own culture is central to all reality" (M. J. Bennett, 1993: 30), whereas the latter is linked to "being comfortable with many standards and customs and to having an ability to adapt behavior and judgments to a variety of interpersonal settings" (ibid.: 26).

In this model, intercultural sensitivity is defined in terms of personal growth and the development of an "intercultural mind – a mindset capable of understanding from within and from without both one's own culture and other cultures" (Bennett et al., 2003: 252). Specifically, the DMIS theorizes that individuals move from ethnocentric stages where one's culture is experienced as "central to reality" (Denial, Defense, Minimization), through ethnorelative stages of greater recognition and acceptance of difference (Acceptance, Adaptation, and Integration) (see Table 2.1 for band descriptors).

Of relevance to study abroad students, the DMIS posits that ethnorelative worldviews have more potential to generate the attitudes, knowledge, and behavior that constitute intercultural competence and facilitate adjustment in a new milieu (Kim, 2001, 2005). For Bennett and Bennett (2004b: 149), intercultural competence is "the ability to communicate

Table 2.1 Developmental Model of Intercultural Sensitivity (DMIS) band descriptors

DMIS stage of development		Descriptor
Ethnocentric stages	Denial	One's own culture is experienced as the only real one and consideration of other cultures is avoided by maintaining psychological or physical isolation from differences.
	Defense	One's own culture (or an adopted culture) is experienced as the only good one, and cultural difference is denigrated.
	Minimization	Elements of one's own cultural worldview are experienced as universal, so that despite acceptable surface differences with other cultures, essentially those cultures are similar to one's own.
Ethnorelative stages	Acceptance	Other cultures are included in experience as equally complex but different constructions of reality.
	Adaptation	One attains the ability to shift perspective in and out of another cultural worldview.
	Integration	One's experience of self is expanded to include movement in and out of different cultural worldviews.

Source: Adapted from Bennett and Bennett, 2004b: 153–8.

effectively in cross-cultural situations and to relate appropriately in a variety of cultural contexts." In the DMIS this construct is viewed as a developmental phenomenon, in harmony with Mezirow's (1994, 2000) transformational learning theory in adult education. The latter posits that adults who engage in critical self-examination may experience a dramatic transformation in response to significant events or difficult stages in their lives (e.g., moving to another country). Within this orientation, intercultural competence is believed to involve a continuous learning process with "new or revised interpretations of the meaning of one's experience" (Mezirow, 1994: 222). Through intercultural contact, people discover cross-cultural differences (and similarities) and face challenges that may lead them to question their usual ways of doing things. As they deepen their awareness and understanding of these differences, they may adjust their mindset (e.g., develop an ethnorelative perspective) and employ new behaviors to help them communicate more effectively and appropriately across cultures. For Mezirow (1994, 2000), this change, in some individuals, can lead to a life-altering transformation and restructuring of their sense of self (e.g., identity reconstruction).

The DMIS assumes a social construction of identity, positioning it as relational and subject to change. This perspective is aligned with contemporary critical and poststructuralist notions of identity (e.g., Guilherme, 2002; Jackson, 2007, 2008; Norton, 2000; Pavlenko and Lantolf, 2000), which recognize the fluid, contradictory nature of this construct. In contrast with traditional views of identity as fixed, static, and unitary, this perspective allows for the impact of globalization and intercultural contact and the evolution of hybrid, global identities.

In sum, the DMIS offers a theory-based explanation of individual effectiveness in intercultural encounters, capturing the elements that Bhawuk and Brislin (1992: 416) argue are key predictors of success in intercultural contexts: "To be effective in another culture, people must be interested in other cultures, be sensitive enough to notice cultural differences, and then also be willing to modify their behavior as an indication of respect for the people of other cultures."

Second language proficiency and intercultural competence

Recently, scholars have attempted to link levels of intercultural competence with proficiency in the second or foreign language (e.g., language of the host community). The development of "an intercultural mindset," according to Bennett, Bennett, and Allen (2003: 252), "resonates positively with communicative competence and proficiency-related theories of language learning." They hypothesize that there is a "typical fit between language proficiency levels and developmental levels of intercultural sensitivity" (ibid.: 255).

> Although language proficiency is not a specific element of the DMIS, the model nevertheless supports the view of language learning as a communication endeavor and as a humanistic enterprise. As a communication endeavor, language competence is defined as the ability to use the language as an *insider*. The DMIS creates a parallel to language competence by defining cultural competence as the ability to interpret and behave within culture as an *insider*. As a humanistic enterprise, language learning creates an awareness and appreciation of language itself. The DMIS parallel is that intercultural sensitivity involves an awareness and appreciation of culture itself.
>
> (Bennett et al., 2003: 253)

More specifically, they suggest that progression through the stages of the DMIS correlates with advances in one's L2 proficiency. For instance, they speculate that learners who have an advanced level of proficiency are apt to be in an ethnorelative stage of cultural development (e.g., Adaptation/Integration). Conversely, those who are novice learners of the language are likely to be in an ethnocentric stage of development (e.g., Denial/Defense). But are intercultural development and L2 proficiency necessarily parallel? What evidence has been gathered that supports or refutes this hypothesis?

Thus far, only a few studies have explored this question. In South Korea, Park (2006) examined the relationship between intercultural sensitivity and linguistic competence in 104 preservice EFL (English as a Foreign Language) teachers. The researcher employed the IDI to measure the participants' level of intercultural sensitivity as outlined in the DMIS (Hammer and Bennett, 2002; Hammer, Bennett, and Wiseman, 2003). The Michigan English Language Assessment Battery (MELAB) was used to assess their level of language competence. Park (2006) found little correlation between the participants' level of intercultural sensitivity and linguistic competence; those with advanced proficiency in English did not necessarily possess a higher level of intercultural sensitivity. The findings suggest that "intercultural competence might not naturally grow with the development of linguistic competence"; in fact, it may progress at a much slower rate than proficiency in a L2. Park (2006) recommends that intercultural competence be taught explicitly, as is the case with second or foreign (international) languages (e.g., formal classroom-based instruction).

To better understand the link between linguistic and intercultural development, Edstrom (2005) interviewed 13 American women (L2 users of Spanish) living in Venezuela. Employing the DMIS as a theoretical framework, she discovered that the following factors influenced the women's participation in L2 conversation: their knowledge of L2 conversational styles, their willingness to accept differences in communication styles, and their interest in the topics of conversation. "[A]lthough an appreciation for the complexity of language and an understanding of the relationship between language and culture do not produce proficient, bilingual learners," Edstrom (2005: 32) concludes that "these concepts may contribute to the formation of informed, tolerant learners who appreciate the difficulty of mastering an L2."

Similar to Park (2006), Edstrom (2005) recommends that intercultural communication theories/strategies be made explicit in L2 education. In particular, she suggests that intercultural sensitivity training and awareness of cross-cultural differences in conversational styles be incorporated into language teaching. In her mind, "exploring the role of personal background and intercultural sensitivity in the language learning process does not ensure learners' successful participation in L2 conversation but it does expose them to the complex relationship between language and its users" (ibid.: 32). Significantly, she was convinced that this awareness "may serve them longer than their L2 skills" (ibid.: 32).

In separate surveys of interculturalists and global education experts, Deardorff and Hunter (2006: 81) found a consensus that "neither language nor education abroad alone makes someone interculturally or globally competent." In both studies, the participants argued that "more language course offerings must include key cultural knowledge that goes beyond the 'tip of the iceberg' of food, music, and holidays to explore and understand the deep cultural knowledge of underlying values, norms, and worldviews" (ibid.: 81). Consistent with Deardorff's (2004) study, Hunter's (2004) respondents maintain that "simply studying abroad, learning a L2, or majoring in international relations is no longer enough to prepare students for the global workforce. The approach to preparedness must be comprehensive" (Deardorff and Hunter, 2006: 79).

Further, a growing number of specialists in intercultural and L2 pedagogy (e.g., Bennett, 1997; Bennett, 2008; Freed, 1995; Kramsch, 1998), cross-cultural psychologists (e.g., Smith et al., 2006), and study abroad researchers (e.g., Jackson, 2008; Park, 2006; Edstrom, 2005) concur with

Ryan's (2003: 132) observation that "[r]esidence in another country does not automatically produce interculturality." Simply put, intercultural contact does not necessarily lead to intercultural communicative competence. Moreover, as Zarate (2003) and Bennett (1997) observe, knowing the grammar and vocabulary of another language does not ensure that people will be able to communicate successfully across cultures in that language. With this in mind, Bennett (1997: 16–21) offers the following depiction of "a fluent fool":

> A fluent fool is someone who speaks a foreign language well but doesn't understand the social or philosophical content of that language. Such people are likely to get into all sorts of trouble because both they themselves and others overestimate their ability. They may be invited into complicated social situations where they cannot understand the events deeply enough to avoid giving or taking offense. Eventually, fluent fools may develop negative opinions of the native speakers whose language they understand but whose basic beliefs and values continue to elude them. ... To avoid becoming a fluent fool, we need to understand more completely the cultural dimension of language.

While the label he uses is pejorative and rather jarring, Bennett's (1997) admonition does raise our awareness of the importance of intercultural competence for language learners who cross cultures.

Empirical research on intercultural/global competence and study abroad

The development of global and intercultural competencies has been the focus of a growing number of studies in recent years due to the acceleration of globalization and increased opportunities for intercultural contact both at home and abroad. In particular, the DMIS has served as the theoretical basis for the investigation of intercultural competence in many diverse populations (e.g., business professionals, medical professionals, educators, international consultants, study abroad students).

Using a mixed-method case study design, for example, Medina-López-Portillo (2004a, 2004b) investigated the intercultural sensitivity of 28 American university students who participated in one of two study abroad language programs: 18 attended a seven-week summer program in Taxco, Mexico, and 10 took part in a sixteen-week semester program in Mexico City. In her comparative study she employed face-to-face interviews, the

IDI, a survey, and a guided journal, drawing on the following theories and models to guide her work: the DMIS (M. J. Bennett, 1993, 1997, 2004), the Intergroup Contact Theory (Allport, 1954), and the Model of the Transformation Process (Kauffmann, Martin, Weaver, and Weaver, 1992). The pre- and postquantitative and qualitative data revealed changes in intercultural sensitivity development in both groups but to different degrees and in different directions. She attributed this to variations in the length of study abroad, the students' initial intercultural sensitivity level, and the location of the program. Those with less time abroad focused on visible, behavioral cultural differences, while the longer-term sojourners developed a deeper understanding of nuances in the host culture. Further, Medina-López-Portillo (2004a, 2004b) observed that the participants had significantly inflated opinions about their level of intercultural sensitivity.

In France, Engle and Engle (2004) investigated the French language learning and intercultural sensitivity of American students who took part in either a one semester or a full-year study abroad program. On entry, the participants had a high intermediate/advanced level of proficiency in their second language, French, as measured by the Test d'Evaluation de Français (TEF). To gauge the development of intercultural competence, the one-semester program participants took the IDI twice: once during the first week of their study abroad and again during the last week of their stay. Full-year students were administered the IDI three times: on entry, after one semester, and at the end of their program. After six semesters of testing, 187 one-semester students and 32 full-year students had participated in the study. Engle and Engle (2004) found that longer-term sojourners made significantly more progress in areas of cultural understanding and intercultural communication, with the most growth in the second term. They suggest that at least one year in the host culture may be needed to trigger significant gains in intercultural sensitivity.

Anderson, Lawton, Rexeisen and Hubbard (2006) employed the IDI to assess the extent to which a short-term, faculty-led study abroad program affected the cross-cultural sensitivity of 23 American business students. The group participated in a one-week management seminar in the US before spending four weeks in Europe. Their study abroad program included site visits and English-medium classes with an American professor and guest lectures by local experts. For two weeks the students lived in a homestay in London; the remainder of their stay was in a dormitory in Ireland. While the students did not experience a "foreign language" environment, they were exposed to other ways of being, informal discourse (e.g., idiomatic expressions), and communication styles that were new to them. The IDI was administered prior to the sojourn and again immediately after re-entry. As a group, the students enhanced their ability to accept and adapt to cultural differences. Preliminary results suggested that short-term non-language-based study abroad programs can have a positive impact on the overall development of cross-cultural sensitivity.

All these studies focused on the intercultural sensitivity development of American students. Would an investigation of L2 sojourners from Asia yield similar results? Would a short stay in the host culture (e.g., five weeks) be long enough for the enhancement of their intercultural communication skills, understanding, and sensitivity? Would the students enhance their L2 proficiency? Is it possible for sojourners to experience identity expansion after such a brief stay in the field? What are realistic outcomes for sojourns of this length? In the remainder of the book I explore these questions by examining the trajectories of Hong Kong students who took part in an intensive, short-term sojourn in England, in accord with the institution's internationalization policy. I examine the extent to which the theories I've reviewed account for the linguistic and intercultural learning of the participants. In particular, I problematize Bennett et al.'s (2003) hypothesized linkage between L2 proficiency and intercultural sensitivity.

Conclusions

In this chapter I have conceptualized key elements related to interculturality and explored theoretical understandings and models of intercultural and global competencies. Drawing on the work of critical theorists, poststructuralists, linguists, and interculturalists, I maintain that we need a deeper, interdisciplinary understanding of what it means to be an effective intercultural communicator in today's global, increasingly hybrid society. In the next chapter, I provide the background for my investigation of the language and cultural development and identity (re)construction of Hong Kong university students both in their home environment and abroad.

3
Groundwork for the Illustrative Case Studies

In this chapter I introduce my ethnographic investigation of the language and (inter)cultural learning of English majors from the Chinese University of Hong Kong who took part in a short-term sojourn in England. To begin, I offer insight into the macro-level sociolinguistic context of Hong Kong and the home institution's internationalization policy. I then describe the presojourn, sojourn, and postsojourn elements of the study abroad program before focusing on the research methodology I employed to track the (inter)cultural and linguistic development of the fourth cohort.

The Hong Kong context – a macro-sociolinguistic perspective

Hong Kong, a city of approximately 1031 square kilometers in the south of China, consists of Hong Kong Island, Kowloon Peninsula, and the New Territories. After China's defeat in the Opium War in 1842, Hong Kong Island was ceded to Britain. Subsequent agreements resulted in the acquisition of further Hong Kong territory by Britain in 1860 and 1898. During this colonial period, English (the colonizers' language) and Cantonese (the vernacular language) formed a diglossic[1] situation in Hong Kong. Both languages were used in different domains for distinct purposes and were accorded different levels of prestige. English officially dominated the formal institutions of government, law, education, and international commerce, providing a link with the world beyond Asia. By contrast, Cantonese, the indigenous language of the vast majority, was used in family and informal daily-life situations and local businesses (Pierson, 1994; Tsui, 2007). With this division, language helped to create a stratified, class-based structure with more power and status given to those with a high level of proficiency in English (e.g., the colonizers, Hong Kong's well-educated Chinese elite).

After more than 160 years of colonial rule, in July 1997 Hong Kong's sovereignty reverted from Britain to the People's Republic of China (PRC). Hong Kong then became a Special Administrative Region (SAR) of the "Motherland"[2] and was assured a high degree of autonomy, except for matters related to defense and foreign relations. Today, "Asia's world city"[3] remains ethnically quite homogenous. Around 95 percent of its population of 7 million is ethnic Chinese; the majority of the older generations either emigrated from the "Motherland" or are descendants of those who did (Mathews, Ma, Lui, 2008). The remainder of the population (5%) is a mix of other ethnic groups. A large number of foreign workers and expatriates also reside in Hong Kong temporarily. Cantonese is still the major language spoken at home and in the community. English remains an official language and the local government continues to emphasize its importance for the city to maintain its international status and competitive edge in the region.

Soon after the Handover, the SAR government announced that a "biliterate and trilingual" policy would be implemented in schools. Hong Kong students are now expected to be proficient in both written English and Chinese, and speak three languages: English (the international language), Cantonese (the vernacular language), and Putonghua (Mandarin, the national language of the PRC). In 1998, Putonghua became a compulsory subject for Primary One (Grade 1) to Secondary Three (Grade 9). A growing number of students are also studying the language as an elective in tertiary institutions of higher education and joining subsidized Putonghua immersion programs in the Mainland. There has also been some sporadic, highly controversial debate about the national language replacing Cantonese as a medium of instruction in schools and tertiary institutions. This notion has been met with strong resistance.

In 1998 Chinese (Cantonese) was officially adopted as the medium of instruction in three-quarters of government-funded secondary schools at the junior secondary levels, with English to be taught as a second language. The remainder were granted permission to operate as English-medium schools. The primary reason given for this "socially stratifying language-in-education policy" (Lin, 2005) was the perceived decline in the standard of English of both teachers and students. Many parents objected to the policy, claiming that Chinese-medium instruction limits their children's chances for advancement. Despite opposition, the government insisted on promoting Chinese and since then numerous educators have cited the benefits of mother tongue teaching (He, Ho, and Man, 2007; Tsui, 2004).

Language use is inextricably bound with identity and a sense of belonging (Jackson, 2008; Mathews, 2000; Meinhof and Galasiński, 2005; Noels, 2009). Accordingly, Tsui (2007: 136) maintains that the postcolonial language policy is strategically designed to foster "the reconstruction of the Chineseness of Hong Kong people." From this perspective, education in a Chinese language is serving as a vehicle to strengthen the bond with the "Motherland" and the larger Chinese family. At the same time, the policy is preserving a unique Hong Kong identity, linking individuals to both Cantonese and English and a hybrid mix of Eastern and Western cultures. Interestingly, the local government is now allowing more curricula in Chinese-medium schools to be taught in English and some senior secondary schools are reverting to English-medium instruction in response to parental pressure (Lai, 2005). This raises further questions about the future role and status of the three languages in Hong Kong. "Given that English is one of the most important mediating tools of globalization," Tsui (2007: 139) reasons that "the push and pull between the nationalism and internationalization in China will be crucial in shaping the language policy in Hong Kong."

The home institution's internationalization policy

Since its inception in 1961, the Chinese University of Hong Kong has promoted bilingualism (Chinese and English) and biculturalism (bridging Chinese and Western cultures). Owing to the acceleration of globalization, in 2004 the University felt compelled to reassess its mission:

> Two major changes, one technological and global, and the other geopolitical and local, have reshaped the environment faced by Hong Kong significantly. First, over the last decade, the information and communication revolution has greatly facilitated and accelerated globalization everywhere. ... Competition is now more global than local. ... There is greater demand in the labor markets for individuals with international knowledge, perspective and skills (including language skills). That is why world-class universities are moving to require that all their undergraduate students spend some time abroad during their undergraduate years.
>
> (Lau, 2004: 2)

Citing the competitive nature of "an increasingly globalized world," the vice-chancellor laid the groundwork for the revitalization of the institution's internationalization policy. He painted a rather rosy picture of the outcomes of intercultural contact and international exchange for undergraduates:

> Their horizons will be broadened, their understanding of diverse cultures will be deepened, and their awareness of the realities of the world will be sharpened. They will develop a greater capacity to communicate, empathize, and tolerate. They will develop the qualities they need to become effective in both work and personal life in an increasingly globalized world. ... By sending our students through the challenge of living abroad as exchange students, where they can immerse themselves completely in a different culture and acquire the perspectives and skills to operate efficiently and independently in a new environment, they will become much better equipped with the kind of versatility, confidence, perspective, and exposure needed to respond creatively to unexpected challenges and opportunities.
>
> (Lau, 2004: 2)

Following Lau's (2004) speech, the institution took further steps to "broaden the student mix" and create "a more diversified campus." This had implications for the language used in some courses. Historically, the University's bilingual (Chinese-English) policy has meant that departments have been free to choose the medium of instruction and the majority of courses have been offered in Cantonese. Plans to increase the number of exchange students, however, would be hampered if too few courses were taught in English. While international students may opt to study Chinese languages and cultures, most are only on campus for one semester and not able to understand Cantonese-medium courses. Moreover, many exchange students from Mainland China have studied English but are unfamiliar with Cantonese. Recognizing this, the administration requested that departments who wished to admit nonlocal students offer at least one section of their required courses in English.

The proposed change was met with protests and skepticism by students and faculty who feared that there would be an erosion of the institution's distinctive Chinese character. There was much confusion about the actual policy and rumors spread quickly that the medium of instruction would switch to English in the majority of courses. In reality, only about 5 percent of courses were affected. The University's bilingual education policy, which makes it unique among tertiary institutions in Hong Kong, would remain in force.[4]

Caught off guard by the hostile reaction on campus, the institution created a commission to reevaluate its bilingual policy. In early 2005, information sessions were held to clear up misconceptions about the recruitment of nonlocal students and the medium of instruction. Once students and professors were reassured that the University would not become an English-medium institution protests diminished. In 2004–5, during this turbulent time, 392 local students took part in semester- or year-long exchange programs. Since then, the number of participants has increased dramatically. Annually, more than 620 now join semester- or academic year-long exchange programs and the University is also welcoming 850 exchange students each year. At present, approximately 7.5 percent of the student body is comprised of non-local students. As the University aims to provide at least one exchange opportunity for every student who wishes it, we have also witnessed a significant increase in the number and diversity of short-term programs, which range from 4 to 7 weeks. Each year, over 2000 students are now participating in these shorter programs or internships, which usually take place during the summer break from May to August.

The Special English Stream:
A short-term study abroad program

In line with the University's desire to internationalize, in 2001 the English Department established the Special English Stream (SES) to provide English majors with a unique study abroad experience in an English-speaking environment. Table 3.1 depicts the learning outcomes that were formulated for participants in this program.

To achieve these aims, the SES consists of presojourn, sojourn, and postsojourn elements. All courses are credit-bearing and integrated into the Bachelor of Arts (BA) program of studies in the home institution. Experiential learning and guided, critical reflection are key ingredients. The sojourn component (a five-week stay in England) is subsidized by a University grant; the students and the Department cover the remainder of the expenses. The following sections provide more details about each phase of the SES 2005 program, the year that the University's revamped internationalization policy was set in motion.

Presojourn elements

In the semester prior to the sojourn, the SES students took several courses that were specially designed for them: literary studies, applied linguistics

Table 3.1   Outcomes for Special English Stream (SES) students

By the end of the program, each student should:

Knowledge	Skills	Attitudes
Understand his/her culture within a global and comparative context (e.g., recognize that his/her culture is one of many diverse cultures and that alternate perceptions and behaviors may be based in cultural differences).	Use knowledge, diverse cultural frames of reference, and alternate perspectives to think critically and solve problems (demonstrate intellectual growth).	Appreciate the language, art, theater, literature, religion, philosophy, and material culture of the host culture.
Demonstrate knowledge of the host culture (e.g., beliefs, values, perspectives, and practices).	Communicate effectively and appropriately with people in the host language in a range of settings for a variety of purposes (e.g., informal social situations) (that is, enhance his/her intercultural communicative competence) (Byram, 1997; Byram and Zarate, 1997; Fantini, 2007; Murphy-Lejeune, 2002, 2003).	Be open to learning and display a positive orientation to new opportunities, ideas, and ways of thinking.
Demonstrate knowledge of effective intercultural communication strategies in the host language.	Enhance his/her sociopragmatic awareness of English in the host culture (i.e., develop a deeper understanding of "the social perceptions underlying participants' interpretation and performance of communicative action" in a particular social context) (Rose and Kasper, 2001: 2).	Recognize and appreciate cultural differences and display tolerance for ambiguity.
	Display more self-confidence and self-efficacy when using the host language in a variety of situations.	Display empathy and the ability to consider multiple perspectives.

(Continued)

Table 3.1 Continued

By the end of the program, each student should:		
Knowledge	Skills	Attitudes
		Demonstrate an ongoing willingness to seek out international or intercultural opportunities (e.g., take the initiative to interact across cultures in English in a wide range of settings).

(ethnographic research), and intercultural communication. Each course lasted 14 weeks (three hours per week).

Literary studies

In the SES literature course, the students explored readings that would prepare them for the literary site visits in England. They were also introduced to the role of the theater in English society. This was especially important as most had never been to a theater and in England they would have the opportunity to experience a wide range of plays, from Shakespearean productions at the Globe Theater in London to contemporary amateur productions in small, intimate theaters in Warwickshire. Included in the literary studies course was an excursion to the Hong Kong International Arts Festival to see a play. This provided the students with the opportunity to observe, critique, and debrief a production in English prior to the sojourn.

Ethnographic research

I introduced the students to the theory and practice of pragmatic ethnographic research, focusing on investigations of linguistic and cultural scenes. The benefits of this approach for language learners on "year-abroad" programs are now well established, especially in Europe, where the LARA (Learning and Residence Abroad) project (Roberts, Byram, Barro, Jordan, and Street, 2001) has been very successful for British learners of French, German, Spanish, etc. I have also found it beneficial for short-term sojourners when adequate preparation and support are provided (Jackson, 2006a, 2006b, 2007, 2008).

In the first half of the course, through a series of weekly tasks, the students honed the skills necessary to carry out ethnographic research (e.g., participant observation, note-taking, diary-keeping, reflexive interviewing, the recording of field notes, the audio-recording, transcribing, and analysis of discourse). They then carried out their own small-scale project, in which they explored some aspects of their cultural world using the tools of ethnographic research. By "making the familiar strange," I hoped that the students would become more aware of their environment and develop a more systematic approach to language and cultural learning. Regular, small-group research advising sessions supported their fieldwork and the preparation of a 20-page report (plus appendices). This process served as a trial run for the fieldwork that they would undertake in England.

Intercultural communication

In the "Communication across cultures" course I emphasized the application of intercultural communication theory to practical communication problems that can occur when people from different cultures interact. I aimed to help the students enhance their cultural self-awareness and better understand how differences in culture, attitudes, and values may affect behavior. Ultimately, through critical reflection and analysis, I hoped they would become more open to diversity, aware of the tendency to stereotype, and learn to communicate more effectively across cultures. Activities in this interactive, experiential course consisted of readings, lectures, observation and analysis of video clips, the preparation of a language and cultural self-identity narrative, interviewing a study abroad returnee or current exchange student, the analysis of intercultural cases and critical incidents, discussions, simulations, and journal-keeping.

Five-week sojourn in England

For five weeks in May–June, the 2005 SES cohort participated in a thematically linked literary, linguistic, and cultural enhancement program at a university in central England. During the sojourn, each student lived with a family in a small community, a short bus ride from the host institution. Their homestay experience was intended to provide them with the opportunity to use English in informal, social settings so they could more fully experience the local culture. For the sojourn there was an English language policy in place to encourage them to take full advantage of the English-speaking environment. As language use is a very sensitive, personal issue, this policy was thoroughly discussed before the sojourn to encourage a full range of views to emerge. As group support for the policy is essential for it to work, all of them would need to understand its aims and believe it was worthwhile. Midway through the course, students from the previous group shared their experiences with "living in English," offering encouragement to the new cohort. Their words reassured those who had been skeptical about the policy.

In England, the academic program (e.g., workshops, talks) was closely linked to excursions (e.g., trips to the theater, literary/cultural sites) with a weekly theme (e.g., Shakespeare and the Elizabethan/Jacobean heritage, Jane Austen and the eighteenth century, Romanticism and the nineteenth century, contemporary multiracial, multicultural England). On Sundays and most weekday afternoons, the students had free time to explore their surroundings and investigate a cultural scene using an ethnographic approach. Every Monday morning a local cultural studies specialist and I facilitated a debriefing session. In a relaxed, supportive environment, we encouraged the students to raise questions about aspects of the host culture that they found confusing, interesting, or unsettling.

As a requirement of their fieldwork course, the students kept a diary in which they recorded their observations and reactions to each day's activities, including their homestay, excursions, ethnographic research, intercultural contact in the community, and lessons. Guidelines were provided to encourage critical reflection and analysis. The student sojourners were also required to prepare a literary reflections paper in which they described and analyzed a play or cultural site visit of their choice. By the beginning of the second week the students had settled on a research topic for their ethnographic project. For most, this involved some aspect of homestay or community life (e.g., hobbies of their hosts, the pub scene). In scheduled research advising sessions and informal chats on excursions, I provided the students with advice and feedback on their individual projects. Discussion sometimes centered on sensitive issues of access and consent. In class we reviewed the interview protocols they prepared and discussed rapport-building strategies to employ with their informants. This process provided additional insight into the development of the students' intercultural sensitivity and attitudes toward the host culture and language.

Postsojourn elements

In the semester following the sojourn the students were free to choose whether to write a 30-page plus dissertation based on the ethnographic data they had collected in England or a library research paper of the same length about a topic in English literature. I supervised the crafting of their ethnographic projects while my literature colleagues worked with those who opted to develop a literary dissertation. When I met with my students each week, I was able to prompt them to reflect more deeply on their intercultural experiences and growth in England (e.g., their ethnographic conversations with their informants). The 2005 cohort also organized a sharing session for the next SES group just as the previous group had done for them. This afforded me additional insight into the impact of their sojourn experience and their intercultural awareness and sensitivity.

Researching the language and cultural learning of SES students

To better understand the language and cultural development of the 2005 cohort, I employed an ethnographic approach as this mode of research is well suited to small-scale, intensive investigations of cultural phenomenon (Crang and Cook, 2007; Gobo, 2008; O'Reilly, 2008). I was fortunate to have the opportunity to observe and spend time with the students in informal and formal situations both in Hong Kong and England. This allowed me to explore aspects of their development that could easily have been overlooked if I had simply employed closed pre- and post surveys and language proficiency tests. This study differed from my previous investigations of SES groups (Jackson, 2005, 2006a, 2006b, 2007, 2008) in that I employed the Intercultural Development Inventory (IDI) to provide an additional, objective measure of the participants' intercultural sensitivity. Hence, for the present research I made use of both qualitative and quantitative data to track the students' language and cultural development over a 16-month period.

Guiding questions

The following questions guided my investigation of the language and (inter)cultural learning and identity reconstruction of the 2005 SES cohort:

1   What are the participants' attitudes toward the languages they speak and their culture/the host culture? What motivates their language and cultural learning? Do their attitudes and motives change over time and space?
2   What are the participants' views about their identity? Do they experience identity reconstruction over the course of the study? If yes, what factors appear to bring about these changes?
3   How culturally sensitive are the participants on entry into the program? Does their level of intercultural sensitivity change after the presojourn preparation and their five-week stay in the host culture? If yes, how does it change?

4 What factors appear to impact on their intercultural communicative competence and willingness to communicate in the host language? Is there a link between their intercultural communicative competence (language awareness, sociopragmatic development, intercultural sensitivity) and identity reconstruction (if any)?

Role(s) of ethnographer

As field research is influenced by the characteristics of the ethnographer, it is important to acknowledge pertinent aspects of my background, biography, and identities. I am a female Canadian (Caucasian) professor who is a native speaker of English. I have taught Chinese university students in Hong Kong for more than 14 years and have researched their language choices, linguistic attitudes, and identities before and after the change of sovereignty in 1997 (Jackson, 2002). As an undergraduate, I majored in French and participated in a "junior year abroad" program at a French Canadian university.

My relationship with the participants evolved over the course of the study as I assumed many responsibilities and roles (e.g., teacher, research adviser, participant observer, conversation partner, evaluator, confident, fellow researcher/explorer, motivator, photographer). I taught two of the presojourn SES courses: ethnographic research and intercultural communication and had informal conversations with the students outside class. During the five-week sojourn in England, I supervised their research projects, helped facilitate weekly debriefing/research advising sessions, joined the students on cultural site visits, and administered weekly surveys. Following the sojourn, I reviewed their fieldwork materials (e.g., diaries, ethnographic portfolios, open-ended survey data, literary report). At the beginning of the next semester, I facilitated debriefing sessions and in the ethnographic research report-writing course I helped the students make sense of the data they had gathered in England. I also observed the sharing session the participants organized for the next group of SES students.

Issues of consent, confidentiality, and trustworthiness

Before the study got underway, in keeping with the ethics guidelines for my university, the students were asked in writing if they would be willing for me to analyze their SES work and follow their progress through the program. They were assured that their participation in the study (or lack of it) would not affect their grades and pseudonyms would be used in subsequent reports. All agreed to participate. They were offered the option of withdrawing from the study at any time. None did.

When introspective data is an integral part of a study, the willingness of the participants to freely disclose their thoughts and feelings is crucial. Throughout the course of this research, I was able to build up relationships of confidence and trust, which facilitated access to student views. An examination of their oral and written narratives revealed that they had been both candid and reflective. While the grading of some of their writing (e.g., diaries, intercultural reflections journal) might have affected their comments, this did not appear to be the case as they expressed both positive and negative sentiments. I found that the students were quite open about critical incidents they had experienced and their reactions to them. This is critical, as Hammersley and Atkinson (1995: 229) warn: "While people are well-placed informants on their own actions, they are no more than that … it may be in a person's interests to misinterpret or misdescribe his or her own actions or to counter the interpretations of the ethnographer." For the most part, this did not seem to be an issue with my students and their revelations provided valuable insight into their personal experience and meaning-making.

Other researchers who work with first-person data (e.g., Pavlenko, 2007; Ochs and Capps, 1996; Riessman, 2002) remind us that narratives are *versions* of reality. Rather than "objective, omniscient accounts," they are "partial representations and evocations of the world" (Ochs and Capps, 1996: 21) as seen through the eyes of the individual at a particular point in time and location. Riessman (2002: 218) explains that "[h]uman agency and imagination determine what gets included and excluded in narrativization, how events are plotted, and what they are supposed to mean." With this in mind, whenever possible, I made an effort to triangulate multiple sources of data relating to the same phenomenon (e.g., different accounts of the same intercultural incident by several SES students, retellings of an event by an individual sojourner in different settings at different points in time). When working with the data, I was also mindful of Hammersley and Atkinson's (2007: 98) advice: "The more effectively we can understand an account and its context – the presuppositions on which it relies, how it was produced, by who, for whom, and why – the better able we are to anticipate the ways in which it may suffer from biases of one kind or another as a source of information." In my analysis I aimed to be mindful of the context, source, and form of the self-reports.

Participants

The 2005 cohort included 14[5] (2 males and 12 females) full-time English majors in the second year of a three-year Bachelor of Arts degree program. The students had an average age of 20.1 years on entry into the program and a grade point average of 3.3. They had an advanced level of proficiency in English with an average of B on the "Use of English" A-level exam at the end of their secondary schooling. All of them grew up in Hong Kong and spoke Cantonese as a first language. Before the sojourn, three had participated in short-term study abroad programs in English-speaking countries (a three- to four-week stay in the US, Australia, or the UK). For most, however, personal contact with non-Chinese had been very limited and their travel experiences had primarily consisted of short family trips to Mainland China or organized tours to other Asian countries.

Prior to joining the SES, none of the participants had ever taken a course in intercultural communication, anti-racist education, or multiculturalism. Their use of English in Hong Kong had largely been restricted to academic settings, with Cantonese playing a dominant role in their personal life. Most had had very limited exposure to informal, social English before traveling to England. Few had ever had a personal relationship with someone from another culture.

Instrumentation

Qualitative measures

Presojourn qualitative data for each student included an application letter to the SES; the language and cultural identity narrative and intercultural reflections journal that were written in the intercultural communication course; the "home ethnography" project portfolio; open-ended surveys; and an interview conducted by a bilingual Hong Kong Chinese research assistant to prompt reflection on cultural socialization, language use, self-identity, previous travels/intercultural contact/study abroad (if any), and aspirations/concerns about the sojourn. The interviewees had the option of expressing their views in English or Cantonese (or code-mixing). All written narratives were in English.

During this phase, I kept field notes based on my observation of the students in the presojourn courses and ethnographic research advising sessions. The orientation session facilitated by previous SES students provided me with the opportunity to observe the reactions and comments/queries of the 2005 group. In my field notes, I recorded my informal, ethnographic conversations with the students as they prepared for the trip to England.

Qualitative data collected during the sojourn included a diary and weekly open-ended surveys designed to draw out student views about such aspects as their intercultural adjustment, cultural differences, their use of English in daily life (e.g., with their hosts, in the community, with other SES students), their identity, their intercultural communication skills and level of sensitivity, and their ethnographic investigations of a cultural scene. All of the writing was in English.

Throughout the five weeks, I participated in the excursions and weekly debriefing sessions and carried out relaxed, informal ethnographic conversations with the students. I kept a daily record of my observations and reflections, which included my review of their ethnographic project materials (e.g., research proposal, interview guides). This added an element of triangulation and helped to further contextualize student experiences.

Postsojourn qualitative data included an open-ended survey in English and an interview about sojourn/reentry experiences that was conducted either in English, Cantonese, or code-mixing, depending on the preference of the interviewee. The bilingual research assistant encouraged the students to reflect on the impact of study abroad on their intercultural awareness and sensitivity, identity, and intercultural communication skills. For a 14-week period, I supervised the development of the ethnographic dissertations that were based on sojourn data. During this phase, I facilitated informal conversations with the students about their sojourn and reentry experiences. I also kept field notes in which I recorded my observations of our debriefing sessions/conversations, the orientation session the group organized for the next cohort, and my reactions to reading their diaries, sojourn surveys, interview transcripts, and ethnographic dissertations.

When any of the discourse (e.g., written narratives in English or translations of interviews that were conducted in Cantonese or code-mixing) was unclear to me, the students were asked to clarify their intended meaning. This was very important as I aimed to accurately represent their voices and offer insight into the ways in which they were making sense of their intercultural experiences both in Hong Kong and England.

Quantitative data

I employed Version 2 of the IDI (Hammer and Bennett, 2002; Hammer, Bennett, and Wiseman, 2003) to measure the students' intercultural sensitivity/worldview orientation to cultural difference as conceptualized in the DMIS (see Chapter 2; M. J. Bennett, 1993). This 50-item psychometric instrument is widely used in study abroad research and has demonstrated construct validity and reliability (Hammer, Bennett, and Wiseman, 2003; Paige, Jacobs-Cassuto, Yershova and DeJaeghere, 2003).

Using a five-point Likert scale, respondents indicate their agreement or disagreement with 50 statements. In addition to measuring overall intercultural sensitivity, referred to as the Developmental Scale (DS), the IDI yields scores for each of the five scales that are described in Table 3.2: Denial and Defense (DD) together, Reversal (R), Minimization (M), Acceptance and Adaptation (AA) combined, and Encapsulated

Table 3.2 Description of IDI (Intercultural Development Inventory) scales

	Scale	Description
Ethnocentricism	Denial and Defense (DD)	Measures a worldview that simplifies and/or polarizes cultural difference. It ranges from disinterest and avoidance to a tendency to view the world in terms of "us" and "them," where "us" is superior.
	Reversal (R)	Measures a worldview that reverses the "us" and "them" polarization, where "them" is superior. It is a "mirror image" of the denial/defense orientation.
	Minimization (M)	Measures a worldview that highlights cultural commonality and universal values through an emphasis on similarity – a tendency to assume that people from other cultures are basically "like us."
Ethnorelativism	Acceptance and Adaptation (AA)	Measures a worldview that can comprehend and accommodate complex cultural difference. It can range from a tendency to recognize patterns of cultural difference in one's own culture and in other cultures (acceptance) to a tendency to alter perception and behavior according to cultural context (adaptation).
	Encapsulated Marginality (EM)	Measures a worldview that incorporates a multicultural identity with confused cultural perspectives as one's identity is separated from any specific cultural context. EM refers to the experience of "cultural marginality"; constructive marginality, the other part of Integration is not measured by the IDI.

Source: Adapted from Hammer and Bennett (2002).

Marginality (EM), a form of integration characterized by plural identities and a sense of alienation. As the EM scale is viewed as an incomplete measure of Integration, it is not used in the calculation of the Overall Developmental Scale.

As well as computing the group's (and individual respondents') fundamental worldview orientation to cultural difference (their progress toward ethnorelativism), the IDI software identifies specific developmental issues within each scale that are not yet resolved (e.g., a tendency to polarize cultural difference by reversing "us and them," whereby "them" is deemed superior). The IDI also measures the group's (and individual respondents') own perception of their intercultural sensitivity and ability.

Procedures and analysis

Once the students had agreed to participate, I set up a project database in NVivo (Bazeley, 2007; Richards, 2005), a hypermedia, qualitative software program. Each piece of data (e.g., interview transcript, intercultural reflections journal, survey, sojourn diary, digital image) was entered into the database soon after it was gathered. By the end of the study, I had a rich database of hundreds of pages of narrative, introspective data, including my own field notes and digital images/video clips.

To make sense of this data, I employed an "open coding" approach (Charmaz, 2006; Grbich, 2007; Strauss and Corbin, 1998); I devised codes to reflect what I saw in the material rather than restrict myself to preconceived categories. Throughout the study, I coded the qualitative data soon after it was entered into NVivo, noting recurrent issues and themes (Bailey, 2007; Berg, 2007; Crang and Cook, 2007). New categories continually emerged and others were reorganized as I better understood the relationship between items. While working with the material I gained new insights and modified the data collection instruments, accordingly (Denzin and Lincoln, 2003; Hesse-Biber and Leavy, 2006; Marshall and Rossman, 2006).

When analyzing these first-person accounts, I heeded Riessman's (2002: 262) advice to pay attention to "nuances of speech, organization of a response, local contexts of production, social discourses that shape what is said, and what cannot be spoken." By triangulating data types and sources, I discovered how the students perceived cultural differences and made sense of intercultural experiences in an unfamiliar linguistic and cultural milieu. In the process, I developed a holistic cultural portrait of the group that incorporated both the views of the students (an emic perspective) and my interpretation (an etic, researcher's perspective).

I also administered the IDI at three intervals: before and after the 14-week presojourn preparation and immediately following the five-week sojourn in England. I then processed the data using IDI software. This provided me with an indication of the actual and perceived levels of intercultural sensitivity of each participant as well as the group as a whole. Since all of the data was dated, it was possible to link the three IDI administrations with the students' oral and written narratives and my field notes. This facilitated another element of triangulation and allowed me to better understand the development of the students' intercultural sensitivity and sociopragmatic awareness over time and space. It also enabled me to see discrepancies between the IDI scores and narratives (see Table 3.3 for the actual and perceived IDI scores of the group at three intervals).

Selection and overview of case participants

To better illustrate variations in the development of intercultural sensitivity and communicative competence, I selected several students for closer scrutiny instead of limiting my discussion to the group as a whole. I began the selection process by eliminating those with previous study abroad experience in an English-speaking country. Next, I examined the language and cultural identity narratives, sojourn diaries, responses on open-ended surveys, and interview transcripts to identify those who had supplied very detailed, frank information about their language and cultural learning before, during, and after the trip to England. I then reviewed their IDI scores and chose four individuals who experienced different developmental trajectories: Nora, Mimi, Lana, and Jade (pseudonyms).

The developmental trajectories of the case participants

The next three chapters focus on the young women's stories, offering insight into the factors that impacted on their language and (inter)cultural learning and evolving self-identity both in Hong Kong and England. Chapter 4 focuses on the presojourn preparation phase, while Chapters 5 and 6 explore their sojourn and reentry experiences. Throughout this book I link their narratives[6] with their IDI scores: on entry, after the presojourn preparation, and postsojourn. When relevant, I interpose

Table 3.3 Actual and perceived IDI Developmental Scores (DS) of SES cohort: On entry, after presojourn preparation, and postsojourn

Students	IDI scores												Gain (+)/Loss (−)			
	Actual						Perceived						Actual		Perceived	
	1	2	3	4	5	6	1	2	3	4	5	6	1	2	3	4
Max (M)	104.90	M	81.20	DD/R	112.49	M	128.23	AA	118.92	AA	131.76	AA	−	+	−	+
*Judi (F)	74.97	DD/R	82.20	DD/R	100.14	M	115.44	AA	120.08	AA	126.67	AA	+	+	+	+
Lana (F)	92.91	M	98.91	M	98.81	M	120.86	AA	122.54	AA	122.26	AA	+	−/+	+	−/+
Mei (F)	83.49	DD/R	76.34	DD/R	99.38	M	118.10	AA	113.16	M	123.08	AA	−	+	−	+
Nina (F)	96.55	M	95.30	M	—	—	122.89	AA	121.86	AA	—	—	−	−	−	−
*Zita (F)	119.97	AA	119.31	AA	115.13	AA	133.71	AA	133.19	AA	132.05	AA	−/+	−	−/+	−
Ella (F)	75.83	DD/R	123.17	AA	124.20	AA	115.09	AA	135.01	AA	137.09	AA	+	+	+	+
Jen (F)	77.66	DD/R	88.31	DD/R	77.20	DD/R	116.04	AA	121.39	AA	117.28	AA	+	−	+	−
Ivan (M)	96.65	M	96.84	M	129.07	AA	123.35	AA	123.52	AA	136.36	AA	−/+	+	−/+	+
Jade (F)	85.87	M	118.50	AA	125.57	AA	117.74	AA	134.69	AA	137.73	AA	+	+	+	+
Sara (F)	91.80	M	86.65	M	93.19	M	123.59	AA	119.84	AA	121.36	AA	−	+	−	+
Mimi (F)	76.02	DD/R	85.59	M	94.87	M	117.15	AA	120.69	AA	125.16	AA	+	+	+	+
*Hidy (F)	90.25	M	114.34	M	106.46	M	122.85	AA	130.85	AA	127.78	AA	+	−	+	−
Nora (F)	68.37	DD/R	80.85	DD/R	86.16	DD/R	114.59	AA	117.99	AA	120.92	AA	+	+	+	+
Full group	88.23	M	96.25	M	104.82	M	120.69	AA	123.84	AA	127.65	AA	+	+	+	+

Note: M = male; F = Female; * = previous short-term study abroad in US, UK or Australia (Nina did not take part in the sojourn, leaving 13 in the study). Developmental Score (DS): DD/R=Denial/Defense or Reversal (55–85), M=Minimization (85.1–115), AA = Acceptance/Adaptation (115.1 +). Actual scores: Columns 1 and 2 (IDI score/Band descriptor on entry into the SES); Columns 3 and 4 (IDI score/Band descriptor after presojourn preparation); Columns 5 and 6 (IDI score/Band descriptor after sojourn). Perceived scores: Columns 1 and 2 (IDI score/Band descriptor on entry into the SES); Columns 3 and 4 (IDI score/Band descriptor after presojourn preparation); Columns 5 and 6 (IDI score/Band descriptor after sojourn). Gain (+) and/or loss (−) in actual intercultural sensitivity: Column 1 (after presojourn preparation); Column 2 (after sojourn). Gain (+) and/or loss (−) in perceived intercultural sensitivity: Column 3 (after presojourn preparation); Column 4 (after sojourn).

an etic (outsider's) perspective, drawing on my field notes, to further contextualize each woman's story. I also draw comparisons and contrasts between the young woman's experiences to better understand the factors impacting on their developmental trajectories.

What follows are the unique stories of the four young women.

4

Presojourn Language and (Inter)Cultural Development

Prior to the sojourn, the four case participants (Nora, Mimi, Lana, and Jade)[1] took part in the predeparture phase of the SES on their home campus in Hong Kong. As their course instructor in the ethnography and intercultural communication courses, we became well acquainted with each other during this 14-week period. As they shared their experiences, thoughts, and emotions, with me, I gained more understanding and appreciation of their language, (inter)cultural, and identity development before the sojourn in England.

After providing a brief profile of each case participant, this chapter offers insight into their presojourn language ability and usage, self-identity, and (inter)cultural sensitivity. I also explore their reaction to the home institution's hotly debated internationalization and medium-of-instruction policies. Throughout this chapter, I link their oral and written narratives[2] with their Intercultural Development Inventory (IDI) scores (on entry and after the presojourn preparation). This allows us to track changes in their intercultural awareness, identity, and readiness for study and residence abroad in the months leading up to the sojourn. The written narratives were in English and excerpts are in their original form. All of the young women opted to do their presojourn interview in Cantonese and efforts were made to retain the nuances and emotions of the discourse in the translation.

Profiles

By way of an interview, surveys, and narrative, all the young women provided insight into their personality, family background, and ambitions. Their revelations help to better understand their unique trajectories.

Nora

When I first met Nora she was quite reserved and often lost in her own thoughts. In the presojourn interview, she described herself as "an introvert," and "the kind of person who's not that passionate." "I may seem very quiet and cool," she explained, "but when I get to know people, I become more talkative and they realize I've got a sense of humor." Nora later revealed more about her personality and interests on her homestay placement form: "I enjoy listening to music and playing the piano. I love singing. Music is my life! Not only am I interested in Canto-pop, I like classical music, operas, and church music. I also like reading and going to the cinema with friends." At University, she opted to major in English and joined several campus organizations: the drama club, the English society, a choral group, and a college society.

An only child, Nora was very close to her parents and decided to live on campus to become more independent. Her father, a secondary school graduate and owner of a publishing company, occasionally communicated with clients in English. Her mother, a housewife, did not complete secondary school and spoke one language, Cantonese. With her family, Nora had visited several South East Asian countries and, as a university student, she had traveled to Taipei and Shanghai with friends. Most trips were short, organized tours for Cantonese speakers. On entry into the SES, Nora aspired to do postgraduate studies in English Literature, drama, or translation and become a reporter for a local English newspaper.

Mimi

Mimi, a vivacious 20-year-old with a flare for the dramatic, saw herself as "friendly, enthusiastic, and cheerful": "I'm an outgoing girl who always wears her smiley face and is, indeed, very talkative. Though hilarious sometimes, I'm also a mature person ready to face different, new challenges" (homestay placement form). She had a wide range of interests: "My hobbies are writing, watching movies and dramas, listening to music, singing, and, of course, reading. I love cooking creatively, too! I love to try fancy and new dishes" (interview). At University, she participated in many student organizations, often assuming a leadership role such as President of the Chinese Association and Chair of the English Society.

Her mother, a widow from Mainland China, had six children, all of whom were born and raised in Hong Kong. Mimi's elder siblings were in the workforce; the younger ones were still in school. None of her family members spoke English at home or interacted across cultures.

Her mother had not completed secondary school and Mimi was the first one in her family to attend university. Except for a brief trip to visit relatives in Mainland China as a child, Mimi had never ventured outside Hong Kong. After finishing her undergraduate degree, she hoped to do postgraduate studies in linguistics or literature and become an English language teacher in a local secondary school.

Lana

Lana, a self-professed introvert, saw herself as "quiet, shy, and thoughtful" (language and cultural identity narrative). In her view, her close friends would describe her as "a funny and interesting person" who was both "genteel" and "cool." As she was "quite patient," she got "along well with different age groups of people" (homestay placement form). At University, she lived in a hostel but, unlike the other case participants, did not join any campus organizations. In her homestay placement form she added: "I like drawing, painting, and cooking. I love watching movies and television. My favorite genres are adventures and romances. I love country music and folk songs but not rock'n roll nor raps."

A middle child, Lana had two sisters; the eldest was a university graduate, while the youngest was still in school. Her father, a high school graduate, had been a teacher in a small village in Mainland China before moving to Hong Kong to work for a company. His wife, a factory worker, completed Form Five (Grade 11) in the Mainland. Although her father and sisters knew some English, they did not use it in their social life. Both of her parents had traveled to other Asian countries but had no personal contact with non-Chinese. Every few years, Lana and her family made short visits to the Fujian province of Mainland China to visit relatives. Similar to Mimi, she had never traveled outside the Chinese-speaking world. On entry, Lana was uncertain about her future but imagined that she might work in some area of business in Hong Kong.

Jade

A "cheerful" extrovert, Jade "loved to smile" and made friends easily. She thought that those who knew her best would describe her as "responsible," "sensible," and "mature" (interview). In her intercultural reflections journal, she wrote: "I'm easy-going. No doubt, this is an advantage for me. I feel comfortable meeting strangers from different ages, backgrounds, and cultures. My easy personality grants me a lot of friendships. I'm just optimistic about everything that happens around me." At University, she lived in a hostel and participated in a range of activities (e.g., a drama competition, the English society, the Rotaract club) "to meet many people from different backgrounds." An "outgoing, adventurous person," Jade had many diverse interests, ranging from music and art to sports.

With her family, she had made short trips to several Asian countries and had also visited South Korea with friends. Of the four case participants, Jade had the most travel experience. As a secondary school student, she joined two brief cultural exchange programs in Mainland China. In her first year of university, she took part in a speech contest in Beijing and a three-week-long French immersion program in France, where she lived in a dormitory.

Similar to Nora, Jade was an only child. Her parents grew up in Hong Kong and had a secondary-school level of education. Her father, a businessman, owned his own company, with branches in Hong Kong and Mainland China. While he spoke some English, he was not fluent. Her mother, a factory manager, knew little English. When she joined the SES, like Lana, Jade hoped to have a career in business but had no concrete plans.

Language ability and usage

All four case participants attended Chinese (Cantonese)-medium primary schools, where they studied English as a second language. Although the majority of junior secondary schools in Hong Kong now use Cantonese as the teaching medium, in Form One (Grade 7) these young women switched to EMI (English as the medium-of-instruction) schools to complete their preuniversity education. From Secondary One to Three (Grades 7–9), they studied Putonghua (Mandarin) as a compulsory subject and then as an elective for their school leaving public examination. In addition to Chinese and English, all of them opted to study other languages in secondary school and at University (e.g., Japanese, French, German). They could also apply to join subsidized language immersion programs linked to these languages, although only Jade chose to do so prior to the SES.[3]

By way of surveys, an interview, and written narratives (e.g., language and cultural identity narrative, intercultural reflections journal), the four women described the role(s) of language in their lives. Their perceptions shed light on the complex linguistic, sociocultural, and psychological factors that influenced their language attitudes and choices prior to the trip to England.

Nora

Nora spoke five languages: Cantonese (her mother tongue), Putonghua, English, Japanese, and French, and also studied sign language. She considered herself "very good" in both Cantonese and Putonghua[4] but only "fair" in French and Japanese. At the end of her secondary schooling, she received an "A" on the A-level "Use of English" examination, the highest score among the four case participants. Even so, she rated her overall proficiency in the language as "good," convinced that her oral skills were "not up to standard." In her interview, she explained: "Sometimes it's hard to express my feelings in English. It's difficult to find the equivalent word that has the same meaning as the Cantonese word I'd like to use." She was most apprehensive about making mistakes when communicating with "native speakers" of English.

As a youngster, Nora was aware of the linguistic capital of English in Hong Kong. The government, media, and her parents continually stressed the importance of "obtaining a good English standard," a phenomenon that has been explained in Chapter 3. Describing the language as "indispensable," Nora displayed a high level of instrumental motivation to enhance her proficiency (e.g., to secure a good job). In her narrative, she wrote:

> The colonization by Britain has affected greatly the education system in Hong Kong. Children learn English together with Cantonese when they are only three or four years old. Same level of importance has been placed on Cantonese and English and, personally, I think both can be considered as the mother languages of Hong Kongers ... I find myself very privileged to have been granted the chance to learn English starting from an early age. I am gratitude to be put in an English-medium secondary school ... As Hong Kong was a colony of Britain, English, the international language, has become an official language so every one is pushed to learn it as its essential in many aspects of our daily lives. ... Besides, the emphasis that the Hong Kong government has put on English seems to indoctrinate its people the notion that English is indispensable and parents should ensure that their children have a good grasp of English, which might guarantee them a brighter future. Though, it may sound a bit aggressive, the stress on the importance of English benefits everyone in Hong Kong. If they are equipped well, they can compete with people from different places as English is essential for every work.

While Nora referred to Cantonese and English as "the mother languages of Hong Kongers," in reality, she "lived in" Cantonese in her family life and in the community, as she disclosed later in an interview:[5] "I haven't had much chance to use English outside of class. Since I'm so close with my mum and dad, I use Cantonese at home. At the moment, I feel there's a kind of distant feeling when I'm using English."

As a young adult and English major, Nora sometimes practiced the language at home: "Once in awhile I read English books and newspapers. Occasionally, I watch English TV programs like David Letterman and America's Next Top Model to improve my listening" (interview). After class, she preferred to use Cantonese to talk with friends who are not from the English Department: "They'd think it was really awkward if I spoke English with them. Besides, if we can speak good Cantonese then why shouldn't we communicate in a language that we're both familiar with?" (interview). While she sometimes discussed "academic stuff" in English with other English majors, she switched to Cantonese "when talking about personal problems or sharing feelings." She and her friends frequently code-mixed (e.g., interjecting some English academic terms into Cantonese discourse), a practice she considered acceptable as long as it was not "too frequent." Her code usage was in line with Trudgill's (2003) observation that the language of bilingual speakers is often associated with particular "sets of domains." Both the social and linguistic context of the communication influenced Nora's perception of which code was appropriate.

Mimi

Mimi spoke Cantonese, Putonghua, English, and a bit of German. She considered her Cantonese to be excellent, her oral skills and listening comprehension in Putonghua to be "very good," and her proficiency in German as "fair." At the end of her secondary schooling, Mimi received a "C" on the A-level "Use of English" examination. Even so, similar to Nora, who had scored an "A," she rated her overall English language ability as "good." While she considered her reading and writing skills in the language to be "very fluent," she was less certain of her oral skills and listening comprehension, describing them as "fairly fluent." In her interview, she contrasted her linguistic ability and confidence level in English and Cantonese:

> When I speak my mother tongue, Cantonese, I feel the most comfortable because of my proficiency in this language and the environment that I live in. As English is not my mother tongue, I'm quite

nervous when I talk with native speakers. Since I'm afraid I'll make mistakes, I try to be more careful about my grammar. Sometimes, this makes me present my ideas in an awkward way. ... My oral skills in English are in great need of improvement.

Like Nora, Mimi sensed external pressure to learn English while growing up: "Under British colonial rule, Hong Kong schools covertly and overtly promoted English as an important tool for students to earn money" (narrative). Her mother reinforced the message that English was "noble, superior, and full of privilege." To please her and do well in society, Mimi felt compelled to master it.

To gain my mother's attention, I needed to seek a way to establish and develop my own strength. I joined tons of extracurricular activities to build up my confidence and win a glance from Mother. Winning English solo-verse speaking competitions several times, my English teachers declared me a genius in speaking English. My mother was, of course, glad to see that. English, to my mother, is something noble, superior, and full of privilege. In her mind, English can make money. Perhaps, imperceptibly influenced by colonialism or by what my mother sees and hears, I also gradually generated such a silly thought (narrative).

Similar to the other case participants, Cantonese was the language Mimi used at home. In an interview she became quite emotional as she recounted a troubling incident in which she had unintentionally spoken in English in the domestic domain. Her older sister accused her of "showing off" and/or disrespecting their mother by using a language that she did not understand:

I always thought that my family, including my mum was very proud of my good English but one day, just after I entered the English Department, she quarreled with my younger sister, and I spontaneously used English to stop them. My elder sister criticized me for using English, saying that she didn't know whether I wanted to show off my English or humiliate my mother because she didn't know English. After this incident, I remind myself not to use English when I'm at home but I still can't avoid code-mixing.

Mimi had violated implicit social rules that determine which language is appropriate in the private arena. In her home, Cantonese symbolizes in-group solidarity and serves as an index of social and cultural identity; hence, her use of English strained interpersonal relations and family harmony. As noted by Canagarajah (1999), Coulmas (2005), and other sociolinguists, tacit social restrictions may profoundly influence language attitudes and choice.

Away from her home environment, Mimi occasionally practiced English with her SES friends as well as her roommate, a journalism major. She appeared to be more accepting of the use of English among Chinese than many of her peers: "Some of my friends think that Chinese should use their own language in their conversations but I'm quite liberal in this aspect. I think it's okay to use English with each other." In her interview, she also remarked that she'd become "much more self-motivated" to learn the language in recent years. Although she seldom tuned into English TV programs, she occasionally watched movies in English, even preferring them to Cantonese films: "I like the style, presentation, and themes of English movies. It's not that I despise local films, it's just that sometimes their themes are just nonsense" (interview). Her comments raise our awareness of the dynamic nature of motivation in second language (L2) learners (Dörnyei, 2005, 2009; Lamb, 2004; S. Ryan, 2006, 2009).

Like Nora, Mimi frequently code-mixed when conversing with friends: "I use English a lot and sometimes don't know how to translate some ideas back to Chinese even though I studied Chinese literature for four years. In the past I wanted to maintain language purity. It seemed that Cantonese was corrupted by code-mixing but now I've just accepted it as normal in this context" (interview). As Coulmas (2005) and Myers-Scotton (2006) observe, this mode of discourse is often a natural consequence of living in a hybrid environment where more than one language is used.

Lana

Lana spoke Cantonese and English and could understand Hokkein (the Min dialect used in the Fujian province of China) as well as some Putonghua. She had also taken several basic French language courses. In an interview she assessed her proficiency in each language:

> I'm most fluent in Cantonese. My English fluency's okay but the others are not good. I can understand Putonghua but can't speak it naturally. If I have to speak the Min dialect, it's possible and others should be able to understand me but I'm not fluent in it. My knowledge of the Min dialect is just barely enough for me to communicate

and survive. My spoken French is not okay at all. I don't really know how to speak it. If I meet a French person, I'd rather speak English.

Of these languages, Lana was most attached to her mother tongue: "Undoubtedly, Cantonese is my preference. All through my school-days, though both Cantonese and English were the medium of instruc-tion, Cantonese has been the language in which I express myself and communicate with others most naturally, most often, and most intimately" (narrative). Her mother tongue "shaped her feelings and emotions" and gave her "a tender feeling." In her interview she added: "I feel I'm myself when speaking it." By contrast, like Nora, she felt rather "distant" from English, as her exposure to it was largely confined to formal, academic settings: "Normally I speak English when I'm in school or when I'm making a speech. It seems that I have another iden-tity when speaking it." Her comments raise our awareness of the com-plex linkage between language, context, and identity that have been noted by sociolinguists in other environments (e.g., Myers-Scotton, 2006; Noels, 2009; Norton, 2000).

Although she spoke Cantonese at home and lived in a Cantonese-speaking society, Lana was concerned that majoring in English was having a detrimental impact on her mother tongue. Her fears draw attention to the potentially subtractive power of the language of prestige (Lambert, 1975): "After a year at university my Cantonese proficiency has been lowered because of being highly immersed in English read-ings, lectures, concepts, and ideas. Sometimes I struggle to find a correct Cantonese word in front of my mother, who doesn't know English, as my mind is occupied by an English word" (narrative). How would she react to being in an English-speaking environment? I wondered if she would resist the host language, fearing that she would become further alienated from Cantonese.

Similar to Mimi, Lana had received a "C" on the A-level "Use of English" examination at the end of her secondary schooling. Of the four case participants, she was the least confident in her overall English language proficiency, rating herself as "fair." While she believed her reading and writing skills were "very fluent," she described her oral skills and listening comprehension as "fairly fluent." In her interview she revealed that, like Nora, she was especially nervous when using the lan-guage with native speakers: "I sometimes feel deaf and dumb because I don't understand what they say. Once I talked to a foreigner on the phone and couldn't understand a single word." She was more relaxed about practicing English with Chinese Hong Kongers who spoke English as an additional language: "We're the same kind of people so there's a closer feeling." Her comments revealed a strong in-group orientation.

Like the other case participants, as a youngster, Lana was aware of the elevated position of English in local society: "English is an amazing language. At first, I learn it because I have to. There seems to be a belief in Hong Kong that having a high proficiency could gain higher respect from the society" (narrative). She was also motivated to learn the language to gain recognition from her family: "I always came in the top three in English. To maintain this 'prestigious' status, I studied hard. I found this a way of drawing my parents' attention. … While I could almost recite every page in the English textbooks, I was an idiot for things beyond. I neglected them as they were not of my parents' concerns" (narrative). Similar to Nora and Mimi, at this age, her motivation was largely extrinsic, that is, driven by a desire to please others.

Witnessing her father's struggle to learn English as an adult heightened Lana's awareness of the power and prestige of the language in Hong Kong. As her own proficiency grew, she began to feel "superior" to her parents:

> Since my father came from China, his English standard is not as good as the local Hong Kong people so when I was in primary school, he intentionally went to an adult school to learn Primary Four, Five and Six English. I appreciated that very much. Perhaps this also made me study English harder. … In the case of father's learning of English it appeared to me that learning English could change one's status. I also found myself more superior to my parents once I gained a higher level of proficiency in English than them because there was something in my mind that they did not understand (narrative).

Lana's attitude toward English continued to evolve as she matured and began to recognize its position on the world stage: "Since English acts as an international language, through it we can communicate with people worldwide so people give it a special rank. Through my university education, I gain more awareness on the position and values of English" (narrative). Her comments underscore the dynamic nature of motivation and attitudes in L2 learners, especially those who are studying English as an international language (Dörnyei, 2009; Lamb, 2004; Ryan, 2009; Yashima, 2009).

For private or personal communication, she preferred to use Cantonese or code-mixing. While she often read English textbooks and websites, she seldom picked up an English magazine or book to read for pleasure.

When she wrote in the language it was usually homework-related although she sometimes used it in ICQ, an instant messaging computer program that is popular among Hong Kong youth. She rarely tuned into English-medium TV programs and appeared to be less invested in the language than the other women.

Like many of her peers, Lana frequently code-mixed with her friends in face-to-face conversation, as well as online. In her interview, she explained her language choices:

> In everyday communication, I naturally replace some Chinese words with English ones. I just utter the words that I first think of. I also code-mix quite a lot in ICQ. Your speed of typing affects the language that you use and it's quicker to type words in English. ... If you get a message in English, you tend to use English to reply, too. But sometimes if you want to express some feelings that can only be conveyed in Chinese terms, then you'll have to type one or two Chinese words in the message.

Lana sometimes denigrated her code-mixing "habit," describing it as "neither pure nor grammatically correct." Similar to Nora, she had rather strict ideas about how much English should be added to Cantonese speech: "If one just code-mixes one or two words, I think it's normal but if one uses code-mixing excessively, e.g., if one uses English words in several sentences or uses some English adjectives or adverbs, I think it's too exaggerated" (interview). Her comments further raise our awareness of the psychological and sociocultural tensions that can surface in bilingual or multilingual situations (Canagarajah, 1999; Dörnyei, 2005; Myers-Scotton, 2006).

Jade

Jade spoke Cantonese, English, Putonghua, and a little French and Japanese. She described herself as "very fluent" in the former, although she lacked confidence in some of the skill areas: "My listening and speaking are fine since it's my mother tongue but my reading skills are just average. My writing used to be very good but I haven't written much in Chinese lately" (interview). In her narrative she added: "I learned to speak Cantonese at home and in daily life. It was the language I was most comfortable with until my English self developed." She rated her Putonghua as "average" and her French listening and speaking skills as "fair." She had forgotten most of the Japanese she'd learned in secondary school.

Jade achieved a "B" on her A-level exam in English and described her overall proficiency as "good." In her estimation, her reading and comprehension skills were "very fluent." She was slightly less confident of her oral and written skills, describing them as "fairly fluent" (predeparture survey). Similar to the other young women, she felt pressured to learn the language while growing up: "My school learning environment pushed me to learn English. I knew from an early age that I must learn it. My parents did not emphasize the importance of Cantonese" (interview). In her narrative Jade provided further insight into "societal attitudes towards English in Hong Kong" which had impacted on her socialization and perceptions of Cantonese and English:

> Hong Kongers have some false values and attitudes towards English. Many think that English is superior and western culture is high. This deep-rooted conception has impacted on my generation, my parents', and maybe my grandparents' generation ever since Hong Kong was colonized. Generally, Hong Kongers fear English but they also see the economic and social advantages that the language has brought about. For practical reasons they are motivated to learn English but the use of English is still very limited to either school or work.

Jade displayed a deeper level of investment in English than many of her peers. She voluntarily kept a diary in the language, read English magazines and newspapers for enjoyment, and interacted with her family's domestic helper in English. She liked to listen to English songs and watch English movies, commenting, "there are not any good Chinese films to see." She often watched television programs in English, such as ER and the news: In a typical day, she claimed to use English 50 percent of the time, primarily in an academic setting.

Conscious of the connection between language, identity, and worldview, Jade wrote in her narrative: "English and Chinese are the languages that I mostly use in Hong Kong. These languages help shape the way I see things, express things, and make sense of the world. They provide me a sense of self." In Noels' (2009) terms, she had begun to internalize both languages into her identity. Similar to most of her peers, however, Jade's mother tongue enveloped her with a sense of "intimacy" and "belonging" whereas she felt "less passionate" when using English. In her narrative, she explained:

> When speaking English, sometimes I don't feel I am Chinese. I become cold and rational when I speak English and tend to be less

demonstrative. I try to understand the difference. Perhaps, English native people belong to individualist culture. When I speak English, I somehow act like them. I think independently and behave more mature. This is how language and culture interact with each other. Apart from that, it may be traced back to my high schooldays which shape my English self. In school, I was taught to be disciplined. It instilled the Christian values and moral integrity into me. Plus, I was trained to think rationally in English debating team. Another possible reason is that Cantonese is the language that I grew up with. The intimacy of a home language allows me to express my emotion freely.

Like Mimi, Jade became anxious about losing the special bond with Cantonese as her "English self" became stronger and more prominent in her academic life: "When I grew up and became proficient in English, my English self sometimes dominates my Chinese self. Now, as an English major, I have more opportunities to use English than Chinese. Chinese nearly falls out of use, especially for writing. I begin to forget some of the Chinese characters" (narrative). Her revelations raise our awareness of the emotional and cognitive risks associated with subtractive bilingualism (Lambert, 1975).

Jade found it acceptable for the Hong Kong Chinese to use English with each other, although, similar to Nora and Lana, she had some reservations about this. In her narrative she explained: "I don't like to judge people. For me, it's people's own choice of language and their own way of communication. I may not find it 'normal' for them to use English but I wouldn't judge it." While the other women were nervous when speaking the language with native speakers, Jade actually preferred it, in part, due to her fear of being out-grouped: "It's great to use English with a native English speaker because people may not stare at you. If I speak English with a local person, people will definitely look strangely at me and think I'm showing off. Then, I'd feel embarrassed and alienated" (interview). Her remarks alert us to linguistic restrictions that may dictate which codes are considered appropriate in certain social situations (Coulmas, 2005; Myers-Scotton, 2006).

Similar to the other case participants, Jade frequently code-mixed when chatting with her friends but, as her narrative showed, she sometimes felt "ashamed" when doing so:

> Due to my lack of vocabulary in Chinese, I subconsciously mix English words in Cantonese conversation. My friends always find it difficult to communicate with me, especially on the phone because

I code-switch so often that they cannot follow. This minute I speak Cantonese. Next minute I speak English. I do not notice any switch in my speech till they raise it to me. Sometimes, I feel sorry when I speak Cantonese sprinkled with large doses of English. I feel ashamed of not being able to speak "pure Cantonese" fluently. It seems that I am losing my mother-tongue. This also makes me feel unsure of myself.

While she sometimes made an effort to refrain from code-mixing in daily conversation, she was rarely successful: "I want to speak pure Cantonese. I code mix all the time unconsciously because I can't think of the Chinese words to replace the English ones." In this interview Jade's concern about her "deteriorating" Cantonese resurfaced, raising concerns about the psychological impact of residing in an English-speaking country, even for a brief sojourn. I wondered if she would retain a subtractive notion of bilingualism (Lambert, 1975) while in an English-speaking environment.

Self-identity formation and change

By way of interviews and written narratives, the young women provided insight into their ethnic, cultural, and personal identity development. I discovered that their sense of self was influenced by a range of socio-historical, political, and situational factors as well as individual and cultural socialization processes. There were differences in the strength of their affiliation with Hong Kong, Britain, and Mainland China. Further, the emotional significance that they attached to their affiliation with local and national groups varied over time. Some valued their personal identity more than membership to their ethnic-cultural group and were periodically very conflicted about their positioning. I also discovered differences in the depth of reflection on this issue; some were more aware of the fluid, dynamic, and relational nature of identity.

Nora

Like many of her generation in Hong Kong, Nora was "caught in a dilemma" when the territory was returned from Britain to Mainland China (the Motherland) in 1997. As the following excerpt reveals, this historical event forced her to question her nationality, ethnicity, and place in the world:

Before the Handover, Hong Kong was part of Britain and I considered myself a British. I still remember clearly that when I filled in personal details on my passport or other forms, I wrote down "British" in the column of nationality. But after the Handover of Hong Kong to China, I had to think for a minute or so what I should write, "Chinese" or "British"? I was bewildered, as one with yellow skin I found no part of me that's similar to the Caucasians, but Asians. While some of my living styles and practices duplicate that of the westerners. I was kind of caught in a dilemma whether I was a Chinese, a British, or Hong Konger (narrative).

After the change in sovereignty, Nora felt pressured to develop a closer attachment to the Motherland. Believing she lacked the "attributes" of an "authentic, patriotic Chinese," she was reluctant to be defined in this way:

The controversial debate of the identity of Hong Kong people has been there for a long time. Some politicians think that after the Handover of Hong Kong to China we should call ourselves "Chinese." Yet, I cannot agree with that. I still lack the attributes that qualify me to be called an authentic "Chinese." For me, "Chinese" is referring to those who are patriotic towards their homeland, China, and are proud to mention it in front of others. Our hearts should be moved when the national anthem is being played and should feel glorified when we can be representatives of our home country. However, I don't feel that I am close to China nor am I willing to sacrifice for my country (narrative).

At this point in time, Nora resisted the imposition of a political Chinese identity, preferring to be referred to as "a Hong Konger" (cultural identity survey). This "label" accorded her a "sense of belonging," linking her to the place and people she loved:

"Hong Konger" is definitely the label that I give to myself because I possess many distinctive qualities of Hong Kong people. For example, the lust for queuing outside restaurants, chat on cell phone in shopping malls, give a helping hands to those who are in need, and finish every task in high speed. "Hong Konger" can represent my sense of belonging to the motherland of mine and the place which I am dearly attached to. As a Hong Konger, the style of thinking is different from the others as inventive ideas can come up very easily and naturally. Some of my characters are nurtured by the cultures of Hong Kong, like the great concern of wise time management, rather high expectation of academic performances, and the never-dying spirit which determined to strive hard all the time in order to attain a better life. My homeland shapes my character and it somehow resolves what a person I am like (narrative).

As she enthused about the positive traits of "Hong Kongers," it became clear that Nora's sense of self and pride were "deeply attached" to her "homeland" (Hong Kong) and the cultural socialization that had instilled her values. She saw a clear linkage between her identity, culture, and the languages she spoke, convinced that "change in any one of them will result in differences in the others." In her narrative, she wrote:

> My identity of Hong Konger is somehow determined by the language that I am most familiar with, which is Cantonese, the common and rather unique code of people living in Hong Kong. With the knowledge of Cantonese, I can interact with people in different contexts, for example, wet markets, restaurants, banks and schools. The dilemma of identity – whether I am a Chinese, British, or Hong Konger, is closely related to language. Hong Kong people code-mix Cantonese and simple English in daily life, this mixture may foreshadow the fact that Hong Kong people are somewhat in between Chinese and British and "Hong Konger" maybe a suitable label for them.

Prior to the sojourn, Nora had already begun to explore the meaning of her cultural membership and affiliations. Feeling "in between Chinese and British," she saw the "Hong Konger" label as a unique, hybrid marker that best reflected her linguistic habits and cultural positioning.

Mimi

In her narrative, Mimi offered insight into the inner turmoil that she'd experienced while trying to define her place in the world. As a rebellious adolescent and teenager, she rejected her "Chineseness," which she linked to "backward" Chinese traditions and morals:

> I wanted to bury my Chinese self. I had a strong desire to ESCAPE. Escape from my ancestral homeland. Escape from the Chinese tradition. ... Since I was little, I have never stepped a single foot-step back to the native soil of China. ... I do not want to have any connections with

them. I dislike the backward Chinese tradition. ... My Chinese self was gradually vanishing. I wish to get rid of the suffocating, moral Chinese world.

Not long after this, Mimi appeared to enter what J. M. Bennett (1993) refers to as a state of "cultural marginality" or "in-betweeness." Describing herself as "rootless," Mimi felt "trapped" between languages and cultures:

> I was perplexed. Somehow I felt as if I was a rootless and homeless girl who belonged to nowhere, got lost inside an enchanted labyrinth and yelled for help but no one answered. "Let me go and set me free ..." I struggled. I wanted to yield and give in. Nonetheless, I had no way out. Being trapped right in the middle of the maze, I suddenly discovered there were two signs Chinese and English leading to different directions. My Chinese self and English self were like bits and pieces of mosaics combating with each other in my body (narrative).

Convinced that she had to choose one language over the other, Mimi "chose the English way" and began to "mimic the British, Americans, or any other English-speaking people," further rejecting her ties to Chinese traditions. From her perspective, she gradually "became westernized" as she "suppressed" her mother tongue. Despite her "best efforts" to promote her "English self," she sensed "an invisible glass wall blocking her path." Mimi explained that no matter how much she tried she'd never become "a native English speaker." Moreover, her rejection of Cantonese and Chinese culture had harmed her emotional well-being. In her narrative, she recounted this chaotic period:

> I started off having great interest in imitating the way English-speaking people speak and even impersonating a native English speaker. Fascinated by the language, I devoted myself to diverse English-related stuff. I never watched any local or Hong Kong-made movies in cinemas, just Hollywood and English ones. I learnt English through singing English songs. ... I even tried to force myself to use English to think in my inner mind. Neglecting the effect of first language attrition, I suppressed my mother tongue Chinese. I was enthusiastic towards foreign things and suddenly discovered I was westernized. Maybe being assimilated to certain extent. Oh! No, no, no ... How can you betray your Chinese identity? Why do you force

yourself to pretend to be a foreigner? Being a counterfeit is a very tough job. ... You cannot deny your Chinese identity. You were born with it. It is inside your blood and your every cell. No matter how good your mimic skill is, you are still a Chinese. There is no point to argue. That is your fate.

After "pretending to be a foreigner," she realized that she could no longer deny her "Chinese identity." In her heart, she longed to draw closer to her family, cultural roots, and L1. For her, Cantonese represented intimacy and a link to her past, while English was tied to the recognition and status she enjoyed in the academic arena: "English helped me build up my self-esteem that I cherished. However, I needed my Chinese self to link myself to my Mother and family intimacy which I treasured." In her narrative she described this epiphany:

I was so naïve to believe that I could easily rip my past off and abandon my Chinese roots by choosing to hide myself under the English roof. I now realize that I could not deny my Chinese self's existence. The ambivalent attitude towards my Chinese self made me suffer. Despite how marvelous my mocking skill was, I was not a foreigner, but a real Chinese. I was born in Hong Kong, in a Chinese family, not in England, America, nor elsewhere. My seed and root developed here in Hong Kong. This fact was as authentic as iron. ... The process of self-discovery and realization bewildered me for a long time but I suddenly saw the light. I was released from the maze. ... I had placed myself on the wrong side and was dislocated. I understood that my English self was somewhere I could hide temporarily whereas my Chinese self was my permanent home. All my haze and doubts were now clear. I found what I had pursued. My real identity. My Chinese self ... Intimacy. Warmth. Ties to my family, my country, and my heritage. ... That's what I've been looking for.

Mimi was relieved that she'd discovered her "real identity" and "won back" her Chinese self – her "permanent home." "Emancipated" from the "psychological knot" that had "tortured" her throughout much of her young life, she appeared to embrace a more balanced perspective: "I have learnt how to navigate, to maintain and to cherish my Chinese self and English self in between the cultural margin. I do not have to sacrifice one in order to maintain the other. They could be present at the same time" (narrative). Mimi believed that she'd discovered how to "respect and maintain" different dimensions of her identity as she inched closer to what Lambert (1975) defines as "additive bilingualism," whereby the L2 is added to the repertoire of language ability at no loss to the first language or cultural identity of the learner.

Just prior to the sojourn, Mimi declared that her cultural identity was Chinese (cultural identity survey). Considering her turbulent journey and earlier rejection of her "Chineseness," it was significant that she was the only one of the four case participants to choose this "label."

Lana

As a young girl, Lana's first trip to Mainland China triggered interest in her identity and family roots: "Before I visited my hometown at nine, I had no concern about who I was and where I came from. Stories from my parents were amusing myths to me." In her narrative, she recalled how this journey had impacted on her sense of self:

> After my first visit to my parents' hometown in Fujian, I realized that there was a world beyond Hong Kong that closely related to me. ... Everything appeared interesting there. The most exciting things were the ways the people treated us. Most relatives looked up to us because of our Hong Kong identity, signaling a wealthier, more prosperous and more advanced life, no matter what the reality was. ... The "fluent" English we spoke also made our cousins surprising and admiring, because they only started learning English in high school. When comparing to them, I felt my Hong Kong identity especially valuable because of the even poorer living conditions in the small village. I could not imagine what my life would be if my father had not gained the passport to Hong Kong.

This visit made her more appreciative of her command of English, further impressing upon her its linguistic capital. It also heightened her awareness of the elevated status of a Hong Kong identity, which, in her mind, was linked to wealth and a greater proficiency in English than that of her Mainland cousins.

Four years later, at the age of 13, Lana witnessed the return of Hong Kong to Mainland China. This was a confusing period for her as she received contradictory messages about the future from the media and those closest to her. In her narrative she explained why she felt alienated from both "British" and "Chinese" identities: "I was joyful to witness the Handover but it was still too abstract for me to understand what the implications could be. At that time I would simply call myself from Hong Kong rather than Chinese. No matter Chinese or British, they are not Hong Kong people; they do not belong to us." She felt deeply connected to her in-group which, at this stage of her life, consisted solely of Hong Kongers of Chinese ethnicity.

As a university student, Lana recognized the impact of Hong Kong culture on her values and beliefs and remained disconnected from the Motherland: "The more I study, the more I realize my cultural identity. ... Hong Kong is where I born and where I receive my education. It is through Hong Kong that I exhibit my existence, gain my values and beliefs. But how can I relate myself to China directly? Is it simply because Hong Kong is part of China?" Just prior to the sojourn she preferred to be identified as a "Chinese Hong Konger" (cultural identity survey). This dual label fused her ethnicity with the city and people she loved.

Jade

Jade cared little about her identity until sociopolitical events and intercultural contact compelled her to reflect on her positioning in local society and beyond. In her narrative, similar to Nora, she revealed that she did not feel "qualified" to be a Chinese. In her estimation, she'd become too westernized:

> For most people, their passports reveal their nationality or give them identity. But it is different for me. As a Hong Konger, I hold a British passport, but I write "Chinese" in the nationality line. Every time I hesitate before I write "Chinese". I can hardly identify myself with Chinese. In spite of my Chinese face and tongue, my living style, my way of thinking and even my value system are all westernized. I do not think I am qualified as being a Chinese.

We have seen that historical, sociopolitical events (e.g., a change in sovereignty) can lead to identity awareness and even disequilibrium. Intercultural contact also has the potential to stimulate profound reflection on selfhood. In Jade's case, her participation in a multicultural social event in Hong Kong underscored her lack of connection to a Chinese identity. In her narrative she recounted the uncertainty and angst that engulfed her when she donned traditional Chinese clothes that did not fit her self-identity:

> Cross-cultural encounters have always triggered my awareness of my identity and brought me an identity crisis. I once joined a fancy-dress party. In the party, there were people from different countries.

We were required to wear our traditional costumes. It puzzled me what to dress. I finally chose to wear "qi bao", a traditional kind of dress for Chinese women. But I did not feel like myself when I wear "qi bao".

At this moment in time, Jade preferred to be identified as a Hong Konger rather than Chinese: "Hong Kong is my root. I was born here; I grow up here and I live here. Not only language, but place and culture are important to provide people a sense of identity. I lost my 'very Chinese' culture and my ethnic identity. I have no reason to identify myself as a Chinese. I identify myself as a Hong Konger" (narrative). While sometimes buffeted between Eastern and Western influences, Jade was determined to chart her own course and make the most of her hybrid environment: "Floating in the middle of the sea, I have no hurry to be on board either China or the West. Instead of struggling I want to navigate so I can have the broadest view of all and be open to differentness. I don't think I'm caught between two worlds. I like my Hong Kong identity. It's the place I'm from and where I belong to." Significantly, she wished to open herself up to cultural differences and undergo further personal expansion.

Owing to her reflective nature and intercultural experiences at home and abroad, Jade had already acquired a more sophisticated understanding of the fluid, relational nature of identity than many of her peers:

Cultural experiences enable me to work out some invisible principles. In international circumstances, there is no distinction between Mainlanders and Hong Kongers. We are all Chinese. It is only within the Chinese community, Hong Kongers cannot be Chinese, or "pure Chinese". In other words, my identity is dynamic and depends very much on the social context. I am regarded as a Hong Konger when I'm with Mainlanders. I am Chinese to foreigners. I am happy with both "labels" but, in general, "Hong Konger" is the label that suits me most (narrative).

During her brief stay in France the previous summer, Jade discovered that her Chineseness was a core part of her identity in the eyes of "foreigners." While she accepted this, she still preferred the "Hong Konger" label due to her lack of attachment to traditional Chinese values and customs. In her narrative, she explained:

In France I became more aware of myself and learned more about my identity. When I knew that some of the French people could not distinguish Hong Kong from Mainland China. I would simply tell them I'm chinois. But some of my friends still insisted on saying that they were Hong Kongers. I was comfortable with the title "Chinese" though sometimes I still wanted to keep my Hong Kong identity. So now, I prefer to see myself as a Chinese Hong Konger.

Just prior to our departure for England, similar to Lana, Jade chose to be identified as a "Chinese Hong Konger," although for different reasons (cultural identity survey).

Intercultural awareness and sensitivity

On entry into the SES and immediately after the presojourn preparation phase, the women completed the IDI, providing a measure of their intercultural sensitivity at these strategic intervals. Their oral and written narratives and my field notes helped to create a more comprehensive picture of their intercultural awareness and sensitivity prior to the sojourn in England.

Nora

While Nora had the highest level of proficiency in English among the case participants when she joined the SES, she received a Developmental Score (DS) of only 68.37 on the IDI. This indicated that she possessed the lowest level of intercultural sensitivity in the SES cohort at this juncture, with her score placing her in the low end of the DD/R (Denial/Defense or Reversal) stage. According to the IDI, the results indicated that her worldview was "protected by exaggerating its positive aspects compared to all other cultures" (M. J. Bennett, 2004). This level is characterized by "us vs. them" thinking and is frequently accompanied by overt negative stereotyping of other cultures. The first administration of the IDI also showed that Nora perceived her level of intercultural sensitivity to be 114.59 in the AA (Acceptance/Adaptation) range, considerably higher than her actual level.

After the intensive presojourn preparation, Nora moved further along the DD/R band on the IDI, gaining 12.48 points. Analysis of the subscales showed that she had developed a tendency to regard another culture as superior while maligning her own. This "dualistic thinking," according to M. J. Bennett (2004), is indicative of an ethnocentric perspective. On the second administration of the IDI, Nora still perceived her level of intercultural sensitivity to be far higher (117.99 in the AA range) than it actually was. I aimed to discover if the oral and written narrative data gathered during the presojourn phase of the SES would support Nora's actual and perceived IDI scores.

In her first semester, Nora chose to live in a hostel on campus and was allocated a roommate from Mainland China who spoke Putonghua and English but no Cantonese. Nora found it difficult to build a relationship with this young woman due to their "different ways of living" and declared that she would not share a room with an exchange student in the future as it was "too challenging to communicate with *them*" [emphasis added] (intercultural reflections journal). She overgeneralized a single, negative experience to be representative of all nonlocal roommates.

Early in the SES much of Nora's discourse revealed that her worldview was protected by exaggerating its positive aspects compared to those of other cultures. In her narratives, she portrayed Hong Kong and Hong Kong Chinese culture as superior, largely ignoring limitations. Overcome with pride, she raved about the city's "many sparkling qualities":

> Hong Kong is renowned for its superman like nature. When I mention it in front of people from other parts of the world, I feel really proud and would probably go on forever in listing out the infinite advantages of Hong Kong. The assiduous people here, the spirit of mutual support to one another, the right to enjoy different kinds of freedom are only some of the many sparkling qualities of Hong Kong (narrative).

At this juncture, similar to many of her peers, Nora had negative opinions of Mainland China and its "barbaric people": "Sometimes, my nerves got racked by the humiliated deeds of some Chinese people. They squat down whenever and wherever they like, furthermore, they speak very loudly and vulgarly in public areas without feeling any shamefulness" (narrative). This perception alienated her from a Chinese identity: "Though I know it's wrong to judge them by looking at just a certain group of people, I can't resist feeling embarrassed by their deeds. I can't help but view them as barbaric people who carry out indecent actions. They are disrespecting themselves and others of their ethnicity." While acknowledging her tendency to stereotype Mainland Chinese, she was unable to push past the derogatory images that were embedded in her mind. This had likely hindered the development of a cordial, respectful relationship with her roommate from Beijing. At this stage, Nora displayed a high level of ethnocentrism, which Bennett (1998: 26) defines as "using one's own set of standards and customs to judge all people, often unconsciously."

Most comfortable and secure in her home environment surrounded by in-group members (Chinese Hong Kongers), Nora was apprehensive about experiencing difference:

> I have been living in Hong Kong ever since I was born and I regard it as the home of mine, which is as dear to me as my family. Everything in Hong Kong is part of my life. ... Though it might be wrong to accept things as they are, I gladly live according to the rules given. ... The feeling of home is so pleasant that it lingers inside me all the time. In Hong Kong, I feel at ease and comfortable. I enjoy very much to be surrounded by flocks of Hong Kongers. The common language that we speak, the similar way that we act, are all signs of family. Once I am with people who look dissimilar or speak a different language as I do, I begin to feel a bit awkward though I appreciate to chat with people from other countries because I can learn more about the distinctive features and cultures of the others. For example, how they see things differently from me and what the view of Hong Kongers are. Unfortunately, I am still not adapted to staying in settings which people around are all unfamiliar and are having different origins (narrative).

As the departure for England drew near, I observed that Nora had become more willing to interact with "foreigners" (e.g., expatriates in her French course). By developing "a more optimistic stance," she was becoming more tolerant of "the discrepancy among people from different cultures." Less fearful of outsiders, her tone had become less judgmental.

Mimi

On entry into the SES, Mimi received a Developmental Score (DS) of 76.02 on the IDI, placing her near the middle of the DD/R (Denial/Defense or Reversal) band. The analysis of the subscales indicated that she had a tendency to see another culture as superior while maligning her own. In the first administration of the IDI, she perceived her level of intercultural sensitivity to be 117.15 in the AA (Acceptance/Adaptation) range; similar to Nora this was far higher than her actual level. After the intensive presojourn preparation, she scored 85.59, in the very beginning of Minimization, the next band level. While she was aware of superficial cultural differences, her score suggests that she had begun to emphasize that all human beings are basically alike. She still perceived her level of intercultural sensitivity to be far greater than it actually was (120.69 in the AA range).

When I read Mimi's narrative, I was struck by her loathing of Chineseness as a child and her alienation from her "backward" relatives in Mainland China. As an adolescent, she sought to embrace a Western persona: "My motive to let myself be westernized and assimilated to foreign cultures was merely owing to the simple and yet childish reason to express my hatred towards my superstitious relatives in China. ... I dislike the backward Chinese tradition. ... I wish to get rid of the suffocating moral Chinese world." Gradually, as she matured, she began to adopt a more balanced view of Chinese and Western cultures and appeared more willing to accept her Chinese roots.

Early in the intercultural communication course she expressed uncertainty about whether ethnocentrism was "good or bad." In her first journal entry she wrote: "To understand another's culture and to be a competent intercultural communicator, we should be conscious enough to use our own culture qualities to classify and interpret the characteristics of those people who are socially and culturally different from us." She had not yet grasped the concept of ethnorelativism.

Toward the end of the presojourn preparation phase, she was encouraged to identify strategies that a sojourner might use to adjust to another cultural milieu. In her journal she offered this advice: "To deal with cultural shock, we need to open up our mind to tolerate cultural differences. Be flexible. We should try to learn and understand their culture to see if their cultural stuffs fit us or not. When we experience a new culture, it doesn't mean that we have to give up our own culture." By crossing cultures, she expected to "better understand her own values and culture." Her entry provided evidence of growth in intercultural awareness and, as in Nora's case, I wondered if she would be able to put these ideals into practice in the host environment.

Looking forward to the sojourn, Mimi aimed to "be respectful" and "step back a little to think" before making "judgments" about English people. At the same time, she believed that she would be uncomfortable adopting their behavior: "It's not appropriate to imitate the way other people act. They may think you're kind of strange" (cultural strategies survey). It was conceivable that this stance would limit her readiness to try out new expressions and ways of being.

Lana

In the first administration of the IDI, Lana received a Developmental Score (DS) of 92.91, indicating that she was in the middle of the transitional state of Minimization. She perceived her level of intercultural sensitivity to be 120.86 in the AA (Acceptance/Adaptation) range; similar to Nora and Mimi, this was much higher than her actual level. After the intensive presojourn preparation, Lana remained in Minimization but moved to 98.91 (a gain of 6 points). In this second administration of the IDI, she continued to perceive her level of intercultural sensitivity to be greater than it was in reality (122.54 in AA). I wondered if her storied experiences would help explain why she made little progress in intercultural competence during the presojourn phase.

When she joined the SES, Lana was convinced that "people could live happily in any place if they can keep to their principles in life, mainly being honest and well-intentioned" (journal). Describing the world as "essentially a global village," she maintained that people in different parts of the world only "differ a little" due to the impact of globalization and subsequent advances in technology. At this stage of her young life she had very limited intercultural contact and demonstrated minimal understanding of the diversity in the world: "I think that village, town, city and country are just arbitrary terms describing the subtle differences between different groups of people. ... The analogy of the world to a village is visualized if we think that different countries are just houses for people." In her journal, she added: "The world is visually large, but people living in it may just differ a little as science and technology improves. Places all around the world are well connected through Internet. People from different places are linked together through phones, emails and ICQ. These bring the world together as a global village."

Even though she accentuated similarities between people from different lands, similar to Nora and Mimi, Lana harbored strong negative perceptions of Mainlanders:

> From my own experience of the Mainland, I have a bad impression that people there are less civilized than Hong Kong people. They are untrustworthy, unfair, and injustice. Bribery and corruption are all around in court, in schools, in companies and even in streets. ... They are less educated in the concepts of hygiene: they squat in toilets, spit around the streets, and throw rubbish all around. ... It is not surprising there are a lot of contagious diseases. The Mainland Chinese are just inferior to us – Hong Kong people. Hence, it is a torture for me to visit my relatives in Mainland (journal).

Shortly after joining the SES, Mimi, like Nora, moved into a hostel and was assigned a Mainland Chinese roommate, who spoke Putonghua and English but no Cantonese. As she learned more about intercultural communication and became better acquainted with her roommate, Lana began to question some of her prejudices. In her journal, a month after they met, she wrote:

> When I knew I had to stay with a Beijing girl for the whole semester, I was quite nervous and disappointed because of my prejudice to Mainland. Nonetheless, after nearly a month's getting along together, I found that there were many things valuable in their mind that we didn't have. For instance, she is hard-working and just sleeps very little. She is polite and sweet to everyone. She is not so uncivilized or dirty as I have imagined. She baths every day, though not usually at night like me. Still, she keeps personal hygiene and her things are clean and packed tidily. ... I realized how unfairly my prejudice made me look down upon our Mainland fellows.

Although her attitude toward Mainlanders was softening, it remained a struggle for her to be "sympathetic" and "appreciate" people from her family's homeland: "Apart from the poor standard of living, Mainlanders are similar to us. They are human beings who want to strive for better life. Still, I cannot easily remove my entire prejudice upon them because it has been built up in my mind since my child-hood. I still think they are different to Hong Kong people" (journal). Nonetheless Lana was determined to overcome her tendency to stereotype: "I'm trying to move from a critical perspective to a sympathetic view, to understand more from their perspectives and to appreciate their valuable, genuine and sincere characters rather than to criticize their place."

While she had no intercultural-intimate relationships, Lana lived vicariously through her best friend, an SES student who was romantically involved with an American. Although convinced that it would take "more time and energy" to cultivate and maintain "an intercultural relationship," Lana began to imagine doing so:

> Personally, I have not confronted the challenges of intercultural communication myself. But I have witnessed what my friend has experienced as she has a western boyfriend. I think the most challenging aspect of communicating with someone from another culture is the cultural differences. To gain more understanding of another culture, people need to move away from their own culture's perspectives to see things from the partner's point of view. ... To gain the new perspective, one may have to reduce one's self-centeredness and pay

more effort to build up the relationship. To understand another's culture, one needs to remove one's prejudices and stereotypes of people from the other culture. It takes time and energy to remove the cultural barrier and build up intercultural relationship (journal).

From her entry, it is clear that Lana had begun to grasp M. J. Bennett's (1993) notion of ethnorelativism and, in one of her last journal entries, she remarked that she was "looking forward to making friends with other cultures in the coming sojourn." As she tended to be quite reticent, I wondered if she would take the initiative to do so.

By the end of the intercultural communication course, Lana believed that she had become more knowledgeable about cultural differences and intercultural communication theories. She hungered to deepen her understanding of intercultural relations through travel and contact with people from other cultures:

> I need a real context where I can experience culture shock to become a good intercultural communicator. I believe experience can make great progress for one to grow. ... The farthest place I have been to by myself is within Hong Kong and the farthest place I have been to with my family is Fujian in Mainland China, where I visit my relatives. Hence, I don't really have anything to say about my own intercultural experience in other places (journal).

When I first met Lana she had no clear career or travel goals. After the intensive presojourn preparation, she imagined leading a very different life: "In the future, I hope to travel overseas or work in international firms or schools to put my intercultural competence into practice and modify through practical experiences. Through gaining experiences of people worldwide, my horizon will be widened" (journal). She could envisage herself with a more international, outgoing persona, interacting with friends and colleagues from other cultures.

Jade

On entry into the SES, Jade received a Developmental Score (DS) of 85.87 on the IDI, which placed her in the very beginning of the Minimization scale, indicating that she had started to emphasize similarities among people from diverse cultures. She perceived her level of intercultural sensitivity to be 117.74 in the AA (Acceptance/Adaptation) range; similar to the other case participants, this was much higher than her actual level. After the intensive presojourn preparation, Jade made a significant gain in intercultural sensitivity (32.63 points), moving from the low end of Minimization, the transitional phase, to AA (118.50), an ethnorelative stage. This time she perceived her level of intercultural sensitivity to be 134.69, in the same range as her actual score.

Early on, Jade displayed awareness of the impact of Hong Kong culture on her socialization. Her travels abroad had exposed her to cultural differences, although on entry into the SES she was not very explicit about these contrasts. "The trip to France was really eye-opening. I came to realize how cultural differences can lead to a feeling of discomfort. ... It is always a shock to know how a culture flows through our veins, and by now, much of Hong Kong flows through mine" (narrative).

Throughout the semester, I was struck by the number of detailed vignettes that she included in her intercultural reflections journal. In the following excerpt, for example, she not only described and analyzed intercultural behavior she'd observed in local classrooms, she offered useful suggestions to facilitate better communication:

> Both the American student and the local students attempt to conform to their own expectations about appropriate classroom behaviors and display of respect. They become judgmental to each other. Very often, when we find that people from other cultures act in a way which is different from us, we tend to look at others' behavior from our own culture and try to judge it. The cultural difference would probably turn into cross-cultural misunderstanding if we do not handle it carefully. The key to deal with cultural difference is to mentally set aside our beliefs and the accompanying evaluative labels. If both sides are able to identify the differences and learn to appreciate the other's culture, the communication can be better.

While many of her peers were either oblivious to or threatened by cultural differences, Jade found them intriguing. Her journal provided further evidence that she was becoming more self-aware and reflective, elements that international educators (e.g., Byram et al., 2002; Deardorff, 2008) consider essential for intercultural competence:

> This is the first course about "cultures" I've ever taken. ... I'm making progress week by week. For example, I begin to question the norms of my culture which I have taken granted. I notice how cultural differences in the way people around me communicate led to misunderstanding. I'm also more aware of my behaviors framed by my cultural background. It's important to confront the communication problem

that occurs when interacting with people from other cultures by reflecting on our own experiences.

Midway through the semester, Jade wrote about the gap between intercultural awareness and effective, respectful communication across cultures in real life. She had developed a better grasp of the complex, on-going process involved in becoming interculturally competent:

> Opening our eyes to see cultural differences is one thing. Opening our heart to accept and respect the differences is another thing. To be open-minded and competent in intercultural contacts, we have to set aside our cultural biases, perceptions about beliefs, values and norms and our expectations on others. This process often involves a lot of internal struggles and anxieties. A way to cope with these internal struggles is to lighten up a bit and be able to laugh about ourselves. The key to deal with cross-culture communication is to have a sense of humor.

In accord with the intercultural experts surveyed by Deardorff (2004), Jade realized that "intercultural communication competence takes time to develop." Recognizing the importance of reflection, she aimed to refrain from making snap judgments about the unfamiliar acts and deeds of people from other cultures. In essence, she aspired to cultivate an ethnorelative orientation (M. J. Bennett, 1993, 2004):

> When interacting with people from a different culture, we may need to adjust our behaviors. I'm still learning to put myself into others' shoes and interpret others' behaviors from their cultural perspectives instead of mine. When I come across people of other cultures violating the rules of our culture, I step back and see the causes of problems in miscommunication before I make negative comments on others. How can we judge anyway if the standard is not the same? (journal).

Interestingly, as Jade's metacognitive competence grew, she lessened her tendency to inflate her level of intercultural sensitivity. While appreciative of the knowledge and skills she was gaining, she realized that she had much more to learn to become a successful intercultural mediator (Alred and Byram, 2002; Byram, 2003). In her journal, she wrote: "I'm happy I've taken my first step – attempting to move beyond the limits of my own cultural experiences to incorporate the perspective of other cultures into my own interpersonal interactions." She believed that an open mindset would serve her well in the five-week sojourn in England.

Attitude toward internationalization policy

Midway through the presojourn preparation, the proposed revitalization of the University's internationalization policy became a hot topic on campus (see Chapter 3 for an overview of the policy). Prior to the full-group discussion, I encouraged the students to express their views about it in small groups as well as in their journal. This provided additional information about their understanding of the issues, their level of intercultural sensitivity, and their attitudes toward intercultural contact and English as an international language.

Nora

When I read Nora's journal, I found that she had misunderstood the policy's implications for the medium of instruction and, like many other students on campus, was quite suspicious of what lay behind the proposed changes:

> Recently, the internationalization of the Chinese University forcing all major courses to be instructed in English triggers students' hot debate on cultural identity. The University used to be branded as our local university because its official language is Chinese. Now, shifting to be an EMI [English-medium] university will inevitably receive censures by patriotic students that we are looking down on our mother tongue and have forgotten our cultural identity. I agree with the internationalization of our university but I have some reservation on forcing lectures to be instructed by English only. Does internationalization only superficially mean to change the university to be an EMI university? Changing to be an EMI university cannot really help to internationalize our university but can only show that the authority is despising the function of our mother tongue.

In the same entry, Nora wrote about "the obligation of educated people" in today's diverse world: "We should recognize our own culture and try to be open-minded to have more international exposure so as to find the difference between our own culture and others. We should treasure and retain the good sides of our culture and learn from the good sides of other cultures to be a better person in this global world." Would she be able to translate these ideals into practice? Would she take further steps to cultivate responsible, intercultural global citizenship (Byram, 2006)?

Mimi

"The objectives" of the internationalization policy, in Mimi's view, were "reasonable under the trend of globalization" and would provide local students with "more intercultural exposure" and "opportunities to enhance their oral English." "Without doubt," she mused, "this policy is meaningful, beneficial and fruitful in this sense."

Realizing that the University would remain bilingual, Mimi disagreed with opponents who feared that the internationalization policy would "devalue the Chinese language and culture." In her mind, it was "reasonable" to offer more courses in English to enable non-Cantonese-speaking students to meet their graduation requirements. She observed that they had "many chances to learn and experience Chinese language and culture because there are Cantonese and Putonghua courses available for them." She did not believe that the presence of more English language speakers on campus would threaten her mother tongue and culture: "In our daily life conversations, most local students use Cantonese to communicate with each other so I wonder how having some more courses in English would profoundly affect their Chinese language and Cantonese abilities. I just don't see the problem and conflict to speak in English in a Chinese University." More supportive of the policy than Nora, she was convinced that local students would benefit from increased exposure to this international language and other worldviews.

Lana

Stressing that Hong Kong was part of the "global village," Lana expressed support for the University's efforts "to promote a multicultural environment" on campus. Nonetheless she had reservations about elements of the policy that she had misunderstood. In her journal entry, she wrote at length about the grievances of students who were convinced that it threatened their mother tongue:

> The Students' Union claims that the change of medium of instruction is not a wholesome measure to promote the global sense on campus. Asking local students to give up their chances of thinking in mother tongue is not fair. Though the proficiency of English language is acceptable for most students, it is still Cantonese which we can share our ideas most fluently and effectively.

As an alternative, Lana suggested that the University "offer special courses for exchange students to learn about Cantonese, Chinese cultures and beliefs," adding that "they could still choose programs offered by different departments in English." Basically she argued for the status quo. As Mimi noted, Lana's first idea was already a reality and the latter did not address the problem of insufficient courses in English for international students and those from Mainland China who did not speak Cantonese.

Jade

Jade displayed a better understanding of the internationalization policy and its implications for the language of instruction than many of her classmates. In her writing, she outlined student concerns and offered a brief analysis of the controversy:

> In the CUHK E-newsletter, the University states that they will recruit more and more students from different countries and regions in order to provide global exposure to students and give them more opportunities to come into contact with different people and cultures. Thus, there is a larger demand for courses that is taught in English for non-local students to fulfill program requirements. However, local students claim that using English as a teaching medium devalues our language (Cantonese) and our culture. They argue that effective learning requires the need to be educated in one's mother tongue. Perhaps, the colonial period has prejudiced Hong Kongers' perception towards the English. Many Hong Kongers think that English is a language of the former colonizer that was imposed on us.

Like Mimi, Jade considered it reasonable to increase the number of courses taught in English to accommodate non-Cantonese-speaking students. When explaining her position, I observed that she attempted to diffuse the tension between the global and the local, portraying English as a "neutral" international tool for communication across cultures: "It's understandable that students want to preserve the local language and culture but having lectures in English doesn't mean belittling Cantonese and Hong Kong culture. I see English as a neutral language since it has long been a common language for intercultural communication." In part, Jade was more accepting of the increase in English usage as she associated the language with a global culture, delinking it from "a privileged group of inner circle countries" (S. Ryan, 2006, 2009; Yashima, 2009). A proponent of intercultural contact and dialogue, she appeared quite comfortable with the use of English to reach out to international students: "Broadening the student mix is good. Global vision and international exposure is important for students. ... The University should organize more activities to bring local and exchange students together." For Jade, internationalization signified an opportunity rather than a threat.

The "home ethnography" project

In the months leading up to the sojourn, the students developed the knowledge and skills necessary to undertake a small-scale "home ethnography" project. This provided a window into their attention to detail, their degree of intercultural sensitivity, the depth of their investment in cultural learning, the state of their interpersonal communication skills, and their interest in the world around them.

Nora

For her project, Nora opted to investigate communication between supervisors and employees in a small company in Hong Kong. Through the act of interviewing and conversing with informants who had a different background, status, and gender, she became more aware of the impact of her communication style on others. She also developed "more independence and self-confidence." In her survey, she added: "The ethnographic research is a great chance for us to get prepared for our stay in England. It trained me to be more open-minded and I didn't get embarrassed or frustrated easily. I've become a more vigilant observer and I think I can find a suitable topic for the next research project in England."

Mimi

For her project, Mimi chose to find out what it was like for a Chinese American to study in his parents' home country. When she began, she had little grasp of the challenges facing an "ABC" (the acronym used in Hong Kong for American-born Chinese). His candid revelations opened her eyes: "I've never imagined the pain that an ABC may suffer inside his heart. I'm pretty surprised that an ABC may not be so fond of being labeled as ABC. From this perspective, I've learnt how to understand and respect different cultural backgrounds" (ethnography research survey). She was convinced that the project had helped her to develop "a better respect and understanding of others with different identities and cultural backgrounds." Despite this perceived gain, Mimi continued to use the ABC label and in her ethnographic report she sometimes displayed a monocultural frame of reference (P. Ryan, 2006); she was not able to fully understand her informant's situation and worldview.

Nonetheless Mimi believed that the project had enhanced her ability to adjust her communication style: "When my informant expressed his inner thoughts, I usually kept silent and listened to him while nodding my head. This non-verbal communication skill just naturally developed throughout the whole research"(ethnography research survey). By the end of the project, she had become more confident of her interpersonal skills and, like Nora, was keen to explore a cultural scene in England using the tools of ethnographic research.

Lana

Lana chose to investigate the linguistic and intercultural adjustment of her roommate, an exchange student from Beijing. In a survey, she reflected on what she'd gained from the research: "When I started the project I had only known my roommate a short time. Our friendship was deepened by the interviews and informal chats." Considering the negative stereotypes of Mainlanders that she had harbored when she began the project, this was significant. Moreover, through their ethnographic conversations and interviews, Lana enhanced her communication skills and became more aware of aspects that needed improvement: "As a communicator, I think that my strength is that I can encourage my informant to talk willingly by keeping good eye contact and response. But perhaps I can improve by learning to ask more related follow-up questions." As her research involved sustained contact with someone outside her in-group, she gained confidence "to converse with different kinds of people."

Further, Lana acquired a deeper understanding of factors that can impact on intercultural adjustment, including proficiency in the host language. In the following excerpt she appeared to recognize the role that "agency" can play in determining sojourn outcomes in a L2 context:

> Through doing the ethnographic research project, I've noticed more about how different people react to a new environment. For example, I found that though given similar environment and supports, willingness of the exchange students to learn a new language did matter a lot. Comparing my informant and one of her Beijing fellows, they acted differently to the new language, Cantonese. My informant was willing to learn and speak while her fellow did not.

Hence, my informant ended up with fluent Cantonese but her fellow did not.

(ethnographic research survey)

I wondered if Lana's discovery would motivate her to take a more active role in her own L2 learning in England. Would she take advantage of linguistic affordances in the community as well as in her homestay? Would she become a "language activist" (Phipps, 2006) in the host culture?

Similar to the other women, Lana believed that her research had increased awareness of the world around her and given her the confidence necessary to carry out research in England. In her survey, she wrote: "From this experience, I'm noticing more about my surroundings and find interesting things to discover. I'm more confident in making a more thorough research in a strange place."

Jade

For her project, Jade explored the reasons why Hong Kong parents may place their children in multiple extracurricular activities, allowing very little time for unstructured play. Realizing that she held firm beliefs that conflicted with those of her main informant, she made a conscious effort to refrain from prejudging the woman. In the postcourse survey, she disclosed the awakenings she experienced as she carried out her project:

> The research deepened my awareness and understanding of my own sub-cultures. I'm in a very different social circle from my informants and new to the ideas of parenting. My idea of education is very different. For me, education is all about academics while activities are simply hobbies. At the beginning of the data collection process, I was at a risk of being judgmental, thinking that my informant is demanding and has unrealistic expectations of her children. Fortunately, I noticed the problem quite soon and was able to adjust and tune myself into a more open-minded mentality.

(ethnographic research survey)

In her study, Jade interacted with two children as well as her adult informant. This facilitated experimentation with a range of questioning techniques and conversation strategies. With practice, she learned to adjust her communication style to develop better rapport with her informants: "I used an informal and softer tone to talk with the children. Since they're very young, they had difficulty understanding my questions so I had to rephrase and repeat my questions form time to time" (ethnographic research survey). On reflection, Jade cited additional benefits of her project work: "I used to be a careless person who overlooks details. After doing this research, I'm more observant and sensitive to things around me. This improvement should prepare me for the research in England." Similar to the other case participants, Jade's confidence and skills evolved as she carried out her research. For all of the case participants, the "home ethnography" project served as a dress rehearsal for their fieldwork in England.

Conclusions

What can we learn from the young women's journeys prior to the sojourn? A review of their oral and written narratives and my field notes revealed that their intercultural development was in line with the actual IDI scores that they received on entry into the SES and after the presojourn preparation. Their perceived IDI scores indicated that most had a very inflated perception of their degree of intercultural sensitivity at all stages and this was also evident in their narratives.

While Nora had the most advanced level of proficiency in English among the case participants, she had the highest level of ethnocentricism in the SES cohort, challenging Bennett et al.'s (2003) linkage between L2 proficiency and intercultural sensitivity. Initially fearful of cultural differences, Nora grew more receptive to intercultural contact during the presojourn preparation phase and began to question some of her entrenched stereotypes.

Mimi has struggled with identity issues throughout her young life, buffeted between her "Chinese self" and "English self." Rejecting her Chineseness, she tried to become more Westernized; this exacerbated her psychological distress and alienated her from her family and L1. When I first met her she seemed trapped in an endless cycle of conflicting emotions. On entry, much of her discourse was ethnocentric; however, as she gained exposure to intercultural communication theories and began to reflect on her attitude and behaviors, she made a genuine effort to develop a more open mindset and embrace an additive form of bilingualism (Lambert, 1975).

Lana remained in Minimization throughout the presojourn preparation. According to the IDI, this indicates a transition from an ethnocentric orientation to a more culturally sensitive worldview. Early on, I noticed her tendency to remain on the periphery rather than take an active role in events. Seemingly content to be a "follower," she was often dominated by her peers and this appeared to curtail her personal expansion.

During this phase, Jade developed the habit of critical reflection and began to reexamine previous intercultural encounters and forays abroad (e.g., her three-week sojourn in France). She made significant gains in cultural understanding, moving from the beginning of Minimization to Acceptance/Adaptation, an ethnorelative stage of development. Among the four case participants, she was the most interculturally sensitive prior to the trip to England. She also demonstrated a greater awareness of the relational, fluid nature of identity. Further, similar to Mimi, I discovered that she suffered from fears of L1 attrition as her proficiency in English grew stronger.

The IDI scores and narratives suggest that it is possible for intensive, appropriately sequenced, intercultural preparation to propel students toward a more ethnorelative mindset on home soil. Guided, critical reflection can enhance their awareness and acceptance of cultural diversity and prompt the setting of appropriate, realistic goals for study and residence abroad. Experiential learning (e.g., ethnographic projects, intercultural activities, interviewing international students) can raise awareness of their self-identity, communication style, and (inter)cultural sensitivity and, ultimately, help them become more systematic explorers of the world around them.

In the next two chapters, we follow the women throughout their five-week sojourn in England and return to Hong Kong.

5
Nora and Mimi's Sojourn and Reentry

In this chapter I focus on the sojourn and reentry experiences of Nora and Mimi. Of the four case participants, they had the lowest levels of intercultural sensitivity on entry into the program according to the IDI (Intercultural Development Inventory). Just prior to the sojourn, Nora was in the second half of DD/R (Denial/Defense or Reversal) (80.85), and after five weeks in the host culture she moved forward into Minimization (86.16), the transitional phase, with a slight gain of 5.31 points. By contrast, Mimi had a Developmental Score (DS) of 85.59 after the presojourn preparation, which placed her in the very beginning of Minimization. By the end of the sojourn, she had gained 9.28 points, moving further into this range. Postsojourn, both women still had inflated perceptions of their intercultural sensitivity, believing themselves to be in the AA (Acceptance/Adaptation) range (120.92 for Nora; 125.16 for Mimi), far higher than it actually was. Would their oral and written narratives (weekly sojourn surveys, sojourn diary,[1] postsojourn interview) and my field notes reflect their actual and perceived IDI scores? What can we learn from their experiences that might explain their trajectories?

In this chapter I begin by discussing Nora's aspirations for the sojourn and her anxieties about living in a foreign country. I track her language, identity, and (inter)cultural development as she explores England and reconsiders her experiences after her return to Hong Kong. As each week unfolds during the sojourn, we see how she adjusts to her new surroundings and intercultural contact. We become familiar with her level of awareness of Self and Other and her attitude toward cultural differences. When relevant, I interpose an etic (outsider's) perspective, drawing on my field notes, to further contextualize her narratives.[2] I follow the same approach when I present Mimi's journey. Throughout, I draw comparisons and contrasts between their perceptions and experiences to better understand the factors impacting on their developmental trajectories.

What follows are the unique stories of Nora and Mimi.

Nora

Predeparture aims and concerns

In her application letter, Nora expressed the desire to join the Special English Stream (SES) to enhance her "personal and social skills" and become "more self-confident and independent." As an only child, "always under the love and care" of her parents, she did not believe that she was "sufficiently self-reliant or mature enough" for a 20-year-old. Further, she wished to develop a better understanding of cultural differences and improve her English language proficiency. Just prior to her departure, she refined her sojourn goals:

> I'd like to improve my English in all aspects, especially listening. I hope to have a better grasp of slangs and idioms used in UK. Ultimately, I want to improve my listening comprehension skills so I can understand foreign movies or TV programs because quite often I fail to catch the funny parts or jokes made by actors. I also want to know about and understand the culture of other people to find out how they live differently, how they see things differently, etc. Besides, I want to be a more independent girl because I somehow find that I rely too much on my parents and friends and sometimes fail to solve problems by myself. I really want to act and think like a 20-year old girl, not a child as I am now (survey).

While excited about the impending sojourn, she was "quite worried" about residing with strangers in a homestay: "As we have different ways of living and don't know each other, in the beginning, it may be difficult to adapt." She was anxious about being away from her family: "I'm afraid I'll get homesick. I haven't left my parents for more than a week and have never stayed in another country for more than five days. It'll be strange not to see my parents for five weeks and I'm nervous about living in a foreign country. Actually, I think the trip's too long. Three weeks would be better" (interview).

Nora's anxiety level seemed to be more elevated than most, as she was also the only one to request that two SES friends be placed in the same homestay "to take care of each other." In her survey, she wrote: "Sometimes you won't know what to do when things happen while you're alone with the host family." While her parents were supportive of the sojourn, they doubted her ability to cope without them: "They're happy I have the chance to experience life there but think the sojourn is too long. They would like it to be two or three weeks. They're concerned about what might happen to me. ... They're worried that I won't be able to take care of myself" (interview). Their lack of faith in her adaptability likely heightened her insecurity.

The language policy for the sojourn

The students were encouraged to use the host language in England to make the most of their stay in an English-speaking environment. Prior to departure, previous SES students shared their experiences with "life in English" and encouraged the new group to use the language to communicate with each other. When Nora first learned of the policy she thought it was "a good idea" as it would provide them with "a chance to use English only." In her interview, she added: "As it's a rule, we should all follow it. We've never tried this in Hong Kong before. I'd like to see if I can express myself well in English." Convinced that it would initially be difficult to "stick to English," she suggested that there be "some kind of penalty" for using Cantonese.

Although supportive of the policy, Nora had some qualms about conversing with her classmates in English during the sojourn. In her pre-departure survey, she wrote: "In Hong Kong we only talk to each other in English during tutorials and lectures so it'll seem odd at first. When we're in an all-English speaking environment, I think we'll gradually change and get used to it." If a classmate spoke to her in Cantonese she imagined she'd respond in kind: "We would definitely continue our conversation in Cantonese and the whole idea of the policy would be abolished." Her comment highlighted her fear of being out-grouped, casting doubt on the success of the policy.

The sojourn

First week – the ups and downs of border crossings

In her first diary entry, Nora wrote about her expectations of English life. In spite of the presojourn preparation, I discovered that she clung to rather idealized, romanticized images of English people and culture. Further, she appeared to overestimate her understanding of England, "an old friend":

> During the flight, the images, or, I should say, my imagination about what England is like and how British people look like, kept lingering in

my mind. In my opinion, Britain is quite a traditional, old-fashioned country. People there are all with perfect propriety. Gentlemen and ladies in nice suits and gowns are the most outstanding images that first come to my mind whenever I think of England. To me, England is just like an old friend of mine since Hong Kong was ruled by British Governors until 1997. ... I felt really excited on the plane, thinking of the coming challenging time with my friends and host in England. I had in mind what my host parents and their children looked like and how big their house would be.

After a two-hour bus ride from Heathrow airport to the host university, one-by-one the students were introduced to their homestay families. In her diary, Nora provided a window into her emotional state: "I was shivering when I heard my name. Standing in front of me was an old couple. They shook hands with me and said 'welcome to England!' I was a bit sad that they didn't have any young children at home." Nora had been placed with a retired couple in their sixties who were experienced hosts. Unfortunately, her first impression was not favorable: "I was frightened since my host mum looked quite cruel. Anyway, I gave them a friendly smile and we left the room together and went home."

Her fears seemed to have been pushed aside when she wrote: "My home in England is really big and comfy. It's quite traditional like. It looked like those in the 18th and 19th century. I called it a replicate of the home of Jane Austen, since the chairs, tables and the stunning fireplace all looked very nice and antique" (diary). Nora's host mother made an effort to make her feel at home and this appeared to ease some of her concerns about living with strangers:

> Host mum was so friendly that she asked if I'd like a cup of English tea. It was milk tea and it tasted really good! Then, she asked if I would like to call her "Elizabeth" or "Mother". I replied that both were fine to me, and she told me to call her "Mother" as it sounded more close. She was nice and welcomed me not as a guest of their house but a new member of their family. I felt so good! (diary).

After a free day to rest and recuperate, Nora met up with some SES friends to take the bus to the University for the first day of classes. Their conversation soon turned to their homestays and Nora believed that she'd not fared as well as the others. Her optimism evaporated: "Jen's host mum brought her out to the supermarket and a car boots sale. Ella had a barbeque with her hosts last night. When I thought of my whole-day stay in the house, I just wished I could change my hosts. I kept on grumbling about my host parents during the short bus trip to school" (diary).

Nora was also finding it difficult to adjust to new kinds of food. In her diary, she bemoaned English people's "obsession" with sandwiches, not recognizing that she and many of her peers had a similar reliance on instant noodles: "In the supermarket I could see lots of sandwiches in the refrigerator. Sandwiches are indispensable in the life of British people. I discover they always have sandwiches as lunch. It seems they never get bored with it." Her malaise was temporarily relieved by the sight of the familiar: "Behind the piles of sandwiches were the shelves full of products from China. I got excited when I saw the familiar soya bean drink which I often drink in Hong Kong. Homesickness was called upon by the shimmering products of my home. I really miss Hong Kong!"

Near the end of the first week, on a group outing to Oxford, Nora and four of her friends asked a local man to take a photo of them together. In her diary, she recounted what transpired:

> When we walked to the Bridge of Sighs, we asked a young British to take picture for us. I sensed that he's really very polite and nice. Again, I could feel the civility of the British people. Unfortunately, after looking at the picture that he took, I was disappointed. We intended to have the five of us standing under the Bridge of Sighs in the photo, but we only saw the five of us. Maybe, British people are so self-centered that they only care about themselves and neglect things around them.

When she saw that the digital image did not include the bridge, she was annoyed and branded "British people" as "self-centered." Similar to her negative experience with her Mainland Chinese roommate, she overgeneralized a meeting with one individual to be representative of all people from Britain (not just England). Further, she did not consider differences in communication styles (e.g., direct vs. indirect) as a possible factor in the miscommunication. As she and her friends had not been explicit in their request, their expectations were not apparent to the young man, who had simply agreed to help them out.

Meanwhile, in her homestay, Nora appeared to be cultivating a positive relationship with her hosts. They demonstrated genuine concern for her well-being and this was not lost on her: "Around 10:30 p.m., I was dropped off in front of my house and saw father anxiously waiting for me. I could really feel that both he and mother care about me! Though it's raining quite heavily and getting cooler, my heart is now filled with warmth" (diary). Nora was positioned as a child in her homestay and seemed quite comfortable with this:

> At around 9:30 p.m., I was home! Mother asked if I ate anything. She didn't mean to hear the answer, "I didn't have my dinner," as shown from her facial expression, she thought that I was like a kid who needs to be spoon-fed. Mother swiftly rushed into the kitchen and cooked me a bowl of soup and roast beef. Thanks Mother, you are really as good as my real mum! (diary).

Although happy to be "spoon-fed," I wondered if she would demonstrate independence and assert herself once she became more familiar with her new environment. Would her hosts' support provide the security she needed to find her feet or would it curtail her personal growth?

Second week – the loss of home and language

Early in the second week, Nora was still suffering from homesickness and seemed to be more unsettled than most of her peers:

> I'm not really surprised about my stress level since I expected it before I come to UK. To be frank, I've been homesick everyday when I am alone in my room. I miss my parents, friends, and everything in Hong Kong so much!!! On the first day, when I look out the window and find that it's not the usual familiar scene which I can view from the window of my bedroom in Hong Kong, I feel strange and a bit nervous. When I received the email from my parents, I burst into tears which reflects that I really miss them so much (survey).

In her diary, Nora laid bare the depth of her distress: "Suddenly, the thought of flying back to Hong Kong pop up in my mind! I miss my parents, friends and everything in Hong Kong." To ease her anxiety she reached out to her parents and SES friends, who gave her "comfort, love, and a sense of belonging."

> The phone calls from my Dad and Mum everyday soothe me. Whenever I hear their voices, I feel better and safe. The email that they send me also comforts me, since they said that I should feel happy all the time as this is a great chance for me to learn the culture

of others and learn to be independent. They asked me not to worry about them. Besides, friends are also important to me. I chat with my SES buddies when I feel stressful and also friends in Hong Kong through ICQ and email. Friends said that after five weeks I would think that time really passes very quickly (survey).

At this stage, I observed that she was more focused on Hong Kong happenings than new experiences in England.

Nora continued to make an effort to cultivate a "grandparents-granddaughter" relationship with her hosts and her homesickness began to subside. She still believed that they were sincerely interested in her and her culture and this motivated her to get to know them better:

I have chats with my host parents every night after dinner when we are watching TV. My host parents are curious about me, my family and everything that happen in Hong Kong and they are willing to share with me their daily experience. Actually, I have got a lot of time to interact with them since both my host parents have retired so they are at home when I go home after school. I think I'm lucky that I can have a grandparents-granddaughter relationship with my host family. The two of them will take great care of me (survey).

While Nora remained silent during the first debriefing session, she closely observed what others were saying, recording some of the topics in her diary (e.g., the "strange tea habit," local people's "obsession" with pets, the high divorce rate, the slower living pace, limited shopping hours). Much of the discussion focused on aspects of the host culture that the students found puzzling or irritating.

After the debriefing, I encouraged the students to talk about possible topics for their ethnographic research projects. Most wished to investigate cultural scenes associated with their host families and Nora was no exception. She chose gardening, a "cultural phenomenon" that was new to her. In a survey administered the same morning, she wrote: "I think my research will go really well since I have good informants (my host parents). They are experts in gardening and spend the whole afternoons looking after their plants. I think I can learn and get a lot of useful information from them." She also believed that the project would enhance her communication with her host family (ethnographic conversation).

While happy to have hosts who "loved and cared for her," Nora saw herself as a "visitor" in her homestay: "We sit in the living room and watch TV together and I help them to clean the table after every meal. Yet, I still find that I'm a visitor of this house, not yet a friend or even family member." She vowed to "do better to develop a more close relationship with them" (survey). Although more comfortable in her homestay, Nora was aware of her status as an "outsider" in the community. In her survey, she wrote: "People give you a warm welcome and that makes you feel better. Yet, there is still some awkward feeling." To overcome this, she aimed to open herself up more to others: "Being an 'outsider', I should learn to observe and share to help bridge the gap between me and the local people. What's needed is time and courage since I find myself quite a shy person when I meet strangers."

She found most locals "helpful" but had become disillusioned with the youth, using a sweeping generalization to negatively characterize all English people of that age group: "I find it quite difficult to accept that young people here drink alcohol and take drugs. On the bus I heard two young Englishmen say that every night they go to pubs. I can't believe that Englishmen are not the gentlemen and ladies that I have thought of" (survey). During the presojourn preparation, we had discussed Fox's (2004: 88) depiction of pub culture as "a central part of English life and culture." This British social anthropologist explains that "pubs are frequented by people of all ages, all social classes, all education-levels, and every conceivable occupation. It would be impossible even to *attempt* to understand Englishness without spending a lot of time in pubs" (ibid.: 88). Despite this groundwork, Nora retained a very negative perception in her mind, associating pubs solely with wild nightclubs and lewd behavior.

When I reviewed Nora's narratives, I discovered that she was routinely contrasting aspects of life in England with what she was familiar with in Hong Kong. While she noticed surface level, "weird" differences, she was oblivious to more subtle nuances (e.g., values, beliefs): "In the supermarket, I could see lots of frozen food, much more than in Hong Kong; British people must depend a lot on frozen food. People also queue in a weird way. Instead of lining up near each cashier, they make one line so the earlier one can be served. I guess this practice seems to be more fair" (survey). The last line is significant as she appeared poised to view an unfamiliar cultural practice in a favorable light, instead of simply rejecting it out of hand.

Although more at ease in her homestay, conflicting understandings of health and wellness hampered her adjustment: "I'm worrying about my health. I feel really tired every day and the food is quite unhealthy, like potatoes. Besides, the routine life here is quite new to me. Everyday we have breakfast at 7:45, lunch at 1:00, then dine at 6:00. I'm not used to this regular lifestyle in Hong Kong" (survey). She was still finding it difficult to accept a different routine and diet.

Third week – adjustment woes

Midway through the sojourn, Nora was in a rather dissatisfied mood: "A bit bored with English life." She berated her proficiency in the host language: "After coming to England, we found that our English was not really good and we should keep on upgrading and training ourselves even during the summer holiday" (survey). When referring to her own limitations, she made use of the collective "we," even though most of her peers were more fully immersed in their new environment and enjoying themselves.

While comfortable with her host family, Nora was still finding it a challenge to accept a new diet and way of life: "I'm happy when I'm with my host parents since they treat me really nice. Yet, I feel homesick always, since I really miss my parents and my friends. I'm homesick for Hong Kong food also, as I have potatoes every day but not rice. I try to 'hypnotize' myself that very soon I can taste Cantonese food again!" (survey). For reassurance, she phoned her Hong Kong parents on a daily basis. Considering these revelations I was surprised when she divulged the following in the same survey: "Adventurous and enthusiastic attitudes are good for people facing a new culture. I think my hosts perceive me as one who is daring or willing to try new things and accept differences in culture." Her self-perception appeared incongruent with much of her behavior, including a negative reaction to ways of being that were new to her.

Nora still wished to enhance her communication skills in English but was not receptive to unfamiliar cultural practices, again citing elements of local society that she disapproved of: "I intend to be more sociable and talkative but not open. I still can't agree with the young people here in UK. They smoke a lot and go clubbing or go to pubs every night and get drunk. I am always cautious about my identity as a Chinese or Hong Konger" (survey). She still tended to overgeneralize and accentuate the negative aspects of the host culture, while elevating her own. While many of her SES friends had ventured into a local pub to enjoy a meal, Nora had refused, holding fast to an unfavorable image of what lay inside.

When reflecting on her adjustment, Nora rated herself "4," using a scale where 1 is feeling like you don't fit in and 6 is feeling like you do fit in. In her survey, she added: "I think my host parents would rate me the same because I've quite a good relationship with them and we share our common tastes and liking towards food and cooking. I thought it would be quite difficult for me to fit in but I find that actually, the life of UK people is not much different from that of Hong Kong." In her survey, she wrote: "When I'm with my host family, I feel really safe and well received because I don't do anything that's particularly 'Cantonese' or 'Chinese'. We enjoy watching the same BBC program and food. I don't find any difference between us. Our common interest in certain fields bridges the gap between us." According to the DMIS (M. J. Bennett, 1993), individuals in the Minimization phase of development tend to believe that differences between cultures are neither deep nor significant. In accord with this stage, Nora had begun to emphasize that people are basically the same (e.g., "just like her").

Her diary entries in the third week were replete with cravings for familiar food. Realizing how much she loved and missed Chinese cuisine, she drew closer to a "Hong Kong Chinese" identity and distanced herself from England, a phenomenon that sociolinguists and study abroad researchers have observed in L2 sojourners in other contexts (e.g., Allen et al., 2007; Block, 2007; Stangor et al., 1996).

I miss the dishes prepared by mum very much! I have been living here for more than two weeks without having any rice. I didn't know that I like rice so much. From it, I learnt more about my identity as a Chinese Hong Konger. When I was in Hong Kong, I prefer having McDonald's or sandwiches from Delifrance. But when I am in England, I don't have any interest towards this kind of western food, I would rather have a Chinese meal! When we are away from home, we begin to realize our bond with it. The confusion over my own identity has been slightly cleared. I no longer really felt proud of my identity as British and would now rather put down "Hong Kong Chinese" whenever I was requested to tell what nationality I am. Being in the community of England, I started to appreciate my identity as a Chinese!

Midweek, Nora wrote about an encounter with her hosts' granddaughter which had a rather profound impact on her. When the young girl expressed interest in Chinese calligraphy, Nora felt a strong sense of pride in being Chinese, not just a Hong Konger. This caught her by surprise:

On the weekend, the granddaughter of my host parents came to visit. She's so lovely and always shows interest in me and the Chinese/Hong Kong culture. She asked me to teach her Chinese writings and she's so amazed by the complicated and beautiful pattern of Chinese characters. Once again, I am reminded of my identity as a Hong Konger and Chinese. I've never thought that by writing simple Chinese characters like numbers can bring me the sense of success and content. I am really proud of being a Chinese (diary).

In an alien environment, cast in the role of "cultural ambassador," Nora further enhanced her appreciation of her "Chineseness."

Fourth week – feeling different: On the periphery of the host culture

As "an outsider" in the community, Nora continued to display a heightened awareness of her ethnicity and peripheral status: "I'm getting used to the slow and peaceful living style and pace. Yet, somehow, I still think I'm an outsider since my outlook and appearance single me out from the UK people" (survey). Feeling "different," she assumed a more passive role in the community than her peers who were initiating conversations with locals outside their homestay (e.g., at the bus stop). Unlike the "languagers" (Phipps, 2006) describes, Nora was reluctant to "engage with the world-in-action" and "develop new dispositions for peptic action" in the host culture (ibid.: 12). In her survey, she wrote: "I'm interacting more with my hosts but not with others in public places. When I do shopping with my host parents, for example, it is them who talk to the cashiers." In the presence of her hosts, Nora was still positioned as a child and seemed accepting of this status.

Prior to the sojourn, Nora had hoped to improve her listening skills in English and develop a "better grasp of local slangs and idioms." Both of these aims were appropriate for informal language learning contexts; however, in the host environment she continued to judge her proficiency (and those of her peers) in purely academic terms. We had discussed the rationale for the policy in Hong Kong but she demonstrated little understanding of it:

I'm able to follow the "English only" policy. It's not as difficult as I thought; however, it's quite abnormal that we're not improving our spoken English but it's worsened. We tend to speak in a rather Cantonese way. It's quite out of my expectation that my English hasn't improved but deteriorated a bit and I make more grammatical mistakes when chatting with my friends. The policy's not as useful and successful as I thought although I am getting used to using English in social situations and I feel more comfortable when speaking English (survey).

While more at ease in social situations, Nora was quite self-critical and frequently lamented her "Cantonese way" of speaking English, seemingly unaware that most of her peers were not conversing in this way. Those who had established stronger bonds across cultures and were more at ease in the host environment were not using this exaggerated style of speech with their friends.

Later that same week, Nora and some of her SES friends visited Chinatown in Birmingham. When she wrote about the outing in her diary it was clear that she was still plagued by homesickness. Longing for the familiar, she still felt uncomfortable as a visible minority in England:

> When we saw the familiar Chinese words, we all had the feeling of being home. ... I wanted to stay there instead of going anywhere else. I wanted to stay with the Chinese people and the Chinese shops and restaurants that reminded me of home! When we're not at home, we tend to find objects that help soothing our homesickness. Once again, I feel my close bond to my parents, friends, my home and everything in Hong Kong! I didn't realize that I cared about the fact that I am the minority here in England.

That weekend the students and I traveled to Yorkshire and spent the weekend in Haworth, where we stayed in a youth hostel. After visiting the Brönte parsonage/museum, the students explored the moors and shops in the village. In her diary Nora described an unpleasant encounter with a shopkeeper:

> Most of the shop owners in Haworth were very friendly. One welcomed us and asked where we come from. However, one old shop owner treated us in a hostile manner, when my friends were choosing souvenirs and looking at those angel figurines. The man shouted to her and said "That's enough!" He didn't like us to touch his products but if we didn't have a good look at them how could we choose the things that we wanted? His rude attitude was presumably rooted from his discrimination towards us, the Asians. His dissatisfying service ruined my impression on the British people (diary).

Nora interpreted the shopkeeper's behavior as xenophobic. It is important to note, however, that six of the SES students had crowded into a tiny shop full of breakable ornaments. While not unusual in Hong Kong, the village shopkeeper was likely overwhelmed and worried that someone would break something. Although no racist words were uttered, Nora perceived the man to be prejudiced against Asians. This darkened her mood and left her with a negative impression of locals.

Fifth week – barriers and facilitating factors in sojourn learning

In the last week, Monday was a free day for the students, so Nora and several of her friends opted to travel to Cambridge. In her diary, she recounted an intercultural incident that disclosed her inflexibility:

> On our Cambridge trip we decided to try punting.[3] Unfortunately, when we found the punting company where we'd booked, we were told that the ride took around 45 minutes but we had to leave around 4:30 to catch the train back to Coventry. So, sorrowfully and unwillingly, we asked if they could cancel the booking. It's quite ridiculous that the girl replied, "Okay, take the money back then." If we were in Hong Kong, the sales girls would try their best to persuade us to try punting. They would even give us discount or ask us if it's possible to change the train. But here, the girl didn't care if she could earn the money but she just wanted to settle the affair. Hong Kongers care more about money and they treat their customers in a polite and friendly way. On the other hand, the British people are not flexible enough (diary).

Nora still had a tendency to judge new behaviors against the yardstick of Hong Kong, with the latter most often cast in a more favorable light. While she viewed the "punting" agent negatively, in this context the woman would have been considered very accommodating and not "pushy." Although the students had made the miscalculation, she refunded their money without question. Nora was unable or unwilling to see the situation from the woman's perspective. In her survey, she wrote: "I thought I could understand almost all the local culture but after the visit to Cambridge I found that some UK people are not polite and quite unfriendly. They are shattering their responsibility and don't have patience to explain to us. Their way of working are quite inflexible." Nora still overestimated her grasp of the local culture and was less open to different practices than many of her peers. In M. J. Bennett's (1993) terms, she displayed an ethnocentric mindset.

Near the end of the sojourn, Nora again rated herself in terms of "fitting in" to the local culture using a scale of 1 to 6 (1 is feeling like you don't fit in and 6 is feeling like you do): "I would say 5 because I find that I fit in the lifestyle here and I communicate with my host parents quite well. I think they would rate me 5 also because I rarely show any disagreement towards anything they do and our habits and practices are more or less the same" (survey). While Nora had found it difficult to adjust to the food and her host family's routine, she minimized cultural differences in "habits and practices" and again inflated her level of adjustment.

As the sojourn drew to a close, the SES students were encouraged to take stock of their learning. When asked if she had changed in any way, Nora cited many developments, ranging from enhanced intercultural communicative competence to a deeper appreciation of a "Hong Kong Chinese" identity:

> I've learnt to interact more successfully with people with different cultural background. My family and friends will find that I'm less shy and more talkative. I can present myself as one with self-confidence and recognition. I've become more mature. I can manage to look after myself which I didn't do that well when I was in Hong Kong as I depend a lot on my parents. Besides, I learn to be more proud of my identity as a Hong Kong Chinese and one who can bring the Chinese culture to my host parents and their families (survey).

Nora had become more relaxed when using English in social situations and felt less like a "foreigner" in the host culture. In her survey, she explained this development: "Speaking the same language as most of the people here motivates me. It helps me think that I'm not a stranger or minority here. Being surrounded by people who speak English encouraged us to speak in English and I'm more confident in communicating with native speakers." Nonetheless she was disappointed with her linguistic gains as she still measured her proficiency in terms of formal language learning (e.g., grammatical accuracy):

> My English hasn't really improved much. I expected my spoken English can be a little bit more fluent and I'd pick up some slang used by local people but I just failed to do so. ... I learnt how to initiate others to talk, yet there's still quite a lot of dead air in the chat. ... A lot of grammar mistakes are made. The main reason is that nobody corrects me when I make the mistake and most of the time I stay with my friends and our English tends to be Cantonese accent. That's why not much improvement has been made. I think my goals were realistic, just that I didn't have as much chance to interact with locals as I expected.

Nora lamented the lack of opportunity to interact with locals and found it difficult to sustain a conversation. By contrast, other participants (e.g., Jade, Mimi) took far more advantage of linguistic affordances and made more of an effort to interact across cultures with people outside their homestay. These "language activists" (Phipps, 2006) better understood the nature of informal language learning and also picked up new expressions and cultural understandings from their peers.

Although she'd experienced many ups and downs and had suffered from homesickness throughout, Nora was very emotional as the departure date approached. While happy to be heading home, she did not wish to part from her host family:

> This morning, when I woke up and went downstairs, mother, as usual, was preparing a nice and big breakfast for me. The sensitive me nearly couldn't control myself at that moment, I just wanted to cry. ... Their love and care overwhelmed me and I just didn't want to leave them. After breakfast, all the memories of the last five weeks kept flooding in my mind. All the happiness and excitement that I had were recalled! This UK trip can be called the most memorable and fruitful one in my life. Though I encountered quite a lot of challenges throughout the trip, these challenges taught me to think in a more mature way and it trained me to be more independent. I could also see the positive changes in all the SES buddies, all of us became more sociable, talkative and independent (diary).

On the last day of the sojourn, Nora offered the following advice to the next cohort of SES students: "They should open up themselves and always be ready to ask and confront ambiguity with questions. They should spend more time with their host family since I'm sure they can learn a lot from them. Furthermore, they should abide by the language policy and get the best out of it" (survey). While she had been less active and open than many of her fellow sojourners, significantly, she advocated this for others.

Postsojourn

A short time after her return to Hong Kong, Nora shared her views about the sojourn in a 40-minute interview, which she opted to do in Cantonese. While happy to be back, she longed for what she had left behind: "In the first week I couldn't get adapted to my life here. I missed my life in England, especially my host family as we'd lived together for five weeks and they treated me very well. I want to visit

England next year because I miss it very much" (interview). Considering her presojourn fears about living with strangers from another culture and her persistent homesickness while abroad, this was a remarkable turnabout.

Once she fell back into her routine, "us vs. them" discourse resurfaced, as she explained that her love of her birthplace had deepened: "I like Hong Kong more because Hong Kong people are nicer than British people" (interview). She still had a tendency to overgeneralize and did not recognize that politeness norms differ across cultures, with positive and negative elements in all societies.

In her interview, Nora still displayed a superficial understanding of cultural differences: "My perceptions of England are more or less the same. To me, it's a place with lots of grasslands and flowers. ... I used to think British people were traditional and gentle but, after I visited London, I think Londoners are similar to the people here. They have a fast pace of life and some dress in a very trendy way" (interview). Focused on visible features, as reflected in her postsojourn IDI scores, she appeared unaware of deeper-level aspects (e.g., beliefs, values) that may vary across cultures.

For Nora, like most of the SES students, the homestay had been the highlight of the sojourn: "If I had stayed on campus, I would not have experienced the life of the British. By living with a host family, I got to know more about their culture and had more chances to communicate with them" (interview). She was pleased that she had been able to develop a friendly relationship with her hosts who had taken "excellent care" of her.

Reflecting on her English language proficiency and intercultural communication skills, Nora was quite self-critical, focusing on her limitations rather than her gains:

> English is more difficult than I thought. On the trip, I found that my English was not that good. There're quite a lot of idioms I don't know. When watching TV in England, I couldn't understand quite a lot of expressions. I also couldn't catch different accents. I think I have to improve my English. Also, we sometimes spoke English with a Cantonese accent and made grammatical mistakes. I need to make more of an effort to improve my oral English and accent. About my intercultural communication skills ... um ... I'm not sure.

Nora also realized that she may have occasionally been overly blunt when communicating across cultures: "Sometimes maybe I spoke in a too direct way to my host family. It would have been better if I'd put my ideas in a more indirect way." Her sociopragmatic awareness appeared to have evolved somewhat during her stay.

Despite her self-professed "limitations," Nora's connection with English had grown closer after five weeks in the host culture: "I speak more English now and sometimes I even think in English first. Before the trip, I would sometimes think in Cantonese and then translate it back to English. But now, the case is sometimes just the opposite." She had also become more relaxed while using English with "native speakers" in informal, social situations as well as with other Chinese: "I think I'll use more English now in my daily life. I no longer feel strange about using it with Hong Kong people" (interview).

When asked if she'd changed due to her sojourn experiences, Nora took some time to reflect before citing a range of personal developments:

> I've become more talkative and less shy as I had to talk and interact with many people in England. I think it's now easier for me to make new friends and get along with them. I'm also more self-confident and independent. I've experienced a lot more things and have become more mature. Even though I was taken care of by my host family, I had to do more things myself and to solve my own problems during the trip. Actually, I think I still need to become more independent and learn to take care of myself. It's not good to be dependent on others (interview).

Throughout the five-week sojourn, I observed that Nora had been positioned as a child in her homestay. Back on home soil, she felt better prepared to assume greater independence. I wondered if she would have gradually taken on more responsibility for herself in England if the sojourn had been longer or if she had been placed with hosts who did not coddle her (e.g., Jade's host).

Even though her transition to English life had not been easy, she was keen to make further forays abroad: "I want to go to England again, because there're still lots of places I haven't visited. I also want to travel to other European countries. I'm thinking about doing postgraduate studies in England." In her own words, the sojourn had been "a life-changing event."

Now, we turn to an examination of Mimi's sojourn and reentry experiences.

Mimi

Predeparture aims and concerns

With almost no travel experience, Mimi was one of the most excited about the sojourn: "I really feel happy and delighted that I'll have the chance to live in England and leave Hong Kong!" (survey). During her stay, she hoped to "further consolidate" her proficiency in English and, in particular: "acquire greater fluency, improve her conversation skills, and develop a wider vocabulary" (survey). She also wished to deepen her understanding of other cultures. In her interview she provided further insight into her aims and aspirations:

RA: What are your personal goals for the trip?
Mimi: To broaden my horizons and explore the world. I've interviewed a German girl and found that she thinks very differently from me. I think people do think differently across cultures so I want to see what the differences are.
RA: How about your academic goals?
Mimi: To strive for perfection.
RA: In which areas?
Mimi: Um ... I want to do well in my studies and improve my communication skills in English and understand some of the British humor. For example, sometimes I don't understand Professor Harvey's British humor in class so I want to learn more about this.

When Mimi joined the SES she worried about her ability to adjust to life in English: "I find myself easily get nervous about whether I can adapt and make myself comfortable with speaking English with locals" (predeparture expectations form). Even so, she felt better equipped for cross-cultural experiences than Nora. From her standpoint, the intensive presojourn preparation, which included interviewing current and former sojourners, had helped ready her for life in England:

I feel I'm prepared for the sojourn. These past few weeks, I've done several interviews with international students about their cultural experiences. Learning from them, I recognize that living in another world where people have very different life style would make you feel quite excited and astonished and yet perhaps alienated. These sorts of exercises help me prepare for that kind of feelings (predeparture survey).

On the eve of departure, most of Mimi's worries had faded away and she was keen to board an airplane for the first time.

From the onset, Mimi was very supportive of the English language policy for the sojourn and believed that it would be relatively easy to follow: "The environment there is an English-speaking one and we all want to improve our English so we should use it, even if all of us are Chinese. I'll be the first one to insist on using English. When I'm talking with my SES friends now, I just start off the topic in English" (interview). Shortly before departure, in a survey, she reaffirmed her desire to make the policy work: "Fully speaking in English the entire five weeks would be really cool and great. We don't really have such a chance to listen, to speak, or to think in English in Hong Kong so I promise I will surely follow the language policy to enrich my ability in speaking English." She was much more confident than Nora that the policy would be a success.

The sojourn

First week – the arrival as a rite of passage

On arrival, in England, Mimi discovered that her host family had been changed while we were en route. The International Student Affairs Officer who greeted us at the airport explained that the couple she'd originally been assigned withdrew due to a family emergency. Another couple, who was already hosting a Japanese exchange student, had agreed to take her. In her diary, Mimi described this unexpected development as a "critical incident" and was clearly shaken: "Gosh! My host has been changed? Why? Why is there such an abrupt change? I don't understand! At that moment, I was a bit stunned. Life is full of uncertainties. This is the conclusion that I could make for the early start of my sojourn. I pretended to be happy but right at the bottom of my heart, unbearable anxiety tortured me" (diary).

While Mimi perceived herself to be self-reliant and tolerant of ambiguities, initially she was thrown into chaos when her expectations were not met. After calming herself, she tried to be positive about what lay ahead: "I suddenly felt that I was so brave. Like a little girl leaving her home without notice, launching her adventurous journey to somewhere she had never been to. Life is not only full of uncertainties, but life is also full of possibilities. You've got to explore it by yourself. Go through it." To her great relief, a retired couple with 20 years of hosting experience warmly greeted her on arrival. The following day, Nora described her new "home sweet home" in enthusiastic, glowing terms: "I've a wonderful and lovely homestay. Judy (mum) and Richard (dad, a good cook!) are funny and talkative people. Their two adult daughters live away but Niko, a 19-year old Japanese boy, lives with them. I love them all. My bedroom (all pink!) is lovely and cozy. Wonderful! Amazing! My new life has started" (diary). While initially shocked and overwhelmed by the sudden change in her homestay arrangement, she recovered rather quickly.

I also observed early on that Mimi displayed the attitudes of openness and curiosity, ingredients that the intercultural experts in Deardorff's (2004) study cite as essential for intercultural competence to grow. At the welcome lunch organized by the host institution, Mimi was thrilled to have the opportunity to taste a range of food from different parts of the world: "I was so happy to have a wonderful lunch in a grand building. I could try different kinds of cuisines (e.g., Indian dishes, Japanese salmon, English salads) – different dishes mixed and mingled. It symbolized people coming from all over the world to meet and share their cultural experiences" (diary). Already, she seemed to have a more open mindset than some of her peers, who were searching for familiar food and reluctant to try anything new.

Further, Mimi felt "good" using English "all the time," and was "often dreaming" in the language: "I think it was a brilliant idea to have the 'English Only' policy. Even if the policy did not impose, we, students, should have the initiation or eagerness to speak in English so as to grasp the chance to speak English in an English-speaking environment" (diary). As she explained in this entry, it helped her to adjust: "It's so good that my spoken English was 100% this week. Even with my friends, we chatted in English as we all thought that speaking it all day really helped us to adapt to the English environment. At least I didn't feel awkward using English in this English-speaking country. I felt good in using English all day."

Despite her enthusiasm, the increased use of English, on occasion, caused Mimi psychological distress: "It sounds weird but sometimes when I speak in English, I don't feel like myself. It's not the real me. I feel like swapping into another person whom I know not. Besides, my strong American accent once again made others think that I am from the States. I am not. I am from Hong Kong. A real Chinese" (diary). Her last comment reminded me of her "home ethnography" project (see Chapter 4). She still did not fully understand the feelings of her American-born Chinese (ABC) informant who was upset when Hong Kongers did not accept him as Chinese. Her revelations further remind us of the complex, emotive connection between language, culture, and context in shaping one's self-perception and attitudes (Dörnyei, 2009; Noels, 2009; Ushioda, 2009).

By chance, Mimi met a former secondary school teacher from Hong Kong, who was studying at the host university. When she began to speak in her mother tongue she found it 'a bit strange'. In dramatic fashion, she recounted her fears that her Cantonese had been "corrupted." Again, she worried she'd lose her facility in the language: "During the conversation, my Cantonese became a bit strange. I mean the accent has been subtly changed ... like mixing with some English accent. ... That's too weird. I don't know why my mother tongue has been corrupted in this way. ... Can I gain it back?" (diary). Would her fears of L1 attrition limit her use of English in the remainder of the sojourn?

During a full-group excursion to Oxford at the end of the first week, Mimi and four of her SES friends went off on their own to explore. In her diary, similar to Nora, she offered an account of what transpired when they asked a local man to take a photo of them together:

> One interesting and funny finding is that I found out even the photo-taking values could differ in different cultures. The reason why I said this was because I asked a British young man to help us take a group photo under the "Bridge of Sighs". Of course, we wanted the bridge as the background. It was so ridiculous that the man just focus on us without the bridge! So, we waited for another group of people to help us. This time we tried to ask another foreigner. Again, the same outcome was found. We felt a bit helpless and frustrated. Moreover, why foreigners would like to focus on people instead of the scenery? I could stereotype this circumstance as a kind of phenomenon. Or may be this finding was not due to cultural differences but personal favors.

Mimi was a bit more cautious than Nora and tried to avoid stereotyping. Nonetheless she too failed to critically examine the event from multiple angles. Since there were five SES students, the young man had little room for the background as he was shooting close to them. Most importantly, they had not made their request explicit. Neither Mimi nor Nora considered this a factor, even though we discussed different styles of communication (e.g., direct, indirect) in the intercultural communication course. It is also relevant to note that when the students showed their digital images at the end of their stay, nearly all were close-ups of themselves alone or with their closest buddies (e.g., Mimi at Blenheim

Palace, Mimi and Nora at Shakespeare's birthplace). Few members of the group took pictures of landscapes without an SES student in the frame.

Second week – new spaces, new awakenings

As Mimi began to relax, she started to notice visible cultural differences in the world around her. After attending her first play in England, for example, she contrasted intermission activities with those in Hong Kong: "It was really interesting to look at the local people in the theatre. During the middle break, most went out to have an ice-cream for relaxation. It's not a common practice in Hong Kong. Perhaps having an ice-cream during breaks helps the audience cool down their nerves before entering back to the play" (survey).

In the small town where we were based, Nora also observed that strangers often greeted one another in the street, including her. Instead of dismissing this practice as "weird," she expressed appreciation for it: "I think people here are extremely nice. No matter they know you or not, they say hello to you. This is definitely different from Hong Kong" (survey). While happy with this custom, she was uncomfortable with another "habit" that she'd observed in her homestay: "My hosts always ask whether I would like something to drink. Sometimes, I feel that's probably too much." At this point in time, she did not recognize this offer as a gesture of hospitality and conversation opener in this context.

A pivotal moment for Mimi occurred in the second week of the sojourn at a local community center when she was invited to sing on karaoke night. In her diary, she wrote: "This was the first time to sing solo in front of people I was so unfamiliar with. Anyway, I went up to the stage to sing the Carpenters' 'Yesterday Once More', my favorite song. Though I was nervous and didn't sing very well, Judy, Richard, and the whole audience gave a big applause to me."

As the only Chinese at this event, the experience heightened her awareness of her ethnicity and nationality. Further, she had difficulty understanding the discourse of locals and this made her feel like an outsider of the language. In her diary, she recalled what transpired:

> Once I stepped into the karaoke room, I started to realize that I was a "foreigner". I was a bit uneasy as I was a minority in the cultural scene. I could sense my Chinese identity suddenly popped up and dominated my body. I don't mean that I didn't fit into the culture. I could get along with the local people very well, but I am not a native. I was not good at English especially listening and speaking. Sometimes they said things and I didn't grasp their meanings. I could

just smile to respond. Language barrier made a distance between us. Maybe they would regard me as impolite, yet I did not mean it. I just did not know how to give a response. I tried hard to hear and understand what they were talking about. Their high pitch intonation and fast speech became obstacles for me.

Mimi could not understand "the local slang and idioms" used by Eric, the master of ceremony (MC), and found that her English "did not work well" in this cultural scene. Unsure how to respond appropriately to his questions, she felt like "a complete idiot in front of the public." In her diary, she recounted one of their exchanges:

> "Where do you come from?" Eric asked.
> I directly replied, "I'm from Hong Kong."
> "Hong Kong? You're from Hong Kong?"
> "Yes, Hong Kong." I was so firm to say that I am from Hong Kong. I am always fond of being a Hong Konger. A Chinese.
> "Is anybody else further than from Hong Kong?"
> I didn't know why he was making fun of me.

Humor often does not translate well across cultures. New to this cultural scene, Mimi misunderstood the MC's intentions. Although embarrassed, this did not prevent her from enjoying the evening. She danced with her hosts and three hours later one of the guests bid her farewell with a song: "It was so kind of him to sing a song for me. On the way home, Richard and Judy told me that I was courageous to sing in front of the public. I also could not believe that I could make it!" Mimi appreciated "these new cultural experiences" facilitated by her hosts: "My gratitude towards them was endless. If they did not bring me here tonight, I would not have this invaluable experience that other classmates do not have. Thanks Judy and Richard!" (diary). Her entries provide evidence of what Byram et al. (2002) refer to as intercultural attitudes (*savoir être*), a positive mindset that they consider a prerequisite for successful intercultural contact and communication.

Excited to be in a new environment, Mimi continued to make an effort to try different foods and practices. While Nora had been reluctant to set foot in a pub, Mimi often went with her hosts and discovered a relaxed gathering place for friends and family. In her diary entry, her enthusiasm and zest for life were evident: "I didn't know how to order drinks so Richard explained the practice. … I had a big plate of fish'n chips with mushy peas. It's good to open up our mind to try new things here."

By this time, Mimi had become very close to her hosts and "felt like part of the family, even like Judy's real daughter." In her diary, she described their relationship with great affection:

> I've really become one of the family members. Having fun with Richard and Judy, sharing our feelings, enjoying our lunch and dinner together, all the happiness I have here become my good memories. At the carnival Richard tried to win a prize from the lucky draw booth/stall. However, he failed and Judy then paid another £1 to buy the tickets to draw and finally she won a little teddy bear and she gave it to me as a present! At that moment, I really felt like I am their daughter. ... I was so touched.

Similar to Nora, Mimi believed that her hosts were genuinely interested in her and this had a positive effect on their relationship. In her diary, she described the warm ties that she was developing in her homestay: "I could feel the love and care from my host parents. They would ask me how my school days were and how I felt about the plays or outings. Besides, they yearned to know more about me! I showed them my pictures with my family members in Hong Kong and they said I should have brought more to let them see!" Her perception was significant, as previous investigations of L2 sojourners (Jackson, 2006a, 2008) have shown that the degree of mutuality and respect in homestays can have a major impact on student learning.

Instead of always waiting for her hosts to make the first move, Mimi initiated conversations in her homestay: "I could tell that Richard was glad to see me actively chat with him and even play crossword puzzles with him. I think it's important to be active to let the host know that you are interested to get to know them" (diary). While many of her SES friends went to Edinburgh on the free weekend, Mimi opted to spend time with her hosts as this was a higher priority for her: "Instead of going to Scotland I will stay with my host mum and dad. I don't want to lose my time to be with them. My plan for the coming weekend – Go wherever my host parents go! Goal for tomorrow: try all the new things and explore the town!" (diary). With a positive, upbeat attitude, she remained open to exploration.

Third week – heightened awareness of Self and Other

The karaoke event left such an impression on Mimi that it was still etched in her mind the following week. "At karaoke night, there were over 80 local people. That experience was quite important in my life since I'd never been in a place where I was the only Chinese. I felt a very strong sense of being a Chinese who came from Hong Kong – without hesitation. This kind of self identity confirmation is very important to me" (survey). In an alien environment, where she was visibly different from locals, Mimi became more attached to her "Chinese self," as she explained in her diary: "I feel happy and a sort of intimacy when I meet Asians. I like the black hair and yellow faces. In the past, when my English self and Chinese self confronted, I would hesitate, or think that both of them could exist at the same time. Now, I have an inclination towards my Chinese self. ... It's become stronger than ever." In an alien environment where she perceived her cultural identity to be under threat, she shifted back to a "subtractive" perception of bilingualism.[4]

Quite relaxed in her "fabulous homestay," Mimi continued to take part in family activities: "I have a great time with my host mum and dad and, Niko, the Japanese exchange student who stays with them. My host parents brought me to different cultural activities like a flea market, having lunch in pubs, going to the fair, etc. I am so happy with my host family" (survey). In contrast with Nora's homestay situation, Mimi's hosts introduced her to a range of cultural scenes, including their favorite pub; this provided her with more exposure to the host language and culture: "After dinner, Richard and Judy were so kind that they brought Sara and me to the pub. I made use of the chance to collect data since three of my informants were in the pub at the same time! Cool! It was so good that we had a new cultural experience tonight drinking beer in a pub!" (diary).

Midway through the sojourn, Mimi revealed that she'd begun to appropriate local greetings: "People here are usually humorous and energetic, like my host mum and dad. I learn to be like them. I'm now friendly to all. I say good-bye or thank-you to the bus driver whenever taking/getting off the bus. This is a very good practice which I like and advocate. I hope I can keep this when I go back to Hong Kong" (survey). Interestingly, before crossing cultures she had been against "imitating the way other people act," convinced that it would be "inappropriate." As her confidence grew, she began to step out of her "habitual ways of speaking" to develop "different, more relational ways of interacting" with host nationals (Phipps, 2006: 12).

When asked how a person might balance his or her own culture with a new one, Mimi outlined her philosophy: "A person should open up his/her mind to try to understand why people behave the way they do and try to experience their culture. But when a particular thing doesn't fit him/her, he/she should politely reject it, since that cup of tea is not everybody's favorite. This is what I'm doing and it fits my situation quite well" (survey). She still did not fully understand that the frequent offers of tea in this context were intended as a social lubricant (Fox, 2004).

Proud of being a "genuine and direct person," Mimi intentionally retained her usual "way of expressing" feelings even if it meant offending people. In her survey, she explained, "Sometimes I don't feel happy with something or I don't agree with something, I would not hypocritically hide my truth feeling. Just as my host mum said I am a down-to-earth person. I know that my directness towards people may unintentionally hurt others but that's what I am, this is the real me." While she saw herself as very culturally sensitive, she did not recognize the merits of adjusting her communication style to put her interlocutors at ease. To borrow from Chen and Starosta (2008), Mimi did not yet possess sufficient "cognitive or intercultural awareness" or "behavioral or intercultural adroitness," elements these interculturalists consider essential for successful intercultural communication competence.

Fourth week – feeling at home in new spaces

In her homestay, Mimi continued to join a wide variety of family activities and made a conscious effort to follow her hosts' conversation:

> I'm getting along very well with my host family. I feel like I'm their daughter and a family member. Moreover, I spend most of my time with them. We talk and I have fun with them. They are so good and caring. We did a lot of things like going for picnic, shopping together, watching TV, chatting, cooking, watching tennis competitions, playing darting, having BBQ, singing karaoke together – many, many activities, and they always treat me in the pubs. It's getting easier to communicate with them because I'm really talkative person. I talk about whatever I want. Sometimes I have a hard time to catch what they say since they speak really fast and my accent is very different from them and my vocabulary is not so rich to help me to understand what they're saying. But I try my best to learn (survey).

A diary entry penned later that same week provided evidence of growth in her sociopragmatic awareness. After observing her hosts in action for several weeks and sharing experiences with her friends, it dawned on her that "frequent offers of coffee or tea" in this context were "a way to start a conversation."

Mimi no longer felt like an "outsider" in the host culture and attributed this to her "open-mindedness" and tolerance of others. While she'd misunderstood local humor and perceived insults when none were intended (e.g., at karaoke night), she believed that she was taking the "high road" by retaining a happy disposition: "I feel comfortable here because I'm open-minded enough to accept a different way of life in England. Besides, even though someone may make fun of me, I actually don't mind. To maintain the atmosphere harmonious I would keep my smiley face to people" (survey). Mimi still possessed an inflated perception of her level of cultural awareness and sensitivity.

Fifth week – fitting in

Similar to Nora, during the sojourn Mimi became close to her hosts through her ethnographic project. By focusing on the local pub scene, Mimi discovered more about English culture and gained wider exposure to the host language in a relaxed social setting.

> I'm happy about my ethnographic research. I have good rapport with my informants and collect data very easily. ... My hosts brought me to many nice pubs to experience the culture. ... They gave me many insights about their experiences in pubs and why they love pubs so much. Through doing the interviews, I had the chance to get to know more about their past. The relationship between us became much closer than before (survey).

The host–sojourner bond was not as close in all of the homestays. Mimi observed that some of her peers "treated the relationship with their hosts as a kind of customer-and-service-provider relationship" (diary). I also noted that some students remained focused on their own needs throughout the sojourn and displayed little recognition of their hosts' efforts to make their stay enjoyable. By contrast, Mimi treasured the time spent with Richard and Judy and demonstrated awareness of the importance of openly expressing gratitude in this context: "Learning how to appreciate the host's effort is important. Judy once told me that she knew that I appreciated their efforts to keep me happy and healthy and bring me to somewhere else to explore, because I would say thank you to them overtly, directly."

While Nora was still suffering from homesickness at the end of her stay, Mimi felt at ease in the host culture: "It's as if I've been living here for many, many years already. I feel so comfortable now, just like being part of the local culture" (survey). Mimi rated her adjustment in the local culture as "6," using a scale of 1 to 6, whereby 1 is feeling like you don't fit in and 6 is feeling like you do. In her estimation, her communication skills had improved during the sojourn:

> Both my verbal and nonverbal intercultural communication skills are better than before. For verbal communication, I've learnt to repeat the questions that I don't understand or ask for repetition or even ask for clarification. In Hong Kong, I was not so keen on requesting repetition as I thought I might disturb the conversation. But now, I find that if I don't ask, I cannot even carry on the conversation. Therefore, I ask if I don't understand (survey).

In particular, Mimi believed that she'd made great strides in terms of her ability to think and communicate orally in English, as she explained in this diary entry:

> Besides the successful homestay program, the English policy was another success. Though I used Cantonese with my family while I phoned back to Hong Kong, I could follow the policy quite well. We had to use English to communicate with our host every day and, most of the time, I would think in English instead of Cantonese. It was like English has embedded in my body, fully. I think my confidence in speaking English was enhanced. In the past, whenever I needed to address a speech or do any form of English presentation, I would draft a speech to think about what kind of words I should use or say. But now, no more draft is needed I bet.

While Mimi maintained that English was now "fully embedded" in her body, she had not learned as much vocabulary as she'd expected: "I guess I was very idealistic that I would learn more English vocabulary in England. In fact, I learnt not as many as I thought. Sometimes, after learning a new word from my host parents, if I did not use it, I would no longer remember it" (diary). By contrast, she was rather pleased with her enhanced ability to understand different accents, as she explained in her diary: "A surprising gain was that my ability to adapt to fast speech and different kind of English accents was increased! This was really unexpected. ... All sort of accents of English I had to adjust to ... Welsh, Londoner, Japanese."

Although happy that she had used English throughout most of the sojourn, Mimi sometimes worried that this brief stay in an English environment might negatively impact on her mother tongue: "Basically, it's a good idea to speak English all the time. Brilliant. But I discover that

I could not speak proper Cantonese when we talked during cooking. This scared me coz I worry the first language attrition may happen to me" (survey). When asked if she thought her family and friends back home would notice any changes in her, she responded: "Maybe they'll think I'm becoming more westernized, like my Cantonese has changed. Nora said my Cantonese accent doesn't sound like real Cantonese, like I'm from overseas. Gosh! I think my friends and my family would sense that as well" (survey). In an English-medium environment her fear of losing her L1 and cultural identity returned as she shifted back to a "subtractive" perception of bilingualism (Lambert, 1975).

Postsojourn

Back on home soil, Mimi shared her views about the sojourn in an interview that lasted more than an hour. Throughout she code-mixed, frequently interjecting English lexical items into her largely Cantonese discourse.

While she experienced some mild reentry culture shock, Mimi quickly readjusted to the familiar environment and way of life: "After coming back home, my cultural shock was related to my feeling of missing life in England. I realized that I saw things differently and kept asking myself why do Chinese people act in this way? I had this question in my mind. There was a change in my values. I also had to get readjusted to a different lifestyle but it didn't take long" (interview). Crossing cultures not only raised her awareness of unique elements in Chinese culture, Mimi had begun to ponder what lay behind behavior that she had once taken for granted. Her comments provide evidence of what Byram et al. (2002) refer to as *savoir s'engager*. These intercultural educators consider this "critical cultural awareness" an essential skill for successful communication across cultures and languages.

In her interview Mimi talked at length about "karaoke night," a pivotal event which impacted on her self-identity:

> There was one cultural shock, actually I don't know if it's a cultural shock. One night, I went to the community centre for karaoke night. I was the only Chinese in the cultural scene, the so-called "alien". I felt afraid as I was the only Chinese there, because I was the minority. And the master of ceremony made fun of me. He said, "Anybody further from Hong Kong?" It was a harmless joke and I didn't mind but the whole situation was quite strange. The sense of my identity as a Chinese became the strongest at that time. Previously, I viewed

myself as a half-British, no, not British, but English, "half-English" and "half-Chinese". Originally, my identity was half-half. But suddenly, my Chinese half became stronger. It was quite a shock to me. ... My Chinese self is now dominating my body. After the trip to England, I feel it's like a watershed. That day, I suddenly felt I was a Chinese ... my language, my appearance ... because when they made fun of me, I didn't know what the jokes meant. I am not a native speaker. I didn't know their idioms. Thus, I suddenly felt my English self became more distant.

Sensitive to her minority status in England, Mimi had become far more accepting of her Chineseness during the sojourn; at times, this distanced her from her "English self." Misinterpreting the banter of the MC she had felt even more like an "outsider." Although this only temporarily alienated her from the host culture it had a significant impact on how she saw herself. While Mimi displayed many of the intercultural attitudes and traits that Byram et al. (2002), Deardorff (2008) and Fantini (2007) consider key for successful intercultural communication, her knowledge (*savoirs*) of the host culture, skills of interpreting and relating (*savoir comprendre*), and sociolinguistic competence were less well developed.

Despite feeling noticeably "different" in England, at times, Mimi believed that she'd adapted to English life rather quickly. In her interview she explained: "I'm a talkative person, and I often took the initiative to talk to people so I established my relationship with my host family quite fast. I didn't feel like a foreigner by the end of my stay although I'm not a native speaker and my appearance doesn't look like them" (interview). She was especially pleased that she'd built up a warm relationship with her hosts, who had exposed her to an array of cultural scenes:

What I liked most about the sojourn was the homestay. I was fortunate to have really great hosts! They treated me like their daughter. If there was a family gathering they always brought me with them. They also took me to many places that my classmates did not see, like to a flea market, a farm, and a community centre. My ethnographic research was about the pub culture in England so they brought me to different kinds of pubs, inviting me for expensive meals there. I really felt happy and appreciated their arrangements for me, bringing me to visit different places, and broadening my mind. My host mum told me she sensed that I appreciated her efforts.

Similar to Nora, Mimi's ethnographic project had provided more opportunity for her to bond with her hosts.

On reflection, Mimi firmly believed that her five-week stay in England was "very important" in her life: "I had never been to a foreign country before. My horizon has been greatly broadened. Previously, I felt I was a frog inside a well, knowing nothing" (survey). Similar to Nora, she credited her sojourn experiences with several areas of personal growth: enhanced self-confidence, a more decisive nature, more "open-mindedness," and a greater willingness to try new things. Notably, many of these elements have been cited by interculturalists (e.g., Chen and Starosta, 2008; Jandt, 2007) as essential for intercultural competence. In her interview, Mimi said:

> I was already independent before the trip but I feel that I've become more self-confident and decisive. It's very good that I've become more determined. The way I dress, the way I eat and my eating style has also changed. For example, although I missed Chinese dim sum, now I realize I like Western food more than before. I brought some English tea back with me as I liked drinking milk tea while in England. I've taught my younger brother and sister how to make it. That's quite good. And, I never wore a short skirt before but I would wear it now. I've become more open-minded.

Mimi was supportive of the "English only" policy for the sojourn and recommended that it remain in place for the next group. In her interview, she outlined its benefits: "The language policy's a fantastic idea because if one just keeps code-mixing Chinese and English, one's language abilities in these two languages will decline. The English-only policy also helped us to adapt to life in England. When we kept speaking in English, we thought in English, too."

In terms of her English language usage, Mimi was convinced that "there was definitely enhancement." In her interview she explained: "I've become less nervous when I speak. Before the sojourn, I needed to think very carefully about which words to choose before speaking out. Now, I use English spontaneously." She had also become more confident using English across cultures, including with strangers: "When I was waiting for a bus in London on my stay-behind trip, a Canadian took the initiative to speak to me. I spoke with her instead of ignoring her. In the past, I would not speak with strangers, but now, I will" (interview). Even so, there were some disappointments: "Before my departure, I was very idealistic. I wished my vocabulary would be greatly enriched but it just expanded a little bit. It's out of my expectation."

Mimi believed that English would play a greater role in her life in the future: "I will definitely use it more in Hong Kong both inside and outside the classroom" (survey). Instead of opting to be interviewed in English, however, she code-mixed throughout; she was the only one of the case participants to do so. While she denigrated this habit, she was unable to stop herself: "In this interview, I used quite a lot of code-mixing. I feel both my Chinese and English are down graded."

After some reflection, Mimi offered advice for future sojourners that centered on behaviors and attitudes that international educators (e.g., Byram et al., 2002; Chen and Starosta, 2008; Fantini, 2007) have associated with successful intercultural mediators:

> The most important thing is the next group should appreciate what their host families do for them and be considerate. They're staying in their hosts' home and not a hotel so they should adjust to their hosts' style instead of making the hosts adjust to theirs. ... Being open-minded and optimistic are also important since you may face obstacles that are unexpected. The next group should be independent enough to help their host do some housework like washing the dishes. They should try to be thoughtful and expressive. They should also do better planning to spend more time with their host (interview).

Mimi was convinced that a positive mindset, a willingness to help out in the homestay, and spending plenty of time in the homestay would lead to successful host–sojourner relationships.

Positive sojourn experiences prompted Mimi to reassess her career goals: "I have a stronger desire to do postgraduate studies, especially in literature. My professional goal is to become a news reporter on the radio. After spending five weeks watching the BBC news every day, I suddenly became more sensitive to current social affairs" (interview). During her short stay abroad, Mimi also became "braver and more adventurous." Having "fallen in love with touring around," Mimi began to arrange future travels: "I've already made plans to visit my host mum next year by myself and I will go to Taiwan in August. I suddenly want to visit different places and I never thought about traveling before." Considering that Mimi had never boarded a plane prior to the sojourn, this was noteworthy.

Conclusions

An examination of Nora and Mimi's oral and written narratives and my field notes revealed that their intercultural development was in line with their actual pre- and postsojourn IDI scores. Their perceived IDI scores indicated that they had a very inflated perception of their level of intercultural sensitivity and there was considerable evidence of this in their narratives and my observations of their behavior.

During the sojourn, Nora was more resistant to new elements than many of her peers and did not display as many of the skills and attributes that Byram et al. (2002), Deardorff (2008), and Chen and Starosta (2008) link to intercultural competence. She suffered from bouts of homesickness throughout and remained in a dependent, child-like role in her homestay. Even so, through her ethnographic research, she became more comfortable using English and established a close bond with her hosts. Although her fears and negative misperceptions of the host culture held her back from fully exploring the world beyond her homestay, by the end of the sojourn, she had moved further into Minimization and become less fearful of cultural differences. While reluctant to embrace her Chineseness on entry into the SES, in an alien environment where she was visibly different, she developed a heightened appreciation of her cultural roots and clung more tightly to a Chinese identity, a phenomenon observed by study abroad researchers in other settings (e.g., Allen et al., 2007; Bateman, 2002; Stroebe et al., 1988; Isabelli-Garçia, 2006). On reentry, Nora cited numerous linguistic, cultural, and personal benefits of the sojourn experience and began to dream of other possibilities for her life.

Throughout the sojourn, Mimi took a much more active role in the host environment than Nora and, consequently, gained more access to English in a variety of settings. While she sometimes misunderstood situations in the host culture and feared L1 attrition (Lambert, 1975), her positive mindset and a willingness to try new things led to personal growth and English language enhancement. By the end of her stay in England, she had moved closer to the second half of Minimization, the transitional phase; she tended to downplay cultural differences, emphasizing common elements across cultures. Although she developed a warm relationship with her hosts, she was mindful that her appearance differentiated her from most locals. Similar to Nora, she clung more tightly to her "Chinese self" in an alien environment and retained an inflated perception of her level of sociopragmatic awareness and intercultural competence. On reentry, she vowed to use English more in her social life and, like Nora, began to imagine more travels abroad.

The developmental trajectories of both women suggest that a short-term sojourn with systematic predeparture preparation, experiential elements, guided critical reflection, and ongoing support can have a positive impact on L2 students who have a high level of ethnocentricism on entry. If the host environment is welcoming and appropriate support is provided, students may be guided toward a more reflective, intercultural mindset. In the process, they can build up the confidence and skills necessary to communicate more appropriately across cultures and begin to consider new possibilities for their life (e.g., intimate-intercultural relationships, further travels, lengthier sojourns, increased use of the host language in a greater variety of domains).

The next chapter explores the journeys of Lana and Mimi who possessed higher levels of intercultural communicative competence and sensitivity.

6
Lana and Jade's Sojourn and Reentry

Of the four case participants, Lana and Jade acquired the highest levels of intercultural sensitivity according to the Intercultural Development Inventory (IDI), although their trajectories were quite different. Following 14 weeks of presojourn preparation, Lana scored 98.91 in Minimization, indicating that she was still in a transitional phase of development. After the five-week sojourn in England, her Developmental Score (DS) barely changed (98.81). Even her perception of her intercultural sensitivity remained constant (122.54 presojourn and 122.26 postsojourn; both were in the Acceptance/Adaptation, AA range). By contrast, just before traveling to England, Jade scored 118.50 in AA, an ethnorelative stage of development. After spending five weeks in the host culture, she gained 7.07 points, advancing to 125.57 in the same range. She perceived her intercultural sensitivity to be 134.69 just before the sojourn and 137.73 afterwards; both were in the high end of the AA range.

As in Nora and Mimi's cases, I wondered if Lana and Jade's oral and written narratives (weekly sojourn surveys, sojourn diary,[1] postsojourn interview) and my field notes would support their actual and perceived IDI scores. In particular, would Lana's narratives offer some clues as to why her intercultural sensitivity remained stalled in Minimization? Would Jade's storied experiences provide evidence that she had developed a higher level of intercultural competence than the other case participants?

Similar to the previous chapter, I track the sojourn and reentry experiences of each woman, beginning with Lana. When relevant, I interpose an etic (outsider's) perspective, drawing on my field notes, to further contextualize each woman's narratives.[2] I also draw comparisons and contrasts between their experiences to better understand the factors impacting on their developmental trajectories.

What follows are the unique stories of Lana and Jade.

Lana

Predeparture aims and concerns

Prior to departure, Lana set language and cultural learning objectives for her stay in England: "I want to improve my ability, confidence, and proficiency in interacting with people from different cultures in English. And I want to master the vocabulary and expressions commonly used in everyday situations" (interview). After witnessing "the benefits of intercultural relationships," she was "looking forward to making friends from other cultures" (intercultural reflections journal). By encountering cultural differences firsthand, she hoped to become more self-aware.

As the departure date approached, she refined her language learning objectives, setting the following targets: "improved conversational skills, better pronunciation, and enhanced spoken English" (language learning strategies survey). She aimed to "speak English fluently and learn more about British culture" (interview). Aspiring to become "more independent and mature," Lana was keen to experience the world outside Hong Kong: "I'm really excited about the trip abroad, new environment, new friends, new culture, new scenes. ... I believe this trip will be one of my most valuable memories in my life."

Similar to Nora, Lana conceded that she had many anxieties about what lay ahead: "I'm really worrying about a lot of things. For example, what will the host family be like, what kind of life will we have there, how much will I spend, what we will do each day, and what will happen" (interview). Just prior to departure she divulged more fears in the predeparture survey: "As this is the first time for me to leave my family for so long, I may suffer from homesickness. I hope that I could learn to tolerate the ambiguities and have a fruitful trip there." While supportive of her trip to England, her family, like Nora's, was anxious about her safety: "They worry about what might happen to me over there" (interview). To cope, Lana planned to e-mail her family "constantly" (survey).

The language policy for the sojourn

When Lana first learned about the English language policy she deemed it "a good idea." In her interview she explained: "When you go to a place in which only English is used, it'll be more natural to use the language so I think we'll be less reluctant to use it there. We won't want to stand out." Nonetheless, similar to Nora, she believed that their group might experience "a certain degree of difficulty" in trying to follow the policy: "Because we're brought up in Cantonese, there are many ideas and feelings that we don't know how to express in English. We haven't learnt English terms for daily life. When you want to ask a foreigner where something is, how can you ask if you don't know how to say what that 'something' is in English?" (interview). She believed that "switching to English" would be the most challenging aspect of the sojourn (survey).

The sojourn

First week – a bystander in a new culture

Lana was both exhausted and excited when she disembarked in London. This had been her first flight and she was looking forward to meeting her homestay family. When introduced to her host mother after the two-hour bus ride, the woman smiled broadly and Lana's fears began to dissipate. On the way to her homestay, Lana learned that Martha and John, a couple in their mid-fifties, had hosted many international students over the past 13 years.

In her diary, Lana described her reaction to what would be her home for the next five weeks: "Though my host family's house was much larger than my flat in Hong Kong, I had imagined it larger, perhaps influenced by TV programs and movies." Despite her disappointment, she loved "this cosy house," adding: "My room is rather spacious for me, though smaller than I've expected. Still, I love it. The colors are light and comfortable. I'm really happy that I could have such a room for my own for five weeks."

From the onset, Lana gave her hosts the impression that she was timid and in need of looking after. On their first morning together, when her host mother gave her a guided tour of the town, more of Lana's idealistic images were shattered. In spite of the presojourn preparation, she had expected to visit utopia: "Martha told me how hard it was to buy a new flat or house in England. I was kind of silly cause I imagined that I was going to visit a heaven-like world where earthly problems were minimized. I now realized there was no such place" (diary).

At the first meal with her host family, Lana appreciated the food provided but was already craving more familiar fare as she adjusted to eating with cutlery instead of chopsticks: "At dinner there were vegetables with meat, placed nicely on a large plate. It was interesting for me. I had never used knife and fork for dinner except in restaurants. Though the food was quite delicious, I was kind of missing noodles and rice" (diary). Lana also found it difficult to understand English humor and, like Mimi, felt like a bystander as her hosts laughed together: "The problem of my listening skills was once again proved. I was so frustrated that I couldn't get the jokes. Everyone was laughing so happily at something which I couldn't understand!" (diary).

While most of her classmates were spending free afternoons with their hosts or exploring the community, Lana was often in the computer room at the University downloading digital images or sending e-mails home. This limited the time she spent with her hosts. Even so, she was developing a very favorable opinion of her host mother: "Martha's really nice and said several times, 'Make yourself at home'. Though I've heard these kinds of phrases in Hong Kong, I felt that they were only spoken for courtesy. However, when Martha told me this in the morning, her eyes were so sincere. This was a touching experience for me."

Second week – mutual respect and appreciation

At the beginning of the second week, Lana joined her classmates and me for the first debriefing session with our English facilitator, a cultural studies specialist. All of the students were encouraged to share their experiences and ask questions about the host culture. During this 90-minute session, like Nora, Lana preferred to observe: "It was great fun to listen to the adventures and explorations of my classmates." Their comments prompted Lana to reflect on aspects of Hong Kong that she missed and treasured, including her L1:

> On one hand, being an "outsider" gives you a sense of loss. You feel you're losing your familiar neighborhood, community, companions, and even your own language. But on the other hand, it's a sense of gain because you gain many things from a new place. As an outsider, I find that it's easier to recognize the small details in life and to treasure more about the things we have taken for granted at home (survey).

After the first debriefing session, each student talked about possible topics for their ethnographic research projects. While most had a clear notion about what they wanted to investigate, Lana was still mulling over several ideas. Mid-week she settled on lace-making, her host mother's hobby, and began to spend more time with Martha when she did her crafts.

Despite some homesickness, Lana was feeling more relaxed in her homestay and felt well looked after: "My host family really treats me as one of their family members and provides everything for me. They are willing to talk with me actively" (survey). Martha displayed genuine interest in Lana and this drew the women closer together: "After dinner my host mum listens to what I've learnt that day. She kindly explains to me the different customs in England and shares her life experiences with me. Sometimes, I feel I'm talking with a very close friend, who I can share every feeling. Sometimes, she's like a mother teaching/reminding me of different details in life" (survey). While Lana found living in a homestay "really memorable," she was still not spending as much time with her hosts as her peers. A diary entry revealed that she planned to change her routine "to get to know more about them."

Noticeably more positive about her new environment than Nora, Lana paid more attention to "the locals' use of language and their manners" explaining that "[t]hey're always very polite, which makes you feel comfortable when talking to them" (survey). In her diary, she added:

> I'm so impressed with the use of language of English people. It seems that they could always be very polite. Even on the bus, instead of saying, "Don't smoke," "Thank you for not smoking" was written on the coach. Also, after every meal, John would say "Thank you, it was a nice meal" to Martha. They always showed their appreciations by saying "lovely". Sometimes their words were so cute as if they were talking to a child. After I took a shower in the evening and told Martha, she said with a fun voice, "A clean girl." I was so happy. Every night, instead of saying "goodnight" to each other, they would say "Night, night" to me.

Similar to Nora, Lana's hosts treated her as a young child and she, too, seemed satisfied with her positioning.

In her diary, Lana wrote a detailed entry about a group excursion to Warwick castle: "When we entered the main entrance, we were all alive. It was just so *gorgeous*, so *marvelous*, so *dazzling* [emphasis added]. This was my first time to visit a castle. ... We were so happy that we rolled down the grounds together. The other visitors were just stunned to see us." As she usually did not use such expressive language, it appeared to me that she was experimenting with the discourse of her hosts. Interestingly, except for a few expressions of politeness, I had not observed this degree of appropriation in Nora and Mimi's writing.

Although she'd only been in an English-speaking environment a short time, Lana was convinced that her English language proficiency was "improving" as she could "speak more fluently and more spontaneously." Lana noted, however, that there was still "a great room for improvement" as she lacked "vocabulary about daily issues." In her survey, she acknowledged another limitation that she aimed to overcome: "My host mother keeps on reminding me that I should speak louder with more confidence. ... I must learn to speak up to communicate better with them."

Similar to Nora, Lana reflected on her language choices and the tendency of her and some of her classmates to use "Chinglish" when conversing with each other.

> Apart from chatting with my family members in Hong Kong, I am quite getting used to speaking in English. The time when I was not speaking English was mainly because my friends wanted to speak in Cantonese, which was more efficient in some ways. Still, when we speak in English, I find that we are developing a kind of Chinglish, which I don't regard as a good phenomenon. We talk in English with a Chinese rhythm. Though it's fun sometimes, it's terrible to find that sometimes I can't switch to more normal English rhythm with my host family (survey).

Unhappy with this development, she worried that this speaking style would have a detrimental impact on her English language fluency. In her writing, she did not consider what may lie behind their style of speech. This nativized, colloquial version of English may have provided a cohesive "insider identity" (Kachru et al., 2006) and sense of security for those who were struggling to adjust to life in English.

As the sojourn unfolded, Lana continued to work on her ethnographic project. To gain a better understanding of "lace making," she observed her host mother in action and, in the process, drew closer to her: "Martha was really a fantastic woman in handcrafts. ... She was just incredible. I loved to watch her make lace. I wish I had time to learn all these skills from her as I really like handcrafts. The programmers really made a good choice for me to be with her. I love to be with her so much" (diary).

Lana also wrote about an incident in her homestay in which she came to the aide of her host: "Unfortunately, Martha burnt her thumb on the oven. Suddenly I thought of how my mother dealt with burns so I went upstairs to take a small pot of white flower oil and poured some oil on her thumb. Martha found it helpful and cooling. She thanked me a lot and even praised me as a lovely nurse." "Delighted" that Martha had appreciated this remedy, Lana shared some Chinese tea with her hosts after dinner: "They loved the tea and commented it's 'gorgeous'" (diary). Her hosts displayed respect and appreciation of Chinese products. Similar to one of my earlier investigations of student sojourners (Jackson, 2008), I found that this enhanced the host–sojourner relationship.

Third week – from dislocations to familiarity

When asked how her experience of "fitting in" to the host culture matched her presojourn expectations, Lana minimized cultural differences and focused on elements that she had in common with locals:

> The experience of fitting in is less complicated than I've expected. Before the trip, I thought that I was going to integrate into a new world where people would have lots of cultural differences from Hong Kong. For example, they might have special kind of entertainment, likes and dislikes which are extremely different from us. But when I stayed here for two weeks, I'm quite surprise to find there are quite a number of similarities in the living styles of British people and Hong Kong people (survey).

Despite this, Lana sometimes felt a bit unsettled in her new surroundings. She loved "the green environment and the nice people," but a sense of "strangeness" sometimes "overwhelmed" her:

> Generally, I've got a strong sense of peacefulness every morning, mixing with a sense of strangeness, and perhaps, stress and anxiety. It's really peaceful and graceful to see cosy houses and green grounds around you every day. Everywhere is full of newness and excitement. This is where the sense of strangeness comes from. Stress and anxiety appear when the sense of strangeness overwhelms me. Usually, all these negative feelings are outweighed by the beauty of the scenery, kindness of people, and peacefulness of the lifestyle (survey).

Although sometimes bothered by "negative feelings," Lana generally appreciated the world around her and found that keeping busy helped her to cope with homesickness. While still missing familiar Chinese food, like Mimi, she expressed gratitude for the meals that her host mother provided: "What I miss most is the food in Hong Kong. But still, I'm happy that my host mother always prepares traditional English meals for me even though it is quite complicated to do so. I know she has paid lots of effort to give me more varieties of dishes" (survey).

While some of her peers (e.g., Mimi) were thinking and even dreaming in English by this stage, Lana was still translating from Cantonese. Instead of focusing on her experiences in England, like Nora, she had maintained daily contact with Hong Kong and her mother tongue: "I learn news from my family through telephone and computer. I find it helpful as I feel that I'm not totally detached from my base" (survey). While this frequent contact eased her homesickness, it may have made it more difficult for her to become immersed in the host culture and language:

> I am able to speak fully in English but I can't help thinking in Cantonese and translating Cantonese from English sometimes. Perhaps one reason is that I still need to keep in contact with my family in Hong Kong, who know Cantonese only. Another reason is perhaps I lack the vocabulary to express my feelings and opinion. When using English to communicate with my host parents, I feel that I'm a child who needs patience to listen to as I'm still not getting used to the rhythms, slangs, and vocabulary of daily life. I'll try to improve this aspect (survey).

Similar to Nora, she felt like a "child" when communicating with her hosts, due, in part, to her perceived weakness in oral English.

Using a scale of 1 to 6 (1 = feeling like you don't fit in and 6 = feeling like you do fit in), Lana rated herself "around 4 or 5." In her survey, she wrote: "I fit in their lifestyle quickly but my listening and spoken skills really need improvements. Now, I can catch up with more British English, but I still cannot express myself fully in English. Most of the time, I lack the vocabulary to express myself." Her explanation centered on her use of the host language rather than cultural elements that might have been impacting on her adjustment and communication with host nationals.

While not as active as her peers, Lana believed that the experience of living in another culture was changing her. In her view, she was becoming more self-reliant and developing a more positive mindset: "I am soaked in a new environment and learn to be more independent and communicate with native English people. I've got plenty of time to reflect on my life. Instead of always focusing on the negative aspects, I try to learn to treasure/to appreciate the positive aspects. This is a valuable experience for me" (survey).

Although Lana had pined for Chinese food early in the sojourn, she had gradually become more open to unfamiliar fare: "In this trip,

I've tried lots of food which I would not eat in Hong Kong, such as, salmon, roasted beef, lamb, and even sausages. They smell a bit strange. Nonetheless, as Martha prepared them so well, I just enjoyed them" (diary). To express appreciation, Lana began to prepare tea for her hosts after meals: "I enjoyed making different kinds for them, Chinese tea, green tea, and fruit tea. We then had a nice time chatting together"(diary). Her social skills were developing along with her self-confidence and, significantly, her efforts were appreciated by her hosts.

By mid-sojourn, Lana was spending more time chatting with Martha as she gathered data for her project: "After lunch, in the summer house I had an informal conversation with Martha concerning the ethno-graphic research. She recently finished a piece of lace which she has worked for three years. She was eager to finish sewing the lace back to the tablecloth and to show the lace-group her product" (diary). Lana also accompanied Martha to a community center where she observed her lace-making group. This provided her with more opportunity to learn about this cultural activity: "Most of the participants were retired elderly ladies. Martha was the youngest. They were energetic when they made lace and chatted about daily issues" (diary). Although Lana pre-ferred to observe the women at work and did not converse with many of them, this site visit did increase her exposure to informal discourse in another cultural scene.

While happy to be with her hosts, she had begun to notice that they treated her differently from their own children and this made her feel somewhat distant from them: "My host parents are willing to listen to me and explain their daily life to me, but they don't treat me as their family member. They greet me differently. They hug and kiss their family members but with me they shake hands/smile. When I see the intense emotion between the family members, I feel like an outsider" (survey). Characterizing her positioning as "somewhere between a guest and a family member," Lana realized that her hosts saw her as "a little child" and spoke to her in a gentler way:

> Whenever I'm in my host family's house, I feel well received, no matter we are preparing/having meals, watching television, or doing gardening. I think my willingness to talk and to integrate into their family, as well as my readiness to accept new changes/strange envi-ronment helps. Everyone in the house chats with me in a friendly way but, sometimes, I feel I'm a small child in the host family. They use nicer tone to speak to me as if they're afraid to scare a little child (survey).

Even with her closest friends, Lana still allowed herself to be cast in a rather passive, dependent role, on the periphery of any decision making. Instead of expressing an opinion or suggesting activities, she just went along with whatever they decided. For example, in her diary, she wrote: "As my classmates had done all the bookings to Cambridge, I knew nearly nothing about the trip." She recognized her tendency to follow others without question but did not take steps to become more proactive.

Later that week Lana called her father in Hong Kong; he encouraged her to make the most of her stay, pointing out that it was "a precious chance." In her diary, Lana reflected on his advice: "I was awakened. Sometimes, I felt lost with myself, wondering why I'm here, spending money, and leading a life which I may never experience again. But he reminded me that it's because this may be the only chance, I should treasure the opportunity to experience the life here." Lana had not embraced the sojourn experience with as much enthusiasm as Mimi and Jade; at times, she likely appeared "lost" and bewildered to her host family and in need of protection.

Fourth week – the stranger as an outsider

At the beginning of the fourth week, Lana offered her impression of the environment and host nationals, making an effort to avoid stereotyping: "I dare not to generalize things in Warwickshire as I still haven't traveled all through it. ... English people are polite but sometimes it's difficult to judge whether they're really talking how they feel." Unfamiliar with frequent, explicit praise, Lana questioned the sincerity of people who expressed themselves in this way. While not fully comfortable with this style of communication, it is interesting that she again appropriated expressive discourse a few days later when describing her trip to Bath: "It was really *splendid* to visit the places appeared in the Jane Austen's movie in person. ... The views from the Royal Crescent were *incredible*. ... The channel in Bath was so *fabulous*" [emphasis added] (diary).

While some of her peers were making an effort to interact with people in the community, like Nora, Lana largely confined her communication to her host family: "In public areas, my conversation with local people is limited to 'Thank you', 'hello', and 'goodbye'" (survey). Lana was still conscious of her peripheral status and lacked confidence in her English language skills: "I'm comfortable with the local culture, at least most of it but I still feel like an outsider. My English is still not fluent enough to communicate thoroughly with my host family or local people. Most of the time I need to rephrase my meanings/sentences to make myself clear." In her survey, she assessed her progress:

> My listening skills have improved after exposure to English people and English media. At first, it was really frustrating that I couldn't understand the TV. For my oral English, I'm still trying hard to improve. I haven't picked up as many English slangs/vocabulary as I'd expected. There're still quite a lot of ideas I don't know how to express. I hope I can grasp the remaining chances to ask and learn.

After revisiting her goals for the sojourn, Lana aimed to accomplish the following in the remainder of her stay: "I really want to improve my oral English so I'll treasure the chance to talk more with local people and ask them more about specific vocabulary" (survey).

Building a relationship with people from another culture in an alien environment enhanced Lana's self-awareness. Realizing that she tended to hide behind others, she vowed to improve her interpersonal communication skills and become more participatory:

> I've realized that one of the reasons for my quiet character is that I really lack the experience of socializing with others. In Hong Kong, I often hide myself with my schoolmates. In these weeks, I've got plenty of time to chat with my host family; however, I'm poor in joining conversations with more than two people. Usually, I just don't know how to "interrupt". I'd like to learn to express myself more (survey).

In the agreement that the host families have with the University they are expected to provide their "guest" with breakfast and dinner on weekdays and a packed lunch for Saturday outings. On Sundays, all meals are provided if the students are at home. On weekdays, some students buy a sandwich from a supermarket or go to a cafeteria; others pack their own lunch. While Lana wished to become more independent, she wrote: "I think it's better for the family to prepare packed lunch for us rather than we prepare it ourselves." While she had written many favorable comments about her host family, I discovered that she still sensed a barrier between them. At the back of her mind, she was always aware that they had received money to provide lodging for her: "They share everything they have for meals and snacks. But we know each other under a contract. I feel uncomfortable that they don't provide the lunch during the week." Her views about her host family were rather contradictory. In the same survey she wrote: "Martha and John really treat me as one of their family members. They tolerate my naivety as if they have a younger daughter. I am so flattered" (diary). With her comments, the issues of agency and level of dependency resurfaced.

Fifth week – life abroad as discovery of Self and Other

During our stay in England, I observed that Lana had become more aware of her identity and cultural socialization. "Through this trip, I see more the specialties of myself as a Hong Konger as compared to English people. I could see more clearly why I am regarded as a Chinese or an Asian, rather than a Westerner." Similar to most of her peers, in an alien environment she also became more appreciative of her family and elements of Hong Kong culture, a phenomenon observed by other study abroad researchers (e.g., Allen et al., 2007; Isabelli-Garçia, 2006). In her survey, she wrote: "This trip was a good time for me to distance myself from a familiar place to a strange one. I'm more aware about small aspects of Chinese culture which I've taken for granted. I will treasure Hong Kong as a mixture of Chinese and western cultures. I love more about my family after not seeing them for a long time."

Overall, Lana believed that she'd adjusted relatively well to life in England. When she assessed her comfort level, I again observed her tendency to downplay cultural differences: "Generally, I feel quite comfortable with the local culture and people most of the time. Though there are some strange things in the local environment, I think it's rather easy for Hong Kong people to adapt to life here as the culture is similar to Hong Kong's" (survey).

In the sojourn survey that was administered a day before our departure, Lana again rated herself in terms of "fitting in" to the local culture using a scale of 1 to 6 (1 is feeling like you don't fit in and 6 is feeling like you do). She offered the following explanation for her choice of 4, focusing on linguistic elements:

> Though I can accept the lifestyle quite naturally, I can't always understand their use of language. Sometimes they speak rather fast and it's difficult for me to follow them. And I still can't follow the dialogues on television programs. For my host family, I think they find me quite fitting in. Basically I eat anything they provide for me and we share our everyday life happily, though I may get stuck on some English words sometimes (survey).

Lana believed that she'd become a more sensitive communicator during her stay abroad: "I am now using English politely to make people feel easier. In the past, I was less careful about other's feelings and sometimes too lazy to speak. Here, I've learned to say 'please' and 'no, thanks'" (survey). In her estimation, her family and friends would find her "more responsible and more polite after exposure to the polite English cultures." Following more reflection, she added: "Perhaps they may find me in need of companions, as I am never alone here except my sleeping time. I think I became more dependent in my daily life as my host family provides me most of the things." In her homestay, like Nora, she had been positioned as "a small child" rather than a young adult and this degree of dependency may have stymied her growth.

Lana revisited the personal goals she'd set for the sojourn and was pleased with her accomplishments: "I've improved quite a lot in my listening skills as I've been fully exposed to the English environment. I love English even more and enjoy using it in daily life. I've also developed a good relationship with my host family. At the same time, I've made friendships with my classmates" (survey). In her diary she cited gains in fluency, which she attributed to exposure to informal English in the host culture:

> When we talked with native speakers, English became our only channel of communication. We had no choice. It was really good for us to speak English with them. Not only can we practice our fluency, we could also learn more vocabulary, pronunciation, rhythm, expressions and slang from them. Though sometimes we might not catch what they meant, we might ask them directly or guess from the situation. In both ways, we could still learn a lot.

While Nora did not believe that she could learn English from her peers, Lana held a very different view: "I've found that through practicing English among ourselves, we might learn and discuss some English phrases from or with each other. For example, I've learnt 'horrendous' from Ivan. We've learnt a lot from each other" (diary).

Lana maintained that she and her hosts had both engaged in a learning process: "It's really amazing that we could learn from each other when we are actually from different parts of the earth" (survey). In the last sojourn survey, she characterized their relationship as "somewhere between friends and family members":

> As a friend, you can talk about anything with them happily, without considering how they expect you to be. They just want to know more

about you and your culture. It is easy to communicate with them. They are willing to answer every question I asked, even if it relates to their private life. But there's something else. You stay with them, eat with them, share their lifestyles but ultimately, they won't hug me/kiss me as they do to their family members.

Lana was also convinced that her research project had enhanced her sojourn: "I joined the lace-meeting group at a community center. I met four lovely old ladies and listened to their stories happily. I also interviewed my host mother about her lace-making and membership in the lace-meeting group and got to know more about her. This research created a great topic for both of us" (survey). Her project afforded her more exposure to the community and helped her to learn more about "the tradition of lace-making and craftwork in England" (survey).

On the eve of departure, similar to her peers, Lana experienced a range of conflicting emotions: "I miss my Hong Kong family and friends and really want to fly back home but I really love the environment here. I know I may never come back again or see my host parents once I leave here. I'll miss them a lot so it's contradictory" (survey). She was "happy to stay in both environments" and had "treasured every day" in England.

This is really a short but long journey. Through the short five-week, I undergo a long internal reflection through the journals. I become more aware of my thoughts, my feelings as well as that of the others. Moreover, through this trip, I've learnt the English way of appreciating life, to make fun of the unhappy things, laugh at them, and forgot them. I think this journey will be an important turning point in my life. As through this peaceful rest, I reflect more about my being a part of the world. I realize what's important in my life. Though I still don't know what I'll do in the future, I learn to treasure everything I have. Overall, this is a valuable experience for me (survey).

Lana believed that she had benefited from the "internal reflection" that had been promoted throughout her stay (e.g., through diary-writing, surveys, informal discussions, debriefing sessions).

Postsojourn

Back in Hong Kong, Lana shared her views about the sojourn in an hour-long interview. Of the four case participants, she was the only one who opted to express her views in English.

While Nora emphasized the virtues of Hong Kong on reentry, Lana adopted a more balanced perspective, expressing appreciation for both the home environment and host culture: "There are advantages in each, in Hong Kong and Britain." When asked if she'd been surprised by anything she'd seen or experienced in England, she cited only a few visual aspects: "I couldn't find major differences between Hong Kong and England ... only some minor ones. For example, they have more cars than I'd expected. The buses are older and without air-conditioning. I'm also surprised by the way they love animals. My host family even talked to their pets." In the Minimalist phase of development according to the IDI, Lana exhibited awareness of only superficial cultural differences and perceived the world to be "smaller" and "more united" than what she'd expected prior to the sojourn. When reflecting on her identity, she remarked that the people she'd met in England "think similar to us." In her interview, she explained:

RA:　How would you describe yourself now in terms of your identity?

Lana:　I still prefer to say Hong Konger rather than Chinese. I met quite a number of people asking me about Hong Kong and China. They just confused the place but I would say that I belong to Hong Kong more than China.

RA:　Has your view of yourself and your position in the world changed?

Lana:　My ideas about my identity have not changed much but after this trip I feel the world is smaller and more united than I expected. The English think similar to us and I was quite surprised by that.

Lana reflected further on her English language skills and observed that she'd become a more confident speaker, especially in social situations: "I now have more vocabulary and better oral skills. ... I had more chances to speak English in England and my listening skills improved. I became more aware of differences in accents and pronunciation. Sometimes I even think more in English than in Cantonese" (interview). While more comfortable expressing herself in English, she remained sensitive to the implicit social sanctions governing appropriate language usage (Coulmas, 2005; Myers-Scotton, 2006). Consequently, she still felt awkward speaking English with other Chinese when not required: "Cantonese is still our major language, and if we use English it's just strange. I still find it strange." When asked if she would use more English in Hong Kong, she responded: "I imagine that I will seldom use English in my daily life except in university or for my job. Language is a tool for communication, but not vice versa. Though I love English even more after this trip, as my environment/surroundings in Hong Kong haven't changed much, I think I will not have a big change in this aspect."

Although happy to be home again, she sometimes longed for her life in England: "I miss the environment there, especially the trees, and my host family had a big house that I don't have in Hong Kong. I also miss the way my host family talked with me about everything. I miss a lot of things." Similar to most of her peers, living with an English family was the most important element of her stay abroad: "I learned more about the way they live and I could also talk more in English in this environment." Even so, she perceived some distance between her and her hosts: "Although my host family tried to treat me like a family member, I still felt like a foreigner, a stranger, because they hugged and kissed each other when they said goodbye but not me."

Back in the security of her familiar surroundings, Lana reflected further on her reliance on others during her stay abroad:

> At first I was more dependent in the UK because I didn't understand everything there. ... I just couldn't handle it. For example, I didn't even know how to call a taxi. My host family prepared all of the meals for me and gave me directions so I wouldn't get lost. Even so, I often got lost and it was really frustrating. I would like to have been treated more independently but maybe I wasn't ready then. ... Looking back, I did make some decisions about my free time. I think the trip gave me the sense that I could be more independent.

More assured of her English language skills and ability to cope in new situations, Lana felt excited about the possibility of further intercultural explorations and travel:

> The sojourn increased my confidence in speaking English and encouraged me to be more independent. Now, I really want to travel abroad to see more of the world and explore different environments. I really hope to improve my English to communicate with people in foreign countries. I think the benefit of understanding different cultures is great because through this you can learn more about yourself.

After taking stock of her growth and limitations, she set new aims for additional personal expansion that would build on her sojourn learning.

In a positive frame of mind, she expressed enthusiasm for the enhancement of her English language and intercultural communication skills.

Lana offered the following advice to the next group of SES students: "They could prepare more Chinese stuff, like photos and tea, to introduce their hosts to Hong Kong culture. They should be active and treasure the chance to communicate with them, to be with them. ... They should try to prepare for change and make an effort to talk more with locals." Although she'd found it challenging to be a "language activist" or "languager" (Phipps, 2006), significantly, she recognized the benefits of becoming fully engaged in the host environment.

Now, we turn to an examination of Jade's sojourn and reentry experiences.

Jade

Predeparture aims and concerns

In her presojourn interview, Jade discussed her personal aims for the sojourn: "I want to experience English in a variety of social contexts. I'd like to see how local people interact in the language both inside and outside the home." She also wished to develop better intonation and improve her conversation skills and overall fluency in the language. Above all, she was looking forward to experiencing daily life in Britain: "I think the lifestyle is very different from that in Hong Kong and I really want to experience it" (interview). Just prior to departure, in a survey she added: "I'm excited because England is my dream place. Having studied English literature for years, I'll finally get a chance to live there for five weeks. I can't wait to explore the culture of England and enjoy my stay there. I hope to enhance my cultural awareness and international exposure."

Despite previous travels, Jade had some doubts about her readiness for the sojourn as she had not been to England before and had never lived with a host family. Nonetheless she was convinced that her optimistic mindset would help her overcome difficulties: "It's easier for me to adapt to new things since I've become more open to them. I think the differences in England will be alright for me. It depends on our attitude if we see differences as negative or positive" (interview). On the eve of departure, she was looking forward to what lay ahead: "Our preparation and my previous experiences will definitely be helpful in case I experience cultural shock. I will not be scared. I'm sure I'll find it easier to adapt to the new culture and be more patient with myself and others this time" (journal).

The language policy for the sojourn

Jade was supportive of the language policy for the sojourn: "It's a good idea because it'll help us to get involved in the place. Also, if we don't speak English in England, it'll be a bit odd. And I expect it will improve my fluency" (interview). Like Mimi, she believed the environment would free them from the social sanctions that restrict their use of the language in Hong Kong: "Since people there all speak English we won't feel strange to speak it. Perhaps, it'll be strange for us to speak Cantonese" (predeparture survey). If a classmate spoke to her in Cantonese she guessed that she would respond in English although she was a bit uncertain as she usually responded "subconsciously" in the language used by her interlocutor.

The sojourn

First week – arrival excitement and fatigue

On arrival at the host institution Jade was nervous about meeting her host family for the first time. When introduced to Tessa, a single mother with two very active children (Kati, aged 7, and Ricky, aged 3), Jade was relieved and delighted:

> When we got off the coach and entered the hall with our heavy luggage our hosts were already there waiting for us. I felt a bit nervous though I looked calm and confident. Who will be my host? Will I be able to get along with my host family well? ... One by one our names were called out and we were matched up with our host families. When my name was called, Mrs. Martin (Tessa), a woman with two kids, waved at me. Oh, I was put into a family with kids! Cool!! In fact, after I put my bags down, I had already noticed the kids, especially the little boy who was holding a toy in his hand and talking loudly. His mother kept asking him to be quiet. I thought it would be great fun to live with the boy (diary).

The day after her arrival, Tessa invited Jade to a community picnic. Although weary with jetlag, she decided to join in, determined to make the most of her stay and forge a bond with her host family. In her diary, Jade wrote: "People spent the afternoon, sitting on the grass, eating, and chatting. I was introduced to Tessa's friends and had a wonderful time. Tessa brought some sandwiches, salad, and wine. Everyone was very hospitable. They offered me a lot of food and asked me to eat more." Her sojourn appeared to be off to a great start.

Later that same evening, however, Jade was suddenly stricken with pangs of homesickness. In her diary she described the unsettling emotions that engulfed her:

> I thought I could adapt to the life here very soon. But when I was alone in my bed, I was in tears. It's difficult to express what I felt at that time. It was just a bit of everything – excited, uncertain, and HOMESICK! I never thought I'd feel homesick. Never!! Since I've traveled a lot, I thought I was independent, tough, and brave enough. Plus, we had had intercultural preparation this time. I could not believe that I had a terrible homesick. I missed my family so much. Perhaps, it was the first time I had homestay. In my previous traveling experiences, I used to live in a hostel with my friends or at least somebody that I knew. I felt so lonely and helpless. I knew my host mom would be anxious if she saw me crying. I retreated to my room. I couldn't understand why I felt so bad. People here were nice to me. Everything was fine. I was angry with myself. Perhaps, I pushed myself too hard to adapt to my new life within a short period of time. Anyway, tears streamed down my cheeks. I hit the rock bottom. It was kind of like an emotional and mental TORNADO. It got noisy when life seemed slow down a bit. In the park, I was fine. But when I was in my room, I felt lost. I wanted to call back to Hong Kong desperately but I did not want to wake my family up. I didn't want them to worry about me. I told myself, "It's just the beginning. I'm sure you'll feel better as time goes." However, it did not sound convincing. Five weeks was too long for me at that moment. I knew I needed to calm down.

To cope, Jade adopted the following strategy; "I took out my MP3 player and listened to my favourite Beethoven symphony LOUD – Loud enough to compete with the thoughts, emotions, and noises that were swirling inside. At last, I fell asleep" (diary). It worked. "After a good sleep, I was like another person. I begin to adjust myself to the living habit. I play with the kids and enjoy meals with my host family. I think it's the preparation that we have in Hong Kong that helped me cope." She also phoned her parents in Hong Kong but did not mention her bout of homesickness.

On the first day of class, Jade walked to the bus stop with two of her classmates. On the way they chatted about their homestays:

> It was pleasant to see everybody again! We all had our own stories to share. I was asked if I got along well with the kids since they were

very active and noisy. It was funny that my friends worried about me. Somebody even suggested that I should talk to Tessa about them. But I appreciate my hosts for what they are. I'm not a tourist living in a hotel who complains about the service. My host family sees me as a member of the family (diary).

While some of her friends often criticized their hosts and "their service," Jade exhibited a more positive attitude. She embraced the opportunity to be a member of her new family and was more realistic about what living in a household with two very young, active children entailed.

Jade's diary also provided evidence that she already possessed a higher level of sociopragmatic/language awareness than most of her peers at this early stage. She was attuned to the world around her and open to experimentation with local norms of politeness:

I observed some cultural practices in the Indian Restaurant. ... It was interesting to see there were quite a lot of interactions between the waiters and customers. The waiters came to ask "How's the meal?" or "Is everything all right" several times when we were eating. Each time Tessa would give a satisfying look and said something good about either the food quality or the service. When she paid the bill, she said to the waiter, "It's lovely. Thank you." At first, I found a bit odd to express satisfaction at intervals while eating. I tried to observe and learn from Tessa. Each time I looked up and smiled. I also expressed thanks to the waiter when I left. At the end of the meal, we even got a little surprise from the restaurant – roses and chocolate! It was really a wonderful experience. The food was great. The service was nice. ... Looking back, the dining experience would not have been that perfect without those words of thanks and compliments. I was brightened up by the dinner. I gained much insight into the importance of expressing appreciation (diary).

Jade considered it a priority to cultivate a close relationship with her host and was thrilled when the woman disclosed her personal experiences, thoughts, and feelings: "Tessa told me a lot about herself and we chatted about everything – family, culture differences, fashion, relationships, and future. She was very friendly and it was easy to talk with her. She would give you valuable advice but also knew where to stop and let you think for yourself" (diary). Her host's warm reception and friendship played "a significant role" in helping Jade adjust: "With Tessa's help,

I become more open-minded and more willing to try new things after I had got the feeling of home and felt more secure" (diary).

Jade noticed early on that the noise level in her new environment was considerably less than what she was used to in Hong Kong. She adjusted her communication style accordingly but some of her peers did not; this upset and embarrassed her: "When Hidy and I were on the upper deck of the bus, we heard our classmates chatting and laughing loudly downstairs. They even gossiped about their hosts. We felt awkward. We both found that some of the classmates were very noisy and attention-seeking, especially when in a small group." Later that same week, Jade analyzed the reasons behind the differences she'd observed, trying to see the situation from multiple vantage points:

> I think the noise was somehow related to cultural differences in the acceptance of silence. Chinese are not very comfortable with silence. In Chinese culture, we believe that it's good to make some sounds. The louder the sound you made, the happier you feel. For example, groups of friends like to talk and laugh loudly in public to show their strong bond of friendship and sense of belonging to the group. However, the English value moderate behavior. I seldom saw local people talking loudly or behave boisterously in public. For example, my host Mom did not allow Ricky to talk loudly in public. She always asked him to calm down when he became excited and jumped on the street. Even when she heard Ricky shouting in the garden, she would say, "Ricky, you will have to go to bed if you keep on shouting!" It is considered as a personal courtesy to lower your voice in public.

Some of Jade's peers were still oblivious to markers of politeness in their new environment and uncomfortable or annoyed by the frequent use of verbal expressions of politeness, finding them insincere or "hypo-critical." By contrast, Jade demonstrated a higher level of intercultural sensitivity and sociopragmatic awareness: "I discovered that there are two important words which should be always on our lips in Britain. One is 'sorry' and another is 'Thank you' or 'Please'". The words could pave a path for avoiding misunderstandings and building better relationship with others" (diary).

Similar to Lana, Jade was quite unhappy with the way some of her peers were talking English with each other on outings: "We heard them speaking Chinglish in a playful way. It was true that they didn't have to speak proper English. They had the right to speak whatever they liked but it was unnecessary to make fun of ENGLISH in ENGLAND. How would the local people feel about their language being humiliated?" (diary). While more culturally sensitive than the other case participants, Jade did not recognize that her peers who were experiencing a more difficult adjustment may have drawn some comfort and a sense of camaraderie (e.g., affiliation with a Hong Konger identity) from speaking English "in a Cantonese way" in an alien environment.

During the presojourn phase, similar to Mimi, Jade had been somewhat anxious about losing her mother tongue, especially her writing skills. This fear of L1 attrition resurfaced on a trip to Stratford:

> I have no contact with Chinese at all. I feel that I'm living in English now. When we visited Shakespeare's birthplace, there were some leaflets printed in different languages. I subconsciously looked for an English version. However, the English one was in short supply. Therefore, I had to resort to a Chinese version. I had a strange feeling when reading the Chinese characters. They were hard to read and difficult to understand. I had to reread each sentence a few times in order to grasp the meaning. Eventually, I ran out of patience and gave up. At that time, my heart felt a bit uneasy. It seemed that my Chinese was gone. Is it unavoidable that you have to forsake one language in order to embrace another? I am confused (diary).

This was only her first week in an English-speaking environment and already she was 'uneasy' and worrying about losing her L1. It was conceivable that her "subtractive" perception of bilingualsm (Lambert, 1975) would limit her use of the host language.

While Nora had been reluctant to set foot in a pub in the first week, Jade accepted an invitation to have lunch in one with her host and the woman's partner. Jade soon became engrossed in the conversation, while keenly observing what was happening around her:

> It was the first time I went to a pub in England. ... It opened my eyes to the pub culture. We first had a round of drinks while the children were playing in the indoor playground. Tessa and I sat around the table and chatted while her boyfriend went to order the food. (Like what I learnt from books, pubs do not offer table service!!) A pub is really a place for people to chat and relax. I began to feel at ease and involved in the discussion. We shared a lot! (diary).

After this successful outing, Jade became more relaxed and her attitude toward English shifted yet again, providing compelling evidence of the dynamic, emotional, contextual nature of language learning (Dörnyei, 2009; Ushioda, 2009): "I'm happy that everything is on track now. I feel comfortable with my homestay. I get along well with my host family. Suddenly, I found that my English improved a lot, especially when I was talking with Tessa. My English self appeared. I began to speak naturally in English. It's a good sign" (diary). Fears about losing her "Chinese self" subsided as she established personal connections across cultures. At this juncture, she appeared more receptive to an "additive" form of bilingualism (Lambert, 1975).

Second week – encountering difference

In the second week, Jade discovered that she and her host differed in their understandings of health and wellness. In her diary, she wrote: "I was very sick today with a dry throat and my voice was rough. ... I asked Tessa where I could get some medicine and her answer surprised me. She asked if I REALLY need to take medicine and suggested me to get some cough sweets in the pharmacy. And today she bought me some throat lozenges." This was not what Jade had expected. In Hong Kong students routinely go to a clinic to get medication for colds. Sharing experiences with her friends led to more discoveries of cultural differences:

> Some classmates said that their host mums still gave them deep fried food and cold food when they got a sore throat. Some said that their hosts did not have a balance diet. It seemed that people here did not care about health. But now I understand that it is the difference in expectations about the right and wrong ways to treat illness and help people. For Chinese, we have a concept of yin and yang. We think that deep fried food is "hot ai". We should not eat fried food (hot) when we have a bad throat (which is considered as hot symptom). Similarly, we should not eat cold food (yin/cold) when we caught a cold (yin/cold). It made sense if we reasoned in Chinese holistic approach. The British also have their own way of thinking. For them, the best treatment for cold and flu is to rest and take plenty of fluids. It has little to do with what kind of food you eat. And in fact, there is no cure available so far. Since antibiotics do not help, it is not necessary to see a doctor.

Instead of rejecting new ideas/remedies out of hand, Jade took the time to reflect on beliefs that govern unfamiliar behaviors and habits. Employing an ethnorelative mindset (M. J. Bennett, 1993), she employed the skills of interpreting and relating (*savoir comprendre*) and critical cultural awareness (*savoir s'engager*) (Byram et al., 2002). She displayed "the ability to decentre from one's own culture and its practices and products and to gain insight into another" (Byram, 2006: 117).

Jade reaped numerous benefits by spending "quality time" with her hosts. As she became more familiar with them and their routine she relaxed and felt more like part of the family. By accepting invitations and taking the initiative to interact with her hosts, she gained more access to their world (e.g., linguistic and cultural practices). Increased intercultural contact afforded her the opportunity to pick-up more local expressions and enhance her conversation skills, one of the goals she'd set prior to the sojourn.

In a diary entry that was written at the end of the week, I was intrigued by her description of "the Winter's Tale," the Shakespearean play that she saw at the Globe Theatre in London. Her lengthy commentary was peppered with uncharacteristically effusive language: "a *remarkable* experience," "a *brilliant* view," "*fantastic* acting," "*advantageous* seats," and "*fabulous* production" [emphasis added]. Similar to Lana, she appeared to be experimenting with the discourse of locals.

Third week – further discoveries of Self and Other

Whereas Nora complained that she did not have enough opportunity to use English in the host community, Jade initiated conversations with people outside her homestay:

> Greetings help to start a friendly conversation. After exchanging greetings, people find it easy to talk with you. I enjoyed engaging in small talk with the people in the bus stop, while waiting for the bus. Sometimes, I had a casual chat with the cashier in the grocery store if nobody was queuing. These small contacts with the locals made me feel like I was fitting in here. It was something that I seldom do in Hong Kong. What a breakthrough! I'm proud that I could create opportunity to interact more with the locals (diary).

Her comments underscore the importance of agency in determining how sojourns unfold. In Phipps' (2006) terms, Jade engaged in "languaging," that is, she "stepped outside" of familiar ways of speaking and experimented with new ways of interacting.

At the beginning of the third week, Jade rated her adjustment to the local culture. Using a scale of 1 to 6 (1 is feeling like you don't fit in and 6 is feeling like you do fit in), she gave herself a "4" for the following reason: "I still have some uncertainty about the way locals behave.

I'll try to sort it out in the coming weeks." She believed that her hosts would rate her higher: "They always say I'm far more independent and open than the Japanese but I think language may be a problem for them." Compared with the other case participants, Jade was more observant of differences between Hong Kong and England and gaps in her knowledge of the host culture.

As she gained more exposure to the new environment and analyzed her intercultural experience, Jade displayed heightened awareness of Self and Other or what Byram et al. (2002) refer to as *savoirs*: "I learn more about myself. When I see people behave differently, I'm also more aware of my own behavior. People never say I did things in a wrong way. They just either look at me strangely or say nothing. I can only learn the correct way by observation" (survey). Similar to most of her peers, Jade was also sensitive to her minority status: "When I go out with my host family, like for a dinner in a restaurant, I feel out of place as people seem to see me differently. It's probably because of my Chinese appearance."

Noticing that some of her friends were cast in a dependent, child-like-role in their homestay, Jade appreciated the more adult relationship that she was developing with Tessa: "I'm glad I have a young and trendy host mum who can actually talk about romance, relationships, and fashion with me. Some of my classmates' host parents treat them like their grandchildren. Their overly caring hosts are very protective" (survey). Her successful homestay placement played an influential role in her sojourn learning.

Jade continued to display a positive attitude both in and outside her homestay and this helped her to cope with her new life and routines: "It's important to try to make a fresh start to do something differently. The first time you do it, you may feel odd but it gets more natural if you do it the second and third times" (diary). While Nora and Lana relied on their hosts in service encounters, Jade was more adventurous in her explorations of the world around her. By gaining more exposure to the host language and culture, she became more self-confident and comfortable using English: "Concerning my own English learning process, it goes quite well. I think my listening skills and spoken English have improved. I feel natural and easy to hear and speak the language." She believed that she had "internalized" the language and "subconsciously begun to function in English." In her survey, she wrote: "I count in English, think in English. I even found it strange when the students from the other Hong Kong group speak Cantonese to me."

Midway through the sojourn, Jade realized that offers of tea in the host culture were linked to local norms of politeness (e.g., hospitality) and an invitation to chat. In the beginning of her stay, similar to Mimi, she had found this practice irksome and had not grasped what lay behind the gesture:

> Most of us noted the drinking habit of the English. Tea is definitely an essential part of their life. It has been a hot topic and sometimes, an inside joke among us. Some of us get really annoyed as our host moms keep offering us tea five times a day. After staying here for several weeks, I found that the English love tea not simply because it's a wonderful drink. It meant much more than that. I decided to figure it out from my observation. ... It's interesting that the English do not expect you to accept every offer. So what is the meaning behind a tea offer? I have made some observations and come up with some ideas. Tessa likes to offer me tea. Most of the time, she offers me tea when she sees me sitting around. I discovered that question like 'Do you want a cup of tea?' 'You want a cuppa?' are in fact ways to show care. It's like another way of saying, 'Are you all right?' Sometimes, an offer of tea can also be used to start up a conversation. For example, Tessa would ask if I want a cuppa once I enter home. Then she would go on, 'how was today?' In addition, Tessa watches television at night. I usually go downstairs and join her after I shower. Each time when she saw me coming into the living room, she would offer me tea. But it actually implies, 'Hey, come and have a sit.'

Recognizing the nature and benefits of informal language learning, Jade took more advantage of linguistic affordances; her understanding and acceptance of "new relational ways of interacting" (Phipps, 2006) grew accordingly.

Fourth week – feeling at home

While some of her peers avoided contact with locals outside their home-stay, I noticed that Jade continued to avail herself of more opportunities to use the host language in a variety of settings: "I now find I can start up a conversation with strangers easily. Each morning I greet people walking on the street. We talk when waiting at the same bus stop. I can even chat with the cashier in the supermarket" (survey). "Very comfort-able with the regular lifestyle and established routines," Jade began to feel like "a member of the community" (diary). In contrast with Nora, her comfort zone extended beyond her homestay.

For her ethnographic project, Jade investigated a youth club organized by her host; this facilitated access to local people in the community close to her own age. "The young people were between 14 and 21. I talked with them and they were indeed very nice. Surprisingly, they don't see me as a foreigner. They just treat me as their friend" (survey). The more she interacted with them the more she felt at home.

Fifth week – appropriating other voices and fitting in

In the final week of the sojourn, Jade was "very comfortable with the local culture": "I'm used to the food, the weather, and the pace of life. I don't feel like a tourist. Instead, I'm moving nearer and nearer to be an insider" (survey). This time Jade gave herself "6" in terms of "fitting in" to the local culture, using a scale of 1 to 6 (1 is feeling like you don't fit in and 6 is feeling like you do), commenting: "I think people from the host culture would rate me 5 because of my appearance. Since I look different, they always try to provide extra help to me as if I'm very new to the local culture."

Similar to her peers, Jade reflected on ways she'd changed during the sojourn: "I begin to see things from the insider's point of view. Instead of finding things or people's behavior strange, I can step in their shoes and look at myself and my behavior which can also be strange to them" (survey). This ethnorelative orientation (M. J. Bennett, 1993, 2004) helped enhance her intercultural communication skills: "I have more self-awareness and am more aware of cultural differences. I think I've become more open-minded to these differences. Besides, I become more observant. I'm aware of my classmates' behavior. I try to learn from their mistakes."

In the last week, I observed that Jade continued to make progress in terms of her sociopragmatic development. She paid much closer attention to the discourse around her than many of her peers and, consequently, was picking up colloquial expressions and deepening her understanding of the local culture:

> The advantage of lodging with a British host family is that I could effortlessly acquire the "real" English. These are the British expressions that I learnt by living the language: "awfully nice/bad", "absolutely fabulous/gorgeous/brilliant", and "bitterly cold". It was easy to get the meaning from the surface of the words. But I could hardly figure out why "awful" went with "nice". Our cultural studies teacher said "awfully" had the same meaning as "very". In the past, "awful" was used to describe something really bad and so unpleasant that

shocked you. Therefore, "awfully" was used to describe something that was extreme and shocking. The British would say something was "awfully nice" when something was extremely good. How interesting to see the progressive change of a word! (diary).

Jade wrote several lengthy diary entries about the meanings of new vocabulary she'd learned. She was the only one of the group to do so. While some listed words that were new to them, Jade explored the sociopragmatic meaning of expressions and paid attention to the context of their usage, as this excerpt illustrates:

> I asked the cultural studies teacher about the pragmatic meanings of some simple words. After living here for almost five weeks, I found that it might not affect our intercultural communication competence if our English was not fluent or we did not acquire enough vocabulary to express ourselves but we had to be very careful with the language use. The very difficulty that I encountered was the pragmatic meaning of words. It directly affected how the linguistic meaning of a discourse was interpreted and it's really a cultural matter. ... I now realize that there is so much to learn about a word besides its linguistic meaning. We had to be careful with the situational context.

Jade appreciated her linguistic achievements. Unlike many of her fellow sojourners, she had focused on social English and the acquisition of colloquial discourse. In her survey, she wrote: "My English language skills have improved, especially for listening. I'm more familiar with the British accent and the pragmatic use of the language. I also learn more British expressions, idioms and slang." She had become "more comfortable using the language in social situations" and "more confident in communicating with native speakers." While disappointed that some of her classmates did not follow the language policy, Jade remained supportive of it, as she explained in her survey: "It's a good idea to have the 'English only' policy because it makes me feel more like part of the community."

She was pleased that she'd chosen to research a youth group that Tessa organized as it brought her closer to her host and provided access to locals outside her homestay. In her survey, she wrote: "I'm happy with the ethnographic data that I collected. My host mum was very helpful. My research enabled me to get into contact with a very different age group of people. It not only helped me to interact across cultures, but also enabled me to see a sub-culture in this environment." Through the process of observing and interviewing her informants, Jade believed that she'd evolved into a more sensitive communicator: "I tried not to be judgmental when I started up conversations with the young people and they became more willing to talk to me" (survey). This mode of experiential learning had served her well.

When reflecting on her personal goals for the sojourn, Jade cited the following gains in her survey: "I've achieved to be open-minded to the local culture and can explore and try new things as much as I can. I also learn to express my appreciation for what others have done for me. For example, after dinner, I thank my host mum or say, 'It's lovely!'" Jade also sensed a broadening of her identity: "I think that my family and friends will find that I've become more 'international'and sophisticated. I feel like a citizen of the world!" (survey). She had experienced personal expansion on many levels. As Lam (2006), Noels (2009), S. Ryan (2006, 2009) and other applied linguists have observed, with increased inter-cultural contact young people may develop "multisite, multilayered cosmopolitan identities" that strengthen their attachment to "a global community."

Postsojourn

Back in Hong Kong, Jade discussed the sojourn in an interview that lasted more than an hour. Similar to Nora, she used Cantonese throughout. While happy to be back home, she was surprised that she'd experienced some reentry culture shock since she had more travel experience than her friends:

> Perhaps I'd been away for too long because when I came back, I found it difficult to adjust to local life and missed England quite a bit. I felt strange during my first two days back in Hong Kong. I don't know where the strange feelings came from. ... I felt the rice was quite heavy and I preferred Western food. ... I've also observed some lifestyle and living habits in Hong Kong that are different from that in England. I just didn't notice this before the sojourn. Anyway, I've gradually adjusted to my life here. I feel I've become more independent. While I was in England and during the post-trip, my ability to adjust was quite strong.

In her interview, Jade compared the sojourn in England with her stay in France the previous summer. This offered insight into her emerging intercultural communicative competence and the impact of the SES presojourn preparation and debriefings (elements that were absent in her previous sojourn experience):

> What made the sojourn so different from the other study tour was that we were prepared. This was very important. It enabled me to have realistic expectations and be more open-minded to cultural differences. The cultural studies sessions in England were also useful. I would have not gained so much from the visits if there had not been workshops introducing the places and its cultural values. I realized the significance of the workshops when I went on the "stay behind" trip. I visited many tourist attractions but found that I didn't learn as much as I did in England for several reasons. In the "stay behind" trip, I felt confused as I had nobody to ask when I encountered difficulty in understanding the cultural pattern. It helps a lot in cultural learning if you have someone to ask. In the sojourn, the cultural studies instructor would tell us many things about British culture. In the Q & A session we could satisfy our curiosity about something that we didn't understand. It enriched my understanding about the real life in Britain. I also realized how little I knew about my own culture. I've became more interested in Chinese culture and this has surprised my parents (diary, postsojourn).

Similar to Lana, Jade realized that she'd benefited from the reflective process that was promoted throughout the program: "I really gained a lot from the sojourn, much more than I'd ever expected. I'm glad I kept a journal each day. It deepens my impression on the whole cultural experience" (diary). Her comments draw attention to the importance of imbedding elements into programs that stimulate deep reflection on language and cultural learning (e.g., regular debriefings, surveys).

Jade was convinced that she'd evolved in many ways after spending five weeks in England: "My attitude has changed. I've become more active and curious about the world around me. As for my intercultural communication skills, I observe more before taking action, instead of just seeing things from my own perspective. And if I have any confusion, I ask for clarification" (interview). Before the sojourn Jade had started on the path toward ethnorelativism (M. J. Bennett, 1993) and her actions and comments provided further evidence that she was continuing to develop an intercultural mindset. The trip to England had been very eye-opening for her: "I hadn't expected to have such a great deal of personal growth during the sojourn. It's really a journey of self-discovery. The homestay experience provided me a chance to get to know myself. My communication skills were improved and I gained insight into the importance of appreciating other's effort."

Jade attributed much of her personal expansion to her host who encouraged her to be self-reliant and explore the world around her: "Tessa did not treat me like a child. Some host moms did everything for my classmates but I did many things myself, including preparing the breakfast. I think it was good because it made me feel at home and I became more self-reliant. Also, I had more freedom" (interview). While some of her peers were coddled in their homestay, Jade willingly assumed more of the roles and responsibilities that would be expected of a 21-year-old in England. Consequently, she became "more self-confident and independent, especially in problem solving." In a postsojourn diary entry, she explained: "I did not turn to others once I encountered problems. Instead, I tried to sort it out myself first. I also became more tolerant and open-minded to differences. It helped a lot in my 'stay behind' trip as I found that I could easily adapt to different environment and changes."

After five weeks in the host culture, Jade also believed that she had become more accepting of cultural differences. In her interview, she explained:

> I've developed a higher degree of tolerance. I'm more open-minded and less judgmental. Though you expect cultural differences when you travel abroad, actually experiencing them in the country is different. You need to adjust to many different situations. You need to step back, think clearly, observe what and how others do things, and follow their steps. This experience was very helpful for my post-trip because I went to many different places with various cultures within a short period of time. We had to adjust to different life styles in different places very quickly.

Jade was one of the most perceptive, observant students in this cohort. She displayed critical cultural awareness (*savoir s'engager*) (Byram et al., 2002), and this spurred her growth: "My self-awareness has been enhanced. When you encounter a new culture, you reflect on your own behavior. After coming back to Hong Kong, this has proved helpful to me. I've become more reflective about a lot of things, including my way of living, my personality, and my way of doing things."

Jade believed that the language policy was "basically successful" due to "the preparation before the trip." In her interview, she added: "Without it, you'd feel you were showing off when speaking English.

When everyone is speaking it, you don't have this concern. Also, it's important for your cultural experience. It makes you feel more part of the community." She recommended that the policy remain in place for the next cohort: "It's a good idea. It helps improve your fluency in the language and you can pick up the new vocabularies that your classmates have learnt." Her last comment is very interesting as some believed it was only worthwhile to learn the language from "native speakers."

While some of the sojourners did not value informal language learning and evaluated their progress in terms of grammatical accuracy, Jade had a much better grasp of what could be gained from her environment. Consequently, she employed more appropriate language learning strategies, took advantage of linguistic affordances, and reaped the benefits. In the process, her feelings about the language changed, a phenomenon observed by social psychologists in other contexts (e.g., Dörnyei, 2009; Noels, 2009; Ushioda, 2009). English became "more part of" her life. In her interview, she explained: "Before the sojourn, English had been mostly just an academic language to me. In England, it was mingled with my life and, as a result, my vocabulary and expression were enriched. I became more willing to use the language with native speakers, even in informal situations. It's easier for me to express myself now." Back in a Chinese context, she made more of an effort to read English novels and talk with exchange students. With her local friends she continued to use her L1: "I haven't used English with nonnative speakers after returning to Hong Kong. We use Chinese with each other. It's not a problem for me. If my friends prefer to use Cantonese, that's what I use." Her comments remind us of the "socially motivated," domain-specific, sensitive nature of language choice (Coulmas, 2005; Myers-Scotton, 2006).

In a lengthy postsojourn diary entry Jade wrote that, much to her surprise, the sojourn had also enhanced her mother tongue:

Strange enough, I've found that my spoken Cantonese has also improved. In the past, I used to speak a mixed code of English and Cantonese. I felt embarrassed when some of my friends jokingly said that I was losing my mother tongue. I hate people saying that. It hurts me. I had no intention to speak a mixed code but I could not help it. Sometimes, I could not think of a proper Chinese word. My mom encouraged me to read more Chinese books but that didn't help much. ... Incredibly, I could speak better Cantonese after the sojourn. It was somehow related to the English-only policy. Having spoken English for five weeks, I developed a natural tendency to speak in English. When I switched to Cantonese in England it was when I deliberately said something to my friends and did not want our hosts to understand. This pushed me to speak in "pure" Cantonese. In other words, I now prefer to speak the whole sentence either in English or in Cantonese.

While abroad, Jade developed an "additive" view of bilingualism (Lambert, 1975). She discovered that she could maintain herself in both "channels" (English and Cantonese); this reduced her fear of losing her Chinese self through L1 attrition. Her attitude toward code-mixing also shifted as she resolved to enhance her fluency in *both* languages.

When asked what she liked most about the sojourn, Jade talked about her warm relationship with Tessa. The mutual respect and openness that she'd experienced in her homestay encouraged her to take an active role in the family and this had enhanced her stay:

> My host mum was really very nice. She had a lot of experience being a host mother so she knew how to get along with you and she respected your culture. That's very important. In addition, she helped me develop a sense of belonging in the family. This made me feel that I was not just a guest living there but part of the family. And I was involved in many of their family affairs. They invited me to join their family activities and also to help solve arguments between the little children.

In her interview, Jade offered the following advice to the next group of SES students who would also reside in a homestay: "Adjust your schedule as soon as possible to interact more with the host family. Don't wait until you come back and regret that you didn't spend enough time with them. Also, try to solve any problems as soon as possible. Just talk with your hosts." She added: "Don't be afraid to ask questions! Seek clarification if there's anything you don't understand about the culture. Instead of complaining about the hosts or other locals, try to be grateful for what they've done for you. This really helps. Also, be brave and explore." After some more thought, Jade recommended the following strategies to make the most of a homestay:

> Be prepared to talk about your home country. Since your hosts may want to know you more or start a conversation with you, they will very likely ask you something about your home culture. Making adjustments to the differences in their home and building a

good relationship with your hosts are the most significant steps in adapting to a new environment. Your classmates will have a different homestay experience than you. Learn to appreciate what you have and see the beauty of your host family. Avoid comparing with others. Sometimes, things may go differently from what you expect. Learn to appreciate! Then, you will have a better mood and enjoy the sojourn a lot.

Her suggestions were much more specific and concrete than many of her peers. She recognized the benefits of a positive attitude and optimistic spirit to overcome challenges in a new environment. Significantly, intercultural communication specialists (e.g., Byram, 1997, 2006; Chen and Starosta, 2008; Deardorff, 2004, 2008) have identified these personal characteristics as vital for successful intercultural communication and adjustment.

In her diary, Jade summed up the impact of the sojourn: "On a whole, it was really a fruitful experience which will remain with me for the rest of my life!" (diary, postsojourn). In her interview she also expressed the desire to do more traveling to experience new cultures and languages. More self-confident about exploring the world independently, she began to contemplate doing postgraduate studies in an English-speaking country.

Conclusions

Throughout the study, Lana remained stalled near the midpoint of Minimization which, according to the IDI, indicates a transition from an ethnocentric orientation to a more culturally sensitive worldview. A review of her narratives revealed that she focused on similarities between cultures, making assumptions that people in the host culture were basically just like her. In her homestay she developed a warm relationship with her hosts but was treated as a child; with her friends she fell into the familiar role of "follower." These positionings and the choices she made in the new environment hampered her linguistic, cultural, and personal development. Interestingly, while carrying out her presojourn ethnography project she displayed awareness of the role that agency can play in language and (inter)cultural learning but did not fully avail herself of the opportunities that the host culture presented her. On return, she expressed the desire to become more independent and active, suggesting possibilities for future self-enhancement and identity expansion.

Jade developed the highest level of intercultural sensitivity among the four case participants and displayed more of the skills and attributes that intercultural experts associate with intercultural communicative competence (e.g., Byram, 1997; Deardorff, 2008; Fantini, 2007; Sercu, 2005) and "enlightened global citizenship" (Byram, 2006, 2008; Chen and Starosta, 2006; Deardorff and Hunter, 2006; Olson and Kroeger, 2001). The discourse of interculturality and "languaging" (Phipps and Gonzalez, 2004) was more evident in her narratives than those of Lana and the other young women. What might account for this?

Early on, Jade developed the habit of critical reflection (*savoir s'engager*) (Byram et al., 2002) and took a more active role in her environment than many of her peers, both at home and abroad. As the sojourn unfolded, she demonstrated a growing recognition and appreciation of cultural differences, going beyond superficial observations. In her homestay she experienced mutuality and camaraderie, which prompted further learning. Where some students saw limitations in the world around them, Jade discovered linguistic and cultural affordances, and became less fearful of L1 attrition. With an optimistic mindset and determination she made better use of the presojourn preparation and sojourn debriefings and more successfully mediated across cultures. By more fully maximizing her short stay abroad, she made gains in cultural understanding (of both Self and Other), enhanced her sociopragmatic awareness, and broadened her view of English. Back on home soil, she continued to set realistic goals for further self-enhancement. Open to the process of identity reconstruction, she began to nurture a broader, more inclusive global identity (Lam, 2006; Noels, 2009; S. Ryan, 2006, 2009).

In the next chapter I link the stories of the four young women with the theories presented in Chapters 1 and 2.

7
New Ways of Being

In this chapter I summarize the trajectories of the focal case participants and revisit the theories that were discussed in Chapters 1 and 2. In particular, I explore the relationship between interculturality, language, and identity (re)construction, and the notions of "intercultural speaker" and "intercultural mediator." I critique the proposed linkage between language proficiency development and intercultural competence put forward by Bennett et al. (2003). In light of the findings, I also discuss the applicability of the Developmental Model of Intercultural Sensitivity (DMIS) and intercultural communicative competence theories for short-term sojourns. In the process, I identify specific program features (e.g., ethnography, intercultural education) that can influence the development of intercultural communicative competence and ethnorelativism in L2 sojourners.

The focal case studies

No two L2 learners travel an identical path in becoming intercultural. In a new environment, sojourners may seek acceptance as full members of the host culture, remain on the periphery, or continuously reject new ways of being. While their aims and development may vary, we can learn a great deal by examining the journeys of L2 students. By identifying the obstacles and opportunities they encounter and their reactions to them, we can acquire a deeper understanding of what propels L2 learners toward higher levels of intercultural communicative competence.

The stories of the case participants offer insight into the ebb and flow of language and cultural learning, both in the home environment and abroad. These case studies are not meant to be representative of all L2 speakers/sojourners; however, these storied experiences do elucidate the complex notions of interculturality and identity reconstruction, providing insight into individual differences and contextual elements that may impact on the development of intercultural communicative competence and global citizenship.

The developmental trajectories of L2 sojourners

While all of the case participants acquired higher levels of intercultural competence, to varying degrees, they experienced different developmental trajectories throughout the course of the study. What can we learn from the young women who acquired higher levels of intercultural communicative competence and experienced a broadening of their sense of self? How do their behavior and choices differ from those of their less ethnorelative peers? What individual and environmental factors might account for differences in sojourn outcomes? The following sections review pivotal moments in their journeys; when appropriate, I refer to the wider group of sojourners to better illustrate the uniqueness or shared nature of their experiences and development.

The young women's oral and written narratives provide perspectives on interculturality and offer insight into the attributes and behaviors of those who more successfully mediated between languages and cultures. What we can see from their stories is that they are not mere recipients of the forces of globalization and internationalization. They are reshaping themselves as they create new spaces of knowledge and understanding, both in their home environment and abroad. Their storied experiences highlight the complexity of individual expansion and help explain variations in developmental trajectories.

On home soil

Language attitudes, learning, and use

From a young age, all of the case participants were keenly aware of the linguistic, symbolic capital of English (Bourdieu, 1991) and its status in their environment. Messages from their parents, teachers, the media, and the community impressed upon them the benefits of mastering the language for instrumental purposes (e.g., to secure a better job and future), and few demonstrated an "internalized thirst" for the language. As Brown (2001: 78) observes,

> schools all too often teach students to play the "game" of pleasing teachers and authorities rather than developing an internalized thirst

for knowledge and experience. ... Over the long haul, such dependency focuses students too exclusively on the material or monetary rewards of an education rather than instilling an appreciation for creativity and for satisfying some of the more basic drives for knowledge and exploration.

Instrumental motives also prompted the young women to major in English at the university. In their home environment, prior to the sojourn, they viewed English primarily as a language for the public domain (e.g., formal, academic situations), preferring to communicate personal thoughts and emotions in their mother tongue, Cantonese. Even though English did not usually feature in their social life (e.g., with friends, family members, people in the community), some were conflicted about its "dominance," fearing L1 attrition. Those who felt torn between competing languages and identities experienced psychological distress and confusion about their bilingual status. For some, it raised uncomfortable questions about language loyalty and the prestige of their L1 (Coulmas, 2005; Fought, 2006; Lambert, 1975; Myers-Scotton, 2006).

Most participants were sensitive to the implicit sanctions that discourage the use of English among Chinese in social situations when everyone present is able to converse in Cantonese. Outside of class, I also observed that these young women exhibited different degrees of motivation and investment in learning English and this changed over time (Dörnyei, 2005, 2009; Norton, 2000). While most had limited use of the language at home, Jade kept a diary in English, read English magazines for pleasure, and watched English TV programs and movies on a regular basis. She was also the only one who preferred to speak English with native speakers; the other case participants were anxious about making mistakes and more at ease practicing the language with other Cantonese speakers.

After exposure to world Englishes and literatures, the participants began to develop a deeper, broader appreciation of this global language. This discovery provided evidence of the dynamic nature of motivation in L2 learners (Dörnyei, 2009). I was interested to discover if their motivation would shift further in an English-speaking environment, with more opportunity to learn and use the language in daily life.

All of the young women frequently indulged in code-mixing, varying their use of Cantonese and English depending on the sociocultural situation, the person being addressed, or the topic. Similar to sociolinguists who have examined this phenomenon in other bilingual settings (e.g., Coulmas, 2005; Myers-Scotton, 2006; Trudgill, 2003), I discovered that the Hong Kong women's code usage was very strategic and complex. For example, they sometimes had multiple reasons for mixing or switching to another language (e.g., to speed up communication; to display a dual identity or membership in both of the cultures that the languages index; to accommodate a lack of proficiency in one or both of the languages; to display expertise in more than one language; to convey a modern, international persona by using some English, a language of "prestige"; to mark their in-group affiliation with other well-educated Hong Kongers of their age group). Several also had very fixed ideas about the amount of code-mixing that was "acceptable" in certain situations. If speakers broke these unwritten rules, they risked being labeled a "show-off." While some of the women had reservations about this "habit," most accepted it as normal for a hybrid environment where more than one language was in use.

Identity (re)construction

Historical events (e.g., the Handover of Hong Kong to Mainland China in 1997) and intercultural contact prompted the young women to reflect on their positioning in local society, Asia, and the world. Since the transfer of sovereignty the Hong Kong government and mass media have emphasized Hong Kong's Chineseness and ties to the Mainland China with mixed results. As Mathews et al. (2008: 97) explain, while most people in the city are immigrants or descendants of recent immigrants from China,

> from the late 1970s on, many Hong Kong people began psychologically to distance themselves from mainland Chinese. The cognitive distance between Hongkongese and Chinese became an important indicator of indigenous cultural identity: the greater the distance between Hong Kong people's self-image and their image of Chinese, the stronger their sense of belonging to the localized culture of Hong Kong became.

This "cognitive distance" impacted on the self-identification of the young women in my study. Most were conflicted about their link with Britain and the "Motherland." Just prior to the sojourn, when asked what "identity label" they preferred, if any, Nora chose "Hong Konger," to emphasize her association with her beloved city and distinguish her from Mainlanders. Just prior to the sojourn, Lana and Jade opted to be identified as "Chinese Hong Kongers." Although neither felt like "authentic Chinese" due to their lack of affiliation with the Mainland, this hybrid label conveyed their pride in their home city and, simultaneously, recognized their Chineseness.

As the most experienced traveler in the group, Jade was more aware of the relational, fluid nature of identity. While in France the previous summer, she had discovered that non-Asians sometimes did not understand the distinction between a Hong Konger and a Mainlander. In this situation, she opted to identify herself as Chinese. Mimi, the young woman who frequently denigrated her "Chinese Self" before entering the program, worked through many of her raw emotions in extensive diary entries; just prior to departure for England, she declared herself willing to be identified as "Chinese" as this linked her to her "family, country, and heritage." The young women's revelations furnished compelling evidence of the basic need for "a sense of belonging" (Meinhof and Galasiński, 2005) and highlighted the dynamic, sometimes contested, nature of identity development (Block, 2007; Hall, 1992) and the inextricable link between language, identity, and culture (Ryan, 2009; Ushioda, 2009). Their narratives also suggested the possibility of further changes during the sojourn.

Intercultural awareness and sensitivity

When the case participants entered the study abroad program, they had an advanced level of proficiency in academic English. Most had had few opportunities to use the language in informal situations, however, and none had ever visited or lived in an English-speaking environment prior to the sojourn. According to the Intercultural Development Inventory (IDI), the young women were at the following levels of intercultural sensitivity on entry: Nora (low end of Denial/Defense or Reversal, DD/R), Mimi (DD/R), Lana (Minimization), and Jade (Minimization). All of them were in an ethnocentric stage of development, with Lana and Jade in the transitional phase, indicating that they were less threatened by cultural differences and more focused on similarities.

After the intensive presojourn preparation (e.g., intercultural communication course, "home ethnography" project, country-specific orientation), all of the women progressed to higher levels of intercultural competence, according to the IDI. Nora made a gain of 12.48 points, advancing further in DD/R. Mimi's IDI score indicated movement from DD/R to Minimization (an increase of 9.57 points). Lana advanced the least (6.0 points), remaining in Minimization. By contrast, Jade made the most significant gain (32.63 points); she progressed from Minimization to AA (Acceptance/Adaptation), an ethnorelative stage of development. A review of the "perceived" IDI scores revealed that all of the women had significantly inflated self-perceptions of their intercultural competence. I aimed to find out if their oral and written narratives and my field notes would resonate with the IDI results and account for differing outcomes.

Cultural socialization

Early in the "communication across cultures" course, the case participants were prompted to write about their cultural background and intercultural contact in relation to such aspects as their verbal and nonverbal styles of communication, their attitudes towards their own and other cultures, and their evolving sense of self. Their narratives disclosed differences in their awareness and appreciation of their own and other cultures. Those who were more ethnorelative (according to the IDI) displayed more awareness of their own social, cultural, and linguistic development. In Byram et al.'s (2002) terms, they possessed more *savoirs*, that is, knowledge of social groups and practices in their own culture. The act of writing raised their awareness of themselves as cultural beings and stimulated further reflection on their self-identity and positioning in the world.

Reflection on intercultural communication

As the intercultural communication course unfolded, the women developed greater awareness of differences and similarities across and within cultures. To link theory with practice, they were continually encouraged to reflect on course content and intercultural encounters and write about their perceptions in a journal. While Jade and Mimi were the most open to experiencing other cultures, initially both displayed only a superficial understanding of differences. Lana viewed the world "essentially as a global village," had little awareness of other cultures, and negatively stereotyped Mainlanders. Among the case participants, Nora was the most apprehensive about intercultural contact; on entry into the SES she felt insecure and threatened unless surrounded by in-group members (Hong Kong Chinese).

As I reviewed their journal entries during the course of the semester, I observed that those who had been very fearful of cultural differences when they joined the SES, slowly but surely, made more of an effort to appreciate diversity. Their writing provided evidence that they were trying to refrain from making quick, negative assessments of cultural practices that were new to them. Notably, those who made the most gains in intercultural sensitivity during this phase of the program provided much more detailed analyses of intercultural encounters and gradually demonstrated the ability to view a situation from different perspectives. Jade, in particular, wrote lengthy entries in which she described and analyzed intercultural encounters in a more sophisticated, balanced way. Her writing provided evidence of a more ethnorelative mindset (M. J. Bennett, 1993, 2004) and several of the *savoirs* that Byram (1997) links to the cultural dimension of the intercultural speaker's competence (e.g., knowledge of Self and Other).

The pragmatic "home ethnography" project

In the 14-week semester preceding the sojourn, the students honed the skills of ethnographic research (e.g., participant observation, note-taking, interviewing, ethnographic conversations, transcribing, qualitative data analysis). After completing a series of tasks, they investigated a cultural scene in their home environment, putting their skills into practice in a small-scale, pragmatic "home ethnography" project (e.g., "The life of an exchange student from Beijing").

Their confidence and level of sensitivity (e.g., awareness of the benefits of adjusting their communication style with different interviewees) evolved as they carried out their project and mediated between their own cultural practices and those of others. Most gained a better understanding of the importance of sensitive word choice and nonverbal communication to build rapport with their informants. While all of the novice researchers aimed to develop an "emic" (insider's) perspective, I observed that Jade was more successful. As well as being a keen observer, she more actively engaged in critical self-analysis; she displayed what Byram (1997: 50) describes as a "willingness to question the values and presuppositions in cultural practices and products" in her own environment. Realizing she had a tendency to negatively judge others whose views differed from her own, she made a concerted effort to overcome this and became a more thoughtful, empathetic listener. By gaining the trust of her informants, she was better positioned to glimpse another worldview.

The ethnographic tasks (e.g., observing interaction in a campus canteen, interviewing an international student) and "home ethnography" project bolstered the students' observational and interviewing skills and heightened their awareness of the importance of interpersonal communication skills to successfully interact with informants. The project enhanced their self-confidence and level of independence and served as a constructive "dress rehearsal" for the fieldwork that they would carry out in England.

During the sojourn

Intercultural awareness and sensitivity

According to the IDI, by the end of the five-week stay in England Nora had progressed from DD/R (Denial/Defense or Reversal) to Minimization (a gain of 5.31 points); Mimi and Lana stayed in Minimization (a gain of 9.28 points for the former and a slight loss of 0.10 points for the latter); and Jade remained in Acceptance/Adaptation (a gain of 7.07 points). Interestingly, their gains were not as great as in the presojourn phase. While all of the participants were in either a transitional or ethnorelative phase by the end of the sojourn, their trajectories differed in rather interesting ways. Nora moved into the transitional phase of intercultural development; Lana remained relatively unchanged. By comparison, Mimi and Jade experienced more growth in intercultural sensitivity. Would these scores resonate with their behavior and attitudes?

As the young women became more intercultural, I observed that they displayed heightened sensitivity and awareness of themselves and those around them. Those who made the most gains in their IDI scores became more attuned to and accepting of cultural differences, going beyond superficial observations (e.g., food, clothing) to noticing less visible cultural differences (e.g., values, beliefs about health and wellness). In line with Chen and Starosta's (2008) theory of intercultural communication competence, these individuals reflected more deeply on their positioning in the world and the impact of their cultural socialization on their relations with others. As their self-awareness and cultural understandings grew, they made more of an effort to avoid stereotyping; their "us vs. them" discourse gradually diminished.

Intercultural attitudes (*savoir être*)

As predicted by Byram et al. (2002), Chen and Starosta (2008) and Deardorff (2004, 2006, 2008), among others, attitude proved to be a key ingredient in determining sojourn outcomes. Those who were "sensitive enough to acknowledge and respect cultural differences" scored higher on the IDI and provided evidence of the following personal characteristics in their oral and written narratives: nonjudgmental attitudes, high self-esteem, open-mindedness, and social relaxation ("the ability to reveal little anxious emotion in intercultural communication") (Chen and Starosta, 2008: 222).

I found significant differences in the sojourners' "readiness to experience the different stages of adaptation to and interaction with" the host culture (Byram, 1997: 50). Those who displayed more curiosity and openness (*savoir être*) attained higher levels of intercultural compe-tence. They were more successful at maintaining a positive attitude and did not let disappointments or setbacks (e.g., critical incidents across cultures, homesickness) deter them for long. Employing a wider range of coping strategies, they were more reflective and resilient in the face of adversity.

Realistic, attainable learning objectives

As well as being more optimistic, the sojourners who developed the high-est levels of intercultural competence in the group set more realistic objectives for a short-term sojourn. In particular, their expectations for language and (inter)cultural learning were more appropriate for the length and nature of their particular sojourn. Realizing that they would have more exposure to informal, social English in the host culture, they were less fixated on improvements in academic English (e.g., grammar). Consequently, they were more satisfied with what they achieved (e.g., more confidence using English in social settings). Their enthusiastic, positive frame of mind set the stage for personal enrichment. By contrast, those who were less appreciative of their accomplishments and more critical of themselves and others experienced a lesser degree of advancement.

Willingness to try new things

I also observed differences in the willingness of the sojourners to try new things. In particular, their reaction to new food proved to be a sig-nificant indicator of intercultural adjustment and competence. Similar to Bhawuk and Brislin (1992) and one of my earlier investigations of the sojourn experience (Jackson, 2008), I discovered that those who were more open to different kinds of cuisine and experiences assumed a more active role in their homestay and community. In Phipps' (2006) terms, they were more effective "languagers." Less fearful of cultural dif-ferences, their enhanced self-confidence and independence motivated them to use English in a variety of settings, including informal situations that were totally foreign to them. Consequently, they gained more expo-sure to social English in a range of cultural scenes (e.g., pubs). In an effort to "fit in" and more fully experience the host community, they experi-mented with speech communication patterns that were new to them and, at times, appropriated the discourse of locals (e.g., colorful, effusive adjectives, idiomatic expressions, discourse markers of politeness). Not surprisingly, these sojourners adjusted better to the host culture; by the end of their stay, they experienced more linguistic development than those who were less open to the English environment.

Culture shock and adjustment

While all of the participants experienced symptoms of culture shock to varying degrees (e.g., trouble sleeping, homesickness, nightmares) (Ward, Bochner, and Furnham, 2001), those who traveled further down the path to interculturality reflected more deeply on their trials and tribulations. Recognizing that culture shock is natural in a new environment, they worked through their malaise and, in the process, developed more awareness of Self and Other (Alred and Byram, 2002; Fantini, 2007; Sercu, 2002), enhanced their self-confidence, and acquired a higher degree of independence and self-efficacy. Their discomfiture served as a springboard to deeper levels of self-analysis and personal growth.

Overall, these women appeared to be better equipped to deal with stress as they rebounded much more quickly from troubling situations (e.g., bouts of homesickness). They employed a range of coping mechanisms which served them well (e.g., writing at length about their feelings in their diaries, drawing on socio-emotional support from friends, hosts). They made better use of the presojourn preparation, took a more active role in debriefing sessions, and more successfully worked through the "downs" that are a natural part of the adjustment process. They quickly refocused on their new environment, reassessed their goals, and remained on course for further personal, linguistic, and cultural expansion.

By contrast, some of their peers were unable to fully overcome their discomfiture and fears in the new environment. In particular, I observed that those with less effective coping strategies were not as motivated to explore the host community and interact with locals outside the confines of the homestay. They spent more time in the computer room at the host institution, which limited exposure to English in diverse cultural scenes. Further, some were positioned as children (e.g., letting their hosts and SES friends make decisions for them) and did not assert themselves. More fixated on home country happenings, they took less advantage of linguistic and cultural affordances in the host environment and experienced less personal growth.

Empathy and the acquisition of interpersonal skills

Another aspect that helped explain the different developmental trajectories was the degree of empathy that each woman displayed for other people (e.g., their hosts, their fellow sojourners). Those who were more interculturally sensitive demonstrated more concern and regard for others and were less preoccupied with their own needs and wants. In their homestay, they recognized and appreciated the efforts of their hosts to make them feel welcome. As well as showing gratitude through acts of kindness (e.g., preparing a meal, helping with daily chores), they began to verbally express their thanks in ways familiar to their hosts. In other words, they became more attuned to local norms of politeness. By demonstrating genuine interest in their interlocutors, the more intercultural speakers also found it easier to sustain conversations and develop warmer, stronger connections across cultures.

By the end of the sojourn, those who had developed a more ethnorelative mindset, like Jade, appeared to be much more socially mindful. These intercultural speakers possessed more behavioral or intercultural adroitness (Chen and Starosta, 2008), demonstrating a greater awareness of sociopragmatic norms and communication styles that are prevalent in the host environment. They displayed the skills of discovery and interaction (*savoir apprendre/faire*), which Byram et al. (2002: 12–13) define as "the ability to acquire new knowledge of a culture and to operate this knowledge in real-time communication." These sojourners developed higher levels of sociopragmatic ability, their social skills were more sophisticated, they displayed more behavioral flexibility, and their behavior in social situations was generally more appropriate. In Chen and Starosta's (2008) terms, their "interaction management" (e.g., ability to initiate and sustain conversations in the host language) was more successful.

Further, a review of their diaries laid bare interesting differences in their response to critical incidents. Those who became more interculturally competent were more inclined to acknowledge the role that their behavior may have played in misunderstandings and, consequently, their learning curve was greater. To borrow from Byram et al. (2002: 12–13), these individuals displayed more critical cultural awareness (*savoir s'engager*) as they were better equipped and more willing "to evaluate critically and on the basis of explicit criteria, perspectives, practices and products in one's own and other cultures and countries." This set them apart from their less ethnorelative peers.

Host receptivity and exposure to new ways of being

Receptivity and mutuality in homestay situations also played a role in how each woman's journey unfolded. Significantly, those who experienced higher levels of acceptance and engagement generally developed more confidence to take an active role in communicative events (e.g., initiating conversations in English more frequently, experimenting with new expressions and behaviors). These sojourners chose to spend more quality time with their hosts and this afforded them more opportunity for the relationship to grow deeper. A positive cycle was set in motion.

Mimi and Jade's hosts involved them in activities both within and outside the homestay (e.g., trips to pubs, fairs, barbecues), whereas Nora and Lana's hosts stayed closer to home. While all four case participants had welcoming, supportive hosts, not all of their peers fared as well. In some cases, hosts were so busy with work and other responsibilities that they had little time or energy left to chat or go on outings. Some demonstrated little or no appreciation of Chinese culture/products (e.g., a gift of Chinese tea); not surprisingly, this negatively impacted on the host–sojourner relationship. Mutuality and the degree and quality of access to the host culture contribute to differing sojourn outcomes. In line with the intergroup contact theory, when Allport's (1954) situational conditions were met, greater intergroup contact was typically associated with reduced prejudice and more positive intercultural relations.

Living the ethnographic life

What role did the ethnographic research projects play in the linguistic and intercultural development of the sojourners? During the five-week stay in England, I noticed differences in the young women's level of interest and time spent in their chosen cultural scene. Those who developed higher levels of intercultural sensitivity were more engrossed in their projects and spent more time immersed in the environment under study. They developed better rapport with their informants and gained more insight into their topic as they engaged in a series of observations, ethnographic conversations, and interviews. I also observed that their field notes and transcripts were richer in detail.

Despite differences in the quality and depth of the material they gathered, it is noteworthy that all of the case participants believed that they had become closer to their informants and acquired a deeper understanding of their chosen cultural scene. They were convinced that they had matured and enhanced their intercultural communication skills by engaging in sustained conversations with people from the host culture. As they gathered their ethnographic data and became more at ease in the cultural setting, their self-efficacy and degree of independence grew. In some cases, their projects also afforded them the opportunity to connect with others outside their homestay and gain exposure to a wider array of communities of practice (Lave and Wenger, 1991). Jade, for example, visited a youth group led by her host, Lana observed a lace-making group that her host mother attended, and Mimi studied pub culture, often frequenting the scene with her host family.

Those who became more intercultural through their ethnographic research also took a much more active role in the host environment – not just in their homestay but also in the community (e.g., conversing with people in shops and at bus stops, joining a fitness run). As these "languagers" (Phipps, 2006) gained more exposure to subcultures and local styles of communication, they had the opportunity to pick up more colloquialisms and informal discourse strategies. By assuming responsibility for their own learning and more fully engaging in "an ethnographic way of life," these sojourners achieved significant personal growth and took further steps toward interculturality.

Identity reconstruction and linguistic expansion

Experiencing a new linguistic and cultural environment prompted the young women to reflect further on their positioning in the world. Those who were more open to the process of identity reconstruction were willing to experiment with elements of the host culture that were new to them (e.g., behaviors, communication styles). In these individuals I observed glimpses of a global identity, which they proudly associated with a more polished, cosmopolitan self, a development observed by other sociolinguists (e.g., Kanno and Norton, 2003; Kinginger, 2008; Lam, 2006; S. Ryan, 2006, 2009). At the same time, I noted that these sojourners developed more awareness, respect, and appreciation of their Chineseness.

Interestingly, some of these same individuals suffered from psychological disequilibrium and identity confusion as they experienced life in English for the first time. While initially fearful that their L1 would suffer, they resolved to "make the most of the sojourn" and took an active role in their homestay and community. As they overcame fears of subtractive bilingualism (Lambert, 1975), they realized that they could develop themselves in multiple languages. No longer viewing Chinese and English as adversaries, they became more appreciative of the enrichment that each language brought to their life. By contrast, some of their peers never felt fully at ease as a visible minority in an English-speaking milieu. Under stress, they frequently spoke "Chinglish in a playful way" with each other; this exaggerated localized variety of Hong Kong English appeared to provide them with a sense of belonging, security, and in-group identification in an alien environment. These individuals rejected more elements of the host culture and clung more tightly to their "Chinese self," a phenomenon observed by other study abroad researchers (e.g., Allen et al., 2007; Bateman, 2002; Stroebe et al., 1988; Isabelli-Garçia, 2006). This discovery further drew my attention to the emotive, context-dependent linkage between language, identity, culture, and positioning (Dörnyei, 2009; Ushioda, 2009).

Perception of the host language

While all of the case participants had focused on the pragmatic, linguistic capital of English before the sojourn (e.g., better job opportunities), those who actively used it in the host culture (e.g., dreaming, reflecting, interacting) modified their perception during their stay. As they became more familiar with life in an English-speaking environment and established close ties across cultures, they began to view the language in much broader terms. By the end of the sojourn, they were expressing appreciation for both its linguistic and cultural capital (ability to provide exposure to new worldviews) (Bourdieu, 1986, 1991). As they used English in their daily family life (and, in many cases, in the community), they no longer saw it simply as a tool for professional or academic communication. They had begun to feel more comfortable expressing their personal thoughts and feelings in the language, not only with host nationals but also with each other. I also observed that those who more successfully mediated between cultures had begun to appreciate the intercultural capital (Lam, 2006) that this international language afforded them. They recognized that English facilitated dialogue and friendship across cultures, both at home and abroad, and were less fearful of L1 attrition.

Back on home soil

Personal, linguistic, and cultural growth

After returning to Hong Kong, the students reflected on their sojourn experiences and reentry in an interview. Most also wrote diary entries, providing further insight into the impact of crossing cultures on their development. Significantly, all were convinced that they had experienced personal growth during their stay in England. For most, it had been their first trip away from home; living in a new environment with people from another culture made them more self-aware and mature. All experienced personal expansion, to varying degrees. Back in familiar surroundings, Lana and Nora, the two who were the "most coddled" by their hosts and SES buddies, expressed the desire to become more independent. They may have gradually taken a more active role and become more self-reliant if the sojourn had been longer. Perhaps the sojourn would have unfolded differently if they had been placed with hosts who encouraged them to assume more responsibility for themselves.

The majority of the students believed that they had enhanced their social skills and become more confident while speaking English with "native speakers" in a range of situations, including informal contexts. Their ethnographic projects had necessitated sustained contact across cultures (e.g., chats, longer interviews) and this had enhanced their awareness of Self and Other or what Byram et al. (2002: 12–13) refer to as *savoirs* – "knowledge of social groups and their products and practices in one's own and interlocutor's country." While all of the case participants made positive comments about the sojourn and their homestay experiences, I noticed that some "us vs. them" discourse and ethnocentric, judgmental comments resurfaced in those who were in the first half of Minimization, the transitional phase of intercultural sensitivity, according to the IDI.

Identity reconstruction

Back in a Chinese environment, all of the young women reflected further on their identity and positioning – both locally and globally. Nora discovered that her love of Hong Kong had grown stronger and some of her ethnocentric discourse reemerged. Never fully at home in an English environment, she had longed for the familiar and more firmly embraced a Chinese identity. Mimi had also been very aware of her minority status in England and had become more attached to her Chineseness. Lana retained her self-identity as a "Chinese Hong Konger" but felt much more connected to the rest of the world. By contrast, Jade embraced hybridity and change. More accepting of an expanded, global identity, she believed she'd become more self-confident and worldly-wise.

While all four women were "physically Chinese," what is significant is that some opted to make their Chineseness the core of their identity, while others chose to de-emphasize it somewhat. I also discovered that their preferences varied over time and space. For example, intercultural contact in the host culture and reentry stimulated changes in their self-identity. This cautions us to avoid affixing rigid identity labels on individuals. As noted by identity theorists, cross-cultural psychologists, and sociolinguists in other contexts (e.g., Rizvi et al., 2005; S. Ryan, 2006; Smith et al., 2006), as a consequence of globalizing forces and increased intercultural contact, people may choose to delink from identities that are tied to nationality, ethnicity, and traditions.

As the SES students developed a heightened awareness of their race and ethnicity in an environment where there were few Chinese, I wondered how their self-identity might have evolved if they'd been housed in a more multicultural setting. Also, due to Hong Kong's colonial past, their perceptions of Britain impacted on their identity and attitudes toward English. It is therefore conceivable that their sense of self and language attitudes might have evolved differently in another English-speaking country (e.g., Australia).

Advice for future sojourners

The advice that the young women offered the next group of sojourners provided a window into their own learning and intercultural communicative competence. All were supportive of the language policy and advocated the use of English to "get the best" out of the five-week stay in an English-speaking environment. They advised future sojourners to be "open-minded" and to talk to their hosts when elements of the host environment were confusing (e.g., "confront ambiguity with questions"). Even those who were not as active in their homestays recommended that sojourners make themselves available to interact with their host families, whenever possible.

Further, those who attained higher levels of ethnorelativism (M. J. Bennett, 1993, 2004) advised future sojourners to adopt a positive, optimistic attitude and express appreciation for their hosts. Those who were more successful intercultural mediators made an effort to adjust to other ways of being instead of rigidly adhering to familiar behaviors. Interestingly, these individuals advocated the adoption of traits and behaviors interculturalists associate with intercultural competence (e.g., Byram, 1997, 2006; Chen and Starosta, 2008; Deardorff, 2004, 2008) and intercultural speakers or mediators (Alred and Byram, 2002; Guilherme, 2004; Kramsch, 1998).

What can we learn from the developmental trajectories of L2 sojourners?

Overall, this small-scale study provided preliminary evidence that intercultural communication/ethnography courses and short-term sojourns, when carefully planned and sequenced, can have a positive impact on student development (e.g., sociopragmatic awareness, enhanced cultural knowledge). With adequate presojourn preparation, students can become more systematic language and cultural learners and, ultimately, enhance their intercultural communicative competence. Through sustained intercultural contact and the habit of deep, critical reflection, they can take steps toward interculturality and responsible global citizenship. Individual characteristics of sojourners (e.g., personality traits, degree of flexibility) and special features in the study abroad program (e.g., experiential learning, ethnographic training, the promotion of critical cultural reflection, debriefing) all play a role in differing sojourn outcomes.

As well as providing direction for meaningful praxis, the analysis of the young women's trajectories helps to understand the merits and limitations of the theories and models that were discussed in Chapters 1 and 2. The following sections highlight key findings that enhance our theoretical understandings of what it means to be intercultural.

Storied experiences and IDI trajectories

In general, the analysis of the young women's oral and written narratives and my field notes supported the primary assumption that underpins the DMIS: "as one's experience of cultural difference becomes more complex and sophisticated, one's competence in intercultural relations increases" (Intercultural Communication Institute, 2004). Those who reached a more ethnorelative stage of development according to the IDI were more aware of cultural differences, going beyond superficial observations by the end of the sojourn. Interestingly, as a whole, the group made the most significant gains in intercultural sensitivity during the presojourn preparation phase (e.g., the intercultural communication and ethnographic research courses, the country-specific orientation). This suggests that Internationalization at Home (IaH) can play a valuable role in developing "global ready" graduates.

Intercultural sensitivity and L2 proficiency

The relationship between language and cultural learning is far more complex than what is presented in Bennett et al. (2003). My study indicates that it is possible for learners to be "advanced" in terms of proficiency in a second language, yet minimally aware of, or uncomfortable with values and modes of behavior (e.g., communication styles) that differ from their own. The developmental sequence of intercultural competence does *not* necessarily parallel linguistic competence.

In the case of L2 learners, intercultural sensitivity and sociopragmatic awareness may lag far behind linguistic development, especially in contexts where the L2 under study is not the language of the community. In the present study, all 14 Hong Kong students had an advanced proficiency in academic English; however, according to the IDI, only one had an ethnorelative mindset on entry into the SES. Moreover, the individual with the highest level of proficiency in English (the best score on the A-level "use of English" exam) at this stage had the highest level of ethnocentrism. This has important implications for the preparation and ongoing support of L2 sojourners, elements that are addressed in Chapter 8.

Inflated perceptions of intercultural competence

Another interesting finding was the tendency of the participants to overestimate their level of intercultural sensitivity/competence. This was also the situation in Edstrom's (2005) investigation of American women in Spain (Spanish as a second language learners), Medina-López-Portillo's (2004a, 2004b) study of American students in Mexico (Spanish as a second language learners), and Park's (2006) study of preservice EFL teachers in South Korea (speakers of English as a second language). In some cases, the SES students estimated their degree of intercultural sensitivity to be several IDI band levels above their actual developmental level. What might account for these inflated self-assessments?

In a review of studies of biased self-assessment, Fischer, Greitemeyer, and Frey (2007) note that most people tend to exhibit positive illusions about their own abilities and personality. Researchers attribute this phenomenon to a variety of reasons, including the desire to maintain a positive sense of self-esteem (e.g., Kruger, 1999; Taylor and Brown, 1988, 1994), selective encoding (Kunda, 1990), and biased reference points (Ditto and Lopez, 1992). In many domains, according to Kruger and Dunning (1999), people who are incompetent may lack sufficient metacognitive ability to be aware of their incompetence and this can lead to inflated self-perceptions. Significantly, these researchers found that "improving the skills of participants, and thus increasing their metacognitive competence, helped them recognize the limitations of their abilities" (ibid.: 1121). This suggests that the promotion of deeper levels of self-awareness has the potential to bring about change.

In the present study, those who acquired the highest levels of intercultural sensitivity were more mindful of gaps in their intercultural communicative competence and knowledge of the host culture. By contrast, those with a more ethnocentric mindset demonstrated less appreciation of the complexity of cultural differences and, in some cases, were blissfully unaware that their style of communication might be hampering relationship building across cultures. Content to just be themselves, they naively assumed that they were more interculturally sensitive than they actually were. Their metacognitive competence was not as well developed as that of their more ethnorelative peers.

The components of intercultural communicative competence

The language and cultural components in Byram's (1997, 2006) model of intercultural communicative competence were deeply involved in the intercultural journeys of the young women. The linguistic elements that he views as characteristic of the intercultural speaker or mediator (linguistic, sociolinguistic, and discourse competencies) were present in those who attained higher levels of ethnorelativism according to the IDI. I also found evidence of the five components or *savoirs* that Byram et al. (2002) link to the cultural dimension of the intercultural speaker's competence (*savoirs, savoir comprendre, savoir être, savoir apprendre/faire*, and *savoir s'engager*) (see Chapter 2 for definitions of each). In particular, the most interculturally sensitive sojourners displayed critical or analytical cultural awareness and a more profound understanding of elements of their own and other cultures.

Byram et al. (2002) consider intercultural attitudes and cultural knowledge prerequisites for successful intercultural communication, which is in line with Chen and Starosta's (2008) model of intercultural communication competence, Hunter's (2004) global competence model, and my own findings. Specific traits and skills have also been cited as characteristic of individuals who more successfully communicate across cultures. In my study, the most ethnorelative students exhibited the following qualities and behaviors: curiosity about the world around them, openness to new experiences, tolerance for ambiguity, empathy and concern for others, an adaptive spirit, respect and awareness of cultural differences, resilience, flexibility, a critical, reflective nature, a sense of humor, and patience. Significantly, these intercultural speakers more actively engaged in critical cultural reflection and analysis or what Byram et al. (2002) refer to as *savoir s'engager*. Committed to developing cordial relationships across cultures, they more effectively dealt with different interpretations of reality (e.g., differing worldviews) and made use of new understandings (e.g., sociopragmatic awareness) to more successfully mediate interaction across cultural boundaries.

Deardorff's (2004, 2006, 2008) process model of intercultural competence identifies certain attitudes, knowledge/comprehension, and skills as essential for intercultural competence. I found that, as predicted, all of these elements could affect the internal and external outcomes of short-term sojourns. While very useful, Deardorff's conceptual framework has some limitations when applied to L2 speakers. It does not sufficiently recognize the role of the interlocutor in the communication process and largely ignores environmental factors (e.g., power, positioning of L2 speakers, degree of mutuality/respect, quality of intergroup contact). All of these elements can impact on intercultural interaction and influence sojourn outcomes (e.g., lead to reduced intergroup prejudice or heightened ethnocentricism) as forecast by Allport's (1954) intergroup contact theory and subsequent investigations by Pettigrew and Tropp (2000).

The analysis of my ethnographic data also revealed that the dispositions of L2 sojourners toward language and cultural learning are variable and linked to the choices they make (e.g., degree of intercultural contact/"languaging" (Phipps and Gonzlez, 2004) as well as contextual factors (e.g., host receptivity). What are the implications of this? Students' motives and expectations for the sojourn, their investment in their growth (e.g., linguistic, cultural, personal, academic), their additive or subtractive perception of bilingualism (Lambert, 1975), their degree of intercultural sensitivity and empathy, and their evolving sense of self must be understood in relation to their personal histories, social psychological factors (e.g., personality traits, self-efficacy) (e.g., Bourhis, El-geledi and Sachdev, 2007), the sociocultural/historical context (e.g., Lantolf, 2000), and the nature of their contact with the host community (e.g., homestay, communities of practice). Access, power, and agency all play a role in the intercultural adjustment, sensitivity, and competence of L2 sojourners. As in Deardorff's (2004) process model, these aspects are often overlooked when educators do not fully acknowledge the dynamic complexity of the language and cultural learning situation. Further, some sojourners, for a variety of reasons, may be less able or willing to adjust to their new environment during a short-term stay. They may resist cultural differences and contact with the host culture (e.g., through the use of avoidance strategies), which, in turn limits their exposure to cultural scenes and the host language. This would then have a negative effect on their sociopragmatic and intercultural sensitivity development. The learning situation of sojourners is far more complex than what is often presented in the literature on study and residence abroad.

Conclusions

Are existing models of intercultural communicative competence relevant to the experiences of L2 students who cross cultures and languages? Can these theoretical frameworks account for variations in developmental trajectories? Byram's (1997) *savoirs* resonated with the journeys of the young women in my study and helped explain why some became more effective intercultural speakers and mediators. I also found that Deardorff's (2004) process model of intercultural communicative competence partially accounted for the intercultural development of my students. Further, the skills and attributes identified by Chen and Starosta (2008) and Hunter (2004) as paramount for globally competent, intercultural communicators were present in the sojourners who possessed an ethnorelative mindset. Finally, the DMIS proved very helpful in understanding the connection between intercultural sensitivity and an individual's awareness of and respect for cultural differences, as measured by the IDI. No single model, however, accounts for the language and cultural learning and identity reconstruction of L2 sojourners. None fully explains the trajectories of those who cross cultures. Our understanding of intercultural communicative competence must continue to evolve as we learn more about the interplay between internal and external elements in intercultural communicative events, both on home soil and abroad.

Additional ethnographic research is needed in a variety of contexts to refine current models of intercultural communicative competence (or create new ones) and more fully explore factors that can affect the language and (inter)cultural development and self-identity of L2 sojourners. Comparative studies, with both qualitative and quantitative data, should also help us better understand the impact of specific program elements, including the nature and form of presojourn preparation (e.g., ethnographic training, intercultural communication courses), sojourn duration, living arrangements during the stay abroad (e.g., homestay, campus residence, shared lodgings with host nationals or international exchange students), mixed classes or intact-group instruction in the host culture, experiential program elements (e.g., ethnographic research projects), debriefings (the promotion of critical reflection), diary-writing, and reentry programming (e.g., sojourner reflection on gains and weaknesses).

In this age of increased global "webs of interconnection" (Inda and Rosaldo, 2006), it is imperative that interculturalists, applied linguists, and study abroad researchers explore the most effective means to propel students toward higher levels of intercultural sensitivity, global competency, and sociopragmatic awareness, both at home and abroad. In today's diverse, ever-changing world, intercultural competence is as important as L2 proficiency and one cannot assume that they will develop simultaneously. As educators, we have the potential and responsibility to empower L2 students to become adept, sensitive global citizens and professionals. Chapter 8 explores practical ways in which international administrators, educators, and study abroad professionals can make a difference.

8
Cultivating Global and Intercultural Competencies

This concluding chapter addresses the practical implications of my findings for the internationalization of campuses and the preparation of "globally competent" graduates.[1] In particular, I focus on the design, delivery, and documentation of study abroad programs for L2 learners. Drawing on the case studies presented in Chapters 4–6 and the theories discussed in Chapters 1, 2, and 7, I suggest concrete steps that can be taken to enhance the global and intercultural competencies of students, both on home soil and abroad.

More specifically, I offer suggestions for the presojourn preparation of student sojourners, ongoing support during the stay abroad, and the reentry phase. Most of the presojourn elements are also relevant for those who remain on campus and forgo participation in a study abroad program. They, too, can experience gains in intercultural communicative competence and develop a more ethnorelative, global mindset through intercultural education, experiential learning (e.g., purposeful contact across cultures), and critical reflection on contact across cultures. This chapter aims to stimulate Internationalization at Home (IaH) initiatives and enhance study abroad programming. In keeping with today's emphasis on outcomes-based assessment and accountability in higher education, I discuss ways to document student learning and provide evidence of successful internationalization efforts.

Establishing program aims and learning outcomes: An integrative approach

As a starting point for any internationalization scheme, program organizers need to address the following questions: What competencies (e.g., linguistic, global, academic, personal) are essential for students to become successful in today's complex globalizing world? What elements should be included in a comprehensive internationalization plan? If study abroad will feature in the scheme, additional questions need to be asked, such as: What are the goals of study abroad? How can educators maximize learning on stays abroad? How can study abroad be integrated into the undergraduate curriculum?

Administrators and faculty engaged in the process of internationalization and outcomes-based assessment may consult Green and Olson (2003) and Olson et al. (2005, 2006) for sample lists of international/intercultural competencies that can easily be tailored to meet the needs of individual institutions and students. While not specifically designed for L2 professionals, these resources helped me to shape the learning outcomes for the study abroad program described in this book.

Documenting student learning: From needs analysis to program outcomes

As a starting point, a thorough needs analysis is vital to provide core information for program planners charged with internationalizing higher education. In addition to reviewing relevant literature in this field, it is important to gain an understanding of the specific needs, interests, desires, and concerns of students and faculty in order to develop international programs and courses that are meaningful and, potentially, transformative.

Outcomes-based assessment can assist institutions in articulating learning outcomes for students and provide direction for the design and delivery of appropriate curricula, pedagogy, and modes of assessment. As learning involves an ongoing process, data should be gathered throughout a program and not be limited to pre- and postmeasures. In the case of study abroad programs, educators may be tempted to apply a single measure to assess student learning (e.g., a language proficiency test) but this is woefully inadequate. It cannot possibly capture the holistic nature of language and culture learning, which includes both formal and informal elements. How, then, can educators enhance current and future programming *and* provide compelling evidence of student growth that can satisfy administrators? Multiple assessment methods (e.g., a range of qualitative and quantitative measures) are needed to track student learning, both in and outside the classroom.

A portfolio approach

To determine the effectiveness of internationalization efforts (e.g., study abroad) and chronicle student development some institutions are now employing a portfolio approach. From their entry into a program until their exit, students can be encouraged to keep track of their learning by way of written, audio, visual, and/or electronic means. Portfolios typically include a personal development plan (e.g., specific objectives for learning) and a focused selection of work accompanied by a reflective commentary (Jacobson, Sleicher, and Burke, 1999; Moon, 2006). The material that students submit may be very diverse and consist of such items as narrative accounts of language and cultural learning, photos of sojourn experiences, illustrations of cultural scenes, personal reflections (e.g., diaries, journals, poems), project work (e.g., pragmatic ethnographies), reports, videos (e.g., the sharing of sojourn experiences after reentry), and audiotapes (e.g., intercultural conversations/interviews).

A portfolio approach not only provides useful data for administrators, it affords educators a window into the learning process. As Steinberg (2007: 15) explains, portfolios have numerous benefits: "students choose what to include, incorporate personal reflections on their work, and become personally conscious of their own academic growth. Portfolios also provide a medium for continued feedback to students." I've also found them to be quite versatile as multiple types of data can be used to develop a holistic picture of the study abroad experience. A significant limitation of this approach, however, is that it is labor intensive. Moreover, the evaluation of portfolios requires training to ensure that the same rubric is applied systematically to all submissions. In formal reviews of programs with large numbers of participants, a sample of student portfolios may be scrutinized by an evaluation team.

Instrumentation

After program planners agree on what it means to be globally and interculturally competent, they can then select appropriate methods and instruments to measure outcomes. Early on, it can be very useful to gather data about such aspects as the participants' level of intercultural sensitivity/competence, L2 use and proficiency (e.g., sociopragmatic awareness), degree of intercultural contact, attitudes toward their own and other cultures, self-identity, and global awareness, among others. If the program includes a study abroad component, educators should also determine the students' preparedness for life in another linguistic and cultural environment. This is essential to develop predeparture materials and activities that address student needs and interests.

In the beginning of a program, surveys can gather data to guide the selection and sequencing of appropriate materials and activities. The following section reviews instruments that provide information about the linguistic/intercultural communicative competence or global competencies of students; most may be administered at strategic intervals to track student learning (e.g., before a program gets underway, after presojourn preparation, midway through a long-term sojourn, immediately postsojourn, six months or a year postsojourn). The findings can suggest interventions that could be made to enhance student learning. An additional benefit of the process of survey writing is that it can heighten students' awareness of their language and (inter)cultural learning and stimulate deeper levels of reflection. Program organizers and administrations may also make use of the data to provide an indication of program effectiveness.

Tools to measure language learning

To gain a deeper understanding of my students' language use and perceived ability, I employ a modified version of the *Entrance Language Contact Profile*, originally developed by Freed, Dewey, Segalowitz, and Halter (2004) and later revised by Cohen, Paige, Shively, Emert, and Hoff (2005). This survey elicits information that is useful for program design and helps students set targets for their learning in the host culture. For study abroad returnees, I administer a modified version of the *Exit Language Contact Profile* developed by Freed et al. (2004) and modified by Cohen et al. (2005). By comparing the results with their *Entrance Language Contact Profile*, I can identify changes in the students' language usage and perceived ability. This data can then be incorporated into program evaluation reports.

To provide a measure of language competency, proficiency tests may play a role but it is essential to select one that is appropriate for the students and their learning situation (e.g., taking into account sojourn duration, the degree of exposure to informal/formal host language). The Simulated Oral Proficiency Interview (SOPI) is a performance-based, tape-mediated test that is often used in study abroad programs to measure speaking proficiency in a variety of foreign languages (e.g., French, Spanish, German). Along with the ACTFL Oral Proficiency Interview, the SOPI can provide pre- and postmeasures of the oral skills of long-term sojourners (e.g., those in semester- or year-long study abroad programs).

In a short-term sojourn that emphasizes informal interaction in the host culture more than formal language lessons, tests designed to measure academic language proficiency (e.g., IELTS, TOEFL®iBT) are inappropriate. Instead, it is more realistic to expect students to develop a broader, more positive perception of the host language and become more willing to use it in a range of domains, including informal, social situations. While administrators may request pre- and post-language proficiency tests to measure the "success" of a program, it is incumbent upon organizers to state a case for more holistic approaches to assessment (e.g., the use of portfolios).

Prior to a sojourn, Discourse Completion Tests (DCTs) may be used to gain insight into students' awareness of culturally appropriate behavior in the host culture. For the SES, I developed a DCT to assess my students' pragmatic ability before and after their stay in England. I focused on requests, refusals, and apologies, as these are common speech acts that my students require in the host culture. All of the scenarios are based on real events involving previous SES sojourners (e.g., host–sojourner interaction). After entering the program, my students read the short scenarios and write down what they think they would say if they were in that situation. Their responses provide an indication of their level of intercultural sensitivity and suggest discourse strategies that should be addressed prior to departure. This is especially important for advanced L2 learners as host nationals often expect more "appropriate" behavior from them, unaware that their language use prior to the sojourn may have largely been limited to formal, academic situations.

Cohen and Shively (2002) also advocate incorporating a sociopragmatics element into the presojourn preparation of L2 students. They developed the *Speech Act Measure*, an indirect assessment of oral pragmatic ability that is in the form of a multiple-rejoinder DCT. It consists of 10 short descriptions of social situations with a prompt for the respondent to perform a particular speech act (apologizing or requesting) by filling in the blanks of a dialogue. Similar to my DCT, it provides an indication of what a student might say in a similar situation.

As part of the *Maximizing Study Abroad through Language and Culture Strategies* research project, resource materials have been developed for three audiences: study abroad students, study abroad program professionals, and language instructors (Cohen et al., 2005). The *Learning Style Survey: Assessing your own Learning Styles* and the *Language Strategy Use Inventory* (Paige, Cohen, Kappler, Chi, and Lassegard, 2006) can be used to gather valuable information for program organizers and, at the same time, help students become more self-aware and systematic language and culture learners.

Tools to measure intercultural and global awareness

One of the most widely used instruments in intercultural training and research is the *Intercultural Development Inventory* (IDI),[2] which is linked to the Developmental Model of Intercultural Sensitivity (DMIS) that was discussed in Chapters 2 and 7. As in the present study, this 50-item survey can be administered at strategic intervals to measure the respondent's intercultural development through ethnocentric and ethnorelative stages (see Table 3.2 for descriptions of the IDI scales). Further, Hammer (1999: 62–3) explains that the IDI can be used "to increase the respondents' understanding of the developmental stages of intercultural sensitivity which enhance intercultural effectiveness ... to evaluate the effectiveness of various training, counseling, and education interventions ... [as] a feedback instrument ... [and] to identify cross-cultural training needs of targeted individuals and groups."

The *Cross-Cultural Adaptability Inventory* (CCAI) (Kelley and Meyers, 1999) is designed as a training tool for intercultural communication programs. I have used it in the needs analysis phase of the SES to assess my students' readiness for residence abroad. The results help me to pinpoint areas that merit attention in the presojourn phase (e.g., lack of awareness of strategies that can ease culture shock). It consists of 50 statements which measure four personal characteristics that have been found to be critical in adapting to other cultures: emotional resilience, flexibility and openness, perceptual acuity (the skills needed to recognize and make sense of cultural cues), and personal autonomy (degree of confidence in one's identity, values, and beliefs and respect for others and their value systems). This self-assessment instrument identifies strengths and weaknesses in intercultural communication skills, raises awareness of potential stressors in the host culture, and prompts individual goal-setting for study abroad. The CCAI Action-Planning Guide (Kelley and Meyers, 1992) facilitates the interpretation of scores and suggests ways respondents can strengthen their intercultural communication skills and cross-cultural adaptability.

Another instrument that I have found to be very effective with study abroad students is the *Culture-Learning Strategies Inventory* (Paige et al., 2006: 29–34). It can raise students' awareness of the knowledge and skills needed to function well in a new environment; at the same time, the findings alert facilitators to aspects that merit attention in the presojourn phase. It consists of 60 items conceptually organized into the following culture-learning categories: adapting to culturally different environs, culture shock/coping strategies, interpreting culture, communicating across cultures, communication styles, nonverbal communication, interacting with culturally different people, homestay strategies, and reentry strategies.

Several instruments have also been developed to measure global awareness and world-mindedness (e.g., The Cross-Cultural World Mindedness Scale by Der-Karabetian, 1992; the Global Awareness Profile (GAPtest) by Corbitt, 1998). As most have been designed with American students in mind, they need to be tested in other contexts with other populations to determine their usefulness. For a list of additional instruments designed to assess global and intercultural competencies and identity development, readers may consult Fantini (2007), Paige (2004), Paige and Stallman (2007), or Stuart (2007).

Presojourn elements at the home institution

As noted in Chapters 2 and 7, intercultural communicative competence is a complex construct that involves multiple components or *savoirs* (e.g., Byram, 1997; Chen and Starosta, 2008; Deardorff, 2006, 2008, 2009). Once program outcomes have been identified, internationalization strategies can nurture these elements in a variety of creative ways (e.g., through coursework in intercultural communication, the organization of campus activities that promote interaction between students from diverse cultural backgrounds, study abroad). Well-designed programs can help students develop the knowledge and skills necessary to make sense of their intercultural encounters. With support and guidance, they can develop a deeper awareness of the impact of their value judgments and behavior (e.g., linguistic, nonverbal) on the communication process and become more competent, mindful "intercultural mediators."

The following section describes a range of practices that can stimulate intercultural communicative competence and global awareness in students on their home campus. While some elements are specifically designed to prepare individuals for study abroad (e.g., homestay life), the majority are equally applicable to those who experience intercultural contact solely in their home environment (e.g., face-to-face, on the Internet). By developing more understanding of, and respect for, other cultures, students may begin to contemplate new possibilities for their life (e.g., intercultural friendships, travel or work outside their home country, study and residence abroad).

Intercultural communication course

In any comprehensive Internationalization at Home (IaH) program, an intercultural communication course is essential. It may be either culture-general (e.g., preparation for life in a multicultural society or study abroad, regardless of destination) or culture-specific (e.g., a predeparture program for Irish students who will participate in a study abroad program in Portugal). Courses of this nature emphasize the application of intercultural communication theories to practical communication problems that can occur when people from different cultures interact (Fowler and Blohm, 2004; Pusch, 2004). By understanding how differences in culture, attitudes, and values affect behavior, students can develop an intellectual framework to make sense of intercultural encounters. As noted in Chapter 2, it is important to avoid homogenizing portrayals of "culture as nationality" (Dervin, 2006; Moon, 2008) and raise students' awareness and appreciation of diversity within and across cultures. Educators can also help students recognize similarities between people from different cultural backgrounds.

Instead of limiting a course to the dissemination of facts and theories, I advocate an experiential approach, drawing on the work of such scholars as Kolb (1984), Kohls and Brussow (1995), and Landis, Bennett, and Bennett (2004). This mode of teaching focuses on the process of learning and encourages participants to assume some responsibility for their own development, beginning with their needs and goals. Educators prompt students to "learn by exploration and discovery, asking questions, formulating and testing hypotheses, solving problems" (Kohls and Brussow, 1995: 5). A range of interactive activities and tasks may stimulate intercultural learning, including observation and analysis of videotapes, small group discussions, dialogue journals, the analysis of cases (problem-based narratives involving intercultural encounters) and critical incidents, simulations, and groupwork (e.g., an ethnographic research project, participation in ethnocultural organizations).

Early in the program the IDI can be administered to assess each student's developmental stage in terms of intercultural sensitivity. The scores can provide a profile of a group of learners so that the curriculum can be tailored to address issues relevant to them. To facilitate this, J. M. Bennett (2004) and Bennett and Bennett (2004a) have developed a range of activities for each stage of development in the DMIS. This careful sequencing of content and pedagogy is critical as "premature challenge for those in ethnocentric stages" can lead to resentment and rejection of different ways of being.

Language and cultural identity narrative

Before delving very far into intercultural communication theories, facilitators need to have an understanding of their students' background, self-identity, degree of intercultural contact, travel experience, and learning goals. The first assignment in my intercultural communication course raises the students' awareness of themselves as cultural beings and helps me to understand their unique journeys. It entails the writing of a personal, descriptive, and analytical narrative in which the students describe their cultural background, socialization, language use, and identity development. With guiding questions, I encourage them to reflect on ways in which messages from their family and society have influenced their communication style (verbal and nonverbal), the way they relate to people from other cultures, their selection of friends, their self-construal, and their affiliation with particular groups (e.g., religious, linguistic, national, ethnic, global). I prompt them to reflect on events or encounters that have caused them to think about or question their identity (e.g., intercultural contact, historical events).

As language, culture, and identity are closely intertwined, I include guiding questions to prompt students to explore their language choices and feelings associated with each language they speak. Sample questions include: What are the connections between your languages and your most important relationships? What experiences in your home, school, or elsewhere have been important in framing your attitudes toward your languages? Do you feel differently when you speak different languages? Do you think of yourself as belonging to particular religious, ethnic, or linguistic groups? How does this impact on your sense of self?

Promoting intercultural contact on campus

Learning about other cultures through lectures, books, and the media is valuable, but knowledge alone does not guarantee interculturality. Educators can take steps to promote intercultural contact by devising meaningful tasks that require sustained interaction and analysis. At the same time, it is important to bear in mind that without this element of critical reflection, real-time experience of crossing cultures may not necessarily result in empathy and enhanced intercultural understanding.

Over the years I have employed a range of strategies to promote linkages between local students and those on exchange. First, I make use of our International Student Society to match up the local students in my intercultural communication course with international exchange students. I also build tasks into my course that require purposeful interaction throughout the semester. For example, my students conduct a series of interviews (or conversations) with their "international partner" to gain a deeper understanding of a cultural topic (e.g., culture shock and adjustment) and then write about their experiences in journal entries. In some offerings of this course, the students work in pairs to carry out a more in-depth investigation of a cultural issue with their "international partner" (e.g., dating practices). They then write a report and share their findings in a presentation to the class or smaller group. Aided by prompts, the students reflect on the communication process and the challenges and successes they have experienced when interacting with their international partner. Through small group discussions and collaborative project work, I also facilitate interaction between local students and any international exchange students who have enrolled in the course; this provides them with opportunities to discover common ground as well as cultural or individual differences.

Intercultural contact exposes local students to other worldviews and communication styles, affords them real-life experiences with intercultural relationship building, and has the potential to stimulate deeper levels of awareness of Self and Other, or what Byram (1997) refers to as *savoirs*. For local students who will participate in a study abroad program, this contact can be helpful in additional ways; it can offer insight into the adjustment process and suggest ways to enhance their own language and culture learning. Further, local students who may initially have been afraid of "outsiders" and never seriously considered traveling or studying abroad may become interested in the lives of their international partners. Some may be inspired to study in their partner's home country or elsewhere.

International exchange students can also benefit from having local "cultural informants" from their own age group. Without this direct link to the local culture, some may restrict themselves to formal classroom settings and spend all of their free time with other international students from their home country. By setting up tasks that require sustained contact over a three to four month period, the partners have the opportunity to cultivate a relationship that goes well beyond the parameters of the assignment. For example, local students may invite international students to their homes or favorite "hang-outs" (e.g., karaoke clubs) and introduce them to other friends, widening the exposure that the international students have to locals and informal cultural scenes. In some cases, genuine friendships have developed in my course and local students have taken their international partners to the Mainland to take part in Lunar New Year festivities in their family's ancestral hometown.

Intercultural reflections journal

Throughout the course, students may also be required to keep a journal to record such aspects as their reactions to readings, videos, simulations, cases, critical incidents, class discussions, and their own intercultural contact. This learning log can serve as a useful vehicle for reflection and enhance personal and intercultural understandings. The act of writing and reviewing one's entries can prompt students to reflect more deeply on their intercultural beliefs and practices.

Journal-writing can take many forms: collaborative or dialogue journals (e.g., written conversations between teachers and students or student–student exchanges), learning logs (student reflections on their experiences and subsequent development), e-journals (electronic journals which allow writers to share their entries with each other by way of an Internet webpage), split-page or double-entry journals (e.g., one side of the page recounts intercultural events; the other is reserved for interpretation/reactions) (Berwick and Whalley, 2000; Chisholm, 2000; Moon, 2006).

As many students may be new to introspective writing, I have found it helpful to provide guidelines to encourage entries that are descriptive, personal, and thoughtfully analytical. At the beginning of the intercultural communication course, I provide my students with a set of optional, guiding questions to stimulate thought and reflection; I also encourage them to write about other issues in intercultural communication that interest them, including their own intercultural experiences. Their entries provide a focus for small group discussions and offer insight into their intercultural learning. For those who will participate in a study abroad program, journal-writing in the presojourn phase serves as valuable groundwork for diary-writing during their stay abroad.

Critical incidents across cultures

For the past 40 years, critical incidents have been used as a tool to stimulate intercultural awareness. Wight (1995: 128) offers the following definition that is particularly relevant for internationalization programs:

> Critical incidents used in cross-cultural training are brief descriptions of situations in which there is a misunderstanding, problem or conflict arising from cultural differences between interacting parties or where there is a problem of cross-cultural adaptation. Each incident gives only enough information to set the stage, describe what happened, and possibly provide the feelings and reactions of the parties involved. It does not explain the cultural differences that the parties

bring to the situation. These are discovered or revealed as a part of the exercise.

To prepare material of this nature, I have found it useful to bear in mind the advice offered by Wang, Brislin, Wang, Williams, and Chao (2000: 8): "The best critical incidents capture an important concept that is useful when thinking about, adjusting to, and interacting in other cultures. ... The combination of a concept and a compelling example is more likely to be remembered than is either element by itself."

In my intercultural communication course I use culture-general critical incidents to raise awareness of aspects that may complicate communication across cultures (e.g., conflicting values, differing concepts of friendship). For predeparture study abroad students, I have developed culture-specific scenarios to depict situations and issues that they may face in the host environment (e.g., in homestay situations). For example, those who travel to England read reality-based incidents that recount misunderstandings between English host families and Hong Kong Chinese sojourners (e.g., differing beliefs about health and wellness) and then discuss/critique possible explanations for each. This activity provides them with virtual experiences in the host culture and raises their awareness of their attitudes and potential reactions in similar situations. Further, this process stimulates critical reflection on ways to enhance host–sojourner relationships and better handle similar incidents in real life.

Pragmatic "home ethnography" projects

The use of ethnography with long-term study abroad students is well documented (Jurasek, Lamson, and O'Maley, 2002; Roberts et al., 2001). As discussed in Chapter 3, I have also found it useful for short-term sojourners, provided there is ample guidance. This experiential mode of learning can help students become more systematic language and cultural learners. It is not intended to transform them into professional ethnographers, as Barro, Jordan, and Roberts (1998: 97) explain:

> The students are not intending to become specialists in social anthropology. They are language students who, we hope, will become even better language students as a result of living the ethnographic life. ... They need the cultural roots for making sense of new intercultural contacts and experiences rather than positivistic facts about other countries, structures and systems which are, despite the text-books'

attempts to freeze-dry them and turn them into fresh-looking, digestible items of information, constantly in a process of contestation and change.

In this approach, students are introduced to the methods of ethnographic exploration (e.g., participant observation, interviewing, note-taking, the recording and analysis of ethnographic conversations/events) and related issues (e.g., ethics, gaining access to cultural scenes). Students may then carry out a series of skill-building tasks and share their findings with each other. Postactivity debriefing is important to raise awareness of potential challenges with this mode of research and focus attention on ways to overcome difficulties. They are then better prepared to undertake their own small-scale project or what Roberts et al. (2001) refer to as a "home ethnography." Damen (1987) uses the term "pragmatic ethnography" to stress the "personal and practical" nature of the project and distinguish it from the theory-building work of professional ethnographers.

Focused training and fieldwork in the home environment have the potential to facilitate communication across cultures. Corbett (2003: 116) points out that "ethnographic observations can be linked to ways of managing intercultural clashes, and the fostering of mediation skills." As learners develop more sophisticated language- and culture-learning strategies, they can become more efficient learners, gain in self-confidence, and display more awareness of the world around them. The expectation is that these ethnographic skills, learning strategies, and new understandings can prepare them to be "languagers" or "language activists" (Phipps, 2006) in diverse linguistic and cultural settings. Prior to their sojourn, my students have explored such diverse topics as the intercultural adjustment and personal transformation of Mainland students in Hong Kong, the daily life of Filipino domestic helpers, SMS (short message service) communication among university students in Hong Kong, interaction in single-sex schools, and reentry culture shock. Their small-scale ethnographic projects have served as essential groundwork for their research in England and encouraged them to be more fully engaged in the host culture.

Languaculture preparation

Much has been written about the connection between language and culture (e.g., Byram, 1997; Kramsch, 1993; Paige and Lange, 2003; Risager, 2006, 2007). Within the framework of internationalization, we cannot overlook the intercultural dimension in L2 instruction. This is important to avoid what Bennett (1997) refers to rather bluntly as the "fluent fool syndrome," whereby a speaker may understand the grammar in the host language but demonstrate little or no awareness of sociopragmatic norms and behaviors in the host culture and find it difficult to communicate effectively and appropriately across cultures.

Maximizing Study Abroad: A Language Instructor's Guide to Strategies for Language and Culture Learning and Use (Cohen, Paige, Kappler, Demmessie, Weaver, Chi, and Lassegard, 2003) offers suggestions for language instructors to help integrate intercultural communication concepts into L2 courses. As well as language learning strategies, language teachers may incorporate sociopragmatics awareness-raising activities into lessons through role plays and DCTs (Cohen and Shively, 2002; House, 2003; Jackson, 2008; Rose and Kasper, 2001).

Study abroad orientation

For students bound for study abroad, an intercultural communication course can provide a solid foundation to help them make sense of their experiences as they cross cultures. Discussion may focus on such issues as culture shock and cross-cultural adjustment, the acculturation process, language- and culture-learning strategies, expectations and goal-setting, identity development and change, health and safety, and preparation for reentry (Thebodo and Marx, 2005; Spencer and Tuma, 2008). This goes well beyond brief predeparture sessions that focus solely on logistics (e.g., banking arrangements, housing, safety, transport).

If groups will travel to the same destination, country-specific information (e.g., history, religion, customs, food, education, popular pastimes) can be included in their preparation. As they prepare for the challenges of living in another culture, students can learn more about themselves and the host culture (Hoff and Kappler, 2005; Littrell and Salas, 2005; Thebodo and Marx, 2005). For those who will live in a homestay, special elements should be incorporated into the orientation that deal with such issues as the aims of these living arrangements, the roles and responsibilities of hosts and "guests," and ways to nurture host–sojourner relationships.

In this predeparture phase, students should also be encouraged to reflect on their expectations and aspirations for their stay abroad. Facilitators can help students set targets that are realistic and concrete (e.g., language learning objectives linked to exposure to informal, social situations in the host language). Survey instruments such as the CCAI and Culture Learning Strategies Inventory can be administered early in the predeparture program to draw attention to areas (personal, linguistic, cultural, academic) that students need to work on to achieve their learning objectives.

Sojourn

How can L2 students who join study abroad programs maximize their learning during their stay in the host culture? What elements of a program can stimulate personal development and the acquisition of global and intercultural competencies? The following sections present a variety of approaches and tasks that I have found useful for students who participate in faculty-led[3] short-term sojourns in the host culture. Much of the advice should be relevant to longer-term sojourners (e.g., L2 students who participate in semester- or year-long stays abroad).

Living the ethnographic life

Sojourners who have received ethnographic training in their home environment may investigate a cultural scene of their choice in the host environment (e.g., engage in participant observation, audiotape ethnographic conversations/interviews, draw sketches of the scene, take photographs, keep detailed field notes). By developing a "thick, rich description" of the cultural scene and facilitating sustained conversations with "informants" from the host culture, they can become more involved in their new environment and, simultaneously, enhance their language and cultural learning and social skills, as Roberts et al. (2001: 237) explain:

> Language learners as ethnographers are inevitably engaged with the otherness of their new environment not just as an opportunity to improve linguistic competence and their ability to produce appropriate utterances, but as a whole social being who are developing, defining, and being defined in terms of their interactions with other social beings. As ethnographers and intercultural speakers, they negotiate a particular relationship with those around them, a relationship traditionally described as participant observation, although this fails to capture the complexity of the reflexive effect on the linguist-ethnographer.

For this approach to be effective, however, the students must be adequately prepared (e.g., through a series of tasks and "home ethnography" project) and have sufficient on-site support and guidance from a qualified mentor. This is especially important in short-term sojourns as time constraints require the students to identify a topic, develop rapport with informants, and gather sufficient data in a very efficient manner. In the last few years I have supervised the ethnographic research projects of nearly 100 Hong Kong short-term sojourners in England. They have explored such diverse topics as interaction in car boot sales, the role of pets in English homes, charity shops, the roles of host families, and life in a retirement home. In most cases, project work has provided the students with more exposure to the host language in a variety of communities of practice and helped them develop closer ties across cultures.

Diaries

To maximize the sojourn experience, it is important for students to record their thoughts and emotions in a diary. Through the process of articulating and critically reflecting on their experiences, they can become attuned to their surroundings, their positioning in the new environment, and the role they are playing in determining the outcomes of intercultural encounters. With a reflective mindset, they can deepen their awareness of their progress (e.g., academic, linguistic, cultural, personal), including their strengths and limitations. This should facilitate more realistic goal-setting and stimulate further learning.

In the study abroad program that is featured in this book, the students keep a reflective diary in which they record their reactions to experiences in the host culture that they found interesting, puzzling, irritating, or otherwise significant, including their ethnographic data collection (e.g., relationship building with informants from another culture). I encourage them to provide sufficient details to contextualize their "stories" and short narratives. They may also write short poems and use metaphors to capture their emotions. Although they've already had the experience of keeping a culture-learning journal, I still find it helpful to provide questions to stimulate reflection, especially in the early stage of the sojourn. Sample prompts are: Think about the values, beliefs and identities that you held before traveling to England. Compare that person with the person you are now. Have you changed in any way? If yes, how?

I encourage the students to write an entry on the day of departure and then several times a week during their stay. Regular entries are crucial as it is very difficult to recollect events in vivid detail if there is a delay in putting pen to paper. To capture their emotions on reentry and stimulate further reflection on what they have gained from their stay abroad, the students write several entries once they are back home and have had some time to reflect on their overall experiences. They date each entry in their diary and use subheadings to capture the theme or topic of each entry. After their return home, they have several weeks to type their diary and e-mail me the file. Some students insert digital images or graphics to complement their narratives. Their diaries provide valuable insight into their language and (inter)cultural learning and adjustment processes. An additional benefit is that the students have a permanent record of their journey.

E-journals and blogs (web logs)

In lieu of traditional paper-based diaries, students may keep an electronic journal (e-journal), which can facilitate the sharing of experiences during the period abroad. A format that is likely to grow in popularity in the near future is blogs. A World Wide Web log or blog, as Moon (2006: 55) explains, is "an internet site on which the written work and editing work of an individual or group is managed through a web browser." She states further that "a blog may be added to at different times or by different people within a pre-determined group, and it is organized by the dates of the additions" (ibid.: 55–6). This method of writing journals or diaries can provide a public vehicle for students to share their sojourn and reentry experiences. They can post digital images and include detailed accounts of their encounters across cultures and reactions to them. Their travel blogs (illustrated, narrated journeys of discovery) can provide future sojourners with insight into the challenges and pleasures of crossing cultures. On *www.BlogAbroad.com*, for example, sojourners can create an account and write their own blog as well as access and respond to other bloggers.

Regular debriefings

While in the host environment, regular debriefing sessions and socio-emotional support are essential to stimulate deeper, critical reflection and promote sustained intercultural contact. Students who are suffering from culture shock and identity confusion may discover that others are experiencing similar symptoms. By sharing experiences with their peers and a sympathetic, supportive facilitator, they can address issues that are troubling or confusing and discuss strategies that can help them move forward to make the most of their stay in a more positive frame of mind. This is one of the most important elements in a program and yet it is often overlooked.

Surveys

At regular intervals (e.g., on a weekly basis in short-term sojourns, on a bi-weekly or monthly basis on longer-term stays), open-ended surveys may be used to stimulate deeper reflection and personal growth. Questions can be designed to encourage students to be more observant of their new world, their positioning, and the state of their intercultural communicative competence. Periodically, they should be encouraged to revisit the learning objectives they set prior to the sojourn. They can then make adjustments as they become more familiar with linguistic and cultural affordances (and restrictions) in their new environment.

Survey results can alert program organizers to adjustment issues and difficulties that merit attention in homestay situations. I have found, for example, that some students are more willing to share their feelings in a survey rather than verbally report difficulties to the on-site homestay coordinator, who is not yet familiar to them. Issues can then be dealt with in a timely manner and, in some cases, concerns shared by many members of the group may be addressed in a debriefing session.

Preparation for reentry

While programs may include a measure of preparation for culture shock in the host environment, an area that is still largely neglected is reentry (reverse) culture shock. If sojourners have not given any thought to reentry issues, even those who participated in short-term programs may be thrown off guard when they return home; much to their surprise, they may experience more malaise than when they traveled abroad. In particular, those who have fully immersed themselves in the host environment, developed strong ties across cultures, experimented with host culture norms/behaviors (e.g., communication styles, values), and acquired a broader, more inclusive, global identity may experience significant readjustment woes. After the initial excitement of seeing familiar faces and places has worn off, depression may set in as those around them lose interest in their sojourn tales and have little understanding of their transformation. In sum, returnees may feel a sense of loss, suffer from identity disequilibrium, and find it difficult to reconnect with friends and family.

Before leaving the host culture, steps can be taken to reduce the negative impact of reentry culture shock. Students can discuss critical incidents that depict typical reentry problems and complete surveys that stimulate reflection on what may lie ahead. Sharing sessions can explore ways to maintain contact with the host culture and language while reestablishing bonds with old friends and family. They can also reflect on ways to nurture their increased independence, global self, and any new interests they've acquired abroad (e.g., love of travel, photography).

Postsojourn

The development of intercultural communicative competence and world-mindedness involves a lifelong process and should not be limited to stays abroad. To maximize the sojourn experience and promote further learning, home institutions should provide opportunities for returnees to make sense of their discoveries and extend their learning. Further, opportunities should be created for returnees to share their new understandings with others (e.g., students who will soon embark on their own study abroad journey).

Debriefing

Providing a safe, open environment to prompt contemplation of such issues as reentry culture shock, language use and choice, and identity reconstruction can enhance and sustain the emotional and psychological well-being of returnees. It can help them make sense of their experiences and encourage them to consider its impact on their lives. During this phase, open-ended surveys, journal-writing, blogs, and discussions can prompt deeper reflection, encourage the setting of new aims for language and culture learning, and provide a focus for debriefing sessions.

Reentry courses

In a small number of institutions of higher education, credit-bearing reentry courses are now being offered to address the needs of returnees (e.g., Saint Mary's College in Notre Dame, Indiana; the University of Minnesota; Duke University in the US). This is a promising development. Recognizing the potentially transformative nature of stays abroad, these courses are designed to spur deeper reflection on sojourn experiences and repatriation. Consequently, they address the affective and behavioral changes students may experience during intercultural transitions. Course content may include intercultural communication theories, models of culture shock and adjustment, readjustment issues, and identity development models (Hoff and Kappler, 2005; Johnson, 2002; Martin and Harrell, 2004; Meyer-Lee, 2005; Spencer and Tuma, 2008; Thebodo and Marx, 2005).

Courses of this nature may incorporate a variety of activities into curricula to promote self-reflection and analysis (e.g., the writing of introspective, narrative accounts of the impact of the sojourn and/or the reentry process; small group problem-solving sessions and discussions; reentry hypermedia blogging; individual or group written or video projects, presentations or poster sessions designed to prepare others for study abroad). Returnees with a positive, open mindset can be valuable resources for those who are considering joining a study abroad program. Campus webpages may also document student learning on stays abroad and motivate others to travel abroad.

Conclusions

Most educators today agree that an undergraduate education should ready students for the challenges of life in an increasingly interdependent world where national borders are permeable and communities are increasingly diverse. How might interculturality be promoted in practice? How can faculty and students become more intercultural? After establishing clear targets for internationalization, institutions of higher education can provide a variety of experiences on campus to promote global and intercultural learning (e.g., offer intercultural communication courses, promote L2 learning, initiate and support international student organizations, develop internationalized curricula and programs, support faculty research in international education, encourage faculty exchange programs). Institutions can also significantly increase opportunities for study abroad (e.g., faculty-led short-term sojourns, semester- or year-long exchanges, internships, service learning) and fully integrate these experiences into curricula on the home campus.

Study abroad, in particular, is widely believed to provide significant benefits to students through increased proficiency in the host language, enhanced understanding of, and respect for, other cultures, and deeper levels of self-awareness and self-efficacy, among others. However, residing in the host culture temporarily, whether for five weeks or a year, does not ensure interculturality. Mastering the grammar of the host language does not necessarily lead to intercultural sensitivity and the enhancement of intercultural communicative competence. On a similar vein, studying intercultural communication theories does not guarantee that one will become an effective intercultural speaker or mediator. Intercultural and global learning is a process that students need to work on before, during, and after a study abroad experience, no matter the length of the sojourn. It entails a lifelong journey.

What then is the potential of a short-term sojourn? A well-designed program that stimulates deep, critical reflection may enhance students' understanding of the host culture and suggest new possibilities for their life (e.g., participation in a longer-term sojourn, postgraduate studies or work abroad, independent travel, intercultural friendships). Comprehensive presojourn preparation, ethnographic training and fieldwork (or other forms of experiential learning), and surveys that promote critical reflection can accelerate language and cultural learning and play a key role in determining sojourn outcomes. If the journey toward ethnorelativism and interculturality is to continue after the return home, adequate postsojourn debriefing must be provided. Further, institutions must create opportunities for returnees to share their experiences with others to fully maximize the benefits of their stay abroad.

In this age of globalization, interculturalists, applied linguists, and study abroad researchers must continue to explore the most effective means to promote interculturality in L2 learners, both at home and abroad. In today's complex, ever-changing world, intercultural competence is as important as L2 competence for responsible global citizens.

Notes

Preface

1. In faculty-led study abroad programs an instructor from the home institution accompanies a group of students during their stay abroad. In this model, the faculty member may liaise with host institution administrators and teach a course (e.g., cultural studies, ethnography, international business). Short-term programs, as defined by the Forum on Education glossary, last from four to seven weeks (Peterson et al. 2007).

1 Globalization, Internationalization, and Study Abroad

1. In his Concentric Circles Model, Kachru (1985: 12) distinguishes between the "the types of spread, the patterns of acquisition and the functional domains in which English is used across cultures and languages." In his *Inner Circle*, English is the primary language of the country (e.g., in Australia, Canada, the United States, the United Kingdom); in the *Outer Circle*, English is a second language (e.g., in multilingual countries like Singapore, India, and the Philippines); and in the *Expanding Circle*, English is studied as a foreign language (e.g., in China, Japan, Korea). "Due to changes in the use of English around the globe," McKay and Bokhorst-Heng (2008: 29–30) observe that "the lines separating these circles have become more permeable." Moreover, the number of speakers of English as an International Language in *Outer and Expanding Circle* countries now far outnumbers those in the *Inner Circle* (Kachru and Smith, 2008).
2. Code-switching refers to "instances when speakers switch between codes (languages, or language varieties) in the course of a conversation. Switches may involve different amounts of speech and different linguistic units – from several consecutive utterances to individual words and morphemes" (Swann et al., 2004: 40).
3. Code-mixing is "[t]he process whereby speakers indulge in code-switching between languages of such rapidity and density, even within sentences and phrases, that it is not really possible to say at any given time which language they are speaking" (Trudgill, 2003: 23).
4. EFL (English as a foreign language) learners typically study a variety of English that is linked to a country in what Kachru (1985) refers to as "the inner circle" (e.g., the UK, the US).
5. The teaching of English as an International Language (EIL) recognizes that mother-tongue varieties of English are not necessarily appropriate targets either for learning or for communication in countries where English is used for cross-cultural or cross-linguistic communication. For example, when a Korean and a Taiwanese use English to negotiate a business deal, the type of

English used will vary according to their mother tongue and the purposes of the interaction (McKay, 2002, 2004).

6. "To be globally literate means seeing, thinking, acting and mobilizing in interculturally mindful ways. It's the sum of the attitudes, beliefs, knowledge, skills, and behaviors needed for success in today's multicultural, global economy" (Rosen and Digh, 2001: 74).

7. The Bologna Process is linked to the Bologna Declaration, which was signed in 1999 by ministers of higher education from 29 European countries. At present, there are 46 European countries who are working together to create a European Higher Education Area that promotes international cooperation and quality-based academic exchange. The Bologna Process is bringing about significant reforms in higher education across Europe at system and institutional levels (see http://www.ond.vlaanderen.be/hogeronderwijs/bologna).

8. The transformational model adopted by the University of Minnesota (USA) to internationalize on-campus courses "emphasizes the importance of movement toward both reflexivity and intentionality" (O'Donovan and Mikelonis, 2005: 92). After creating a sense of community and trust, the facilitators raise the intercultural and global awareness of faculty through critical thinking activities and self-reflective exercises. With new insights and understandings, the participants design curricula that reflect diverse, international perspectives. Their globalized syllabi are then shared with colleagues at faculty gatherings.

9. In transnational education students study on home soil (even in their own home) and receive their degree (or other credential) from a foreign institution (Rauhvargers, 2001).

10. Since its inception in 1987, more than 1.5 million students have received ERASMUS (European Community Action Scheme for the Mobility of University Students) grants. This number is expected to rise to around 3 million by 2012 (Forrest, 2008).

11. International service-learning programs integrate academic study with substantive volunteer service (e.g., community development projects) to enhance the participants' (inter)cultural, personal, and academic growth.

2 Intercultural and Global Competencies

1. Acculturation refers to the degree of identity change and adaptation that occurs when individuals move from a familiar environment to an unfamiliar one and come into contact with another culture (Smith et al., 2006; Ting-Toomey and Chung, 2005).

2. Habitus from Pierre Bourdieu's perspective includes the "durable motivations, perceptions and forms of knowledge that people carry around in their heads as a result of living in particular social environments and that predispose them to act in certain ways" (Layder, 1997: 236).

3 Groundwork for the Illustrative Case Studies

1. Fishman (1965) extended the notion of diglossia to illustrate how speakers in a bilingual community may use certain languages in specific domains.

For example, one language (or form) may be used for education, politics, and commerce, while another for domestic and informal settings. While the former is deemed more prestigious, the other may be quite acceptable in the contexts in which it is used (e.g., Spanish is the "high" language in Paraguay and Guarani, the language of everyday life).

2. The People's Republic of China (PRC) is sometimes referred to as the "Motherland" in Hong Kong, particularly, by older Chinese residents who feel some attachment to their ancestral home. Prior to the colonization of Hong Kong by Britain, the territory was part of the PRC. On July 1, 1997, sovereignty over Hong Kong reverted from Britain to the PRC.

3. After the change in sovereignty, the slogan "Asia's world city" was adopted by the Hong Kong government to emphasize the city's position in the region.

4. English is the official medium of instruction at most tertiary institutions in Hong Kong, although Cantonese or code-mixing (English-Chinese) may be used in lectures and tutorials.

5. One female student, Nina (pseudonym), did not participate in the sojourn due to an illness in her family.

6. For interviews that took place in Cantonese, efforts were made to retain the nuances and emotions of the discourse in the English translation.

4 Presojourn Language and (Inter)Cultural Development

1. Pseudonyms are used for the four case participants. To preserve their anonymity, the case participants are not featured in the photo that appears on the cover of the book.

2. Presojourn oral and written narratives include an interview conducted in Cantonese or English (or code-mixing), depending on the preference of the interviewee, a letter of application to the SES, surveys with open-ended questions, a language and cultural identity narrative, and an intercultural reflections journal; all written narratives were produced in English.

3. Jade participated in a three-week long French immersion program in France during her first year of University. As a secondary school student, she joined two brief cultural exchange programs in Mainland China.

4. The scale for the self-ratings of language ability ranged from 1 = very poor to 6 = excellent.

5. Nora's somewhat contradictory comments raise our awareness of the need to consider the context, timeframe, and "linguistic, rhetorical, and interactional properties" of "discursive constructions" (Pavlenko, 2007: 180–1); when analyzing sojourner narratives, whenever possible, it is best to include the element of triangulation (e.g., data from multiple sources).

5 Nora and Mimi's Sojourn and Reentry

1. As each diary entry was dated it was possible to link the participants' writing with their sojourn surveys and events.

2. As in the previous chapter, all of the excerpts from narratives written in English are in their original form. Nora opted to do her postsojourn interview

in Cantonese and Mimi code-mixed; efforts were made to retain the nuances and emotions of their discourse in the translation.
3. A punt is a flat-bottomed boat with broad, square ends that is propelled by a single long pole. Punting takes places in shallow water and is a popular tourist attraction in Oxford and Cambridge.
4. In the theory of additive-subtractive bilingualism (Lambert, 1975), a subtractive bilingual situation is one in which a second language becomes so dominant that it eventually replaces the first language, jeopardizing the learner's native language and cultural identity. In additive bilingualism, a second language is added to the individual's linguistic repertoire at no loss to the first language and cultural identity of the learner.

6   Lana and Jade's Sojourn and Reentry

1. As each diary entry was dated it was possible to link the participants' writing with their sojourn surveys and events.
2. All of the excerpts written in English are in their original form. While Lana opted to do her postsojourn interview in English, Jade chose Cantonese. In the transcription process, efforts were made to retain the nuances and emotions of her discourse in the translation.

8   Cultivating Global and Intercultural Competencies

1. NASULGC (2004) defines global competence as the ability of faculty, staff, and students "not only to contribute to knowledge, but also to comprehend, analyze, and evaluate its meaning in the context of an increasingly globalized world." Brustein (2007: 382–3) notes that "the skills that form the foundation of global competence include the ability to work effectively in international settings; awareness of and adaptability to diverse cultures, perceptions, and approaches; familiarity with the major currents of global change and the issues they raise; and the capacity for effective communication across cultural and linguistic boundaries."
2. The Intercultural Development Inventory (IDI) and analysis software are available to educators/administrators who have successfully completed a three-day qualifying seminar organized by IDI, LLC (or, previously, by the Intercultural Development Institute). (Contact www.idiinventory.com.)
3. In "faculty-led" sojourns an educator from the home institution accompanies a group of students on their sojourn; this individual may teach a course in the host culture, supervise student projects (e.g., ethnographic research), and liaise with administrators/educators in the host institution.

Bibliography

Allen, H. W., Dristas, V., and Mills, N. (2007). Cultural learning outcomes and summer study abroad, in M. Mantero (ed.), *Identity and Second Language Learning: Culture, Inquiry, and Dialogic Activity in Educational Contexts* (pp. 189–215). Charlotte, NC: Information Age Publishing.

Allport, G. W. (1954). *The Nature of Prejudice*. Reading, MA: Addison-Wesley.

Alptekin, C. (2002). Towards intercultural communicative competence in ELT. *ELT Journal*, 56 (1), 57–64.

Alred, G. and Byram, M. (2002). Becoming an intercultural mediator: A longitudinal study of residence abroad. *Journal of Multilingual and Multicultural Development*, 23 (5), 339–52.

Alred, G., Byram, M., and Fleming, M. (2003). *Intercultural Experience and Education*. Clevedon, UK: Multilingual Matters.

Alred, G., Byram, M., and Fleming, M. (2006). *Education for Intercultural Citizenship: Concepts and Comparisons*. Clevedon, UK: Multilingual Matters.

Altbach, P. G. (2008, September & October). The imperial tongue: English as the dominating academic language. *International Educator*, 56–9.

Altbach, P. G. and Knight, J. (2007). The internationalization of higher education: Motivations and realities. *Journal of Studies in International Education*, 11 (3/4), 290–305.

Anderson, L. C. (2005). *Internationalizing Undergraduate Education: Integrating Study Abroad into the Curriculum*. Minneapolis, MN: University of Minnesota.

Anderson, P. H., Lawton, L., Rexeisen, R. J., and Hubbard, A. C. (2006). Short-term study abroad and intercultural sensitivity: A pilot study. *International Journal of Intercultural Relations*, 30, 457–69.

Appadurai, A. (1990). Disjuncture and difference in the global cultural economy, in M. Featherstone (ed.), *Global Culture: Nationalism, Globalization and Modernity* (pp. 295–310). London: Sage Publications.

Arnett, J. J. (2002). The psychology of globalization. *American Psychologist*, 57, 774–83.

Bailey, C. (2007). *A Guide to Qualitative Field Research* (2nd edn). Thousand Oaks, CA: Pine Forge Press.

Baraldi, C. (2006). New forms of intercultural communication in a globalized world. *International Communication Gazette*, 68 (1), 53–69.

Barro, A., Jordan, S., and Roberts, C. (1998). Cultural practice in everyday life: The language learner as ethnographer, in M. Byram and M. Fleming (eds), *Language Learning in Intercultural Perspective: Approaches through Drama and Ethnography* (pp. 76–97). Cambridge: Cambridge University Press.

Bateman, B. E. (2002). Promoting openness towards culture learning: Ethnographic interviews for students of Spanish. *The Modern Language Journal*, 86, 318–31.

Bazeley, P. (2007). *Qualitative Data Analysis with NVivo*. London: Sage Publications.

Beelen, J. (ed.) (2007). *Implementing Internationalisation at Home*. EAIE's Professional Development Series for International Educators. Amsterdam: European Association for International Education.

Bennett, J. M. (1993). Cultural marginality: Identity issues in intercultural training, in R. M. Paige (ed.), *Education for the Intercultural Experience* (pp. 109–36). Yarmouth, ME: Intercultural Press.

Bennett, J. M. (2004). Turning frogs into interculturalists: A student-centered developmental approach to teaching intercultural competence, in R. A. Goodman, M. E. Phillips, and N. A. Boyacigiller (eds), *Crossing Cultures: Insights from Master Teachers* (pp. 312–42). London: Routledge.

Bennett, J. M. (2008). On becoming a global soul: A path to engagement during study abroad, in V. Savicki (ed.), *Developing Intercultural Competence and Transformation: Theory, Research, and Application in International Education* (pp. 13–31). Sterling, VA: Stylus.

Bennett, J. M. and Bennett, M. J. (2004a). *Developing Intercultural Competence: A Reader*. Portland, OR: Intercultural Communication Institute.

Bennett, J. M. and Bennett, M. J. (2004b). Developing intercultural sensitivity: An integrative approach to global and domestic diversity, in D. Landis, J. M. Bennett, and M. J. Bennett (eds), *Handbook of Intercultural Training* (3rd edn) (pp. 145–67). Thousand Oaks, CA: Sage Publications.

Bennett, J. M., Bennett, M. J., and Allen, W. (2003). Developing intercultural competence in the language classroom, in D. Lange and M. Paige (eds), *Culture as the Core: Perspectives on Culture in Second Language Learning* (pp. 237–70). Greenwich, CT: Information Age Publishing.

Bennett, M. J. (1993). Towards ethnorelativism: A developmental model of intercultural sensitivity, in R. M. Paige (ed.), *Education for the Intercultural Experience* (pp. 21–71). Yarmouth, ME: Intercultural Press.

Bennett, M. J. (1997). How not to be a fluent fool: Understanding the cultural dimensions of language, in A. E. Fantini (vol. ed.) and J. C. Richards (series ed.), *New Ways in Teaching Culture. New Ways in TESOL Series II: Innovative Classroom Techniques* (pp. 16–21). Alexandria, VA: TESOL.

Bennett, M. J. (1998). Intercultural communication: A current perspective, in M. J. Bennett (ed.), *Basic Concepts of Intercultural Communication: Selected Readings* (pp. 1–34). Yarmouth, ME: Intercultural Press.

Bennett, M. J. (2004). Becoming interculturally competent, in J. Wurzel (ed.), *Toward Multiculturalism: A Reader in Multicultural Education* (2nd edn) (pp. 62–77). Newton, MA: Intercultural Resource Corporation.

Berg, B. L. (2007). *Qualitative Research Methods for the Social Sciences* (6th edn). Boston: Allyn and Bacon.

Berwick, R. F. and Whalley, T. R. (2000). The experiential bases of culture learning: A case study of Canadian high schoolers in Japan. *International Journal of Intercultural Research*, 24 (3), 325–40.

Bhawuk, D. P. S. and Brislin, R. W. (1992). The measurement of cultural sensitivity using the concepts of individualism and collectivism. *International Journal of Intercultural Relations*, 16, 413–36.

Block, D. (2007). *Second Language Identities*. London: Continuum.

Bolen, M. C. (ed.) (2007). *A Guide to Outcomes Assessment in Education Abroad*. Carlisle, PA: Forum on Education Abroad.

Bourdieu, P. (1977). *Outline of a Theory of Practice* (trans. R. Nice). Cambridge: Cambridge University Press.

Bourdieu, P. (1986). The forms of capital, in J. Richardson (ed.), *The Handbook of Theory and Research in the Sociology of Education* (pp. 241–58). New York: Greenwood Press.

Bourdieu, P. (1991) *Language and Symbolic Power*. Boston: Harvard University Press.

Bourhis, R. Y., El-geledi, S., and Sachdev, I. (2007). Language, ethnicity, and intergroup relations, in A. Weatherall (ed.), *Language, Discourse, and Social Psychology* (pp. 15–50). Basingstoke, Hampshire: Palgrave Macmillan.

Bredella, L. (2003). What does it mean to be intercultural? in G. Alred, M. Byram, and M. Fleming (eds), *Intercultural Experience and Education* (pp. 225–39). Clevedon, UK: Multilingual Matters.

Brown, H. D. (2001). *Teaching by Principles: An Interactive Approach to Language Pedagogy* (2nd edn). Englewood Cliffs, NJ: Prentice Hall Regents.

Brown, K. (2006). Models, methods, and curriculum for ELT preparation, in B. B. Kachru, Y. Kachru, and C. L. Nelson (eds), *The Handbook of World Englishes* (pp. 680–93). Oxford: Blackwell Publishing.

Brustein, W. I. (2007). The global campus: Challenges and Opportunities for Higher Education in North America. *Journal of Studies in International Education*, 11 (3/4), 382–91.

Byram, M. (1995). Intercultural competence and mobility in multinational contexts: A European view, in M. L. Tickoo (ed.), *Language and Culture in Multilingual Societies* (pp. 21–36). Singapore: SEAMEO Regional Language Centre.

Byram, M. (1997). *Teaching and Assessing Intercultural Communicative Competence*. Clevedon, UK: Multilingual Matters.

Byram, M. (2003). On being "bicultural" and "intercultural," in G. Alred, M. Byram, and M. Fleming (eds), *Intercultural Experience and Education* (pp. 50–66). Clevedon, UK: Multilingual Matters.

Byram, M. (2006). Developing a concept of intercultural citizenship, in *Education for Intercultural Citizenship: Concepts and Comparisons* (pp. 109–29). Clevedon, UK: Multilingual Matters.

Byram, M. S. (2008). *From Foreign Language Education to Education for Intercultural Citizenship. Essays and Reflection*. Clevedon, UK: Multilingual Matters.

Byram, M., Gribkova, B., and Starkey, H. (2002). *Developing the Intercultural Dimension in Language Teaching: A Practical Introduction for Teachers*. Strasbourg: Council of Europe.

Byram, M. and Zarate, G. (1997). Defining and assessing intercultural competence: some principles and proposals for the European context. *Language Teaching*, 29, 14–8.

Canagarajah, A. S. (1999). *Resisting Linguistic Imperialism in English Language Teaching*. Oxford: Oxford University Press.

Canagarajah, A. S. (2005). Accommodating tensions in language-in-education policies: An afterword, in A. M. Y. Lin and P. W. Martin (eds), *Decolonisation, Globalisation: Language-in-Education Policy and Practice*. (pp. 194–201). Clevedon, UK: Multilingual Matters.

Charmaz, K. (2006). *Constructing Grounded Theory: A Practical Guide Through Qualitative Analysis*. London: Sage Publications.

Chen, G-M. and Starosta, W. J. (2006). Intercultural awareness, in L. A. Samovar, R. E. Porter, and E. R. McDaniel (eds), *Intercultural Communication: A Reader* (pp. 357–66). Belmont, CA: Wadsworth.

Chen, G-M and Starosta, W. J. (2008). Intercultural communication competence: A synthesis, in M. K. Asante, Y. Miike, and J. Yin (eds), *The Global Intercultural Communication Reader* (pp. 215–37). New York: Routledge.

Chieffo, L. and Griffiths, L. G. (2003, Fall). What's a month worth? Student perceptions of what they learned abroad. *International Educator*, vol. XII, no. 5, 26–31.

Chisholm, L. A. (2000). *Charting a Hero's Journey*. New York: The International
Partnership for Service-Learning and Leadership.

Chiu, C-y and Hong, Y-y. (2006). *Social Psychology of Culture*. New York: Psychology
Press.

Cohen, A. D. and Shively, R. L. (2002). *Speech Act Measure of Language Gain*.
Minneapolis, MN: Center for Advanced Research on Language Acquisition,
University of Minnesota.

Cohen, A. D., Paige, R. M., Kappler, B., Demmessie, M., Weaver, S. J., Chi, J. C., and
Lassegard, J. P. (2003). *Maximizing Study Abroad: A Language Instructor's Guide to
Strategies for Language and Culture Learning and Use*. Minneapolis, MN: Center for
Advanced Research on Language Acquisition, University of Minnesota.

Cohen, A. D., Paige, R. M., Shively, R. L., Emert, H. A., and Hoff, J. G. (2005).
*Maximizing Study Abroad through Language and Culture Strategies: Research
on Students, Study Abroad Program Professionals and Language Instructors*.
Minneapolis, MN: Center for Advanced Research on Language Acquisition,
University of Minnesota.

Cohen, R. and Kennedy, P. (2000). *Global Sociology*. New York: New York University Press.

Corbett, J. (2003). *An Intercultural Approach to English Language Teaching*.
Clevedon, UK: Multilingual Matters.

Corbitt, J. N. (1998). *Global Awareness Profile*. Yarmouth, ME: Intercultural Press.

Coulmas, F. (2005). *Sociolinguistics: The Study of Speakers' Choices*. Cambridge:
Cambridge University Press.

Crang, M. and Cook, I. (2007). *Doing Ethnographies*. London: Sage Publications.

Cushner, K. and Karim, A. U. (2004). Study abroad at the university level,
in D. Landis, J. M. Bennett, and M. J. Bennett (eds), *Handbook of Intercultural
Training* (pp. 289–308). Thousand Oaks, CA: SAGE Publications.

Dahlen, T. (1997). *Among the Interculturalists: An Emergent Profession and its
Packaging of Knowledge*. Stockholm, Sweden: Stockholm University, Department
of Social Anthropology.

Damen, L. (1987). *Culture Learning: The Fifth Dimension in the Language Classroom*.
Reading, MA: Addison-Wesley.

Davis, T. M. (2003). *Atlas of Student Mobility*. New York: Institute of International
Education.

Deardorff, D. K. (2004). The Identification and Assessment of Intercultural Com-
petence as a Student Outcome of Internationalization at Institutions of Higher
Education in the United States. Unpublished dissertation. Raleigh, NC: North
Carolina State University.

Deardorff, D. K. (2006). Identification and assessment of intercultural competence as a student outcome of internationalization. *Journal of Studies in
International Education*, 10 (3), 241–66.

Deardorff, D. K. (2008). Intercultural competence: A definition, model, and
implications for education abroad, in V. Savicki (ed), *Developing Intercultural
Competence and Transformation: Theory, Research, and Application in International
Education* (pp. 32–52). Sterling, VA: Stylus.

Deardorff, D. K. (ed). (2009). *The SAGE Handbook of Intercultural Competence*.
Thousand Oaks, CA: Sage Publications.

Deardorff, D. K. and Hunter, W. D. (2006, May–June). Educating global-ready graduates. *International Educator*, 72–83.

Denzin, N. K. and Lincoln, Y. S. (2003). *Collecting and Interpreting Qualitative Materials*. Thousand Oaks, CA: Sage Publications.

Der-Karabetian, A. (1992). World-mindedness Scale and the nuclear threat: A multinational study. *Journal of Social Behavior and Personality*, 7, 293–308.

Dervin F. (2006). Quality in Intercultural Education: The Development of Proteophilic Competence. *EU-Bildung 2010, Regionalveranstaltung fur Wien, Niederosterreich und Burgenland*. BM: BWK, Stadtschulrat fur Wien.

Dervin, F. and Dirba, M. (2006). On Liquid Interculturality. Finnish and Latvian student teachers' perceptions of intercultural competence, in P. Pietilä, P. Lintunen, and H-M. Järvinen (eds), *Language Learners of Today*. Jyväskylä: Suomen soveltavan kielitieteen yhdistyksen (AFinLA) julkaisuja, no. 64, 257–73.

Dessoff, A. (2007, March–April). Branching Out. *International Educator*, 24–30.

Dissanayake, W. (2006). Cultural studies and discursive constructions of world Englishes, in B. B. Kachru, Y. Kachru, and C. L. Nelson (eds), *The Handbook of World Englishes* (pp. 545–66). Oxford: Blackwell Publishing.

Ditto, P. H. and Lopez, D. F. (1992). Motivated skepticism: Use of differential decision criteria for preferred and nonpreferred conclusions. *Journal of Personality and Social Psychology*, 91, 1–15.

Dixon, M. (2006). Globalisation and international higher education: Contested positionings. *Journal of Studies in International Education*, 10 (4), 319–33.

Dolby, N. (2007). Reflections on nation: American undergraduates and education abroad. *Journal of Studies in International Education*, 11 (2), 141–56.

Donatelli, L., Yngve, K., Miller, M., and Ellis, J. (2005). Technology and education abroad, in J. L. Brockington, W. W. Hoffa, and P. C. Martin (eds), *NAFSA's Guide to Education Abroad for Advisors and Administrators* (pp. 129–150). Washington, DC: NAFSA: Association of International Educators.

Dörnyei, Z. (2005). *The Psychology of the Language Learner: Individual Differences in Second Language Acquisition*. Mahwah, NJ: Lawrence Erlbaum Associates.

Dörnyei, Z. (2009). The L2 motivational self system, in Z. Dörnyei and E. Ushioda (eds), *Motivation, Language Identity and the L2 Self* (pp. 9–42). Clevedon, UK: Multilingual Matters.

Dunstan, P. (2003). Cultural diversity for life: A case study from Australia. *Journal of Studies in International Education*, 7 (1), 64–76.

Edstrom, A. M. (2005). Female, nonnative perspectives on second language conversation: Connecting participation with intercultural sensitivity. *Foreign Language Annals*, 38 (1), 25–34.

Edwards, J., Hoffa, W., and Kanach, N. (2005). Education abroad at the beginning of the twenty-first century, in J. L. Brockington, W. W. Hoffa, and P. C. Martin (eds), *NAFSA's Guide to Education Abroad for Advisers and Administrators* (pp. 5–24). Washington, DC: NAFSA: Association of International Educators.

Engle, L. and Engle, J. (2004). Assessing language acquisition and intercultural sensitivity development in relation to study abroad program design. *Frontiers: The Interdisciplinary Journal of Study Abroad*, X, 219–36.

Fantini, A. E. (2007). *Exploring and Assessing Intercultural Competence*. St. Louis, MI: Center for Social Development, Global Service Institute, Washington University in St Louis (CSD Research Report).

Ferguson, G. (2008). *Language Planning and Education*. Edinburgh: Edinburgh University Press.

Fischer, P., Greitemeyer, T., and Frey, D. (2007). Ego depletion and positive illusions: Does the construction of positivity require regulatory resources? *Personal and Social Psychology Bulletin*, 33 (9), 1306–21.

Fishman, J. A. (1965). Who speaks what language, to whom and when? *La Linguistique*, 2, 67–88.

Forrest, S. (2008, May–June). Staying competitive with Europe. *International Educator*, 88–91.

Fought, C. (2006). *Language and Ethnicity*. Cambridge: Cambridge University Press.

Fowler, S. M. and Blohm, J. M. (2004). An analysis of methods for intercultural training, in D. Landis, J. M. Bennett, and M. J. Bennett (eds), *Handbook of Intercultural Training* (pp. 37–84). Thousand Oaks, CA: Sage Publications:

Fox, K. (2004). *Watching the English: The Hidden Rules of English Behaviour*. London: Hodder and Stoughton.

Freed, B. F. (1995). *Second Language Acquisition in a Study Abroad Context*. Amsterdam: John Benjamins.

Freed, B. F., Dewey, D. P., Segalowitz, N., and Halter, R. (2004). The Language Contact Profile. *Studies in Second Language Acquisition*, 26 (2), 349–56.

Gacel-Ávila, J. (2005). The internationalization of higher education: A paradigm for global citizenry. *Journal of Studies in International Education*, 9 (2), 121–36.

García Canclini, N. (2006). Narratives on culture: From socio-semiotics to globalization, in J. R. Baldwin, S. L. Faulkner, M. L. Hecht, and S. L. Lindsley (eds), *Redefining Culture: Perspectives Across the Disciplines* (pp. 117–26). Mahwah, NJ: Lawrence Erlbaum Assoc. Publishers.

Giddens, A. (1990). *The Consequences of Modernity*. Stanford: Stanford University Press.

Giroux, H. A. (1992). *Border Crossings: Cultural Workers and the Politics of Education*. New York: Routledge.

Gobo, G. (2008). *Doing Ethnography*. Thousand Oaks, CA: Sage Publications.

Grbich, C. (2007). *Qualitative Data Analysis*. London: Sage Publications.

Green, M. F. and Olson, C. L. (2003). *Internationalizing the Campus: A User's Guide*. Washington, DC: American Council on Education, Center for Institutional and International Initiatives.

Gudykunst, W. B. (2004). *Bridging Differences: Effective Intergroup Communication* (4th edn). Thousand Oaks, CA: Sage Publications.

Guilherme, M. (2002). *Critical Citizens for an Intercultural World: Foreign Language Education as Cultural Politics*. Clevedon, UK: Multilingual Matters.

Guilherme, M. (2004). Intercultural competence, in M. Byram (ed), *Routledge Encyclopedia of Language Teaching and Learning* (pp. 297–300). London: Routledge.

Hall, S. (1992). The question of identity, in S. Hall, D. Held, and A. McGrew (eds), *Modernity and Its Futures* (pp. 274–316). Cambridge: Policy Press.

Hammer, M. R. (1999). A measure of intercultural sensitivity: The Intercultural Development Inventory, in S. M. Fowler and M. G. Fowler (eds), *The Intercultural Sourcebook* (vol. 2, pp. 61–72). Yarmouth, ME: Intercultural Press.

Hammer, M. R. and Bennett, M. J. (2002). *The Intercultural Development Inventory: Manual*. Portland, OR: Intercultural Communication Institute.

Hammer, M. R., Bennett, M. J., and Wiseman, R. L. (2003). Measuring intercultural sensitivity: The intercultural development inventory. *International Journal of Intercultural Relations*, 27 (3), 421–43.

Hammersley, M. and Atkinson, P. (1995). *Ethnography: Principles in Practice* (2nd edn). London: Routledge.

Hammersley, M. and Atkinson, P. (2007). *Ethnography: Principles in Practice* (3rd edn). London: Routledge.

He, R., Ho, E. S-c, Man, E. Y-f (2007). *Student Performance in Chinese-medium-of-instruction (CMI) and English medium-of-instruction (EMI) schools: What we Learned from the PISA Study*. Hong Kong: Hong Kong Institute of Educational Research, Chinese University of Hong Kong.

Held, D., McGrew, A., Goldblatt, D., and Perraton, J. (1999). *Global Transformations: Politics, Economics, and Culture*. Cambridge: Polity Press.

Hesse-Biber, S. N. and Leavy, P. (2006). *The Practice of Qualitative Research*. Thousand Oaks, CA: Sage Publications.

Heyward, M. (2002). From international to intercultural: Redefining the international school for a globalized world. *Journal of Research in International Education*, 1 (1), 9–32.

Hoff, J. G. and Kappler, B. (2005). Integrating intercultural learning in education abroad programming, in J. L. Brockington, W. W. Hoffa, and P. C. Martin (eds), *NAFSA's Guide to Education Abroad for Advisers and Administrators* (pp. 193–206). Washington, DC: NAFSA: Association of International Educators.

Holliday, A. (2005). *The Struggle to Teach English as an International Language*. Oxford: Oxford University Press.

House, J. (2003). Teaching and learning pragmatic fluency in a foreign language: The case of English as a lingua franca, in A. Martinez Flor, E. Usó Juan, and A. Fernández Guerra (eds), *Pragmatic Competence and Foreign Language Teaching* (pp. 133–59). Castelló de la Plana, Spain: Publicacions de la Universitat Jaume 1.

Hunter, W. D. (2004). Knowledge, Skills, Attitudes, and Experience Necessary to Become Globally Competent. Unpublished PhD dissertation, Lehigh University, Bethlehem, Pennsylvania.

Inda, J. Xavier and Rosaldo, R. (2006). Introduction: A world in motion, in J. X. Inda and R. Rosaldo (eds), *The Anthropology of Globalization* (pp. 1–34). Oxford: Blackwell.

Intercultural Communication Institute (2004). *The Developmental Model of Intercultural Sensitivity*. http://www.intercultural.org.

Isabelli-García, C. (2006). Study abroad social networks, motivation and attitudes: Implications for second language acquisition, in M. A. Dufon and E. Churchill (eds), *Language Learners in Study Abroad Contexts* (pp. 231–58). Clevedon, UK: Multilingual Matters.

Jackson, J. (2002). Cultural identity and language choice: English majors in Hong Kong, in C. Lee and W. Littlewood (eds), *Culture, Communication and Language Pedagogy* (pp. 37–50). Hong Kong: Baptist University.

Jackson, J. (2005). Assessing intercultural learning through introspective accounts. *Frontiers: The Interdisciplinary Journal of Study Abroad*, XI, 165–86.

Jackson, J. (2006a). Ethnographic pedagogy and evaluation for short-term study and residence abroad, in M. Byram and A. Feng (eds), *Living and Studying Abroad* (pp. 134–56). Clevedon, UK: Multilingual Matters.

Jackson, J. (2006b). Ethnographic preparation for short-term study and residence in the target culture. *The International Journal of Intercultural Relations*, 30 (1), 77–98.

Jackson, J. (2007, March). Mutuality, engagement, and agency: Negotiating identity on stays abroad. Paper presented at an invited colloquium, the 17th International Pragmatics and Language Learning conference, Honolulu, Hawaii, USA.

Jackson, J. (2008). *Language, Identity, and Study Abroad: Sociocultural Perspectives*. London: Equinox.

Jacobson, W., Sleicher, D., and Burke, M. (1999). Portfolio assessment of intercultural competence. *International Journal of Intercultural Relations*, 23 (3), 467–92.

Jandt, F. E. (2007). *An Introduction to Intercultural Communication: Identities in a Global Community*. Thousand Oaks, CA: Sage Publications.

Johnson, M. C. (2002). *Intercultural Transitions: Designing Undergraduate Courses at a US Liberal Arts College*. An unpublished Master of Intercultural Relations, School of International Studies, University of the Pacific, Stockton, CA: and the Intercultural Communication Institute, Portland, OR, USA.

Jurasek, R., Lamson, H., and O'Maley, P. (2002). Ethnographic learning while studying abroad. *Frontiers: The Interdisciplinary Journal of Study Abroad*, 2 (2), 1–25.

Kachru, B. B. (1985). Standards, codification, and sociolinguistic realm: The English language in the outer circle, in R. Quirk and H. G. Widdowson (eds), *English in the World* (pp. 11–30). Cambridge: Cambridge University Press.

Kachru, B. B. (2005). *Asian Englishes: Beyond the Canon*. Hong Kong: Hong Kong University Press.

Kachru, B. B., Kachru, Y., and Nelson, C. L. (2006). Preface (pp. xvii–xix), in B.B. Kachru, Y. Kachru, and C. L. Nelson (eds), *The Handbook of World Englishes*. Oxford: Blackwell Publishing.

Kachru, Y. and Smith, L. E. (2008). *Cultures, Contexts, and World Englishes*. New York: Routledge.

Kälvermark, T. and van der Wende, M. C. (1997). *National Policies for Internationalization of Higher Education in Europe*. Stockholm: National Agency for Higher Education.

Kanno, Y. and Norton, B. (2003). Imagined communities and educational possibilities: Introduction. *Journal of Language, Identity, and Education*, 2 (4), 241–9.

Kashima, Y. (2000). Conceptions of culture and person for psychology. *Journal of Cross-Cultural Psychology*, 31, 14–32.

Kauffmann, N. L., Martin, J. N., Weaver, H. D., and Weaver, J. (1992). *Students Abroad: Strangers at Home*. Yarmouth, ME: Intercultural Press.

Kelley, C. and Meyers, J. (1992). *Action-Planning Guide, Cross-Cultural Adaptability Inventory*. Minneapolis, MN: Pearson, Inc.

Kelley, C. and Meyers, J. (1999). The cross-cultural adaptability inventory, in S. M. Fowler and M. G. Mumford (eds), *Intercultural Sourcebook: Cross-cultural Training Methods* (vol. 2, pp. 53–60). Yarmouth, ME: Intercultural Press.

Kim, Y. Y. (2001). *Becoming Intercultural: An Integrative Theory of Communication and Cross-cultural Adaptation*. Thousand Oaks, CA: Sage Publications.

Kim, Y. Y. (2005). Adapting to a new culture: An integrative communication theory, in W. Gudykunst (ed.), *Theorizing about Intercultural Communication* (pp. 375–400). Thousand Oaks, CA: Sage Publications.

Kim, Y. Y. (2008). Intercultural personhood: Globalization and a way of being. *International Journal of Intercultural Relations*, 32 (4), 359–68.

Kinginger, C. (2008). Language learning in study abroad: Case studies of Americans in France. *Modern Language Journal*, 92 (1), 1–131.

Knight, J. (1999). Internationalization of higher education, in J. Knight (ed.), *Quality of Internationalization in Higher Education* (pp. 13–28). Paris: OECD.

Knight, J. (2003). Internationalization: Developing an Institutional Self-Portrait. Readings for EOTU Project. http://www.eotu.uiuc.edu/events/2003-04global .htm, retrieved November 3, 2007.

Knight, J. (2004). Internationalization remodeled: Definition, approaches, and rationales. *Journal of Studies in International Education*, 8 (1), 5–31.

Knight, J. (2007). Internationalization brings important benefits as well as risks. *International Educator*, 16 (6), 59–62.

Knight, J. and de Wit, H. (eds) (1997). *Internationalization of Higher Education in Asia Pacific Countries*. Amsterdam: European Association for International Education.

Knight, J. and de Wit, H. (eds) (1999). *Quality and Internationalisation in Higher Education*. Paris: Organisation for Economic Co-operation and Development.

Kohls, L. R. and Brussow, H. L. (1995). *Training Know-How for Cross Cultural and Diversity Trainers*. Duncanville, TX: Adult Learning Systems, Inc.

Kolb, D. A. (1984). *Experiential Learning*. Englewood Cliffs, NJ: Prentice Hall.

Kraidy, M. M. (2005). *Hybridity: Or the Cultural Logic of Globalization*. Philadelphia: Temple.

Kramsch, C. J. (1993). *Context and Culture in Language Teaching*. New York: Oxford University Press.

Kramsch, C. J. (1998). The privilege of the intercultural speaker, in M. Byram and M. Fleming (eds), *Language Learning in Intercultural Perspective: Approaches through Drama and Ethnography* (pp. 16–31). Cambridge: Cambridge University Press.

Kramsch, C. J. (1999). Global and local identities in the contact zone, in C. Gnutzmann (ed), *Teaching and Learning English as a Global Language – Native and Non-native Perspectives* (pp. 131–46). Tübingen: Stauffenberg-Verlag.

Kramsch, C. J. (2002). In search of the intercultural. *Journal of Sociolinguistics*, 6 (2), 275–85.

Kritz, M. M. (2006). Globalisation and Internationalisation of Tertiary Education. Paper presented at the International Symposium on International Migration and Development. Turin, Italy. http://www.un.org/esa/population/migration/ turin/Symposium_Turin_files/P02_KRITZ_Rev3_Augst21.pdf.

Kroeber, A. L. and Kluckhohn, C. (1952). *Culture: A Critical Review of Concepts and Definitions*. Cambridge: Harvard University Press.

Kruger, J. (1999). Lake Wobegon be gone! The "below-average effect" and the egocentric nature of comparative ability judgments. *Journal of Personality and Social Psychology*, 77 (2), 221–32.

Kruger, J. and Dunning, D. (1999). Unskilled and unaware of it: How difficulties in recognizing one's own incompetence lead to inflated self-assessments. *Journal of Personality and Social Psychology*, 77 (6), 1121–34.

Kunda, Z. (1990). The case for motivated reasoning. *Psychological Bulletin*, 108 (3), 480–98.

Lai, M-L. (2005). Language attitudes of the first postcolonial generation in Hong Kong secondary schools. *Language in Society*, 34, 363–88.

Lam, W. S. E. (2006). Culture and learning in the context of globalization: Research directions. *Review of Research in Education*, 30 (1), 213–37.

Lamb, M. (2004). Integrative motivation in a globalizing world. *System*, 32, 3–19.

Lambert, R. D. (1996). Parsing the concept of global competence. *Educational Exchange and Global Competence*. New York: Council on International Educational Exchange.

Lambert, W. E. (1975). Culture and language as factors in learning and education, in A. Wolfgang (ed.), *Education of Immigrant Students* (pp .55–83). Toronto: Ontario Institute for Studies in Education.

Landis, D., Bennett, J. M., and Bennett, M. J. (eds) (2004). *Handbook of Intercultural Training* (3rd edn). Thousand Oaks, CA: Sage Publications.

Lantolf, J. P. (2000). Introducing sociocultural theory, in J. Lantolf (ed.), *Sociocultural Theory and Second Language Learning* (pp. 2–26). Oxford: Oxford University Press.

Lau, L. J. (2004). Installation of the New Vice-Chancellor, inaugural address by Professor Lawrence J. Lau (December 9, 2004) Hong Kong: The Chinese University of Hong Kong.

Lave, J. and Wenger, E. (1991). *Situated Learning: Legitimate Peripheral Participation*. Cambridge: Cambridge University Press.

Layder, D. (1997). *Modern Social Theory: Key Debates and New Directions*. London: UCL Press.

Leclercq, J-M. (2003). *Facets of Interculturality in Education*. Strasbourg Cedex, France: Council of Europe Publishing.

Lewin, T. (2008). US universities rush to set up outposts abroad. *New York Times*, February 10.

Lin, A. M. Y. (2005). Critical, transdisciplinary perspectives on language-in-education policy and practice in postcolonial contexts: The case of Hong Kong, in A. M. Y. Lin and P. W. Martin (eds), *Decolonisation, Globalisation: Language-in-Education Policy and Practice* (pp. 38–54). Clevedon, UK: Multilingual Matters.

Lin, A. M. Y. and Martin, P. W. (2005). From a critical deconstruction paradigm to a critical construction paradigm: An introduction to decolonization, globalization and language-in-education policy and practice, in A. M. Y. Lin and P. W. Martin (eds), *Decolonisation, Globalisation: Language-in-Education Policy and Practice* (pp. 1–19). Clevedon, UK: Multilingual Matters.

Lindahl, R. (2006). The right to education in a globalized world. *Journal of Studies in International Education*.10 (1), 5–26.

Littrell, L. N. and Salas, E. (2005). A review of cross-cultural training: Best practices, guidelines, and research needs. *Human Resource Development Review*, 4 (3), 305–34.

Lustig, M. W. and Koester, J. (2006). *Intercultural Competence: Interpersonal Communication across Cultures* (5th edn). New York: Longman.

Marshall, C. and Rossman, G. B. (2006). *Designing Qualitative Research* (4th edn). Thousand Oaks, CA: Sage Publications.

Martin, J. N. and Harrell, T. (2004). Intercultural reentry of students and professionals, in D. Landis, J. M. Bennett and M. J. Bennett (eds), *Handbook of Intercultural Training* (pp. 309–36). Thousand Oaks, CA: Sage Publications.

Mathews, G. (2000). *Global Culture/Individual Identity: Searching for Home in the Cultural Supermarket*. Abingdon, Oxon, and New York: Routledge.

Mathews, G., Ma, E. K-w, and Lui, T-l. (2008). *Hong Kong, China: Learning to Belong to a Nation*. Abingdon, Oxon, UK and NY: Routledge.

McArthur, T. (1998). *The Oxford Companion to the English Language.* Oxford. Oxford University Press.

McBurnie, G. and Ziguras, C. (2006, Spring). The international branch campus. *The Institute of International Education (IIE) Networker,* 35–7.

McCabe, L. T. (2001). Globalization and internationalization: The impact on education abroad programs. *Journal of Studies in International Education,* 5 (2), 138–45.

McConnell, J. (2000). Language, identity and the Asian crisis: Is English causing an identity crisis? in W. Jung and X. B. Li (eds), *Asia's Crisis and New Paradigm* (pp. 139–48). Lanham, MD: University Press of America.

McGrew, A. (1992). A global society? in S. Hall, D. Held, and A. McGrew (eds), *Modernity and its Futures* (pp. 61–102). Cambridge: Polity.

McKay, S. L. (2002). *Teaching English as an International Language: Rethinking Goals and Approaches.* Oxford: Oxford University Press.

McKay, S. L. (2004). Western culture and the teaching of English as an international language. *English Teaching Forum,* 42 (2).

McKay, S. L. and Bokhorst-Heng, W. D. (2008). *International English in Its Sociolinguistic Contexts.* New York: Routledge.

Medina-López-Portillo, A. (2004a). Intercultural learning assessment: The link between program duration and the development of intercultural sensitivity. *Frontiers: The Interdisciplinary Journal of Study Abroad,* X, 179–99.

Medina-López-Portillo, A. (2004b). College Students' Intercultural Sensitivity Development as a Result of their Studying Abroad: A Comparative Description of Two Types of Study Abroad Programs. A PhD thesis, Baltimore: University of Maryland.

Meinhof, U. H. and Galasiński, D. (2005). *The Language of Belonging.* Basingstoke, Hampshire and New York: Palgrave Macmillan.

Meyer-Lee, E. (2005). Bringing it home: Follow-up courses for study abroad returnees in *Internationalizing Undergraduate Education: Integrating Study Abroad into the Curriculum* (pp. 114–16). Minneapolis, MN: University of Minnesota.

Mezirow, J. (1994). Understanding transformative theory. *Adult Education Quarterly,* 44, 222–32.

Mezirow, J. (2000). Learning to think like an adult, in J. Mezirow and Associates (eds), *Learning as Transformation: Critical Perspectives on a Theory in Progress* (pp. 3–33). San Francisco: Jossey-Bass.

Moon, D. (2008). Concepts of "culture": Implications for intercultural communication research, in M. K. Asante, Y. Miike, and J. Yin (eds), *The Global Intercultural Communication Reader* (pp. 11–26). New York: Routledge.

Moon, J. A. (2006). *Learning Journals: A Handbook for Reflective Practice and Professional Development* (2nd edn). Abingdon, Oxon: Routledge.

Murphy-Lejeune, E. (2002). *Student Mobility and Narrative in Europe: The New Strangers.* London: Routledge.

Murphy-Lejeune, E. (2003). An experience of interculturality: Student travelers abroad, in G. Alred, M. Byram, and M. Fleming (eds), *Intercultural Experience and Education* (pp. 101–13). Clevedon, UK: Multilingual Matters.

Myers-Scotton, C. (2006). *Multiple Voices: An Introduction to Bilingualism.* Oxford: Blackwell Publishing.

Naidoo, V. (2006). International education: A tertiary-level industry update. *Journal of Research in International Education,* 5 (3), 323–45.

National Association of State Universities and Land-Grant Colleges (NASULGC) (2004, October). *A call to leadership: The presidential role in internationalizing the university*. A Report of the NASULGC Task Force on International Education. Washington, D.C.: NASULGC.

Nederveen Pieterse, J. (1994). *Globalization and Culture: Global Mélange*. Oxford: Rowman and Littlefield.

Nilsson, B. (2003). Internationalisation at home from a Swedish perspective: The case of Malmö. *Journal of Studies in International Education*, 7 (1), 27–40.

Noels, K. A. (2009). The internationalization of language learning into the self and social identity, in Z. Dörnyei and E. Ushioda (eds), *Motivation, Language Identity and the L2 Self* (pp. 295–313). Clevedon, UK: Multilingual Matters.

Norton, B. (2000). *Identity and Language Learning: Gender, Ethnicity and Educational Change*. Harlow, England: Pearson Education Ltd.

Ochs, E. and Capps, L. (1996). Narrating the self. *Annual Review of Anthropology*, 25, 19–43.

O'Donovan, K. F. and Mikelonis, V. M. (2005). Internationalizing on-campus courses: A faculty development program to integrate global perspectives into undergraduate course syllabi, in L. C. Anderson (ed.), *Internationalizing Undergraduate Education: Integrating Study Abroad into the Curriculum* (pp. 91–5). Minneapolis, MN: The Learning Abroad Center, Office for International Programs, University of Minnesota.

O'Dowd, R. (2003). Understanding the "other side": Intercultural learning in a Spanish-English e-mail exchange. *Language Learning and Technology*, 7 (2), 118–44.

Olson, C. L. and Kroeger, K. R. (2001). Global competency and intercultural sensitivity. *Journal of Studies in International Education*, 5 (2), 116–37.

Olson, C. L., Green, M. F., and Hill, B. A. (2005). *Building a Strategic Framework for Comprehensive Internationalization*. Washington, DC: American Council on Education.

Olson, C. L., Green, M. F., and Hill, B. A. (2006). *A Handbook for Advancing Comprehensive Internationalization: What Institutions can do and what students should learn*. Washington, DC: American Council on Education.

O'Reilly, K. (2008). *Key Concepts in Ethnography*. Thousand Oaks, CA: Sage Publications.

Organisation for Economic Co-operation and Development (OECD) (2009). *Education at a Glance. 2009*. Paris: OECD Centre for Educational Research and Innovation. http://www.oecd.org/document/24/0,3343,en_2649_39263238_43586328_1_1_1_1,00.html, retrieved 30 October 2009.

Paige, R. M. (2003). The American case: The University of Minnesota. *Journal of Studies in Education*, 7 (1), 52–63.

Paige, R. M. (2004). Instrumentation in intercultural training, in D. Landis, J. M. Bennett, and M. J. Bennett (eds), *Handbook of Intercultural Training* (pp. 85–128). Thousand Oaks, CA: Sage Publications.

Paige, R. M. and Lange, D. L. (eds) (2003). *Culture as the Core: Perspectives on Culture in Second Language Learning*. Greenwich, CT: Information Age Publishing.

Paige, R. M. and Stallman, E. M. (2007). Using instruments in education abroad outcomes assessment, in M. C. Bolen (ed.). *A Guide to Outcomes Assessment in Education Abroad* (pp. 137–61). Carlisle, PA: The Forum on Education Abroad.

Paige, R. M., Cohen, A. D., Kappler, B., Chi, J. C., and Lassegard, J. P. (2006). *Maximizing Study Abroad: A Student's Guide to Strategies for Language and Culture Learning and Use* (2nd edn). Minneapolis, MN: University of Minnesota.

Paige, R. M., Jacobs-Cassuto, M., Yershova, Y. A., and DeJaeghere, J. (2003). Assessing intercultural sensitivity: An empirical analysis of the Hammer and Bennett Intercultural Development Inventory. *International Journal of Intercultural Relations*, 27 (4), 467–86.

Pang, N. S-K. (2006). Globalization and educational change, in N. S-K Pang (ed.), *Globalization: Educational Research, Change and Reform* (pp. 1–24). Hong Kong: The Chinese University Press.

Park, M. (2006). A relational study of intercultural sensitivity with linguistic competence in English-as-a-Foreign-language (EFL) pre-service teachers in Korea. Unpublished PhD thesis. The University of Mississippi.

Pavlenko, A. (2007). Autobiographic narratives as data in applied linguistics. *Applied Linguistics*, 28 (2), 163–88.

Pavlenko, A. and Lantolf, J. P. (2000). Second language learning as participation and the (re)construction of selves, in J. P. Lantolf (ed.), *Sociocultural Theory and Second Language Learning* (pp. 155–77). Oxford: Oxford University Press.

Pavlenko, A. and Norton, B. (2007). Imagined communities, identity, and English language learning, in J. Cummins and C. Davison (eds), *International Handbook of English Language Teaching* (pp. 669–80). Dordrecht, the Netherlands: Springer.

Pennycook, A. (2000). English, politics, ideology: From colonial celebration to postcolonial performativity, in T. Ricento (ed.), *Ideology, Politics and Language Policies: Focus on English* (pp. 107–19). Amsterdam: John Benjamins.

Peterson, C., Engle, L., Kenney, L., Kreutzer, K., Nolting, W., and Ogden, A. (2007). Defining terms for use in designing outcomes projects, in M. C. Bolen (ed.), *A Guide to Outcomes Assessment in Education Abroad* (pp. 163–203). Boston: Forum on Education Abroad.

Pettigrew, T. F. and Tropp, L. R. (2000). Does intergroup contact reduce prejudice? Recent meat-analytic findings, in S. Oskamp (ed.), *Reducing Prejudice and Discrimination: Social Psychological Perspectives* (pp. 93–114). Mahwah, NJ: Erlbaum.

Phipps, A. M. (2006). *Learning the Arts of Linguistic Survival: Languaging, Tourism, Life*. Clevedon, UK: Multilingual Matters.

Phipps, A. M. and Gonzalez, M. (2004). *Modern Languages: Learning and Teaching in an Intercultural Field*. Thousand Oaks, CA: Sage Publications.

Pierson, H. (1994). Ethnolinguistic vitality during a period of decolonization without independence: Perceived vitality in Hong Kong. *International Journal of the Sociology of Language*, 108, 43–61.

Pusch, M. D. (2004). Intercultural training in historical perspective, in D. Landis, J. M. Bennett, and M. J. Bennett (eds), *Handbook of Intercultural Training* (pp. 13–36). Thousand Oaks, CA: Sage Publications.

Rauhvargers, A. (2001, Spring). Recognition problems and solutions of transnational education – the code of good practice. *EAIE (European Association of International Education) Forum*, 28–9.

Reagan, T. and Schreffler, S. (2005). Higher education language policy and the challenge of linguistic imperialism: A Turkish case study, in A. M. Y. Lin and P. W. Martin (eds), *Decolonisation, Globalisation: Language-in-Education Policy and Practice* (pp. 115–30). Clevedon, UK: Multilingual Matters.

Richards, L. (2005). *Handling Qualitative Data*. Thousand Oaks, CA: SAGE Publications.

Riessman, C. K. (2002). Narrative analysis, in A. M. Huberman and M. B. Miles (eds), *The Qualitative Researcher's Companion* (pp. 217–70). Thousand Oaks, CA: Sage Publications.

Risager, K. (2006). *Language and Culture: Global Flows and Local Complexity*. Clevedon, UK: Multilingual Matters.

Risager, K. (2007). *Language and Culture Pedagogy: From a National to a Transnational Paradigm*. Clevedon, UK: Multilingual Matters.

Rizvi, F. (2006). Internationalization at home: Rethinking internationalization of higher education, in H. Teekens (ed.), *Internationalization at Home: A Global Perspective* (pp. 19–32). The Hague: Netherlands Organization for International Cooperation in Higher Education.

Rizvi, F. (2007). Internationalization of the curriculum: A critical perspective, in Hayden, M., Levy, D., and Thomson, J. (eds), *The SAGE Handbook of Research in International Education* (pp. 390–403). London: Sage Publications.

Rizvi, F., Engel, L., Nandyala, A., Rutkowski, D., and Sparks, J. (2005). Globalization and Recent Shifts in Educational Policy in the Asia Pacific: An Overview of Some Critical Issues. A report prepared for UNESCO Asia Pacific Regional Bureau for Education, Bangkok, Thailand.

Roberts, C., Byram, M., Barro, A., Jordan, S., and Street, B. (2001). *Language Learners as Ethnographers*. Clevedon, UK: Multilingual Matters.

Robertson, R. (1992). Globalization: Social Theory and Global culture. Newbury Park, CA: Sage Publications.

Rogers, E. M. and Hart, W. B. (2002). The histories of intercultural, international, and development communication, in W. B. Gudykunst and B. Mody (eds), *Handbook of International and Intercultural Communication* (pp. 1–18). Thousand Oaks, CA: Sage Publications.

Rose, K. and Kasper, G. (2001). *Pragmatics in Language Teaching*. Cambridge: Cambridge University Press.

Rosen, R. and Digh, P. (2001, May). Developing globally literate leaders. TD, 70–81.

Rowe, W. and Schelling, V. (1991). *Memory and Modernity: Popular Culture in Latin America*. London: Verso.

Rubin, K. (2008, January–February). Singapore's Push for Foreign Students. *International Educator*, 56–9.

Ryan, P. M. (2003). Searching for the intercultural person, in G. Alred, M. Byram, and M. Fleming (eds), *Intercultural Experience and Education* (pp. 131–54). Clevedon, UK: Multilingual Matters.

Ryan, P. M. (2006). Interculturality, identity, and citizenship education in Mexico, in G. Alred, M. Byram, and M. Fleming (eds), *Education for Intercultural Citizenship: Concepts and Comparisons* (pp. 11–22). Clevedon, UK: Multilingual Matters.

Ryan, S. (2006). Language learning motivation within the context of globalization: an L2 self within an imagined global community. *Critical Inquiry in Language Studies: An International Journal*, 3 (1), 23–45.

Ryan, S. (2009). Self and identity in L2 motivation in Japan: The ideal L2 self and Japanese learners of English, in Z. Dörnyei and E. Ushioda (eds), *Motivation, Language Identity and the L2 Self* (pp. 120–43). Clevedon, UK: Multilingual Matters.

Scharito, T. and Webb, J. (2003). *Understanding Globalization*. London: Sage Publications.

Schmelkes, S. (2006). Interculturality in basic education. Paper presented to the Intergovernmental Committee of the Regional Education Project for Latin America and the Caribbean, Santiago de Chile, May 11–13, 2006.

Scholte, J. A. (2000). *Globalization: A Critical Introduction*. London: Palgrave Macmillan.

Schoorman, D. (1999). The pedagogical implications of diverse conceptualizations of internationalization: A US-based case study. *Journal of Studies in International Education*, 3, 19–46.

Schuerholz-Lehr, S. (2007). Teaching for global literacy in higher education: How prepared are the educators? *Journal of Studies in International Education*, 11 (2), 180–204.

Seelye, N. (1997). Cultural goals for achieving intercultural communicative competence, in A. E. Fantini (ed.), *New Ways in Teaching Culture* (pp. 22–7). Alexandria, VA: TESOL, Inc.

Sehlaoui, A. S. (2001). Developing cross-cultural communicative competence in pre-service ESL/EFL teachers: A critical perspective. *Language, Culture and Curriculum*, 14 (1), 42–57.

Sercu, L. (2002). Autonomous learning and the acquisition of intercultural communicative competence: Some implications for course development. *Language, Culture and Curriculum*, 15 (1), 61–74.

Sercu, L. (2005). Teaching foreign languages in an intercultural world, in L. Sercu, E. Bandura, P. Castro, L. Davcheva, C. Laskaridou, U. Lundgren, M. del Carmen, M. García, and P. M. Ryan (eds), *Foreign Language Teachers and Intercultural Competence: An International Investigation* (pp. 1–18). Clevedon, UK: Multilingual Matters.

Smith, P. B., Bond, M. H., and Kagitçibasi, Ç. (2006). *Understanding Social Psychology across Cultures: Living and Working in a Changing World*. London: Sage Publications.

Spencer, S. E. and Tuma, K. (eds) (2008). *The Guide to Successful Short-term Programs Abroad* (2nd edn). Washington, DC: NAFSA: Association of International Educators.

Stangor, C., Jonas, K., Stroebe, W., and Hewstone, M. (1996). Influence of student exchange on national stereotypes, attitudes and perceived group variability. *European Journal of Social Psychology*, 26 (4), 663–75.

Stanley Foundation (2003). Educator support Programs. http://www.stanley foundation.org/programs/esp/index.html, retrieved March 3, 2008.

Steinberg, M. (2007). The place of outcomes assessment in higher education today and the implications for education abroad, in M. C. Bolen (ed.), *A Guide to Outcomes Assessment in Education Abroad* (pp. 7–22). Carlisle, PA: Forum on Education Abroad.

Strauss, A. and Corbin, J. M. (1998). *Basics of Qualitative Research* (2nd edn). Thousand Oaks, CA: Sage Publications.

Stroebe, W., Lenkert, A., and Jonas, K. (1988). Familiarity may breed contempt: The impact of student exchange on national stereotypes and attitudes, in W. Stroebe, A. W. Kruglanski, D. Bar-Tal, and M. Hewstone (eds), *The Social Psychology of Intergroup Conflict: Theory, Research and Applications*. New York: Springer.

Stromquist, N. P. and Monkman, K. (2000). Defining globalization and assessing its implications on knowledge and education, in N. P. Stromquist and K. Monkman (eds), *Globalisation and Education: Integration and Contestation across Cultures* (pp. 3–26). Lanham, MD: Rowman and Littlefield.

Stuart, D. (2007). Assessment instruments for the global workforce. http://www.shrm.org/memberkit/sub_pages/whitepapers/CMS_022010.asp, retrieved January 5, 2008.

Swann, J., Deumert, A., Lillis, T. M., and Mesthrie, R. (2004). *A Dictionary of Sociolinguistics*. Edinburgh: Edinburgh University Press.

Taylor, E. W. (1994). Intercultural competency: A transformative learning process. *Adult Education Quarterly*, 44 (3), 154–74.

Taylor, J. (2004). Toward a strategy for internationalization: Lessons and practice from four universities. *Journal of Studies in International Education*, 8 (2), 149–71.

Taylor, S. E. and Brown, J. D. (1988). Illusion and well-being: A social psychological perspective on mental health. *Psychological Bulletin*, 103, 193–210.

Taylor, S. E. and Brown, J. D. (1994). Positive illusions and well-being revisited: Separating fact from fiction. *Psychological Bulletin*, 116 (1), 21–7.

Teekens, H. (2003). The requirement to develop specific skills for teaching in an intercultural setting. *Journal of Studies in International Education*, 7 (1), 108–19.

Teekens, H. (2007). *Internationalisation at Home: Ideas and Ideals*. EAIE Occasional Papers. Amsterdam: European Association for International Education.

Teichler, U. (2004). The changing debate on internationalization of higher education. *Higher Education*, 48, 5–26.

Thebodo, S. W. and Marx, L. E. (2005). Predeparture orientation and reentry programming, in J. L. Brockington, W. W. Hoffa, and P. C. Martin (eds), *NAFSA's Guide to Education Abroad for Advisors and Administrators* (pp. 293–312). Washington, DC: NAFSA: Association of International Educators.

Ting-Toomey, S. and Chung, L. C. (2005). *Understanding Intercultural Communication*. Los Angeles: Roxbury Publishing Co.

Trudgill, P. (2003). *A Glossary of Sociolinguistics*. Edinburgh: Edinburgh University Press.

Tsui, A. B. M. (2004). Medium of instruction in Hong Kong: One country, two systems, whose language? in J. W. Tollefson and A. B. M. Tsui (eds), *Medium of Instruction Policies: Which Agenda? Whose agenda?* Mahwah, NJ: Lawrence Erlbaum, Associates, Inc.

Tsui, A. B. M. (2007). Language policy and the social construction of identity: The case of Hong Kong, in A. B. M. Tsui and J. W. Tollefson (eds), *Language Policy, Culture, and Identity in Asian Contexts* (pp. 121–41). Mahwah, NJ: Lawrence Erlbaum, Associates, Inc.

Turner, Y. and Robson, S. (2008). *Internationalizing the University*. London and New York: Continuum.

Ushioda, E. (2009). A person-in-context relational view of emergent motivation, self, and identity, in Z. Dörnyei and E. Ushioda (eds), *Motivation, Language Identity and the L2 Self* (pp. 215–28). Clevedon, UK: Multilingual Matters.

van der Wende, M. C. (1994). Internationalisation as a process of educational change, in Pilot project on regional co-operation in reforming higher education, seminar II: Mobility in higher education (pp. 37–49). Paris: European Commission/Organization for Economic Cooperation and Development.

Verbik, L. (2007). The international branch campus: Models and trends. *International Higher Education*, 46, 14.

Verlag, J. Raabe (2006). *EUA Bologna Handbook: Making Bologna Work*. Berlin: EUA, www.bologna-handbook.com.

Wang, M. M., Brislin, R. W., Wang, W., Williams, D., and Chao, J. H. (2000). *Turning Bricks into Jade: Critical Incidents for Mutual Understanding among Chinese and Americans*. Yarmouth, ME: Intercultural Press.

Ward, C. A., Bochner, S., and Furnham, A. (2001) *The Psychology of Culture Shock*. London: Routledge.

Warschauer, M. (2000). The changing global economy and the future of English teaching. *TESOL Quarterly*, 34, 511–35.

West, C. (2008, January–February). Abroad after graduation, English style. *International Educator*, 50–4.

Wight, A. R. (1995). The critical incident as a training tool, in S. M. Fowler and M. G. Mumford (eds), *Intercultural Sourcebook: Cross-Cultural Training Methods*, vol. 1 (pp. 127–40). Yarmouth, ME: Intercultural Press.

Wilkie, D. (2007, September–October). Canada's innovative internationalization. *International Educator*, 46–51.

Williams, R. M. (1947). *The Reduction of Intergroup Tensions: A Survey of Research on Problems of Ethnic, Racial, and Religious Group Relations*. New York: Social Science Research Council.

Yashima, T. (2009). International posture and the ideal L2 self in the Japanese EFL context, in Z. Dörnyei and E. Ushioda (eds), *Motivation, Language Identity and the L2 Self* (pp. 144–63). Clevedon, UK: Multilingual Matters.

Zarate, G. (2003). Identities and plurilingualism: Preconditions for the recognition of intercultural competences, in M. Byram (ed.), *Intercultural Competence* (pp. 84–119). Strasbourg: Council of Europe Publishing.

Index

IN-SERVICE:

School Library/Media Workshops and Conferences

by
NANCY POLETTE

The Scarecrow Press, Inc.
Metuchen, N. J.   1973

Library of Congress Cataloging in Publication Data

Polette, Nancy.
   In-service: school library/media workshops and
conferences.

    1. School libraries--Congresses.   2. Instructional
materials centers--Congresses.   3. Teachers--In-
service training--Congresses.   I. Title.
Z675.S3P59   020'.7'15   73-12095
ISBN 0-8108-0658-4

FOREWORD

When the author first talked to me about dealing with in-service workshops and conferences, I tried to think of any others on this general topic I had seen in the past. If there is such a book, it has escaped my notice. That makes this book so much more an important contribution to the literature. For the first time there is one source of help for the person having responsibility for planning and executing a workshop or conference for persons working and/or interested in the media field.

The organization of this book makes it possible to follow easily, step-by-step, things that are necessary for the successful workshop--whether it be local, state, or national. While the amount of material will vary depending on the length of a workshop, the steps in planning for the material will be essentially the same. Anyone who has attended meetings and workshops knows the results of neglecting important details of planning.

Mrs. Polette has had wide experience in planning in-service workshops and conferences. Her suggestions, along with examples of programs held in many places, will be very helpful by suggesting possible topics and materials to be covered. These examples also indicate the wide range of topics and kinds of material that are appropriate for such meetings.

It is with real pleasure that I commend this book to anyone who gets the responsibility of planning an in-service workshop. Following the many suggestions within these pages should result in more worthwhile time spent in workshops and conferences dealing with library/media topics.

Eldon H. Madison, Ph. D.
Chairman, Dept. of
Instructional Technology
Southern Illinois University

iii

ACKNOWLEDGMENTS

The author is indebted to the following persons and institutions for their help and willingness in sharing their in-service programs with others through inclusion in this book.

The American Association of School Librarians
Dorothy Seitz, St. Charles (Mo.) Public School District
The St. Charles (Mo.) Librarian's Council
Wesley Beck, Jr., Asst. Supt., Stillwater (Okla.) Public Schools
Elfrieda McCauley, Coordinator of Libraries, Greenwich (Conn.) Public Schools
Glenn W. Cook, IMC Director, Plymouth River (Mass.) School
Mary Belle England, Director Library Services, Fulton County (Ga.) Board of Education
Lynn S. Simpson, Supervisor in Education, Mass. Dept. of Education
Charles Strantz, Jr., Hazlewood (Mo.) School District
Agatha Parks, Director of Libraries, Hazlewood (Mo.) School Dist.
Leatha Garrison, Director Ed. Materials, School Board of Volusia County (Fla.)
Miriam Morrow, Elem. Librarian, Ladue (Mo.) School District
Lois M. McCallum, Elem. Library Coordinator, Dillon (S. C.) School Dist. #2
Arabelle Grant, Director Educational Media, Bay County (Fla.) Educational Media Center
Leonard L. Johnson, Director Media Services, Greensboro (N. C.) Public Schools
William D. Grindeland, Dir. Instructional Materials Center Unified School Dist. #1, Racine, Wisc.
Elizabeth M. Stephens, Director, Library Services, School Board of Pinellas County (Fla.)
Bernard Franckowiak, School Library Supervisor, Wisc. Dept. of Public Instruction
Carl F. Sitze, State School Library Supervisor, State Dept. of Education (Mo.)

Maxine Larson Hough, Exec. Secretary, Michigan Assoc.
School Librarians
Charles Economous, Pennsylvania Association of School
Librarians
Jean A. Coleman, Chairman Committee on Instruction in
Libraries, American Library Association
John H. Cely, Jr., Program Director Edgefield County
(S. C.) Dept. of Education
Stella Farley, Director of Libraries, Ferguson/Florissant
(Mo.) School District
Dan Burns, President, St. Louis (Mo.) Suburban Media
Directors Assoc.
Martin Hente, Sharon Bogard, Linda Coleman, Jackie Dillon,
Students, Lindenwood College, St. Charles (Mo.)
Pattonville (Mo.) School District
Massachusetts School Library Association
The Missouri Association of School Librarians
T. J. Lawson, Asst. Supt. Hazelwood School District (Mo.)
Eldon Madison, Prof. Instructional Technology, Southern
Illinois University, Edwardsville, Ill.
Joan Berry, Promotion Manager, University of California
Extension, Santa Cruz
Guy Garrison, Dean, Graduate School of Library Science,
Drexel University (Pa.)
Robert Foley, Director, Media & Materials, Cedar Rapids
(Iowa) Community Schools
Mendel Sherman, Director, Div. of Instructional Systems
Technology, Indiana University, Bloomington, Ind.
Otis McBride, Prof. of Education, University of Colorado,
Boulder, Colorado
Donna Harsh, Asst. Prof. Education, Fort Hays Kansas
State College
Minda Sanders, Director, Dept. of Educational Media,
Millersville (Pa.) State College
William J. Quinly, Director, Media Center, Florida State
University, Tallahassee, Fla.

CONTENTS

viii

APPENDICES

PART I

LIBRARY/MEDIA TRAINING FOR TEACHERS

1

1. PLANNING AND IMPLEMENTING THE TEACHER IN-SERVICE PROGRAM

In most educational complexes the announcement of an in-service training meeting for the purpose of upgrading professional competency within a particular teaching area is greeted with something less than enthusiasm by the instructional staff. As recently as ten years ago the typical educator's reaction to such an announcement was one of resigned martyrdom. Today, the reaction is more likely to be overt protest. Yet, in examining the reluctance of teachers or administrators toward additional educational exposure, one meets a paradox. Our educational scene is a reflection of our national scene. It is one of constant and rapid change. In an age of technological advancement new methods and materials become outdated almost before printing presses have cooled. The prolific spawning of satellite companies in the field of education from larger parent companies has made the instructional market so fiercely competitive, and so pervaded with surveys, studies, new products, and materials, that it has become difficult if not impossible for today's educators to examine and select the best methods and media for use with students. It is an era of constant search, examination, retraining and rethinking of instructional objectives, procedures and processes. Why, then, the reluctance on the part of those directly involved in these processes to update and upgrade competencies through in-service programs?

The answer lies in part in the traditional type of in-service training offered to educators. The typical in-service session finds tired teachers sleeping through a lecture given by an "expert" brought in from outside the local program (usually selected by the administration), expounding a topic which may or may not (usually the latter) have applicability to the local teaching/learning situation. As long as teachers were willing to suffer in silence, such workshop situations tended to perpetuate themselves.

The new breed of teacher, including those who work in the field of media, has not been silent in its protests against such practices on the part of school administrations. Wise administrators--some of them themselves among the new breed--have opened their ears as well as their doors, and have not only begun to involve the instructional staff in workshop planning, but have re-worked traditional school calendars to provide a time for in-service training that will be conducive to learning.

Criteria for Successful Workshops

Successful workshop planning, then, including the development of training meetings in instructional media, must be based in part on the following criteria:

1. Determination of workshop procedures and content must be a cooperative endeavor of all educators involved.

2. The material presented must be relevant and applicable to the particular teaching-learning situation of the conferees.

3. Provision must be made for immediate use of the materials or information presented.

4. Provision must be made for active involvement of participants.

5. Released time from daily teaching duties is essential for creating a receptive audience.

Cooperative Planning

The tendency of library or media directors to bemoan the general lack of teacher knowledge in the instructional media field often leads to the planning of workshops designed to "give teachers what is considered good for them." Such workshops may be planned exclusively by the library/media director with the approval of the district administration and with no trace of teacher involvement, since "teachers don't know enough to know what they need to know anyway." Such an attitude on the part of media personnel is bound to lead to an unsuccessful in-service

program. Teachers do know better than anyone else the
strengths, weaknesses and basic needs of the students with
whom they work. They also know the subject area content
they are expected to teach and the basic skills necessary
for attaining competency in these areas. New methods and
new materials for upgrading the teaching/learning process
will be welcomed only when teachers are assured that their
basic needs will be met in any in-service program in which
they take part. This calls for cooperative planning.

The initial step in the selection of a planning committee is contact with the district administration. Before
approaching the administration the library/media director
should have some evidence of the need for in-service training
of teachers in more effective use of instructional materials.
Information from both national and local surveys should be
readily available at the time of the meeting with the administration.

An excellent general statement on the need for continued exposure of educators to new ideas is that by Alice
Miel:

> A good way to develop openness to experience is
> to help the individual to have an experience in
> which he can get a different view of a familiar
> landscape. When a teacher is in a position to
> look at the curriculum as a whole, old information
> falls into new relationships and calls for new in-
> formation. Representing the school on a respon-
> sible school or community committee, interpreting
> the school program to the public through speaking
> or writing, attending a ... workshop or conference
> with a definite responsibility for contributing to the
> insights of the stay-at-homes, all give opportunity
> to acquire a new view. [1]

Research in In-Service Training

For the administrator who wants to know what "research has to say" or "what is being done nationally" concerning in-service training in instructional materials, a
number of excellent studies are available. The studies cited
here are from Shirley Louise Arron's "A Review of Selected
Research Studies in School Librarianship 1967-1971," which
appeared in the Summer 1972 issue of School Libraries,

published by the American Association of School Librarians.
A complete reading of this article is highly recommended.
These studies show clearly the need for in-service training
of educators in the more effective use of both print and non-
print media.

An investigation by Elton Tielke of three elementary
school libraries was based on exhaustive case studies of
these institutions and their patrons. The study concluded
that: 1) classroom teachers generally have not realized the
potential of the library in the instructional program; 2) in-
service programs for teachers and librarians which stress
extensive use of library resources are lacking; 3) commit-
ments made by the school district to the library program
are low; and 4) the library program in a school is developed
through the initiative of the librarians with little or no participation by the teachers, principals, or other professional
personnel.[2] This study is representative of a situation
which exists in far too many elementary schools today.

Four hundred and sixty school districts in Oklahoma
were evaluated by Kenneth King to determine whether there
was a relationship between teacher utilization of selected educational media and the level of sophistication of the educational media program. Two conclusions of the study were:
1) educational media programs were much more effective
when teachers and administrators were committed to their
provision and use; and 2) a positive relationship exists between well-established media programs and teacher utilization of media in these schools.[3]

Hilda Jay questioned 88 teachers and 1,240 students
to determine why greater use is not made of school library/
media centers in secondary schools. Teachers' reasons for
lack of use included time, accessibility, familiarity with library materials, and lack of conviction that these materials
were necessary to the teaching of their subject. Among de-
terrents mentioned by students were instructional methods
employed by teachers, limited numbers of materials required
by students through their courses, and lack of access to non-
book materials.[4]

Additional studies by Williams and McMahan support
the hypothesis that additional training is needed in the field
of library/media use by teachers. The Williams study
dealt with the pre-service education of teachers and the
methods by which prospective teachers are taught. Exten-

sive data was gathered from colleges and universities in
Florida having teacher education programs to determine the
nature and extent of preparation which graduates will have
had in educational media in required education courses.
Major findings of the study indicated that in the institutions
surveyed instruction on the whole was traditional, and that
the use of media as content in a course or as part of the
instructional process was opposed rather than accepted. [5]

The McMahan study was an effort to design a system
for developing media competencies in existing education and
methods courses. The system was designed from judgments
of representative elementary education professors, from system design procedures from the literature, and from testing
on a pilot basis in one course the systems procedures for
developing media selection and utilization competencies. Two
conclusions of the study were: 1) media competencies in
prospective elementary education teachers were lacking, and
2) there was a substantial need for improving current methods for developing these competencies. [6]

A seven-year study of teacher use of instructional
materials centers in the Pattonville School District in St.
Louis County, Missouri involved 20 public and private elementary schools and three secondary schools. Approximately 15,000 students and 600 teachers were surveyed after the
second, fourth, and seventh year of involvement in the program. Conclusions drawn from surveys and from stan-
dardized achievement tests at the end of the second year indicated little involvement of teachers and students with the
IMC program. The IMC was viewed by teachers as a "nice"
(but not really necessary) supplement to the educational program. Students showed little gain in the development of
work-study skills on the Iowa Test of Basic Skills.

Following extensive in-service training of teachers
over the next two years, both teacher and student use of
instructional materials showed dramatic increase. Subsequent survey instruments indicated that at the end of four
years teachers saw the use of the Instructional Materials
Center as an integral part of the educational program. Students showed a 60 per cent gain in development of work/study
skills, moving from a district-wide average of the 20th percentile in 1965 to the 80th percentile in 1969. In 1972, the
district average on the California Test of Basic Skills showed
students achieving one year or more above their expected
level of achievement in the work-study skills area. [7]

While the foregoing studies are regional in character, additional studies all seem to support the same conclusions: that teachers as a whole are not trained in the effective use of media in the classroom, and that they do not allow their students opportunities to learn through making full use of the instructional materials center in the school, even though the use of such media or facilities to individualize instruction generally creates a more favorable learning situation.

While national studies are helpful in indicating a general trend in a teaching-learning area, or in spotlighting the current state of the teaching art, local administrators may be more concerned with studies or surveys undertaken within their own geographic area. An excellent survey instrument for use with both public and private schools throughout a county-wide area was developed by the St. Charles (Missouri) Librarians' Council and distributed in informational meetings with faculty members in almost every elementary and secondary school in that county. The major purpose of the questionnaire was "to help establish and improve ... communication and cooperation between teachers and librarians at all levels."[8] In addition, an examination of responses indicated to the members of the Librarians' Council how teachers were using media and library resources available to them--a most important item for examination prior to determining workshop or in-service training need.

The questionnaire, reproduced here by permission of the St. Charles Librarians' Council, can be easily adapted to individual local situations. Its use should be helpful in revealing teacher attitudes and knowledge concerning effective library use.

1. When the library you use doesn't have the information you need, do you
   Go to another library
   Give up
   Ask the librarian to borrow it from another library

2. How often do you use a library for your own needs, professional and personal?
   Daily
   Once a week
   Once a month
   Once a semester

Once a year
Never
Two times a month (added by teachers)

3. Are you normally able to find the materials which
   your students need in the St. Charles area li-
   braries?
   Always
   Frequently
   Sometimes
   Never

4. What percentage of your assignments require
   students' use of a library?
   0
   20%
   50%
   70%
   90%
   0-20% (added by teachers)

5. Do you make a library assignment as part of a
   unit of study on library skills?
   Never
   Once a year
   Once a semester
   Once a month
   Once a week
   Daily

6. When you plan an assignment for which students
   will need to use both school and public libraries,
   do you
   Visit each library and tell the librarian
   Ask your school librarian to inform the public
   libraries
   Make the assignment without informing the libraries

7. Do you direct your students to use a particular
   library when an assignment is made?
   Yes
   No

   If so, which one?
   Own school
   Another school--please name

Public library
Other--please name

8. How do you check to see if the libraries have
    what you need before making an assignment?
    Contact the librarian
    Check the card catalog yourself
    Send a student to check
    Do not do so

9. Do you find library employees helpful and courte-
    ous in assisting you in the use of the library?
    Always
    Frequently
    Sometimes
    Never

10. If there is a library in your school, do you send
    students there for independent study and research?
    Never
    Occasionally
    Frequently
    Constantly
    Classroom Library (added by teachers)

11. If you are receiving less than excellent service,
    which factors are the cause?
    Inconvenient library hours
    Inconvenient location
    Incompetent or discourteous staff
    Lack of leisure time
    No need for library materials
    Lack of skills needed to use the library
    Lack of needed materials in the library col-
    lection
    Comments:
    Use of other resources (added by teachers)

12. Library service could be improved by:
    More books
    Better books
    More audio-visual materials
    More frequent bookmobile service
    Book delivery on request rather than bookmo-
    bile service
    More library branches

Conferences between librarians and teachers to
select materials and plan ways for the library
to become an integral part of classroom learn-
ing
Teaching of library skills to children
Simplifying the procedure for finding books
Printing the card catalog in book form so
there can be a library catalog in each class-
room
More permissive policies about book use--
longer loan periods, overnight loan of refer-
ence books, etc.
Keeping the library open longer
More knowledgeable library staff
More staff members
More study space in the library
Photocopy equipment
Better location for the library
Better arrangement of library materials
Other:

        When results of this questionnaire are tabulated, a
careful study should be made of responses. If, for example,
teachers indicate that they give up easily if they do not find
the information they are seeking, perhaps training is needed
in research methods or in helping staff members become
familiar with their school library/media resources. If
teachers indicate that they rarely require students to use
the school library for independent study or assignments, an
attitudinal workshop to help teachers broaden their thinking
about the independent study process is called for. One of
the major roles of the school media center should certainly
be helping students to learn how to learn. This does require a retraining of teachers who, from lack of knowledge
or from tradition, are textbook oriented. Beggs and Buffie
state the problem in this way:

        Educational tradition has not placed the emphasis
        on independent study. Most teachers in the schools
        had little experience of this nature when they were
        students. Few professional education courses have
        dealt with both the rationale and techniques of en-
        couraging independent study.

        An in-service program for independent study is a
        long range enterprise if it is to realize its maxi-

mum effectiveness. Asking teachers to encourage
independent study is an easy matter. Giving them
the tools to implement it over a sustained period
is another issue. Experience has shown that a
school which places a high value on independent
study needs to devote a healthy portion of its staff
meeting time to the subject. Staff meetings are
not enough. A varied program must be conducted
within the school staff. [9]

The final two questions on the survey can be most revealing
concerning teacher attitudes and competencies involved in
media center use. If the teacher indicates either a lack of
time or no need for library materials as reasons for avoiding IMC use, one must question where the teacher places his
or her priorities in the instructional program. Here again,
in-service training designed to change attitudes is necessary.

Traditional teachers will generally respond to the final question by noting that library service could be improved
by "more books." Progressive teachers will usually indicate
the desire for additional library staff members and for planning conferences with librarians to select materials and plan
ways for the library to become an integral part of classroom
learning. This pattern of conflict between traditional and
progressive teachers must be considered in both the selection of planning committees and in workshop content. Biddle
and Ellena highlight the problem:

> The public school system is plagued by controver-
> sy, the most basic between traditional and pro-
> gressive teaching methods. Although long exposed
> to progressive education in summer school and
> through educational literature, most older teachers
> hold (somewhat defensively) to traditionalism. This
> may have to do with the mold in which they were
> set as young teachers. Perhaps they abandoned
> what progressive experimentation they may have
> attempted as their age distance from students in-
> creased. The young teachers ... trained during a
> period when progressive education was being intro-
> duced generally align themselves with the progres-
> sive school. The two ideologies often are used for
> name calling purposes in a broader pattern of con-
> flict between older and young teachers. [10]

This is not to say that traditional and progressive teachers cannot work together toward the common goal of improving the educational program in the school. Care must be taken, however, in structuring workshop planning committees to secure members from both groups. This will help to insure that the needs of more teachers are met and that one group is not accused of attempting to force its ideas on another.

While the preceding questionnaire dealt with county-wide services, it may be more helpful in some cases to use a survey instrument related directly to the individual district's instructional materials center program, such as the one which follows. It is usually better to ask staff members completing the survey not to sign their names; responses are more likely to be honest if the respondent is not called upon to identify himself. A survey of the responses will usually reveal areas where more extended training is desirable.

Another major use of the survey lies in its informational value. Media personnel often decry the fact that teachers do not take advantage of the materials or services offered by the library/media center, when the real difficulty is that many teachers are not aware that the materials or services exist. An answer key can be included at the end of the survey to inform staff members of those materials and services available to them.

WHAT GOES ON IN THE IMC???

Test Your Know-How of the Materials and Services
Available to You

ADMINISTRATION

1. Does your district have a library/media coordinator or supervisor?
    (a) yes
    (b) no
    (c) don't know

2. Where are your school's IMC materials cataloged, processed and made ready for your instructional materials center?
    (a) in your school
    (b) in a district central processing center

    (c) in a county processing center
    (d) don't know

3.   How are the librarians or media personnel able to see new materials and equipment before purchase?
    (a) not able to do so
    (b) ask representatives of companies to come to the school
    (c) examine special displays set up in the district's media service center
    (d) don't know

4.   Who develops and produces most of the non-commercial skills programs and materials for use in teaching work/study and library skills to students, and where are these materials produced?
    (a) the librarian in the school
    (b) the library/media coordinator at the district service center
    (c) county library supervisor at the county library
    (d) don't know

5.   How are materials selected for purchase for your IMC?
    (a) librarian reads reviews of materials
    (b) teachers request materials for purchase
    (c) materials are previewed before purchase when possible
    (d) pupils request materials
    (e) all of these
    (f) don't know

6.   Is librarian or media specialist in your school a certified teacher with additional training in instructional materials and/or librarianship?
    (a) yes
    (b) no
    (c) don't know

SERVICES

1.   Which of the following services does the librarian or media specialist in your school provide?
    (a) charges books to students
    (b) catalogs and processes books for the IMC
    (c) sends collections of materials to the classroom on teacher request

(d) meets with teachers planning new units of work
(e) introduces materials to classes beginning new
     units of work
(f) teaches work/study skills needed at each grade
     level for independent study activities
(g) holds story hours and book talks for students to
     develop a greater love of reading and of books
(h) guides individual and small group research activi-
     ties
(i) demonstrates on request the use of audio-visual
     equipment and materials and supervises student
     use of such materials
(j) provides any printed bibliographies of materials
     available in your IMC on any topic for student
     use during a unit of work if requested to do so
     by the teacher
(k) assists students in selection of materials
(l) informs teachers of new materials added to the
     collection
(m) prepares tapes and transparencies for teacher use

MATERIALS AND EQUIPMENT

1. Which of the following materials does your school li-
    brary contain for your use and the use of your stu-
    dents?

Materials

(a)	books	(m)	slides
(b)	records	(n)	books on microfiche
(c)	reel to reel tapes	(o)	8mm loops
(d)	cassette tapes	(p)	flannel board materials
(e)	silent filmstrips	(q)	maps
(f)	sound filmstrips	(r)	globes
(g)	posters	(s)	pamphlets
(h)	charts	(t)	book/record sets
(i)	study prints		(talking books)
(j)	picture sets	(u)	short strips
(k)	art prints	(v)	models
(l)	transparencies	(w)	museum artifacts

Equipment (for library use)

(a)	16mm projector	(d)	slide projector
(b)	television	(e)	filmstrip viewers
(c)	filmstrip projector	(f)	shortstrip viewers

(g) cassette recorder   (m) overhead projector
(h) reel to reel recorder (n) radio
(i) tape player   (o) hot press
(j) opaque projector   (p) copy machine
(k) record player   (q) duplicating machine
(l) microfiche reader   (r) 8mm loop projector

TEACHER-STUDENT USE OF MATERIALS

1. I make regular use of audio-visual materials from the central library in my teaching.
   (a) frequently   (b) sometimes   (c) never

2. When beginning a new unit of work I contact the librarian and request that she introduce the materials for this unit to my class and teach the skills necessary for independent use by my students.
   (a) frequently   (b) sometimes   (c) never

3. When requesting a story hour I give the librarian a topic or theme so that the story will be related to classroom studies or activities.
   (a) frequently   (b) sometimes   (c) never

4. I inform the librarian of students who need special help in selecting reading materials on their level.
   (a) frequently   (b) sometimes   (c) never

5. I send groups of students for research projects related to units of work in order that they can seek knowledge independently.
   (a) frequently   (b) sometimes   (c) never

6. I send students to the IMC to preview filmstrips or recordings so that they can then present them to the class.
   (a) frequently   (b) sometimes   (c) never

7. When I find new materials that I feel would be valuable to have in the school I turn in a request to the librarian so that they can be added to the library.
   (a) frequently   (b) sometimes   (c) never

8. I visit the library before planning a new unit to examine the materials available for use by my students during the unit. I plan my unit with these materials

in mind.
(a) frequently   (b) sometimes   (c) never

9. I inform the librarian of topics being studied in the
   classroom before scheduling skills classes so that
   students can immediately apply the skills learned.
   (a) frequently   (b) sometimes   (c) never

Data gathered from such surveys should provide administrators with concrete evidence of the need for in-service training in the more effective use of media.

The administrator's knowledge of the interests and
abilities of individual district staff members should be invaluable in assisting the media supervisor in forming a workshop planning committee. As noted previously, committee
members should represent a variety of grade levels and
points of view, but care should be taken that the planning
committee does not grow so large as to be unworkable.
While involving the administration in selection of the planning committee, it should be stressed that arrangements
must be made for committee members to meet during the
school day. If each committee member's planning period is
scheduled to follow a lunch period it might be possible for
the committee to meet weekly at luncheon-planning meetings.
Other possibilities, including hiring half-day substitutes for
committee members, can be explored by a creative administration for providing released time.

The In-Service Planning Committee

The committee for planning in-service library/media
training will probably be chaired by the district library/
media supervisor or by the person from whom the impetus
for the training sessions came. Before assigning specific
responsibilities to committee members, an overview of survey results should be carefully studied by the committee as
a whole. It is important to stress that the training needs
revealed by the survey may not be those specific learning
activities desired by the instructional staff for in-service
training activities. For this reason, before the committee
begins its work an additional, more specific survey may be
needed. A survey such as the one which follows will indicate the specific interests of teachers and the information or
skills they wish to have offered in a workshop.

INSTRUCTIONAL MEDIA SURVEY

Any planning of in-service programs must take into consideration the desires of the instructional staff in order
to make such workshops of direct and applicable aid to
the teaching-learning process. Would you take a few
minutes to complete this questionnaire? Indicate within
each category by number, your choices of items you
might like to see included in an in-service workshop. A
number one would indicate first choice, a number two,
second choice, etc.

I. Learning Activities Using Audio-Visual Media
    ___ a) Developing listening skills
    ___ b) Developing viewing skills
    ___ c) Creative writing activities
    ___ d) Development of learning packages

II. The Research Process in the IMC
    ___ a) Writing behavioral objectives as they relate
            to student IMC use
    ___ b) Individualizing instruction
    ___ c) The independent study process
    ___ d) Developing research skills
    ___ e) Teaching children to "learn how to learn"
    ___ f) Content of basic reference tools and methods
            for use by students

III. Reading Guidance
    ___ a) A review of high interest/low vocabulary ma-
            terials available for use
    ___ b) Methods for utilizing the IMC in the reading
            program
    ___ c) A review of fiction available in the IMC pub-
            lished in the last five years
    ___ d) A review of new acquisitions in the non-
            fiction area for your grade level
    ___ e) Examination and review of non-book materials
            available for use in the reading program

IV. Selection and Utilization of Materials
    ___ a) Examination of new materials for possible
            purchase
    ___ b) A review of filmstrips available for use
    ___ c) A review of tape and disc recordings avail-
            able for use

___ d) A review of transparencies, charts, study
prints, and microfiche materials available
for use

___ e) Development of selection committees and
processes in curriculum areas

V.   Production of Materials (number as many choices as
you wish)
___ a) Filmstrip production
___ b) Producing 8mm films
___ c) Photography
___ d) Preparation of transparencies
___ e) Making tape recordings
___ f) Producing slide-tape programs
___ g) Posters and bulletin boards
___ h) Laminating and dry mounting
___ i) Making color lifts
___ j) Preparing flannel board materials
___ k) Student production of media

VI. Operation and Use of Equipment (number as many
choices as you wish)
___ a) 16mm projector
___ b) tape recorders (cassette and reel-to-reel)
___ c) microfiche reader
___ d) overhead projector
___ e) filmstrip and slide projectors
___ f) copy and duplicating machines
___ g) opaque and microprojectors
___ h) utilization of mobile science laboratory
___ i) video tape equipment

VII. If time will permit, which of the following workshop
areas would be most useful to you? Please give
first and second choice.
___ a) Learning Activities using Audio-Visual Media
___ b) The Research Process in the IMC
___ c) Reading Guidance
___ d) Selection and Utilization of Materials
___ e) Production of Materials
___ f) Operation and Use of Equipment

VIII. Other workshop topics you would like to propose.
List below:

Determining Behavioral Objectives

With the results of such a survey in hand, the committee is ready to begin work. The tabulation of responses will indicate the major areas of interest. When a specific area has been determined, committee members should then examine the information or skills contained within that area and set definite behavioral objectives. Stated another way, it is essential to know beforehand the specific changes in knowledge, attitudes, or behavior expected to occur as a result of workshop participation. Based on the six major areas noted in the preceding survey instrument, the following behavioral objectives might be developed for each area.

I. Learning Activities Using Audio-Visual Media

A. Teachers will develop purposes for listening in the classroom and send groups of children to the IMC to listen to designated recordings (tape or disc). The listening activity will result in a demonstrable acquisition of skills or knowledge on the part of the students.

B. Teachers will use films in the classroom directly related to specific educational objectives.

C. Teachers will borrow viewers and filmstrips (or send students to the IMC to view filmstrips) for the purpose of developing new concepts on the part of students related to classroom studies.

D. Teachers will encourage students to use story records, films and filmstrips independently to help develop a love of literature, reading and books.

E. Teachers will use study prints, filmstrips, films and recordings as the basis for stimulating creative writing activities among students.

F. Each workshop participant will develop one learning package for use in his or her classroom for a specific learning activity.

II. The Research Process in the IMC

A. Teachers will be able to state in behavioral terms

the specific research skills students are to acquire using the instructional materials center.

B.   Teachers will show a demonstrable change in attitude in working with their classes by planning
many more activities specifically for individual
students and involving the use of the IMC.

C.   Teachers will send individuals, and small groups
of students to the library daily to work independently in supporting concepts or developing new
concepts or skills.

D.   Teachers will request work/study skills materials
from the librarian to use with their students in
developing such skills and will work closely with
the librarian in an ongoing program of skills development.

E.   Teachers will demonstrate both knowledge and use
of reference materials and will provide many opportunities for their students to consult such materials.

III. Reading Guidance

A.   Teachers will be able to select books for students
with reading problems which will be at both the
vocabulary and interest level of the student.

B.   Teachers will schedule classes in the IMC when
beginning a new reading unit in order that the librarian can review books of interest for students
to read during the unit, and demonstrate audio-
visual materials for student use.

C.   Each teacher will be able to discuss five to ten
new books of fiction and will read several of
these to her class during the school year.

D.   Each teacher will be able to recommend to her
students one or more new books available for a
particular unit of work.

E.   Each teacher will be familiar with five filmstrips
and five recordings for her grade level in the
field of childrens' literature and will use these

audio-visual materials with her class during the
course of the school year.

IV. Selection and Utilization of Audio-Visual Materials

    A.   Workshop participants will examine a variety of
new materials and request at least five new additions for possible purchase.

    B.   Each teacher will preview at least 20 filmstrips
in his or her area of instruction and will use a
sizable portion of these in teaching throughout the
year.

    C.   Each teacher will preview at least 20 recordings
in his or her area of instruction and will use a
sizable portion of these in teaching throughout the
year.

    D.   Each teacher will preview transparencies, charts,
study prints, and microfiche materials suitable
for her grade level and will request a number of
these materials for use throughout the school
year.

    E.   One fourth of the participants will volunteer to
work on materials selection committees and will
continue to recommend throughout the year materials for possible purchase.

V. Production of Materials

    A.   The teacher production of each type of material
indicated will be based on specific educational objectives.

    B.   Each participant will produce one filmstrip for
use in the classroom and will teach and encourage
student production of filmstrips where applicable
to a particular learning situation.

    C.   Each participant will produce one 8mm film and
will supervise students in the production of such
films where applicable to a particular learning
situation.

D. Each participant will make a box camera and will
shoot and develop six photographs. Participants
will teach students these procedures when applicable to a particular learning situation.

E. Each teacher will prepare four transparencies,
including one color lift, demonstrating particular
concepts taught at their grade level. They will
supervise and teach students the production of
transparencies when applicable to a particular
learning situation.

F. Each participant will make one tape recording
and one slide-tape program to teach a particular
concept to students. Teachers will work with
students in developing slide-tape programs to
demonstrate skills or concepts to be acquired.

G. Each participant will make two posters and design
one bulletin board using materials which have been
laminated by the participant, dry mounted, or
lettered.

H. Each participant will prepare a flannel board and
accompanying materials and will present a story
or concept to the group using these materials.
Materials will also be used in the classroom with
students.

VI. Operation and Use of Equipment

A. Each participant will be able to load and show a
film in the 16mm projector, rewind the film, and
replace the sound bulb, projection lamp and fan
belt.

B. Each participant will be able correctly to operate
both reel-to-reel and cassette recorders in both
record and play positions and will be able to
splice a broken tape.

C. Each participant will be able to operate the microfiche reader and will list in writing six ways that
the reader can be used by students.

D. Each teacher will correctly demonstrate the use
of the overhead projector and will be able to re-

place the projection lamp.

E. Each teacher will be able to operate the filmstrip
    and slide projectors and will be able to replace
    the projection lamps in these projectors.

F. Each participant will develop one science unit in-
    corporating the use of the science laboratory and
    will demonstrate the major concepts to be developed
    in the unit to the other workshop members.

G. Each participant will prepare and demonstrate a
    mini-lesson to be video-taped. Each participant
    will act as both demonstrator and cameraman.
    Teachers will be able to supervise students in the
    operation and use of video tape equipment.

Once the need for in-service training in the library/
media field has been demonstrated, and training areas based
on teacher requests have been determined, the planning committee as a whole is ready to develop guidelines and assign
specific areas of responsibility.

Developing Guidelines for Conference Planning

Basic decisions concerning the content and overall
structure of any in-service program should be developed by
the committee to determine the answers to the following
questions:

1. When and where will the conference be held?

2. Will it be a single session or several sessions? How
    many?

3. Are outside agencies to be involved? Universities?
    Exhibitors? Others?

4. Who are the conference participants? How many parti-
    cipants?

5. How can released time from teaching duties be ob-
    tained for participants?

6. What is the basic goal of the conference?

7. What specific behavioral outcomes do we expect from the conference?

8. What specific program(s) and activities will help to meet these behavioral objectives? (Set forth in outline form.)

9. Who will direct the in-service training?

10. What speakers, consultants, instructors will be needed?

11. How is the in-service training program to be financed? What will it cost?

12. Are fees to be charged?

13. Who shall be responsible for collection and disbursement of funds?

14. What specific materials need to be developed for the program? What handouts? Forms? Publicity releases? Programs? Other materials?

15. What materials and equipment are needed? Where can these items be procured?

16. Who is responsible for loss or damage to borrowed equipment or materials?

17. Are commercial exhibits desirable? If so, what exhibitors should be contacted?

18. Is any type of food to be served? If so, where is it obtained? Who pays for it? Are facilities available for serving? Are food personnel needed?

19. How shall areas of responsibility be assigned?

20. What time-table should be developed for each committee member to follow in carrying out a specific area of responsibility?

Assigning Areas of Responsibility

When content, objectives and guidelines have been determined by the committee, specific responsibilities should be assigned in the following areas:

A. Program

1. Determine sources of financing the program and establish budget.

2. Determine the title of the program.

3. Develop description and outline of program content.

4. Determine participants. (elementary teachers, secondary teachers?)

5. Determine speakers, consultants, instructors.

6. Contact consultants, instructors, etc., to determine availability and fee.

7. Make commitment for consultants desired.

8. Arrange to meet consultant's plane, train, etc., if necessary, and make necessary local accommodations for speaker if needed. Arrange to return to plane following workshop if necessary.

9. Develop printed materials (handouts) for participant use.

10. Determine method of evaluation.

B. Facilities

1. Examine program content to determine type of facilities needed. (Small group work? Large group meeting? Both?)

2. Arrange for suitable program site.

3. Consider--
    a) Size of group participating.
    b) Availability and comfortable arrangement of seating.
    c) Will work tables be needed?
    d) Will shelving for materials be needed?
    e) Is a speaker's platform with microphone needed?

f) Does the site have sufficient electrical outlets?
g) Is a source of running water necessary?
h) If audio-visual materials are used in the consultant's presentation, is the site such for ease of viewing by all?
i) Are acoustics good for ease of hearing?
j) If the workshop is to be held in the summer, are air-conditioned quarters available? If in winter, is heating control good?
k) Can the room be darkened for viewing purposes if necessary?

C. Audio-Visual Materials and Equipment

1. Contact consultants for list of equipment and materials needed.

2. Secure equipment and materials.

3. Provide extra extension cords, projection bulbs, tape reels, speakers, adaptors.

4. Arrange for security of materials and equipment when in use and when stored awaiting use.

5. Determine responsibility for equipment replacement in case of loss or damage.

6. Check all equipment shortly before meeting time to assure good working order.

7. Provide staff members to set up and dismantle equipment, and to pick up and return equipment to proper location.

D. Exhibits

1. Determine with program chairman desirable exhibits.

2. Contact exhibitors with prepared exhibit form. Information on the form should include the following:

Workshop Title
_____

Sponsor
_____

Dates:_____   Location_____

Exhibitor_____   Address_____
(Name)   (street, city, state, zip)

Phone:_____

Items included
in the exhibit: _____   _____   _____

_____   _____   _____

Space
required: _____

Equipment
required: _____   _____   _____

_____   _____   _____

Special needs: _____

_____

Exhibit to be
set up: Date_____   Time_____

Exhibit to be
removed: Date_____   Time_____

Responsibility for
security of exhibit
items: _____
(Name)   (Address)

Charge to   Exhibits Chairman_____
exhibitor:_____   (Name)

_____
(Address)

_____
(Phone)

Include a map of the exhibit area and amount of space available per exhibitor.

---

3. Notify facilities chairman of number of exhibits, space requirements, equipment requirements and special needs by a specified date.

4. Assign exhibit spaces and notify exhibitors of space allocations.

5. Be on hand to greet and direct exhibitors to exhibit area. Assist exhibitors with any problems that may arise.

E. Conference Materials

1. Obtain from the chairman a list of materials needed by participants (blank tapes, acetate sheets, transparency film, etc.).

2. Ascertain the source of materials including source of funds for obtaining materials.

3. Obtain materials in sufficient quantity to accommodate all participants.

4. Confer with conference chairman on types of printed handouts needed.

5. Prepare and duplicate handouts. (Have chairman approve before duplication.)

6. Arrange for staff to supervise distribution of each type of material or handout when needed.

F. Publicity

1. Ascertain date, time, place and basic program content at earliest possible date.

2. Compile a list of all possible conference participants.

3. Prepare publicity release (have approved by chairman).

4. Arrange for distribution to all interested parties.

5. Arrange for a central telephone number which can be called for those desiring further information.

6. Keep district administration fully informed of all publicity.

7. Write publicity release for local papers. Send to papers after approval by chairman and administration if required.

8. Develop conference summary at close of conference to be distributed to conference participants and to all news media.

It is essential at the outset for each committee member charged with a specific area of responsibility to be given a time-table for completion of assigned tasks. Committee members should be ready with alternate plans if initial planning cannot be carried out for any reason. It is desirable for the committee as a whole to meet at frequent intervals to review and modify program plans as the necessity arises. Both careful planning and a well-informed planning committee are essential to assure a successful in-service training program.

Notes

1. Alice Miel, Creativity in Teaching (Wadsworth Publishing Co., 1961), p. 242.

2. Elton Tielke, "A Study of the Relationship of Selected Environmental Factors to the Development of Elementary School Libraries" (Ed. D. diss., Univ. of Texas, Austin, 1968).

3. Kenneth King, "An Evaluation of Teacher Utilization of Selected Educational Media in Relation to the Level of Sophistication of the Educational Media Program in Selected Oklahoma Public Schools" (Ed. D. diss., Univ. of Oklahoma, 1969).

4. Hilda Jay, "Increasing the Use of Secondary School Libraries as a Teaching Tool" (Ed. D. diss., New York University, 1969).

5. Marjorie Williams, "Educational Media as Content and
    Process in Teacher Education in Florida" (Ed. D.
    diss., Univ. of Florida, 1969).

6. Marie E. McMahan, "A Study of the Feasibility of a
    System of Pre-Service Teacher Education in Media"
    (Ed. D. diss., Michigan State University, 1969).

7. Nancy Polette, "A Survey of Teacher Attitude and Pupil
    Achievement in IMC Use in the Pattonville School
    District, 1965-1972" (Pattonville School District,
    St. Louis County, Missouri).

8. St. Charles, Missouri Librarians' Council, "Report on
    Teacher Questionnaires to the Librarians' Council"
    (St. Charles, Missouri, May 1971).

9. David W. Beggs and Edward G. Buffie, Independent
    Study, Bold New Venture (Indiana University Press,
    1965), pp. 187-188.

10. Brice J. Biddle and William J. Ellena, eds., Contem-
    porary Research on Teacher Effectiveness (Holt,
    Rinehart & Winston, 1964), p. 312.

2. A SURVEY OF IN-SERVICE PROGRAMS FOR TEACHERS

One of the major areas identified by most teachers as most lacking in their professional training is the use of media centers and the wide variety of instructional materials available in the schools today. In an effort to fill this training gap and help teachers keep abreast of new developments in the field of education, many school districts throughout the United States have developed excellent in-service training programs. In some of these programs, school districts carry the total responsibility for training. In others, cooperative efforts with local colleges or universities have produced effective in-service training programs.

The majority of the programs which follow have goals based on specific behavioral objectives; provide opportunity for participants to become involved in the training process; develop techniques or concepts which can be related directly to the participant's needs; provide for voluntary teacher participation; and have developed means of evaluation of the in-service training.

The programs are presented here as models. Their goals, objectives, procedure, activities and materials used can be easily adapted to specific school situations where a need for a particular type of in-service training program has been demonstrated. While in some cases it is difficult to present a variety of programs in a basic format, an attempt has been made to provide the following pertinent details for each district's program:

1. The title of the in-service training program.
2. The sponsor (including address for more information).
3. The date or dates, number of sessions and place held.
4. The director.
5. The participants.

6. The basic theme.
7. In-service training objectives.
8. Speakers and consultants.
9. An outline of content.
10. Activities of participants.
11. Commercial materials used.
12. Materials prepared locally for use.
13. Means of evaluation.

EXAMPLE (1)

LIBRARIES

(In-Service Training)

SPONSOR: St. Charles School District, St. Charles, Mo. Dr. Frank Colaw, Superintendent.

CO-SPONSORS: St. Charles County Librarian's Council; University of Missouri Extension Council --St. Charles County.

DATE(S):   Fall, 1972--Twenty hours of instruction.

NO. OF SESSIONS: Eight (8) two and one-half hour weekly sessions beginning 7:00 to 9:30 p. m.

DIRECTOR: Mrs. Lynn McIntosh, Reference Librarian, Kathryn Linnemann Public Library, St. Charles, Mo.

PARTICIPANTS: Designed for elementary teachers and library assistants.

BASIC THEME: To provide teachers with a working knowledge of libraries and instructional materials centers and the manner in which they can be of assistance in curriculum development and individualized study.

IN-SERVICE
TRAINING
OBJECTIVES: To encourage teachers and students to make more and better use of library materials and services in their educational activities.

SPEAKERS--
CONSULTANTS: A highly qualified staff of professionals assisted the instructor. A professional from each specific area of interest worked with the group each week.

33

Among the speakers were: Chuck Mad-
den, Dean, Webster College, St. Louis,
Mo.; Gene Martin, Director, Daniel
Boone Regional Library (Mo.); Mary
Thornton, St. Charles High School Li-
brarian; Nelson Smith, Principal, St.
Ann School, St. Ann, Mo.; Conrad
Erickson, Director, School Libraries
City of St. Louis.

OUTLINE OF CONTENT

I.   The library as an important part of innovative teaching
     techniques and new fields of study:

     A. Hooked on Books, Fader
     B. How Children Learn, Holt
     C. Independent study
     D. Individualized reading
     E. Use of instructional materials in the classroom
     F. Sesame Street's effect on education
     G. New courses, example: Ecology

II. How libraries operate -- 2 sessions:

     A. Library organization and management

         1. Types of libraries and the orientation of their
             collections
         2. Educational background of librarians
         3. How libraries are arranged and why
             (Melvil Dewey as a necessary evil)
         4. Library hardware and its functions
         5. Library services and policies--loan periods,
             circulating vs. reference collections, etc.
         6. Care and handling of library materials
         7. Budgeting

     B. Library collections

         1. The variety of media in libraries and why
             they're purchased, ex.: value of a book com-
             pared to value of a periodical; film vs. print,
             etc.
         2. The selection process
         3. The concept of collection-building

4. Recent trends in children's and young adult
literature

III. The teacher's role in the library:

A. The library as a resource for planning study units,
reinforcing what happens in the classroom, source
of materials to use in the classroom, professional
development
B. Teacher-librarian relationship--symbiotic (conferences, etc.)
C. Other library services--reserves, ILL, bibliographies, current awareness, etc.
D. Role in selection and budgeting

IV. How to give a library study unit (different age levels)
--2 sessions:

A. How to use a card catalog and find the book you
want (film, "Finding Information")
B. Basic reference tools (could use a variety of techniques to teach this to show teachers what's available for a library skills unit--filmstrip, transparency, live demonstration, etc.)
C. Planning for student use of the library

V. Future library developments:

A. Media
B. Info storage and retrieval
C. Book catalogs
D. Closed circuit TV

VI. Field trip and summary:

A. Visit to Curriculum Library, Eden Webster Li-
braries--7:00 p.m.
B. Summary--meeting room at Eden Webster Libraries

Activities

Lectures   Large and Small Group Discussions
Films   Evaluation of Materials
Demonstrations   Storytelling
Developed, demonstrated and implemented an independent
study plan for use with students
Examination and use of basic reference tools

Field trip to Webster College Curriculum Library

Commercial Materials Used

McGraw Hill filmstrip #402391 Using Books

Recordings: Black Beauty (RCA); Call It Courage (Miller
              Brody)

Weston Woods Sound Filmstrips: The Happy Owls and The
                                 Three Robbers

Pied Piper Productions: Sound filmstrip, Distant Lands

Milliken Publishing Company: Basic Library Skills (12 visu-
                               als--24 worksheets)

Creative Visuals: Visual Series, 124 transparencies, Using
                    the IMC Effectively

Creative Tapes: Tape Series, Library and Reference Skills
                  for Middle Grades: The Right Book for You

Evaluation

        Each session was evaluated individually with stress
on how useful the material presented would be to the teachers on situation.
        Due to popular demand the entire workshop was re-
peated in the spring for another group of the district's
teachers.

EXAMPLE (2)

SELECTION OF INSTRUCTIONAL MATERIALS

(Workshop)

SPONSOR:	Pattonville R-3 School District, 115 Harding, Maryland Heights, Mo. 63043.
DATE(S):	April 2, 1970.
PLACE:	St. Ann School, 3721 St. Bridget Lane, St. Ann, Mo.
NO. OF SESSIONS:	One (full day).
PARTICIPANTS:	450 elementary teachers, grades K-6.
BASIC THEME:	The careful selection of instructional materials for use with and by elementary school students should combine two factors: a thorough knowledge of basic selection criteria and a personal previewing of materials.
IN-SERVICE TRAINING OBJECTIVES:	1. To acquaint teachers with the basic criteria for evaluating both print and non-print materials. 2. To provide teachers with a wide variety of instructional materials for the purpose of examination, evaluation and selection. 3. To provide teachers with an opportunity to share with each other effective utilization practices concerning instructional materials.
SPEAKERS-- CONSULTANTS:	1. Dr. Eldon Madison, Chairman Instructional Technology Dept., Southern Illinois University, Edwardsville.

2.   Elementary Media Specialists (7),
     Pattonville School District.

OUTLINE OF CONTENT

I.   Research on the effectiveness of a multi-media ap-
      proach to teaching:

      A. How children learn
      B. Need for involvement of all five senses
      C. Need for a multi-media approach
      D. Multi-media and the requirements of innovative
          school programs
      E. Techniques for effective use of multi-media
          1.   Listening activities
          2.   Viewing activities
          3.   Research activities
          4.   Fostering creativity through multi-media

II.   Criteria for selection of instructional materials:

      A. Suitability for the age and grade level for which
          intended.
      B. Demands of the curriculum.   What materials are
          needed?
      C. Recency.   How recent is the material?   Is re-
          cency a factor to be considered?
      D. Method of presentation.   Will it keep the interest
          of the reader, listener or viewer?
      E. Authority.   Who prepared the material?   Is this
          person an authority in the field?
      F. Scope.   How broad or narrow is the coverage of
          the subject?
      G. Style.   Is it suitable for the subject?
      H. Format.   In what format can the information best
          be presented?
      I. Demand.   Does the demand justify the cost?
      J. Technical quality.   Good?   Fair?   Poor?
      K. Comparison.   How does the material compare with
          other materials on the subject in similar format?

Activities

1.   Conference participants as a group heard one major
      speaker give an overview of the problems involved in se-
      lection and the use of instructional materials.

2. Participants divided into grade level groups and each group received several items of both good and poor quality to evaluate using the evaluative criteria presented. Small group evaluations were briefly presented to the entire group.

3. Evaluation and selection. Participants moved to a large selection area to examine materials on display. Materials were those used in various schools in the district and displays by commercial exhibitors. Each participant had selection sheets to complete noting those items they would like to have purchased for their school's instructional materials center.

4. During the selection phase of the workshop, teachers in schools which had materials which were not available in other schools discussed the way in which they and their students used these materials.

Commercial Materials Used

Displays of materials from several commercial companies including Eyegate, McGraw Hill, SVE, Phelan Audiovisual Aids, Britt Visual Aids.

Local Materials Used

Materials displayed from local materials centers--books, filmstrips, maps, charts, study prints, slides, records, tapes, reference books, art prints, recent fiction and nonfiction.

Local Materials Prepared for Participants

1. Sheet listing evaluative criteria for selection of materials
2. Statement on Selection of Materials

Selection of Materials

It is essential that careful planning in the selection of IMC materials precede the expenditure of funds allocated for this purpose. All purchase orders for new materials will be prepared by the elementary librarian in cooperation with teachers and principals and must be approved by the director of elementary education. Materials will be selected in keeping with the Pattonville Criteria for selection as outlined in

Policies, Procedures and Practices, Section 6.105, and with
the requirements of the Missouri State Board of Education.
The collection of print and non-print materials shall be balanced as follows:

General Reference	2.5%	Fine Arts	4.0%
Philosophy	.3%	Literature	4.0%
Religion	.8%	History-travel	
Social Science	9.0%	Biography	21.0%
Language	.4%	Fiction	20.0%
Pure Science	12.0%	Easy Books	19.0%
Applied Science	6.0%		

3.   Selection Form as follows.

4.   Evaluation Form as follows.

SELECTION FORM--BOOKS

Author_____   Author_____
Title_____   Title_____
Copyright_____Price_____   Copyright_____Price_____
Publisher_____   Publisher_____
Cat. Used_____   Cat. Used_____

Author_____   Author_____
Title_____   Title_____
Copyright_____Price_____   Copyright_____Price_____
Publisher_____   Publisher_____
Cat. Used_____   Cat. Used_____

SELECTION FORM--AUDIO-VISUAL MATERIALS

Filmstrips   Picture Sets

Title_____   Title_____
No. in Set_____Price_____   No. in Set_____Price_____
Cat. Used_____   Cat. Used_____
Company_____   Company_____

Title_____   Title_____
No. in Set_____Price_____   No. in Set_____Price_____
Cat. Used_____   Cat. Used_____
Company_____   Company_____

(List all others on back--records, pamphlets, etc.)

EVALUATION FORM

INSTRUCTIONAL MATERIALS CENTER QUESTIONNAIRE
(April 1, 1970)

New Missouri Standards for Accreditation will require elementary libraries in the schools of the State for the first
time beginning July 1, 1969. We have tried to develop an
elementary library program based on the best practices in
library services recommended by the American Library Association. However, we are always concerned with improving the program to provide those services that will most
help you in reaching your goals for students and to aid each
student in reaching his full educational growth. We would
appreciate your answers to the following questions. It is
not necessary to sign this questionnaire. Please complete
before leaving the gym this morning and leave on the table
by the door.

1. School_____

2. Which of the following goals do you feel is most im-
    portant for your students to reach in using the materials
    centers this year? Check two.

    a. Develop concepts independently through use of a wide
        variety of materials.
    b. Develop proficiency in working alone.
    c. Develop greater discrimination in his selection of
        materials.
    d. Develop a greater love of reading and books.
    e. Become independent in use of audio-visual materials.
    f. Become more proficient in note taking, outlining and
        organization of material.
    g. Improve listening and viewing skills.
    h. Other_____

3. In which of the following ways are library services most
    helpful to you in reaching your goals for students?
    Check two.

    a. Materials sent to classrooms on teacher request.
    b. Materials introduced to classes centered around
        units of work.

    c.   Work/study skill classes.
    d.   Helping students in selection of reading materials.
    e.   Helping students in selection and use of audio-visual materials.
    f.   Supervising and assisting students in individual research activities.
    g.   Assisting small groups of students or individual students in research activities.
    h.   Book talks related to units of work.
    i.   Other_____

4.   In what way do you feel the use of library facilities would be most helpful to your students?

    a.   Library facilities available to any child at any time the librarian is on duty, (for group or individual work or selection of materials by small groups of individuals).
    b.   Classes scheduled at any time the teacher requests to work on particular skills or present materials for units of work.
    c.   A combination of A and B.
    d.   One regularly scheduled weekly class visit.
    e.   Other_____

5.   Please add any other comments on this sheet that would help us in improving the IMC program.

Evaluation of the workshop on "Selection of Instructional Materials."

1.   Did you find the workshop helpful to you as a teacher? (a) to a great degree (b) to a moderate degree (c) not at all

2.   Which part of the workshop was most helpful (number choices 1--2--3)
    a.   overview of the selection and use of instructional materials
    b.   small group evaluations of materials
    c.   previewing and selection of materials
    d.   discussions with other teachers concerning use of materials

3.   How could the workshop have been improved?

EXAMPLE (3)

MEDIA IN SERVICE

(In-Service Program)

SPONSOR:	Stillwater City Schools, 314 S. Lewis, Stillwater, Oklahoma 74074.
DATE(S):	12 weeks, 1970.
PLACE:	Stillwater City Public Schools.
DIRECTORS:	Dr. Wesley Beck, Jr., Asst. Supt., Stillwater Public Schools; Dr. Gene Post, Prof. Education, Oklahoma State University; Mr. Calvin McIntire, Director Media Development, Stillwater Schools; Mr. Winston Smith.
PARTICIPANTS:	67 classroom teachers, 30 student aides.
BASIC THEME:	The basic goal was to involve students, teachers, and teacher-aides in reaching more pupils on a one-to-one basis in the classroom. This was to be achieved by training high school students, as well as teachers and para-professionals, to serve as media technicians in the Stillwater Schools.
IN-SERVICE TRAINING OBJECTIVES:	1. To help teachers to be more creative in using media to individualize instruction. 2. To train student aides to assist teachers in the use of media. 3. To provide vocational training in the media field for economically and scholastically less advantaged students who were not achieving success in the typical classroom situation.

43

4. To promote more efficient and more
    frequent use of media in the classroom.

THE PROGRAM

The Stillwater Schools in-service education program
was held during 1970 over a twelve-week period.   A two-
week session directed by Dr. Gene Post was designed to
train 27 teachers for the following tasks:

1. Operate audio and video tape recorders, record play-
    ers, and projectors (16mm, slide, opaque, and over-
    head)
2. Organize groups to observe instructional television
    and films
3. Make overhead transparencies
4. Coordinate and order films, slides and tapes
5. Assist with effective bulletin board displays
6. Drymount pictures for class use
7. Supervise high school students placed as media tech-
    nicians in the Stillwater Schools.

During the summer of 1970 a one-week workshop involving 40 classroom teachers was conducted by Mr. Calvin
McIntire and Dr. Wesley Beck, Jr.   In this workshop teachers were apprised of the kind of services they could expect
to receive from the aides and high school students and were
given the opportunity to acquire television production and utilization skills.

A final nine-week training session for less advantaged
students was conducted by Mr. Winston Smith.   General objectives for these students were:

1. To train high school less advantaged students for main-
    tenance positions in media.

2. To place high school less advantaged students as media
    technicians in Stillwater Schools, Oklahoma State Univer-
    sity and the community.   Students attending this training
    session were enrolled in a high school Vocational Techni-
    cal Exemplary course in audio-visual maintenance and
    operation.   They were expected to cover three proficiency
    levels for each of the following machines:

16mm projector   video recorder
slide projector   overhead projector
video camera   tape recorder
filmstrip projector   video monitor
opaque projector

Basic Components of the Stillwater Program

1. Maintenance and Utilization

    Each school has a media aide responsible for the super-
    vision of the student media technicians and for the total
    media support program in the individual school.   A main-
    tenance shop is maintained at the district level where
    one technician supervises student media technicians.

2. Production and Distribution

    Stillwater teachers identify those areas of the curriculum
    where support and enrichment are most needed.   Color
    video tapes are produced by teachers and students to
    meet this need.   Mini-studies in each school provide stu-
    dents with the opportunity to be creative through local
    production of television programs under the direction of
    their teacher.

Evaluation

        Constant, ongoing evaluation is a part of the continu-
ing objectives of the Stillwater Program which include:

1. Expansion into a cooperative effort supplying video taped
    lessons, in-service training for teachers, and video tape
    recorders to approximately 48 school districts in Payne,
    Lincoln and Creek Counties

2. Continuation of teacher pre-service and in-service train-
    ing through closed circuit television

3. Continuation of a program to promote student learning
    of communication skills

4. Development of a complete color studio for the produc-
    tion and distribution of video tape lessons

The Stillwater City Schools received the 1971 National
Association for Educational Communications and Technol-
ogy/Encyclopaedia Britannica Education Corporation Award
for its new Media In-Service Education Program.

EXAMPLE (4)

EFFECTIVE USE OF MEDIA
AND OF EDUCATIONAL TELEVISION

(In-Service Training)

SPONSOR: Greenwich Public Schools, Greenwich High School Media Center, Hillside Road, Greenwich, Conn. 06830

DATE(S): On-going program throughout the school year.

PLACE: Greenwich Public Schools.

DIRECTOR: Elfrieda McCauley, Coordinator, Secondary School Libraries.

PARTICIPANTS: All classroom teachers.

TRAINING SESSIONS: Afternoon and evening classes for teachers. Day sessions for volunteers (80 volunteers serve 12 elementary schools assisting teachers and students in the use of educational television).

BASIC THEME: Specific Program Description

The Effective Use of Educational Television--(An on-going program for the training of teachers and parent volunteers in the instructional uses of TV and effective use of equipment).

Forms of In-Service Training

1. Orientation of new teachers
2. "Hands on" instructional equipment seminars
3. TV operation and production

47

4. New equipment demonstrations
5. New book exhibits
6. Encouragement of instructional staff to attend workshops and conferences outside the school district.

IN-SERVICE
TRAINING
OBJECTIVES:

1. To use the unique features of TV to provide educational opportunities not otherwise available.
2. To produce quality controlled presentations and be able to retrieve them indefinitely.
3. To magnify objects and processes.
4. To provide resources otherwise unavailable.
5. To improve communication within the educational community.
6. To help the student to discover a new method of self-expression.
7. To help the teacher better communicate to students new information and ideas.

Activities

Teachers are given the following questionnaire, statement of purpose of the Greenwich High School Audio-Visual Program, and brochure listing suggestions for effective utilization of instructional television. Media personnel and technicians are available to assist the teacher in developing competencies to meet those specific educational needs indicated by the teacher on the questionnaire.

Local Materials Used

The following questionnaire, general statement of purpose and brochure on television use were prepared by Robert W. Markarian of the Greenwich Schools.

Greenwich Public Schools

Please indicate the kind of TV activity which you would like
to explore, and return this form to the volunteer mail-box
in the main office.   A TV volunteer will contact you.

.... CLASS OBSERVATION & INSTANT REPLAY   Requested
(a tape of your class in session)   date _____

.... AN INTRODUCTION TO CLOSED CIRCUIT
TELEVISION

       A live presentation of the TV story told   date _____
with overhead projectuals explaining the
history of TV and how it works.

       A videotape of this presentation is also
available.

       A brief live taping is done to orient
the class to CCTV.

.... MAGNIFICATION

       Small objects, processes, demonstra-   date _____
tions and visuals can be enlarged to
the full size of the TV screen to give
every student a good view of what is
being shown.

.... REPLAY OF A PROGRAM FROM THE TV
TAPE LIBRARY

       Title_____   date _____

**

I WOULD LIKE TO TALK ABOUT THE USE OF TV IN MY
CLASSES.

       date _____

Name _____ Room No. _____

School _____

# #

Greenwich Public Schools

GENERAL STATEMENT OF PURPOSE

The purpose of the Greenwich High School Audiovisual Program is to enrich and support instruction in order to achieve the goals of the school curriculum.

Specific Goals

    I. Physical Goals
       A. To fully equip the Audiovisual Center to meet the demands of the instructional program.
       B. To provide materials necessary to the instructional process.
       C. To provide work areas for teachers to produce instructional materials.
       D. To purchase equipment necessary for the implementation of individualized instruction.

    II. Organizational Goals
       A. To train teachers and students in the proper use of electronic audiovisual equipment.
       B. To assist teachers in the selection and evaluation of instructional materials.
       C. To promote the proper use of equipment and materials by students in the Media Center.

    III. Instructional Goals
       A. To assist teachers in the most efficient utilization of audiovisual materials and equipment.
       B. To train teachers in the use of a "systems" approach to education.
       C. To foster the use of audiovisual materials as integral segments of the curriculum.

Additional Specific Information

    A. Organizational Goals
       About 50 teachers currently enrolled in in-service TV courses.

    B. Instructional Goals
       Four 10-week mini-courses for high school students next year in TV studio.

Specific TV Tapes Made this Year:

1. Orientation to New School by Headmaster
2. Orientation to the Media Center
3. Use of the "On Line" School Computer
4. Use of the MTST Computer
5. Tour of the Town Sewage Plant
6. 50 Teacher Self-Appraisal Tapes
7. Alliance Francais Meeting
8. Dr. Charles Silberman
9. Freedom Shrine Dedication
10. Media Center Open House

Television In-Service for Greenwich Teachers

OUTLINE OF GENERAL GOALS

I. To use the unique features of TV to provide educational opportunities otherwise unavailable.

    A. To provide the opportunity for self-observation:

        1. Show and tell (primary grades).

        2. Tape a 20-30 minute segment of a regular class day and replay it for the class to see. Be sure to discuss the activity so that the class can become aware of good and bad behavior. Stimulate suggestions for improvement.

        3. Tape activity of students during individualized activities. Replay it for them and be sure to discuss and appraise various activities.

        4. Tape students in small groups at various activities, e.g., student reports, pantomine, short plays, athletic activities, book reports, student tutors working with other students, games, and subject discussions. Play it back for students and discuss performance according to prepared criteria.

        5. Tape any one of your classes and examine it closely for activity you may have missed.

Teachers are usually surprised at how much
specific behavior can elude them during class.

6. Examine your own teaching technique.   One
    cannot really know how he appears in front of
    a class until he sees himself on TV.   Fre-
    quent use of TV erases all unnaturalness that
    may characterize a first experience.

7. Let children role play situations.   A class
    viewing of students role playing common diffi-
    cult situations (especially those that arise in
    school, e.g., teacher-student confrontation)
    can make for valuable class discussion and
    perhaps new insights for the children that may
    result in improved behavior.

B. To produce quality controlled presentations and be
    able to retrieve them indefinitely:

1. Teachers are sometimes required to explain
    or repeat a single presentation (especially a
    demonstration) several times.   If such a pre-
    sentation is put on videotape, it can be played
    when needed thus releasing the teacher from
    the front of the room and permitting him to
    devote himself to immediate needs in the class.
    Videotape allows the teacher to examine the
    presentation making whatever improvements he
    wishes before the tape is finalized.

2. The TV circulation office will enable teachers
    to use taped lessons made by other teachers
    in the district.   The office is just starting but
    will eventually circulate video tapes the same
    way the Media Services Center now circulates
    films.

C. To magnify objects and processes:

By simply training a portable camera over his
shoulder a teacher can sit at his desk and demonstrate proper technique in any process.   If this
demonstration is video taped the teacher is freed
from the desk and can circulate among students
giving individual help as needed.

D. To provide resources otherwise unavailable:

1. Share guest speakers--A guest addressing one
    class can be videotaped and made available to
    all other classes and in independent study
    centers. The TV circulation office will list
    these resources monthly. Be sure to inform
    them via your school TV volunteers of any
    contributions you can make.

2. Lightweight, battery-operated TV equipment
    can be taken virtually anywhere to record in-
    formation. Our own units have gone to the
    United Nations, Metropolitan Art Museum, lo-
    cal factories, financial business institutions,
    the airport, the local waterworks and China-
    town.

    These videotapes are not meant to substitute
    for students' visits but are designed to be used
    when visits are not practical.

E. To improve communication within the educational
    community

    Parents are often surprised and delighted to see
    segments of actual classes on tape during visits to
    the school. An otherwise disbelieving parent can
    be convinced of a child's behavior in class when he
    sees it on tape. Misconceptions about class activi-
    ties can often be cleared up when parents are in-
    vited to see a video tape of a class with the teach-
    er setting the context for the tape and explaining
    what is happening while parents view the tape.

II. To help the student to discover a new method of self-
     expression.

Let students use TV to express their own creativeness.

They can:
1. Write and perform an original skit.
2. Create a commercial for a real or imaginary prod-
    uct.
3. Research a favorite famous person and assume his
    identity in an interview.
4. Create and perform a satire on something familiar

around school, in society or on broadcast TV.
5. Produce a documentary, especially about the local
   environment--the school, the neighborhood or the
   town.
6. Prepare dramatized lessons for other students on
   social behavior in particular situations, e. g., the
   classroom, the lunchroom, at home with the family,
   and in their peer groups (especially when faced
   with pressure to take part in activity of which they
   disapprove).

Of course most of the above activities could be performed without being video taped but television invari-
ably serves as an added incentive during preparation.
And the playback increases satisfaction and often helps
the child learn more about his own real image.

III.   To help the teacher to better communicate to students
        specific information and ideas.

        Many of these applications have already been dis-
cussed in Part I.   They include bringing outside resources
to the classroom, showing special taped presentations done
by subject specialists in the school district, magnifying objects and processes and taping simple demonstrations for
replay in order to release the teacher.

        It is important that any classroom teacher who de-
velops a useful technique with TV communicate that experience to the TV specialists through the TV volunteers so
that other teachers in the district can profit from the technique.

        Trained volunteers are available to provide TV ser-
vices for teachers and students in every elementary school
in the district.   These volunteers can effect all of the activities suggested here and are particularly eager to work
with small groups of students (under the overall direction of
the teacher) using television creatively.

        We know that TV is an effective teaching tool but it
will be successful only when the classroom teacher is convinced of its value and integrates it as a standard resource.
We are attempting through our volunteer program to make
it as easy as possible for an already busy teacher to experiment with still another tool.

We are eager to have the opportunity to service you and your students.   Please fill out the attached TV form and drop in the TV volunteers mail box in the main office.

EXAMPLE (5)

"DO TOUCH" LEARNING TO USE MULTI-MEDIA

(In-Service Training)

SPONSOR:	Plymouth River Elementary School, Region 2, Hingham, Massachusetts 02045.
DATE(S):	Ongoing program throughout the year.
PLACE:	Plymouth River Elementary School.
DIRECTOR:	Glenn W. Cook, IMC Director, Plymouth River Elementary School.
PARTICIPANTS:	29 teachers and 850 students.
BASIC THEME:	Teachers and students alike are encouraged to handle audio-visual equipment, helping teachers to see results and gain incentive to use more media more effectively.
IN-SERVICE TRAINING OBJECTIVES:	1. To help the faculty become better teachers by attaining proficiency in media use, and acquiring a desire to capitalize on this knowledge in the classroom.
	2. To assist children in becoming better communicators in a media minded world.
SPEAKERS-- CONSULTANTS:	IMC staff of the Plymouth River School.

PROGRAM DESCRIPTION

Teachers and students alike are encouraged to handle the equipment, experiment with it, use it, gain confidence in themselves and their technical expertise with it, even take it home if they like.

Teachers and students simultaneously learn how to use the hardware and employ effective techniques. During weekly sessions faculty and students are exposed to a wide variety of media and equipment. The following are the print and non-print oriented skills covered in the program:

The Decimal System	Use of opaque, slide and over-
Reference	head projectors
Folklore	Photography
Storytelling methods	Drymounting
Book reporting ideas	Animation
Use of tape recorders	Poster making
Use of films	Lettering
Use of filmstrips	Video tape recording

According to Mr. Cook, "While teachers are using video-tape recordings for self-evaluation and extensive lesson planning, fourth, fifth and sixth graders are broadcasting news three mornings a week over PRS CTTV Channel 9. Seeing their children respond so well to sophisticated media motivates the Plymouth River faculty to become equally expert. And this has been the basis for the school's successful in-service training program--reaching teachers through children. "

EXAMPLE (6)

ORIENTATION OF FIRST-YEAR TEACHERS IN LIBRARY SERVICES AND RESOURCES

(In-Service Training)

SPONSORING AGENCY:	Library/Audio Visual Department of the Fulton County Board of Education, 786 Cleveland Ave., Atlanta, Georgia 30315.
DIRECTOR:	Mary Belle England, Director of Library Services.
DATE(S):	Annually in 6-8 one and one-half hour training meetings.
PARTICIPANTS:	Small groups of first year teachers.
BASIC THEME:	To acquaint first year teachers with the services and resources available to them through the library and audio visual departments of the Fulton County School System.
IN-SERVICE TRAINING OBJECTIVES:	1. To provide opportunity for nonprint review sessions. 2. To provide information concerning the resources and services available for organized reading courses. 3. To provide for examination of new books. 4. To provide instruction in the production and use of non-book materials.
SPEAKERS-- CONSULTANTS:	Mary Belle England, Director Library Services; Elizabeth Whitehead, Asst. Director; Mr. S. M. Richenberg, Director AV Dept.; Mr. C. T. Gervais, Associate Director AV Dept.

OUTLINE OF CONTENT

I. Levels of IMC Services

    A. School system level
    B. Local school level

II. Teacher-Librarian Cooperation

    A. Steps in cooperative planning
    B. Development of library-reference skills
    C. Enrichment learning

III. Types of Materials

    A. Special types for subject areas
    B. Instructional television
    C. Professional library
    D. Periodical collection
    E. Pamphlets

IV. Services and Regulations

    A. Requesting materials in the collections
    B. Requesting new materials
    C. Basic services
    D. Basic regulations

Activities

Teachers are divided into groups, each group meeting separately for a presentation of services from the library and audio-visual departments.

Separate orientation meetings are held with directors of specialized curriculum areas such as art, music and physical education.

Locally Produced Materials

The library department has produced an audio-visual presentation of the resources and services available from the Fulton County Central Library Department and has also included special suggestions for utilizing the resources and services of the local school library. The presentation was planned by outlining the services, central and local, that it was felt should be emphasized and which would be informative and interesting to the groups viewing the presentation. Settings were selected as examples and pictures were made and developed into slides. From the outline, scripts were written and oral descriptions were recorded on tape. Slides were arranged and coordinated with the taped descriptions.

A sample tape script follows.

Script: For new teacher orientation of resources and services available from the Fulton County Library Department

SCHOOL LIBRARY MEDIA SERVICES

Fulton County School System
Atlanta, Georgia

In the Fulton County School System, instructional materials services or library media services are provided at two levels; at the school system level and at the local school level. The library media center in each local school, under the direction of a professionally trained librarian, offers convenient and supportive service for all types of classroom activities. Each librarian, eager to give good service and to know the library needs of the school, suggests several ideas for teacher-librarian cooperation to insure maximum use of the school library as a base for education:

1. Make an effort to know the librarian; feel free to ask for help in planning class activities. The librarians believe that they are most effective when they work with the teacher through the instructional program, for example:

   a. The teacher decides on the unit and outlines its scope.

   b. The teacher meets with the librarian to plan use of materials, and they consult the card catalog for suggestions for pamphlets, pictures, books, recordings, filmstrips, and other materials.

   c. The teacher and the librarian evaluate the proposed materials to determine the suitability for the unit of study.

d. The teacher and the librarian decide which materials
should stay in the library and which should be sent
to the classroom.

2. Accompany class groups to the library to help the librarian to know the needs and abilities of the children
in the group.

3. Make use of unscheduled periods to send individual
children or small groups for reading, research, listening, and/or viewing experiences.

4. Make plans with the librarian to teach the use of library-
reference skills, for example, card catalog, the dictionary, abridged readers' guide, maps and globes.

5. Encourage enrichment through personal reading, storytelling, sharing ideas, and home circulation.

Special types of materials are provided for some subject areas. Several examples illustrate this part of the library media program:

1. Albums of recordings are available to use with the music
textbooks.

2. The library collection includes many of the recordings
used on the physical education television programs.

3. The Magic Book Programs are the WETV library television programs for primary and elementary grades.
Each week a story teller or author presents interesting
books to read for pleasure. These books and related
titles are available for individual or group reading in
most library collections.

Cover to Cover, a telecourse in literary appreciation,
designed for the fifth and sixth grades, and A Matter of Fiction, a telecourse in literary appreciation, designed for the
junior high school student, were produced by the public television station in Washington, D.C. and are also available
from WETV.

The Teachers' Professional Library and the Audio-
Visual Department expand and enrich library instructional
materials services at the system level. These services are
housed in and administered from the Fulton County Services

building.

        In every school system there should be small collec-
tions of professional materials available to teachers in the
individual school libraries; but there should also be a comprehensive systemwide library for teachers.   In the Fulton
County School System there is such a library.   It is called
the Fulton County Teachers' Library and is as accessible as
the telephone and school mail to all of the teachers in the
Fulton County schools.

        The materials available in the Teachers' Library are:
books, periodicals, pamphlets and recordings.   The collection contains approximately 6,000 books on a wide range of
subjects, such as: administration, supervision, philosophy
of education, methods, grouping of children, building units
of study, discipline, independent study, and all subject areas
in the curriculum.   The library subscribes to about 170
periodicals.   Many of these periodicals are indexed in the
Education Index, so that articles on almost any educational
subject can be located.   Articles in recent issues of periodicals supply the newest material available on a subject.
Since the library has back files of many of the periodicals
which are indexed, a wealth of information is available.   A
list of the periodicals to which the library subscribes has
been sent to each school librarian.

        The pamphlet collection is filed in pamphlet boxes,
arranged and cataloged by subject.   The collection of recordings is one which supplements school collections, especially
in the fields of elementary music, foreign languages, and
holidays.   Recordings may be requested on the audio-visual
requisition forms which the A-V coordinator has.

        There is another special collection of books in the
Central Library Department.   This department is a deposi-
tory for examination copies of new books from about 65 publishers.   These books cover most subject areas and are
available for examination any time the teachers should desire
to see them.   They would be of great assistance in recommending materials for purchase in the local school library.
The librarians spend a great deal of time examining and reviewing the new books.

        The Teachers' Library offers various special services,
such as: providing materials for college and university
classes, for extension courses offered through the Atlanta

Area Teacher Education Service, for teaching modern foreign languages, for faculty study groups, and for summer school study.   One of the most popular services is the furnishing of books, pamphlets and periodicals to teachers attending summer school.   Teachers may borrow materials for a whole summer school session instead of having to depend on overnight or hourly use of reserved material.   If several Fulton County teachers are taking the same course, they may borrow a quantity of materials and pass them around among themselves for the duration of the summer session.

A sheet describing services of and regulations for the use of the library was distributed at the beginning of this meeting.   It states that materials may be requested in three ways: 1) by telephone, 2) school mail, or 3) a personal visit.   Materials requested by telephone or school mail will be sent directly to teachers at their local schools.   Teachers are urged to visit the professional library to examine materials and to use the card catalog which indexes all materials in the collection.   Please feel free to request assistance from the central library staff in meeting any professional reading or study needs.   There is a great deal of leniency in the length of time that materials may be kept.   The only thing that is asked of the teachers is that they pay for anything that is damaged or lost, and that they return the material within a reasonable period of time or when somebody else needs it.   No fines are charged for overdue materials.

Since the library is for the teachers of Fulton County, they should feel free to suggest titles of materials that they consider very good and believe would be worthwhile additions to the collection.   They will surely run across titles of books in professional periodicals, or may actually see books, pamphlets, periodicals, or other materials which they feel would also be very useful to other teachers.   The aim of the library is to serve all of the teachers as much as possible; and any requests and suggestions will be helpful in making the library one which is truly for everybody in the school system.

EXAMPLE (7)

THE 21-INCH CLASSROOM

(Media Utilization Workshops)

SPONSOR: Department of Education, Commonwealth of Massachusetts.

PARTICIPANTS: Membership in the 21-Inch Classroom, which broadcasts programs every day over Channel 57 WGBY, involves the public school system in a given city or town and provides among its free services, in-service workshops and media consulting services.

PROGRAM DESCRIPTION

The Media Utilization Workshop Series offers the following programs for in-service teacher training:

The 21-Inch Offerings

Workshop Series

1. Theory and use of ETV and 21-Inch Programs:
 Information on ETV and The 21-Inch Classroom viewing of particular programs, studying program guides, discussion of in-class utilization procedures.

 Separate sessions can be arranged for specific grade levels and for subject areas.

2. Classroom Media Techniques:
 dealing with requests from teachers, can include making transparencies, posters, charts, bulletin boards, duplicating, mounting, laminating, audio devices.

 One or more sessions.

3. Preparing a Multi-media Presentation:
    deals with choosing a topic and discovering the most
    effective means of presentation of ideas, i. e., how to
    translate a topic into media; use of variety of appro-
    priate techniques and equipment.

    Three or more sessions.

4. Producing a Videotape Program:
    may include use of all equipment, camera work,
    script writing, in-class use, etc.

    Three or more sessions.

5. Producing an 8mm or 16mm Film:
    may include camera technique, script writing, editing,
    use of equipment, silent continuous film loop, etc.

    Three or more sessions.

6. Producing a Slide-Tape Presentation:
    may include camera work or handdrawn slides, script
    writing for audio and visual effects, in-class use,
    filmstrip techniques.

    Two or more sessions.

7. Still Photography and On-the-spot Developing:
    may include camera technique and skill in shooting,
    developing, mounting photos.

    One 2-1/2 hour session.

8. Technical Consultation Services:
    includes discussion of budget systems, antenna, cost
    accounting, future hardware planning.

Objectives

Sample objectives follow for three of the program series:
the film workshop, the videorecorder and the photo module.

FILM WORKSHOP

This workshop will teach you to shoot, screen and edit your

films. Discussions will address technical and creative issues in film making as well as how and why teach it in the
classroom.

Technical Objectives of Production Classes

    1. understanding the equipment (what do you need?)
    2. exploring the camera
    3. planning a film and shooting
    4. screening the rushes
    5. editing a film
    6. presenting your own completed film.

Long Range Educational Goals for Classroom Use

1. developing an awareness of the objectivity/subjectivity
    continuum
    a. learning to recognize how much of "self" shapes
       reality
    b. recognizing and understanding biases in the work of
       others and the effects of one's own biases of one's
       work
    c. learning to view television analytically

2. explore the process of documentation
    a. gathering data
    b. interpreting data
    c. selection and arranging data
    d. presenting data

3. sharpen skills needed to create a documentary
    a. observing and recording
    b. recognizing primary and secondary sources of infor-
       mation
    c. developing organizational abilities
    d. developing greater awareness of purpose, and audi-
       ence

4. recognize difference in style between narrative and docu-
    mentary films.

VIDEORECORDER

At the conclusion of a videorecorder workshop teacher
should:

1. feel confident to handle the camera, recorder and monitor without any fear of equipment

2. have a working knowledge of:
    a. camera, i.e., aperture, focus, zoom, on-off standby button, trigger
    b. recorder, i.e., threading, rewind, record and fast forward controls
    c. monitor, i.e., on-off button

3. have an understanding of how the image travels from camera onto recorder to monitor while recording; also, playback from recorder to monitor

4. have a general understanding of wiring, i.e., camera plugged up to recorder, monitor plugged up to recorder, recorder plugged into wall socket

5. a working knowledge of camera techniques including tilting, panning (tripod)

6. be able to write a script and be able to produce a short video tape of that script.

PHOTO MODULE

At the conclusion of a photography workshop teachers should:

1. have working knowledge of exposure controls, i.e., shutter speed and aperture and an awareness of the effects of these controls

2. understand the function and visual effects produced by various lenses

3. an awareness of the many types of color and black and white films available in addition to a knowledge of their working characteristics

4. understand the basics of black and white developing and printing in regard to methods and materials

5. be aware of various technical source books available

6. be enthused and anxious to use these basics as a springboard for personal exploration.

EXAMPLE (8)

AN IN-SERVICE CATALOG OF
MEDIA WORKSHOP COMPONENTS

(In-Service Training)

SPONSOR: Volusia County Public Schools, Deland, Florida. Leatha Garrison, Director, Educational Materials and Related Services.

PROCEDURE: The following are summaries of Media Workshop components prepared for the in-service catalog of the Volusia County Public Schools.

Workshops listed in the catalog are available to teachers and carry credit points in in-service education for participants.

Component Title: MEDIA WORKSHOP - SELECTION AND UTILIZATION OF INSTRUCTIONAL MEDIA

General Objective
    Each participant will become proficient in the selection of appropriate materials and equipment and the operation of the equipment.

Specific Objectives

1. Upon completion of the workshop, participants will be able to select the equipment most appropriate to implement a given concept.
2. Upon completion of the workshop, each participant will demonstrate ability to operate each piece of equipment presented in the workshop.
3. Upon completion of the workshop, each participant will demonstrate ability to select appropriate materials to support an instructional objective.

68

Summary Statement
A workshop to instruct participants in methods of selection and utilization of instructional media.

Evaluative Procedure
Evaluation will be by observation of instructor and by
completion of an objective test with at least 70% accuracy.

Component Title: VIDEO PRODUCTION WORKSHOP

General Objective
To give all school personnel involved with video work
a basic course in video production.

Specific Objective
After participation in the workshop, learners will be
able to script and produce a video tape program, operating
and maintaining the equipment.

Summary Statement
Participants will learn to operate and maintain video
taping equipment.   Participants will learn basic techniques
of video production.

Evaluative Procedure
Instructor observation, and finished tape.

Component Title: MEDIA WORKSHOP - PRODUCTION OF
                   MATERIALS

General Objective
Teachers should be able to produce various instructional materials (software) for use in the classroom.

Specific Objectives

1. Upon completion of the workshop, participants will under-
    stand how to produce various instructional materials for
    use in the classroom.
2. Upon completion of the workshop, participants will dem-
    onstrate their ability to produce instructional materials
    by producing materials for evaluation by the instructor.

Summary Statement
A workshop to instruct participants in production of

instructional materials for use in the classroom.

Evaluative Procedure
         The product will serve as the evaluation.

Component Title: DEVELOPMENT OF EDUCATIONAL SPECI-
                  FICATIONS FOR HARDWARE SELECTION

General Objective
         To revise educational specifications for media hard-
ware.

Specific Objective
         After receiving instructions in criteria, participants
will develop updated specifications for selecting media hardware.

Summary Statement
         A committee consisting of 15 members, selected by
the Director of Educational Materials, will be instructed in
the criteria to apply in assessing the quality of educational
media hardware. They will then develop specifications for
this equipment.

Evaluative Procedure
         New specifications for media equipment.

Component Title: MEDIA WORKSHOP - CURRICULUM
                  GUIDE

General Objective
         Media librarians should provide students a compre-
hensive program of instruction in use, care and interpretation of a variety of materials.

Specific Objective
         To specifically detail a program of instruction in stu-
dents' utilization of materials in a sequential listing of competencies.

Summary Statement
         The document will be written by 15 media librarians
working in six sessions.

Evaluative Procedure
     The guide, complete with evaluative instruments will
serve as the evaluation.

Component Title: TEXTBOOK ADOPTION WORKSHOP

General Objective
     The committee will study and evaluate books of the
subject areas to be considered in the 1972-73 Florida Textbook adoption.

Specific Objectives

1.   The committee will evaluate the books for state adoption
     in relation to the criteria developed by the Florida State
     Course of Study Committee.
2.   The committee will recommend from the state adoption
     those books which will fulfill the county adoption needs.

Summary Statement
     The county-wide committee(s) (one for each of the subject
areas up for adoption) shall consist of the supervisor(s) concerned, three principals of school levels concerned, 1 to 15
teachers, and two lay members.   The co-chairman shall consist of the Chairman of the CTD Curriculum and Textbook
Committee or designate or the appropriate Specialist (county
level) or County Textbook Management Representatives.
     Each committee member will participate for an average
of 21 hours in evaluating books for state adoption and recommending from the state adoption, books which will fulfill the
county adoption.

Evaluative Procedure
     The completed evaluation studies and the recommenda-
tions filed by the committee will be the evaluative procedure.

Component Title: MEDIA WORKSHOP - SELECTION AND
                   UTILIZATION OF HARDWARE

General Objective
     Each participant will become proficient in the selec-
tion of appropriate equipment and the operation of the equipment.

Specific Objectives

1. Upon completion of the workshop, participants will be able to select the equipment most appropriate to implement a given concept.
2. Upon completion of the workshop, each participant will demonstrate ability to operate each piece of equipment presented in the workshop.

Summary Statement
    This workshop is intended to be conducted at the faculty level in a number of schools during after duty hours for teachers.   Leadership will be provided by the Media Specialist on the faculty.

Evaluative Procedure
    Each participant will be rated by instructor observations and will score 70 per cent or higher on an objective test covering content.

EXAMPLE (9)

MAIL BOX -- MATERIALS AND ACTIVITIES
FOR INDIVIDUALIZED LEARNING
(Development of Learning Packages)

(In-Service Training)

SPONSOR: Hazelwood School District, Hazelwood, Missouri. Mrs. Agatha Parks, Director of Libraries.

DATE(S): Ongoing participation 1972-73 school year.

PLACE: Permanent facilities established for the year's work.

PARTICIPANTS: Teachers and media specialists released from teaching duties to devote full time to the development of the learning package program for an entire school year.

BASIC THEME: To develop learning packages which will meet both district wide and building needs to foster individualized learning activities of students.

PROGRAM DESCRIPTION

Teachers and administrators were selected to serve on the Steering Committee and Task Force. They were divided into four groups and discussed and formulated answers to the following questions concerning the program:

I. ROLE OF THE TASK FORCE

Q. How do we make the Task Force a viable member of the TEAM?
A. By face to face contact with members of primary

73

staff (K-3) and other interested personnel.

Q. Who or what determines the functioning of the Task Force?
A. District wide needs in terms of curriculum; broad needs, then building needs.

Q. How do we inform professional staff of the function of the Task Force?
A. Through administrative meetings; principals set up faculty meetings with Task Force.

Q. What are the goals for the Task Force?
A. Determine the needs and priorities of district through questionnaire and personal contact with teachers.

Q. How does the Task Force function above the level of teacher aides?
A. By determining the needs of the district with a wide perspective. Coming up with creative ideas to meet these needs is beyond capacity of a teacher aide.

Q. What are the limitations of the Task Force?
A. Determine the areas of needs of district first.

Q. Should Task Force be writing a proposal for Federal Funding?
A. YES. The Task Force has a qualified member to do this. As a one year program the Task Force would just be getting oriented - next year the real effectiveness of the Task Force would be seen.

II.   WHAT IS A LEARNING PACKAGE?

Individuals have preconceived ideas of learning packages --to dispel this we will give the packages a new name: MAIL BOX. (Materials and Activities for Individualized Learning)

Q. What should learning packages do?
A. They should be capable of being used by any child or any group of children with the same need of a certain concept, whether remediation, enrichment, etc. The aim is to implement the present curricu-

lum.

Q. What format should packages have?
A. They should have four main parts in simple form.
    The pretest may not necessarily be a part of the
    "box." Teacher assessment may be the pretest.
    (1) Motivational statement including the concept to
         be learned in behavioral terms.   Pre-requisite
         skills needed to use this box.
    (2) List of materials contained in MAIL box and
         list of materials needed to complete activity.
    (3) Sequencing of the activity or activities which
         would be suited to various learning styles (not
         just pencil and paper).   Could be audio, kines-
         thetic, or visual approach.   Dependent upon
         needs of student-skill could do one of many of
         all of the activities if necessary.
    (4) Each MAIL box would include some types of
         evaluation which would go back to the initial
         statement so that child could demonstrate
         mastery of the concept.

Q. Would skills in the package pyramid other skills?
A. Prerequisite skills defined before child starts pack-
    age and skills would pyramid within the package
    but the package (box) would be an entity within it-
    self.

Q. How does package fit program of individualized in-
    struction?
A. The MAIL box could be used by any child (pro-
    viding flexibility).

Q. Does package provide capability for creative teach-
    ing?
A. The MAIL box will provide a variety of activities
    and teacher will need to select the activities which
    the child will need.

Q. How do we identify a package?
A. Labels will be best, no color coding for grade
    level, etc.   For instance, a box on telling time
    could be used by any child in any grade level, de-
    pendent upon the needs of that child.   EXAMPLE
    of label:

MAIL box "TIME"
(the major concept to teach)

Q. How sophisticated should a package be?
A. Task Force is not in manufacturing business.
    Packaging and layout should be as simple as pos-
    sible although sophisticated concepts could be dealt
    with.

Q. Should reproduction of a successful box be the job
    of Task Force?
A. No. After the initial idea and field test, box could
    possibly reach the stage to be reproduced by teach-
    er aides, etc.

III. PROCEDURES FOR TASK FORCE

Q. How do we inform the professional staff?
A. When Principal meets with the staff for the first
    time to talk about the Task Force, several mem-
    bers should be present, and also something should
    be in written form to explain purpose of the Task
    Force so the teachers could read and respond.
    Coordinator of Task Force would make dates and
    times available when Task Force members could
    come to each building.

Q. How do we develop communications between Task
    Force and buildings?
A. A newsletter should come out by the Task Force.
    At administrative meetings a Task Force repre-
    sentative would make reports which would be car-
    ried back to the buildings by the principals. Prin-
    cipals would also request Task Force to come for
    grade level meetings or with certain groups of in-
    dividuals.

Q. How do we meet needs of teachers?
A. Prepare a form that principals could put in the
    hands of the teachers to tell the Task Force what
    kinds of problems to work on. The form determines
    basic needs and is sent back to the principals and IS
    people (instructional specialists) for screening.
    Some of these ideas could be carried out by teacher
    aide or IS person in individual buildings. Then form
    is returned to Task Force. This would be more

business-like and would commit the teachers to initiate the request. Things to be included on form might be: name of teacher, room, grade level, school, and type of problem.
No major job of getting important things to be worked on by the Task Force should be done in the buildings first.

Q. Who implements the package?
A. It will be implemented in the building in accordance with the arrangements of the Principal. Possibilities of implementation:
(1) Teacher does the actual implementation--materials brought in and left for the teacher to use and evaluate.
(2) Task Force member presents the entire thing to class.
(3) Combination of Task Force and teacher implementation.
The teacher should have something to say concerning which method to use.

Q. Should package originate from the Task Force?
A. If Task Force has a package that worked unusually well, this should be made known in the Newsletter or Task Force Coordinator should make it known to the principals so that they can use it immediately instead of waiting their turn to use it.

Q. How should teacher feedback be handled?
A. A second form should be made to evaluate a package being used by a teacher in order that there be information on whether the package has merit with one or more teachers. If the form does not provide enough information, then another personal contact should be made.
The form and the personal contact should be able to tell whether or not the package worked or the teacher didn't follow through, etc.

Q. Should there be a package library?
A. There should be a central storage--after unit is used goes back to a central place and is cataloged. If a package is successful, each building should be notified. Each building should then make provisions to have one of the packages. The Task Force should have a budget from which to draw to

duplicate these materials.   Package would be duplicated by teacher aides, students, F. T. A. people,
etc.

IV.   FOCUS

Q.   Should district wide needs be met or individual
building needs FIRST?
A.   Attack individual building needs.

Suggestions for identifying needs:
(1) Meet faculty members, clarify role of Task
Force.
(2) Identify the learning package.
(3) Open up discussion to entire group.
(4) Start with one grade level and IS person per
building.
(5) Identify areas where skills need to be furthered
and develop package from these needs.
(6) Instructional Specialist should keep list of areas
of needs and make these available to the Task
Force.

Q.   Should package originate from the Task Force?
A.   NO.   Ideas should originate from the teachers, not
from curriculum guides.   After needs (ideas) are
expressed, find out what materials in the building
would do the job or how teacher aid could make or
should Task Force develop it?

Q.   What curriculum to zero in on first?
A.   Depends upon the needs of individual teachers.

Q.   How to field test the package?
A.   (1) Send self-explanatory package through the IS
people.
(2) Demonstrate package in classrooms at request
of teacher.
(3) Team approach--teacher and Task Force member.
(4) Brief meeting on grade level with demonstration by Task Force member if package has
been requested by a grade level.
(5) Workshop held by I. S. on how to develop and
make learning packages.

Following development of the rationale for the implementation of the Learning Package Program, media personnel of the Hazelwood District, under the direction of Charles Stranz, Jr., developed a series of five in-service workshops for classroom teachers, to acquaint them with the competencies necessary for the development of a successful learning package and with basic techniques for effective utilization of audio-visual materials in the classroom. A brief summary of each of the workshops follows:

HAZELWOOD SCHOOL DISTRICT
LEARNING PACKAGE WORKSHOP

(2 sessions--2 hours each session)

Sponsor: Hazelwood School District, Hazelwood, Mo.
Charles Stranz, Jr., Media Consultant

The objectives of the course will be to produce a learning unit using visual aids and to integrate these instructional materials into classroom and/or student use.
In order to complete the project in the allotted time the following prerequisites are necessary:
Participant must know how to:
1. Make transparencies using the thermofax machine and/or hot press.
2. Produce slides using the thermofax machine and/or hot press.
3. Mount pictures using the hot press and/or rubber cement method.
4. Laminate visuals using the hot press and/or cold laminating process.

The above techniques will be briefly reviewed. Each participant will be expected to provide his own materials. Most schools have the following:
1. Seal-lamin
2. M-T5
3. Chartex
4. Transparency frames
5. Magic-markers
6. Transparency pens
7. Pencils, paper, rulers, scissors
8. Magazines, newspapers (artistic expression optional)

Contact paper can be purchased in most department stores. Slide mounts can be purchased at Stanley Photo. Interested staff members should complete a Professional Development form and return it to the Administration Building through their building principal.

Outline

I.   Review of preparation and utilization of Instructional Materials
     A.   Thermo-fax
     B.   Hot press
     C.   Contact paper
     D.   Rubber cement

II. Planning Unit Package
     A.   Topic/subject area
     B.   Decide way(s) to develop concept
     C.   Plan production of package in outline form
     D.   Production of materials for class use
     E.   Presentation to class (15 days from first meeting date)

III. Learning Package
     A.   Explain package produced
     B.   Show to class

HAZELWOOD SCHOOL DISTRICT
BASIC PHOTOGRAPHY WORKSHOP

(2 two-hour sessions)

Sponsor: Hazelwood School District, Hazelwood, Missouri
           Charles Stranz, Jr., Media Consultant

Participants will learn the basic fundamentals of operating any camera and will be given the opportunity to develop their own slides. The art of picture taking will be taught.

Objectives

Participants will be able to:

1.   Take good quality pictures using any camera.   35mm, instamatic, or polaroid (35mm SLR preferred).
2.   Describe how a camera works.

3. Develop own 35mm color slides.
4. Mount own 35mm slides.
5. Produce a slide/tape presentation on a particular topic.
6. Correlate various subject areas with slide/tape presentations.
    a. Social Studies--Pictures of the community
    b. Art/Music--Creative expression
    c. Math/Geometry--Architectural design shows lines and various geometric shapes used in construction of buildings. Pictures of shapes and designs all around us
    d. Science/Ecology--Man and his environment (wise use and misuse of)
    e. Language Arts/Reading--Shots of signs, advertising, words used in the community.

Materials and Equipment Needed for the Course--Photography

1. 35mm camera preferred.   Others accepted.
2. 35mm slide mounts--1-1/2 cents at Stanley Photo
3. 35mm film developing kit--$1.99 develops 4 rolls of 20 slides.
4. Black bag for darkroom (optional).
5. Developing tank with 2 reels (36 exposure) for developing film.
6. Thermometer.
7. 8-16 oz. bottles.
8. 32 oz. glass measuring cup.
9. Cassette tapes (2 per student).
10. Film furnished by participant.

HAZELWOOD SCHOOL DISTRICT
LEARNING CENTER WORKSHOP

(two sessions--two hours each session)
(1/2 hour credit)

Sponsor: Hazelwood School District, Hazelwood, Missouri
          Charles Stranz, Jr., Media Consultant

Objective
        Set up "Learning Centers" using a variety of equipment.

Prerequisite
        A basic understanding in operation of following:

1. 16mm projector
2. Tape recorders--reel to reel and/or cassette
3. Record players
4. Filmstrip viewers--individual and group
5. Overhead projector
6. Headsets

Outline

I. Discussion centering around uses that have been made
    of equipment in the classroom
    A. Class use of equipment
    B. Small group use of equipment
    C. Individual use of equipment

II. Learning Centers--How equipment can be used to help
    teachers individualize instruction
    A. Set-up
    B. Practical uses in classroom
    C. Discussion

HAZELWOOD SCHOOL DISTRICT
MEDIA WORKSHOPS

Sponsor: Hazelwood School District, Hazelwood, Missouri
          Charles Stranz, Jr., Media Consultant

Workshop I
Basic Operation and Utilization of Audio-Visual Equipment

(2 two-hour sessions)

Session One:
    A. Operation and Utilization of Various Projectors
        1. 16mm film projector
        2. 35mm filmstrip projector
        3. Overhead projector
        4. Opaque projector
        5. Microprojector (Science)
        6. Filmstrip previewers
           a. individual
           b. rear screen (small group)
        7. Discussion and sharing of ideas
        8. Kodak Carousel slide projector

Session Two:
- A. Operation and Utilization of Various Tape Recorders
  1. Cassette recorders
     a. for use by individual student
     b. for use with Jack-Box for small group instruction
  2. Sony recorder
  3. Wollensak
  4. Stereo tape recorders
  5. Record players--individual and group instruction using headsets
  6. Discussion and sharing of ideas

- B. Operational Set-ups of Video Tape Recorders

  A specialist in the field of production of educational video tape recordings for industry and public school education will be present to demonstrate and answer questions.
  1. Operational checklist--basic setup procedures
  2. Discussion of safety precautions
  3. Making manual adjustments
  4. Uses of TV camera and V. T. R.
  5. Problems encountered with use of V. T. R.
  6. Discussion and sharing of ideas.

Workshop II
Preparation and Utilization of Instructional Materials

(2 two-hour sessions)

Session One:
     Use of the Thermofax machine to make instructional aids

  1. Thermofax machine--uses
     a. Single copy making
     b. Spirit master making
     c. Transparencies
     d. Stencil making
     e. Laminating
     f. Slide making
     g. Discussion and sharing of ideas
     h. Kodak Carousel slide projector

Session Two:
    Use of the Hot Press to make instructional aids
1. Slide tape presentation--step-by-step procedures for dry mounting
2. Laminating using the hot press
3. Chartex-map making
4. Transparency and slide construction
5. Discussion and sharing of ideas

EXAMPLE (10)

IN-SERVICE TRAINING PROGRAMS FOR TEACHERS IN THE
FERGUSON-FLORISSANT SCHOOL DISTRICT
ST. LOUIS COUNTY, MISSOURI

Stella Farley - Director of Library/Media Services

Introduction

Planning for in-service training programs for teachers is a never-ending process. The ongoing development of
new equipment and materials calls for continuous development of training programs. Once a successful program has
been completed it is not possible to relax and feel that the
job of in-service training has been done.

The summary which follows covers the activities of
one school district in ongoing in-service teacher education
in effective use of library/media services. A careful study
of the summary will reveal a variety of programs, each designed to meet specific needs as those needs were demonstrated.

Summary

The realization by educators that individualization of
instruction is greatly dependent upon availability of re-
sources--both print and non-print materials and human re-
sources--has made it imperative that teachers in the school
district be made fully aware of what these resources are
and how they may be utilized. This information can be dis-
seminated through personal contact of the teaching staff by
librarians and audiovisual personnel or media specialists.
Attempts to reach larger numbers of people, however, have
been made through workshops and conferences.

In the Ferguson-Florissant School District, St. Louis
County, Missouri, many workshops have been scheduled for
this purpose.

85

On the elementary level, programs have often been
presented on an area basis (four or five schools constituting
an area) throughout the school year. One such program used
as its theme, teaching the social studies through books of
fiction. Books were used to illustrate geographical factors
and their impact upon people who live in any given area,
and also to provide insight into the people themselves--indi-
cating the universal likenesses of all mankind.

Another program which was repeated in all areas
dealt with sixty-one ways in which to share books--ways to
"review" or report on books. Suggestions demonstrated included the "time capsule" technique, "recipes, " slides, dio-
ramas, movies and puppets.

Other workshops stressed services available to teachers and practical sessions on teacher-produced materials.
Teachers were taught how to laminate materials, how to
make slides, how to make transparencies and how to use the
overhead projector most advantageously, and how to make
8mm movies. One recent workshop was "Photography" for
teachers. The use of the electric quiz board had been
demonstrated and incorporated into learning activity packages.

On the secondary level similar workshops have emphasized the display and discussion of both print and non-
print material centers. Workshops on equipment and software to achieve instructional objectives involved representatives of commercial firms as well as educators who had
used multi-media in their own programs. In their programs
the effective use of 8mm films, microfilm, copying machines,
and amplified telephone facilities were among items studied.

Other workshops included reports of staff who had
visited schools with exemplary programs. The reports included not only comments by the visitors but also slide presentations of the sites and programs observed. Teachers
were able to share observations from: Oak Park-River
Forest High School Library (a Knapp project library) and its
random access retrieval system; the Nova Schools at Fort
Lauderdale, Florida--the resource center concept; Evanston
High School at Evanston, Illinois--the four schools within a
school concept, with the central library and four resource
centers with teachers' offices in the library, and the use of
automated circulation procedures; Guibor High School at
Waterloo, Illinois, with an inexpensive but effective audio-
retrieval system; and Lakeview-Decatur High School at

Decatur, Illinois, with its independent study program.

Other workshops included dissemination of evaluations of ESEA Title II programs by visiting consultants. Librarians and teachers benefitted from suggestions for improvement in the report on facilities, resources, and personnel at McCluer High School and Walnut Grove Elementary School made by Dr. Alice Lohrer of the University of Illinois Library School, Miss Lura Crawford of Oak Park-River Forest High School, and Mr. Richard Halsey of CEMREL.

Librarians, audio-visual specialists and staff manning or supervising resource centers were assisted by Dr. Frederick Mundt's (Southern Illinois University, Edwardsville) evaluation of the instructional materials centers and resource centers. The strong points of the program were developed further and the weak points were subjected to review and action for improvement.

Commercial software and hardware exhibits have been set up not only in the instructional materials centers but in classrooms and faculty rooms so that teachers might preview and assess media.

Various schools have had workshops and conferences to provide in-service for teachers and students.

At McCluer High School special orientation programs have been provided. New teachers have been given tours, shown materials especially relevant to their disciplines, given lists of periodicals of interest to them specifically, informed of production services and facilities, and given explicit details of library services such as bibliographic services, recommendations and acquisitions of materials, classroom loans and library instruction.

Explanation of library instruction services includes unipacs for individualized or group instruction on the card catalog, Dewey Decimal System, Readers' Guide, and biographical, literary, historical and general reference sources.

Workshops have often taken place in the form of library teas and by participation of librarians and display of materials in departmental meetings.

At Ferguson Junior High, workshops have included: special displays in specific disciplines such as materials available to the Foreign Language student, the use of learning activity packages, contests and book fairs, and special tours to introduce facilities and services to new teachers.

Florissant Junior High has an elaborate, lengthy orientation program for seventh graders. The program teaches library arrangement and organization and research methods in conjunction with units on folklore and composition. Students are introduced to the library by a set of slides made at Florissant, accompanied by a taped commentary which discusses location of materials in this specific library and the rules of procedure there. The voices on the tape are their teachers' and the librarians'. The program has been effective in getting the students to use the library and dispels some of their feeling of strangeness in a new environment.

In-service programs at Cross Keys Junior High include:

1. Library Skills and Instruction--In addition to cooperating with all the teachers in needed library instruction at the specific needed time, Cross Keys has a special program used in eighth grade--a unipac program. It is introduced by a pre-test which determines what units the students need to study. This same program, expanded, is used in teaching alphabetizing, card catalog, Dewey Decimal System and reference skills to student assistants. This year Cross Keys is beginning work with the eighth grade social studies teachers on special United States history reference tools and on library know-how (the history section of the card catalog and the geography-history sections of Dewey).

2. Book Talks and Reviews--Cross Keys' library staff encourages English teachers to use the library for their oral book reports, and find that this is very successful. As a part of Book Week and/or National Library Week the library has provided book talks by students, teachers (including science, industrial arts, and principals) and the librarian. The library staff has published a ten-page pamphlet of the books students recommend to other students, with signed brief recommendations; the name for this, chosen in an all-school contest, was The Good Book Book. Later the eighth grade English teachers and the librarian worked together to choose the very best from the Junior High School Catalog and its supplements, and to print in booklet form the titles and reviews of these fifty books.

3. <u>Bibliographies</u>--By the score--to help any and all teachers and students find the material available in the library on the subjects that are chosen or assigned.

PART II

TRAINING PARAPROFESSIONALS,
AIDES AND VOLUNTEERS

3. RELEASING THE TIME OF
PROFESSIONAL PERSONNEL

The time of the trained professional media person is too valuable to be utilized in the variety of routine tasks required for the efficient operation of any library/media center. The major duties of the professional librarian or media director should lie in the areas of curriculum design (including the overall objectives of library/media services as they relate to the curriculum); cooperative instructional planning with faculty members; team teaching; development of media center policies; staff supervision, planning and evaluation of services; training of teachers and students for competent use of media; development and implementation of the work/study skills program; direct assistance to students in independent study projects; implementation of a strong reading guidance program; reference and bibliographic services; supervision of production services; professional materials selection; and overall responsibility for establishing and maintaining a well-organized, easily accessible collection of print and non-print materials and equipment.

Within these broad major areas are a variety of tasks performed by the professional. The School Library Personnel Task Analysis Survey (ALA 1969), prepared by the Research Division of the National Education Association as a part of the School Library Manpower Project, lists over two hundred specific tasks required of the professional media person which should not be assigned to members of the supportive staff. A survey of these tasks leads one to define the role of the school librarian or media director as that of trained administrator, knowledgeable educator, and master teacher. However, this role can be fulfilled only if enough supportive staff is available to allow professional media personnel to perform those duties for which they were trained.

The need for supportive staff. The lack of under-

92

standing among many administrators and teachers of the roles of both the professional media person and members of the supportive staff has led to the existence in the nation's schools of a number of undesirable situations.   Among these are:

1.   The use of clerical aides in place of trained librarians in elementary school libraries.

2.   The heavy clerical workload carried by many professional media personnel throughout the schools in the country. (The Manpower report cited earlier indicates that from 50 to 85 per cent of all librarians, including heads of media centers, are responsible for both clerical and secretarial duties.)

3.   The lack of state standards for school media programs which require a realistic ratio of professional, paraprofessional, and clerical personnel in school library/media programs.

4.   The scarcity of trained paraprofessionals to handle many vital audiovisual and production services.

With the advent of the Elementary and Secondary Education Act of 1965, a number of changes occurred in school library/media centers throughout the nation.   Pilot programs funded under this Act have proven the value of the library/media program in the schools.   Teachers and administrators in schools where pilot programs in media services have been initiated have undergone a change in philosophy and methods as both relate to the teaching-learning process.   The value of the trained professional has been proven and the need for supportive staff has been clearly demonstrated.

The Paraprofessional

Recent years have seen the emergence of college and university training programs geared especially to the education of the library/media paraprofessional.   Forward-looking institutions like the Florissant Valley Community College in Florissant, Missouri, and its neighboring institution across the Missouri River, Lindenwood College of St. Charles, have instituted training programs culminating in the Associate in Arts Degree for the library/media paraprofessional.   These colleges work closely with local school districts in determining the specific training program and the competencies needed in the field. Graduates of these and of similar programs throughout the nation have become jewels in the crowns of those library/media professionals fortunate enough to obtain them. Unfortunately, such training programs are few and in most schools (once the need for the paraprofessional has been demonstrated) the task of on-the-job training falls upon the professional librarian or media director.

Duties of the Library/Media Paraprofessional

In any active and busy instructional materials program, duties performed by professional personnel, the paraprofessional, library/media clerks and volunteers will overlap. However, defining the duties of various members of the supportive staff should assist administrators in developing needed job descriptions and effective in-service training programs.

The compilation of a complete list of the duties of the paraprofessional is extremely difficult since the level of sophistication of the media program will determine the extent of the tasks performed. However, within six broad areas, major duties will be among those that follow:

Selection of Materials and Equipment

1.   Should be alert to expressed needs of students and teachers and refer these requests to the librarian or media director.

2.   Assists in the development of equipment specifications and selection.

3.   Maintains the materials request file.

4.   Maintains a selection file of teacher-student evaluations of audio-visual materials.

5.   Maintains selection aides for locating new material.

Acquisition of Materials and Equipment

1.   Unpacks and checks invoices for new materials.

2.   Inspects new materials for damage.

3. Returns damaged materials.

Preparation of Materials

1. Assists in the processing of materials for circulation.

2. Mounts pictures, slides, and transparencies.

3. Checks and prepares new equipment forms.

Production of Materials

1. Develops learning packages.

2. Handles graphics production services.

3. Prepares bulletin boards and displays.

4. Handles print shop operations.

5. Provides photographic production services.

6. Programs materials for computer use.

7. Prepares and duplicates instructional tapes.

8. Microfilms print materials.

9. Prepares instructional models.

10. Handles television production facilities.

11. Directs radio broadcasting facilities.

Maintenance of Materials

1. Assists teachers and students with equipment failures.

2. Maintains all equipment.

3. Repairs faulty equipment.

4. Schedules use of equipment.

5. Inspects nonprint materials for damage.

Instruction

1. Instructs teachers and students in use of all equipment.

2. Supervises student aides in use of equipment.

3. Instructs teachers and students in graphics techniques.

4. Instructs teachers and students in photographic techniques.

5. Instructs teachers and students in radio and television broadcasting techniques.

6. Supervises student preparation of models.

7. Supervises student use of dial access systems.

The Library/Media Aide

The library/media aide seems to have found no middle ground in the subjective evaluation processes undertaken by professional media personnel. The aide, in many instances, is either eulogized by the librarian or media director as "My strong right arm, " or depicted as "the latest reject from some administrator's secretarial pool. " Those media personnel who have gained the "strong right arm" find the aide capable of undertaking almost any routine task required in the instructional materials program. In addition, where there is a staff shortage, many of the responsibilities generally assumed by the paraprofessional or the professional staff have been very capably handled by trained aides under careful supervision. At the other end of the scale, the untrained instructional aide or assistant who shows an obvious lack of enthusiasm and/or dedication for assigned tasks can produce careless, sloppy work which complicates rather than eases the workload of the professional. Thus it is obvious that any in-service training program for library aides should encompass not only training in the basic routines, but should attempt to build positive attitudes concerning the importance of the work as it relates to the total instructional program.

Duties of the Library/Media Aide

Once again, before an effective in-service training program can be developed it is important to define the duties of the library/media aide. While the duties listed below are those most commonly performed by aides and are chiefly clerical in nature, it may be found in many schools that aides also assist in library media orientation for teachers and students, aid individual students and small groups in independent study activities, assist students and teachers in materials selection, and prepare and conduct story hours for primary grades.

Among the most frequently performed tasks of library aides are the following:

Fills out request slips
Checks request slips against the shelf list
Checks selection aides for bibliographical data
Prepares orders for printed cards
Types materials orders
Files order cards
Maintains order files
Unpacks new materials and checks invoices
Checks new materials for damage
Keeps the periodical record
Matches printed cards with materials
Assigns accession numbers and records on cards and
    materials
Records classification number (assigned by professional)
    on spine
Types book cards and pockets
Pastes pockets and date slips in books
Stamps new materials with school stamp
Files catalog and shelf list cards
Shelves materials
Clips and mounts pictures
Maintains pamphlet and information file
Prepares books for the bindery
Mends books and other materials
Maintains circulation record
Charges books to students
Types bibliographies
Maintains a record of reference questions asked
Prepares, sends and follows up overdue notices
Duplicates printed material
Types correspondence
Maintains correspondence file
Charges and discharges equipment
Locates requested materials
Delivers and collects materials and equipment
Keeps library/media center attendance record

In comparing the duties of the paraprofessional and of the library aide one can easily see the far more extensive training required of the former, and the necessity for more college training programs in this field. However, the competent library/media director who does not have access to graduates of such programs can and must provide on-the-job training for persons wishing to gain expertise within areas defined as belonging to the paraprofessional. Only in this way can the library/media director's time be released for work directly with students and teachers.

The training of the library aide is usually done on the job. As new programs, equipment and services are added, the training becomes more complex. In large school systems which utilize the services of a number of aides, time and energy can be conserved and more effective in-service training achieved through the in-service training workshop.

The Library/Media Volunteer

The use of volunteer mothers has become a way of life in many elementary school libraries--one that has on many occasions proven to be highly successful and of great benefit to library/media programs. At other times the use of volunteers has proved to be disastrous. The difference lies chiefly in the manner in which the volunteer's services are to be used. In a well-organized program staffed by trained, professional personnel who possess, in addition to their formal training, tact, patience, dipolomacy and a sense of humor, the volunteer mother can be an asset to the instructional media program.

When volunteers do not work under the direction of trained media personnel or are used in place of such personnel, the program will usually be less than successful. Volunteers who attempt to establish an elementary library program without professional help and guidance see such a program as a "place where children get books to read for fun." This becomes the total purpose of such a program, with teachers, mothers and students never looking beyond to see the vital role that the materials center can play in developing independent study habits, individualizing instruction, helping students to acquire efficient work/study skills, and building concepts through the efficient use of a wide variety of materials.

Even in the well-organized program directed by professionals the use of volunteers can cause problems if difficulties are not foreseen and provided for. Among problems encountered with the use of volunteer aides (unless provision is made to avoid them) are the following:

Problem
An ill child at home or an unexpected invitation may cause the volunteer not to appear at the expected time.
Solution
Provision should be made for substitutes to be called when a volunteer cannot be present at the assigned time.

Problem
One mother corrects another's child and difficulties between families arise.
Solution
In-service training of volunteers should stress that all discipline in the media center should be handled by professional personnel.

Problem
The volunteer overhears a teacher's or student's conversation concerning school problems or activities and carries unfounded rumors to other parents.
Solution
Teachers should be informed when volunteers are on duty, and of the advisability of being discreet in their conversation. Volunteers should be cautioned that the problems of individual students should never be discussed.

Problem
Volunteers attempt to "run the media center" or tell professional personnel what to do.
Solution
Each volunteer should be well trained in carefully defined tasks and kept busy at those tasks during the work period. Suggestions should be heard courteously but at the outset, the manner in which decision making processes are carried out should be made clear.

Problem
Volunteer tasks are performed in different ways, thus confusing the next volunteer who performs the task.
Solution
A volunteer handbook outlining duties and the manner in which each duty is performed is a must.

Problem
    Volunteers tire or become bored with the job assigned to
    them and soon do not return.
Solution
    A careful pre-screening of volunteers to determine inte-
    rests and abilities will help in fitting the right job to the
    right person. Media personnel need to be alert to the
    attitudes of individual volunteers and make provision for
    reassigning duties if necessary.

Problem
    The volunteer does not feel appreciated after donating
    hours of work time and thus derives no satisfaction from
    the activity.
Solution
    Appreciation is voiced often by media personnel. Volun-
    teers are always treated with tact, patience and diplo-
    macy. Provision should be made periodically for some
    form of concrete recognition for volunteer services.

Duties of the Volunteer Aide

        The following duties can be performed by volunteers
when careful training and supervision are provided:

    Charging and discharging materials to students
    Sorting and filing book cards
    Issuing overdue notices
    Keeping attendance records
    Assisting students in locating materials
    Filling requests for teachers
    Preparing new books and materials
    Repairing books
    Shelving returned books and materials
    Reading shelves
    Assisting with the annual inventory
    Checking lists with holdings for future orders
    Filing catalog cards
    Typing lists of new books
    Typing book card replacements
    Typing catalog cards
    Typing bibliographies
    Telling stories to primary children
    Preparing bulletin boards and displays

The Volunteer Handbook

A major requirement for media personnel considering the use of volunteers in the instructional materials center program is the development of a volunteer handbook. Volunteers should not be recruited, nor training sessions scheduled, until such a handbook has been developed and made ready to place in the hands of each volunteer. Basic content of the handbook should include:

1. The Goals and Objectives of the Library/Media Program

2. Everyday Procedures for the Materials Center
    A. Checking the date stamp
    B. Circulation routines
    C. Handling returned materials
    D. Shelving materials
    E. Rules for filing book cards
    F. Method for reading shelves
    G. Procedures for sending overdue notices
    H. Policy on fines

3. Special Help and Library Tasks
    A. Procedures for processing materials
    B. Procedures for typing book cards and catalog cards
    C. Filing rules
    D. Procedures for mending books

4. Explanatory Sheets if Necessary

5. Glossary of Terms Used in Libraries

An excellent example of a simply constructed, clear and easily understandable handbook for volunteer mothers is the Ladue Library Handbook for use in the elementary materials centers of the Ladue School District, St. Louis County, Missouri. Portions of the Handbook are reprinted here with permission.

LADUE LIBRARY HANDBOOK
prepared by
The Staff of the Elementary Libraries
of the
School District of the City of Ladue

Miriam Morrow, Chairman
Elizabeth James   Fran Marks
Rae Meyer   Betty Myers

Portions reprinted by permission of Miriam Morrow
School District of the City of Ladue, 1970
9703 Conway Road, St. Louis, Missouri 63124
(pp. 1-8)

Objectives of the Elementary Library

The primary objective of the elementary school library is to enrich and support the educational program of
the school. Other objectives are to satisfy the personel
needs of the individual child and to contribute to the development of his social and intellectual values.

To achieve these goals it is necessary that the library be available to students at all times during the school
day. Mother librarians are indispensable to the achievement
of this ideal.

Everyday Procedures for All Libraries

I.   CHECK DATE STAMP

      1.   It should be set one week ahead of current date
            except when the date would fall on a holiday.

      2.   Then it should be set forward to the first regu-
            lar school day.
            Example: If class comes in on a Tuesday, set
            date stamp for the first Tuesday after vacation.

II.   CHECK-OUT PROCEDURE FOR LIBRARY BOOKS

      1.   Child signs name on the first blank line of the
            book card.   The first name and initial of the
            last name is sufficient. He places the number
            of his grade or room designation after his name.

      2.   Stamp the date due on slip in book and on book
            card with the date due in left hand space on
            card.   Be sure to stamp card and book clearly
            to avoid delay in finding cards.

3. The book card is retained by the librarian to be filed at the end of the library period.

4. Teachers who check out books sign their names on book cards and on date-due slip in book. These cards are filed behind teachers' names.

5. Reference books, encyclopedias and atlases may not be taken from the library and are never checked out.

III. RETURNED BOOKS

1. Children should return books to designated place.

2. Note last date-due stamp on date-due slip in back of book.

3. Look behind date in tray and find book card.

4. Compare accession number on card with one in book to be sure they are exactly the same.

5. Put card in book-pocket and put on cart for books to be shelved.

6. Shelve in proper place when time permits.

IV. SHELVE RETURNED BOOKS BY CALL NUMBERS ON THE SPINES

1. Fiction books, E and F (jF or FIC), are shelved in alphabetical order according to the last names of the authors.

2. Classified books (non-fiction numbered 0--to 999) should be arranged by numbers including decimal points in proper place on the shelves. If there are a number of books with the same classification number, they are arranged in alphabetical order by the author's last names.

V. FILE THE BOOK CARDS OF BOOKS CHECKED OUT AT THE END OF YOUR LIBRARY PERIOD.

VI. READ SHELVES TO SEE THAT BOOKS ARE IN ORDER.

"A book out of place is a book lost."

VII.   SEND OVERDUE NOTICES

    1.   Slips are found in the desk drawer.

    2.   A listing of children in each grade is found in the desk drawer.

VIII. CLOSING THE LIBRARY

    1.   Put date stamp and ink pad in the top drawer.

    2.   Check for books left on top of shelves or tables.

IX.   FINES: SEE RULES FOR YOUR LIBRARY

X.   DAMAGED OR LOST BOOKS: Such books are set aside for consideration of the librarian and administration.

XI.   SPECIAL HELP AND LIBRARY TASKS

    1.   From time to time there are special tasks that librarians can do to keep the library running smoothly. Notes will be left asking for such aid when they occur.

    2.   Preparing and processing new books, checking the card catalog against book lists, filing, typing catalog and book cards, mending books, etc. are a great help.

    3.   We welcome any suggestions as to procedures, bulletin boards, etc.

    4.   If you have any questions about procedure, please feel free to ask the librarian. IF IN DOUBT, ASK!

Procedures for Processing Library Books

I.   NEW BOOKS ARE CHECKED AGAINST ORDERS AND/OR INVOICES. This procedure is usually done by the librarian or the school secretary.

II. BOOKS ARE EXAMINED FOR DEFECTS.

III. BOOKS ARE STAMPED WITH THE SCHOOL STAMP.

1. On the title page and inside front cover.

2. On page 21 or if unpaged, near the center of the book.

IV. IF AN ACCESSION BOOK IS USED, BOOKS ARE AC-CESSIONED IN THE BOOK ACCORDING TO THE HEADINGS IN THE BOOK. The accession number is also written in ink on the stamped marks after no.

V. REMOVE BOOK JACKETS AND SAVE. These may be filed for future use by teachers and librarians after clipping those desired.

VI. CLIP BOOK JACKETS IF ...

1. The book is for the upper grades and has pertinent information about authors or content.

2. Do NOT clip jackets of easy books or publisher's blurbs about other books.

3. Take care not to mar the covers for display.

VII. PREPARE POCKETS AND BOOK CARDS ON THE TYPEWRITER.
See explanatory sheet 1.

VIII. PASTE POCKETS INSIDE BACK COVER; DATE-DUE SLIPS OPPOSITE; AND THE CLIPPINGS, IF ANY, INSIDE THE FRONT COVER.

IX. PRINTED CATALOG CARDS SUCH AS WILSON, LIBRARY JOURNAL, CCC ETC.

1. Call numbers must sometimes be added. These are provided by the librarian.

2. Author or biographee letters must sometimes be added to the classification numbers.

3. Shelf List Cards must have the following information added in a line just below any printing

on the card: Accession number (4 spaces) date
book was received (4 spaces) price of book (4
spaces) dealer (may be abbreviated).

    4.   See explanatory sheet 2.

X.   CATALOG CARD FORM FOR BOOKS WITHOUT
PRINTED CARDS.
See explanatory sheet 3.

    1.   Books will be cataloged (classified) by the li-
brarian.

    2.   Order cards will provide price, etc.

XI.   LETTER SPINES WITH THE CALL NUMBER OF
THE BOOK AS ON THE BOOK CARD AND POCKET
AND CATALOG CARDS.
Call numbers include:

    1.   The classification (numbers or letter).

    2.   Plus the first three letters of the author's or
biographee's last name.

XII.   IF TAPE IS USED FOR CALL NUMBERS, TAPE
SHOULD EXTEND ABOUT 1/2 INCH IN FRONT AND
BACK OF THE GROOVES OF THE SPINE AND BE
FIRMLY PRESSED IN THE RIDGES OF THE SPINE
WITH A LIBRARIAN'S BONE OR A CASE KNIFE.

XIII. COVER CALL NUMBER WITH PLASTIC TAPE AS
XII.

XIV. SHELVE NEW BOOKS WITH OTHERS ON SHELVES
BY CALL NUMBERS.

XV.   FILE CATALOG CARDS IN THE TWO FILES:

    1.   SHELF LIST FILE (For inventory, library re-
cords, etc.) This file is for teachers and librarians and is not open to children.   Cards
are arranged in this file as the books are arranged on the shelves.
       (1)   Classified (Non-fiction) cards are filed nu-
merically by call number, then alphabeti-
cally by author's last name.

    (2) Fiction books (F and E) are filed alphabetically by author.

    (3) Individual biography (92 or B) is filed alphabetically the last name of the subject of the biography.

    (4) There is only ONE card in the shelf list for each title in the library. Duplicate copies have accession numbers listed on the shelf list card.

2. GENERAL CATALOG FILE is the second file that is located in the library for general use of students and teachers.

    (1) There may be many cards for each book in the library. There are usually an AUTHOR CARD and a TITLE CARD. There is also at least one SUBJECT CARD and sometimes several if the book covers several topics.

    (2) These cards are filed alphabetically by the "Word-by-Word" filing system according to the top lines of the card.

    (3) See: Rules for "Word-by-Word" filing.

"Word-By-Word" Filing Rules

General Rule: All cards are filed in ABC order by words beginning with the top line.

1. Nothing comes before something.
    Example: Hawaii comes before Hawaiian.
                New York comes before newspaper.

2. Abbreviations are filed as though spelled out.
    Example: St. Louis is filed Saint Louis.
                Dr. Dolittle is filed Doctor Dolittle.

3. A, AN and THE are ignored at the beginning of a title. (But only at the beginning.)
    Example: The Little House is filed Little House.

4. Numbers are filed as though spelled out.
    Example: 101 Riddles is filed One Hundred One Riddles.

5. Prefixes M', Mc, Mac are filed as though all were spelled MAC.

Example: McCloskey is filed before MacDonald.
            McFarland is filed before MacGregor.

6. If the first word is identical, go on to the second word,
    etc.

7. If the first lines of two cards are identical, go on to
    the second line, etc.

4. TRAINING PROGRAMS FOR PARAPROFESSIONALS,
   LIBRARY AIDES AND VOLUNTEERS

   The basic concepts involved in successful in-service
training of teachers presented in Part I apply equally well
to the in-service training of paraprofessionals, library/media
aides and volunteers. Released time must be provided for
district personnel; the interests and needs of participants
must be considered; provision should be made for direct involvement of participants; and cooperative planning of objectives, content and activities should be done by the school administration, professional media personnel and the paraprofessionals, library/media aides, or volunteers for whom the
workshop is intended.

   The following items should be considered in planning:

1. Basic Goal of the Workshop (Example: To pre-
    sent information? To demonstrate techniques?
    To develop specific skills? To change attitudes?)

2. Behavioral Objectives (Exactly what should the
    participants know, be able to do, or what attitude
    should be present at the close of the workshop?)

3. Determination of Program Content

4. Assigning Responsibility for Instruction

5. Selection of Site

6. Determination and Acquisition of Needed Equip-
    ment

7. Preparation of the Physical Facilities

8. Publicity (Informing participants of the workshop)

9. Preparation of Workshop Materials (slides, tapes, transparencies, duplicated materials, handbooks, etc.)

10. Provision for Evaluation

The examples which follow provide program descriptions and samples of materials prepared for use in highly successful in-service training programs for supportive staff members and volunteers in school library/media programs.

EXAMPLE (1)

Library Aides Workshop
(multi-session)

Sessions: 14 weekly meetings designed for in-service training of paid library aides.

Sponsor: Dillon School District #2, Dillon, South Carolina. Lois McCallum, Elementary Library Coordinator.

Coordinated by: Pee Dee Supplementary Education Center, Florence, S.C. Dr. John W. Baucum, Director.

Goal: To train library aides in those competencies necessary for the efficient operation of nine elementary school libraries.

Objectives:

1. Administrative procedures and policies
2. The learning process
3. Clerical records
4. Circulation filing
5. Materials--Tools of selection and processing
    Production and repair
    Preparing and arranging on shelves
    Content-reference
6. Audio-visual services--equipment, demonstration and storage
7. Inventory procedures
8. Role of the librarian--role of aides

Speakers and consultants:
    Eight different resource people were brought in to speak and demonstrate various competencies.

Activities:
    Speakers

111

112   In-Service

Demonstrations
Opportunities for aides to demonstrate competencies
acquired

Outline of Content:

Session 1   - Orientation - Administrative Procedures, School
              Policies, Chain of Command - Mr. H. E.
              Corley, Superintendent Role of Librarian -
              Role of Aides - Mrs. Lois McCallum, Li-
              brary Coordinator Dillon School District #2

Session 2   - Child Development and The Learning Process -
              Dr. Jaren Van Den Heuvel, Psychologist
              Pee Dee Education Center

Session 3   - Clerical Records - Mrs. Lois McCallum, Dillon
              School District #2

Session 4   - Circulation Filing - Mrs. Lois McCallum, Dil-
              lon School District #2

Session 5   - Materials - Tools of Selection and Processing -
              Miss Nancy Jane Day, Library Services
              Mrs. Margaret Ehrhardt, Library Services
              State Department of Education

Session 6   - Materials - Production and Repair - Miss Nancy
              Jane Day, Library Services, Mrs. Margaret
              Ehrhardt, Library Services, State Depart-
              ment of Education

Session 7   - Materials - Preparing and Arranging On Shelves -
              Miss Nancy Jane Day, Library Services
              Mrs. Margaret Ehrhardt, Library Services
              State Department of Education

Session 8   - Materials - Content - Reference - Miss Nancy
              Jane Day, Library Services, Mrs. Margaret
              Ehrhardt, Library Services Story Telling -
              Mr. John Richardson, Pee Dee Education
              Center

Session 9   - Audio-Visual - Recommended Equipment -
              (K-6) (7-12) - Cataloging - Miss Nancy
              Matthews, Pee Dee Education Center

Session 10 - Audio-Visual - Equipment Demonstration -
Miss Nancy Matthews, Pee Dee Education
Center

Session 11 - Audio-Visual - Aides Demonstrating Equipment -
Miss Nancy Matthews, Pee Dee Education
Center

Session 12 - Audio-Visual - Aides Demonstrating Equipment -
Miss Nancy Matthews, Pee Dee Education
Center

Session 13 - Inventory - Storage - Miss Nancy Jane Day -
State Department of Education

Session 14 - Evaluation - Role of Librarian - Role of Aides -
Robert C. Scott, Jr. - Pee Dee Education
Center

EXAMPLE (2)

<u>Teacher Aide Workshop</u>

Sponsor: Hazelwood School District, St. Louis County, Mo.

Dates: One-week workshop within the district following two weeks of intensive teacher aide training at Florissant Valley Community College, Florissant, Mo. Summer 1971.

Place: Hazelwood Senior High School.

Participants: Full time and part time teacher and instructional aides.

Basic Themes: Survey of AV Materials and Equipment; Child Growth and Development.

<u>Course Descriptions:</u>

(1) Survey of AV Materials and Equipment
   This course will offer experience in making audiovisual materials and in the operation of various types of commonly used audiovisual equipment found in the classroom.

(2) Child Growth and Development
   This course will include a survey of the growth and development of the child from conception through adolescence. There will be an emphasis on development as it relates to physical growth, physical activities of children and information on first aid and safety in the supervision of children in group activities. In addition there will be an analysis of interpersonal relations and the role of a teacher aide in the school situation.

<u>Daily Schedule:</u>

Monday
   a. m.   Preparing visual aids. Transparencies and

114

bulletin boards.
Routine service of equipment.
Small group discussion on responsibilities of
teacher aides

p. m.   Principles and techniques of setting up and
operating equipment.   Including video tape recorders, movie projectors, tape recorder,
opaque projectors.

Tuesday
a. m.   Principles and techniques of setting up and
operating equipment.
Video tape recorders
Movie projectors
Laminating Materials
Other av equipment
Duties of teacher aides

p. m.   General library information
Small group discussion to share new ideas and
experiences on the job

Wednesday
a. m.   Child growth and development

p. m.   General school philosophy

Thursday
a. m.   Child growth and development
Small group and large group discipline
Supervision of students
Cafeteria services

p. m.   Health, first aid and emergency situations
Job description and performance standards
Instructional aides
Inside and outside activities

Friday
a. m.   Small group discussions on teacher aide relationships with students, teachers and parents.
Student discipline in relation to the teacher
aides role

p. m.   Question and answer period over material
covered.
Evaluation by students and teachers

WORKSHOP EVALUATION   School_____

                    Name (optional)_____

1. Do you feel this workshop has added to your knowledge
    of the role of the teachers aid in our schools? Yes___
    No___   Please explain in detail:

2. What phase of this week's program has been <u>most</u> bene-
    ficial to you?_____
    (refer to list below)

        ___Audio Visual lab instruction
        ___Small group discussions on responsibilities of teach-
           ers' aides
        ___General Library Information
        ___Child Growth and Development Presentations (Mrs.
           Ann Eaddows)
        ___General School Philosophy (Mrs. Hinda Dillinger)
        ___Film and Guidance Presentation (Mr. Collins Henson)
        ___Discussion on Group Discipline and Supervision
        ___Food Services (Mrs. Ruby Chapman)
        ___Health, First Aid, and Emergency Procedures (Mrs.
           Loyola Bushnell)
        ___Activities--Inside, Outside (Mr. Roy Tanner)
        ___Small group discussions--Personal Relationships

3. In the blank to the left of each item above, begin with
    number 1 and rate the items in order of your personal
    preference of importance. (1-11)

4. In future workshops, what improvements and/or addi-
    tions would you suggest? Your ideas would be of utmost
    importance in future planning.

    What, if any, areas could be deleted from future pre-
    parations?

    COMMENTS: (on workshop in general)

SUGGESTIONS FROM HAZELWOOD
TEACHER AIDE WORKSHOP

1. Written rules should be developed within schools.
    Teacher-aides should be included in the formulation
    along with teachers and principal.

2. All rules should be distributed and made known to all
    teachers, aides, children and parents.

3. There should be support for teacher-aides on rules,
    from the principal and the teachers.

4. Aides should meet with teachers once per quarter to
    exchange ideas and keep communication lines open.

5. Communication should be made with aides as to special
    problems of individual children. (e.g. Muscular Dys-
    trophy, Diabetes, Epilepsy, Hyperactivity or other crip-
    pling or chronic diseases particularly if the child is on
    medication.)

6. Larger buildings should employ more teacher-aides for
    more effective supervision.

7. The use of children as monitors when teachers are
    away and aides are supervising is a questionable prac-
    tice. The aides feel as a group that it causes many
    problems for them.

TRAINING THE LIBRARY VOLUNTEER

The three programs which follow were designed to train volunteer library/media aides for specific roles within each district. In the Ladue School District, volunteer mothers are trained annually to serve on a regular schedule in the district's elementary libraries. The Greenfield Public Schools have both paid aides and volunteer aides, with volunteers being on call when needed. The training program of the Edgefield Schools began as a volunteer program and expanded into providing opportunities for formal training. The three programs are presented as representative of the varied types of training that can be made available to volunteer teacher or instructional media aides.

EXAMPLE (3)

Library Workshop for Volunteer Mother Aides
(single session)

Sponsor: Ladue School District, St. Louis County, Missouri.

Dates: Annual one-half day workshop.

Place: Board of Education Building-School District of Ladue.

Participants: 25-50 volunteer mother aides.

Basic Theme: To provide professional instruction in the area of Library Science.

In-Service Training Objectives:
1. To acquaint volunteer mother aides in the operation, organization, and purposes of the Ladue elementary library program.

   2. To assist volunteer mother aides in improving their library skills.

Speakers and consultants:
Professional elementary library staff of the District.

Outline of Content:
   1. The Purposes and Goals for Mother Librarians
   2. Defining Library Terms
   3. Introduction to the Dewey Decimal System
   4. Introduction to the Card Catalog
   5. Introduction to Reference Books

Activities:
Because of the large number of mother librarians the same workshop is repeated morning and afternoon.

The group is divided into two smaller groups for forty minute sessions. All topics are presented in the two forty-minute sessions. A coffee break is provided between the two sessions to allow mothers to meet with each other to exchange experiences and ideas.

Commercial Materials Provided:
Workshop materials from the T. S. Dennison Library Skills series by Vera Pace.

Local Materials Produced: (samples of these materials follow)
   1. Letter of Invitation
   2. Flyer on the duties of mother librarians
   3. Form for reply
   4. Workshop program
   5. Mother librarian's handbook (portions of which were reproduced earlier in this chapter)

School District of the City of Ladue

9703 CONWAY ROAD

St. Louis, Missouri 63124

OFFICE OF THE
DIRECTOR OF SPECIAL SERVICES

TELEPHONE:
994-7080

September 21, 1970

Dear

The value of your library service is greatly appreciated, not only by the teachers and students in your school, but by the

Ladue School District as well. Without your skills and assistance in performing the many detailed tasks which are required to maintain an efficient library, our elementary library program would be greatly reduced.

Because many parents have shown much interest in improving their library skills, a workshop has been planned which will provide professional instruction in the area of library science.

You are invited to attend the library workshop which will be held on Thursday, October 22, at the Board of Education Building located at the rear of East Junior High, 9703 Conway Road.   You may make a choice of either the morning session (9:15-11:15 a. m.) or the afternoon session (1:00-3:00 p. m.).

The program will be identical for both sessions and will consist of teacher demonstrations, dialogues, and a brief work session.   The purpose of the workshop is to give you further instruction by which you may improve your skills, and to solicit from you your ideas and suggestions for an improved elementary library program.

Please complete the attached form and return to your principal as soon as possible, so we can begin to prepare adequately for a profitable workshop.

Sincerely yours,

Richard P. Bouchard

Richard P. Bouchard, Ph. D.
Library Committee
Instructional Division
Ladue School

RPB:lgb

Mother Librarians Can Do These Things
to Improve Library Services to Elementary Children

At the Desk

Check out books
Sort and file book cards
Issue overdue notices
Put cards in returned books
Keep records of attendance

At the Shelves

Shelving returned books
Reading shelves to keep them
   in order
Helping shift books when neces-
   sary
Helping with annual inventory

For Students and Teachers

Helping students locate materials
   1.   On the shelves
   2.   In the Card Catalog
Filling requests of teachers

At the Card Catalog

Checking lists with our holdings
   for future orders
Making bibliographies for curriculum
Filing cards for new books
   "above the rods"

Preparing New Books and Materials

Preparing printed cards and
   pockets

Do You Type?

We need:
Typed lists of new books

Stamping school ownership
Labelling spines
Pasting pockets and date-
   slips
Checking magazines
   Also:
Repairing books
Filling out order cards
Preparing rebound books

Typed book card replacements
Catalog cards for some books
   and materials
Typed bibliographies

Do You Like to Tell Stories?
Do You Like to Draw Pictures?

We have birthday books to acknowledge.
We have primary and kindergarten story hours.
We use bookmarks and bulletin boards to stimulate reading.
We can use your Talents!

Ladue Library Workshop

I will be able to attend the Library Workshop on Thursday,
October 22, 1970 for the following session (check one).

   __ Morning   9:15 to 11:15 a. m.

   __ Afternoon   1:00 to 3:00 p. m.

What I would like to see included in the library workshop is:

_____   _____
Name   School

Please return to your elementary school principal by October 9.

LIBRARY WORKSHOP

Morning Session Agenda
October 22, 1970

Sponsored by
Ladue School District, 9703 Conway Road,
St. Louis, Missouri 63124

Instructed by
Mrs. Miriam Morrow, Mrs. Elisabeth James,
Mrs. Rae Meyer, Mrs. Betty Myers and
Mrs. Fran Marks

9:15 - 9:30   Registration and Introductions - Board Room

9:30 - 10:10   Group I - Upstairs - Board Room
                Mrs. Miriam Morrow - Purposes and
                Goals for Mother Librarians
                Mrs. Fran Marks - Glossary of Terms
                Mrs. Betty Myers - Dewey Decimal System

9:30 - 10:10   Group II - Downstairs - IPC Room
                Mrs. Elisabeth James - Card Catalog
                Mrs. Rae Meyer - Reference Books

10:15 - 10:30   COFFEE BREAK - Board Room

10:35 - 11:15   Group II - Upstairs - Board Room
                Mrs. Miriam Morrow - Purposes and
                Goals for Mother Librarians
                Mrs. Fran Marks - Glossary of Terms
                Mrs. Betty Myers - Dewey Decimal System

10:35 - 11:15   Group I - Downstairs - IPC Room
                Mrs. Elisabeth James - Card Catalog
                Mrs. Rae Meyer - Reference Books

11:15   DISMISSAL

EXAMPLE (4)

INSTRUCTIONAL TECHNOLOGY

(In-Service Seminar for Teacher Aides and Related Staff)

SPONSOR: Greenwich, Connecticut Public Schools.

DATE(S): February 29, 1972. Full-day seminar.

PLACE: Greenwich High School, Hillside Road, Greenwich, Conn. 06830.

DIRECTOR(S): Instructional Media Staff, Greenwich Media Center; Elfrieda McCauley, Co-ordinator, Secondary School Libraries.

PARTICIPANTS: 30 clerical, teacher and instructional aides.

BASIC THEME: To develop expertise on the part of teacher aides in four categories of instructional technology: projection, recording, duplicating equipment and graphics.

IN-SERVICE TRAINING OBJECTIVES:
1. To develop techniques of duplication: stencils, ditto, xerox, photography, prints, filmmaking, slides, darkroom facilities.
2. To develop techniques for use of mounting and laminating equipment.
3. To develop enlarging and reduction techniques.
4. To develop techniques for making overhead transparencies.
5. To develop techniques in the use of recording equipment: dubbing, use of phonograph, reel to reel playbacks, audio cassettes, Coxco.
6. To develop techniques in the use of

124

projection equipment: loop projectors,
Technicolor 1000, 8mm, 16mm, filmstrip and carousel projectors.

Outline of Content and Activities

1. Orientation to the Instructional Materials Center.

2. Six One-Hour Sessions on Tape Recorders, Graphics,
Duplicating and Projection.

A. The morning from 8:30 to 12:30 was divided into
four one hour sessions. Students were assigned to
four groups and by groups traveled to each of the
four locations where teachers explained and demonstrated all the kinds of equipment assembled by
category.

B. Two one-hour sessions in the afternoon gave students a chance to select a session according to their
own preferences. Activities included:
1. Threading projectors
2. Dubbing a tape
3. Laminating a print
4. Making a Reneo stencil
5. Making a transparency.

C. Take home materials on the various kinds of equipment and processes covered in the seminar sessions
were distributed.

Evaluation

Ms. McCauley evaluates the seminar in the following
manner: "Without reservations, the Seminar was a success.
Although attendance was more or less compulsory, the cap-
tive student body was enthusiastic about having a seminar of
this kind available to them. They seemed to have enjoyed
the learning experience, and apparently found the instruction
suited to their needs. Teachers and administrators who
have overheard comments by those who attended have reported good things to us. Several teachers have expressed
an interest in having a similar seminar to which teachers
should be invited. "

Local Materials Used

ing:
  Materials prepared locally for use include the follow-

1. Orientation to the Greenwich Instructional Materials Center (including a list of production equipment available at
the IMC and the respective materials produced).

2. Mounting and Laminating Using the Dry Mount Press.

3. The advantages, disadvantages and use of the opaque
projector, filmstrip projector, 2 x 2 slides, transparencies, tape recordings, discs, motion pictures.

ORIENTATION TO INSTRUCTIONAL MATERIALS CENTER

  The Instructional Materials Center and the IMC staff
are here to help you to provide an ever-improving educational program for the children and youth in the Greenwich
Public Schools.

  In the basement of the Havemeyer Building, adjacent
to the Print Shop, is the IMC Repair and Maintenance Department and the film and tape storage area. Here films
are packed to fill teachers' orders and upon their return are
checked for damage, repaired when necessary, and stored
or repacked for the next user.

  The collection of instructional materials at the Center
contains over 7,000 items. Instructional materials catalogs
and the file of film guides housed in each school are used
by teachers in selecting appropriate instructional materials
prior to preinstructional previewing, which is recommended.

  One of the major tasks of the Center is to distribute
these materials in response to teacher requests.

  In addition to the instructional materials collections,
the Center has certain equipment available for production of
instructional materials. You are welcome to make an appointment to come to the Center to use this equipment with
supervision. Request for production service will be filled
as time and schedule permit.

  Here is a partial list of production equipment available at the IMC and the respective materials produced:

Equipment	Materials
Drawing table and graphics kit	Overhead transparencies, masters, layouts for photo-copy work, etc.
Thermofax Secretary) Addofax)	Paper copies, overhead transparencies, spirit reflex masters
Protoprinter & Protocoupler	Diazo copies on acetate (for OH projection) or paper
Ozalid Ozamatic	(Same as above, for multiple copies only)
Vari-typer Headliner	Photographic lettering for transparency masters, layouts, etc.
Translifter	OH transparencies lifted from clay-coated magazine material, plastic lamination of pictures, et al.
Dry Mount Press	Dry mounting pictures and other material, lamination
Magnetic Tape Copier	Multiple copies of tape recordings
Photorapid	OH transparencies, paper copies, matte copies to be used as diazo masters
Copy cameras	2x2 slides 3-1/4x4 slides

Please familiarize yourself with the Instructional Materials Catalog, the location of the file of film guides, the collection(s) of instructional materials, and the instructional and production equipment in your school.

Suggestions for the improved operation of the Center

are welcome.

Robert A. Fischer, Jr.
IMC Manager

MOUNTING AND LAMINATING
USING THE DRY MOUNT PRESS

The mounting and preserving of flat pictorial and
graphic imagery is one of the most important and basic
areas in the production of visual materials. The heat processes of mounting and laminating have become very popular
because the application of heat and pressure forms a fast,
clean mounting within seconds. Mounting involves a visual
backed by a dry adhesive sheet which is placed on an appropriate mounting surface. Dry mounting tissue is a thin
sheet of paper which is covered on both sides with a coating
of high grade thermoplastic or wax type adhesive. The
thermo plastic adhesive forms a permanent mount and the
wax type adhesive can be removed when re-exposed to heat.

Permanent Tissue

Seal MT5 and Kodak Dry Mounting tissue are permanent
tissues. Steps in using a permanent tissue:

1. The visual should be dry and free of wrinkles; if it is
   not insert it in the heated press with a protective sheet
   on top for about ten seconds.

2. IMPORTANT - Always turn the heat press on and set
   temperature control at the proper temperature setting
   some time before putting it to use (225° F).

3. Heating the press up to temperature will also dry out
   any moisture that may have accumulated because of
   humidity.

4. Choose a piece of dry mounting tissue which is exactly
   the same size as the visual or a bit larger so that it
   can be trimmed with the visual after it has been
   "tacked" in place.

5. Place the tissue on the back of the visual.

6.   Tack it in two or three places near the center with a heated taking iron or the tip of a hand iron.

7.   After the dry mounting tissue is securely tacked to the back of the visual, carefully trim it to the desired size, making sure that no mounting tissue extends beyond the margin of the picture.

8.   Attach the visual and tissue to the mounting board. Since the tissue is not sticky, it can be positioned as desired on the board.

9.   Tack it onto the board by lifting any two opposite corners and by touching the tip of the tacking iron to the tissue. (This will keep the visual in place during the actual mounting.)

10.   Check to see that the press is up to desired temperature.

11.   Insert the visual into the press with a clean sheet of paper on top to protect the surface.

12.   Close the press for the recommended time (15 sec.).

13.   After visual is removed from the press, it is best to allow it to cool under pressure.

Removable Tissue

Seal Fotoflat has a waxy finish and mounts at a temperature of 180° F. It should not be used in mounting visuals that are to be exposed to heat for any length of time (ex. visuals placed over heaters or in warm window-display areas). For mounting follow the same steps as the permanent mounting tissue.

To Remove a Visual From It's Backing

1.   Place the visual in the heated press (200° F) for about one minute.

2.   Do not lock the press down.

3.   Quickly remove the visual and lift one corner.

4.   Gently peel the material from the base.

5. If material is large it may require reheating to complete the process.

Permanent mounting tissues are used on flat or textured surfaces and acetates. Removable tissues are used on rough surfaces, and hold well on wood or cloth surfaces. Fotoflat works very well on flannel or felt for making flannelboard materials.

Laminating

Laminating is simply laying a thin layer of coating over another material. Adhering a thin coating of transparent film as a protective surface over a visual not only preserves it but also gives it great flexibility in use. The process usually involves some type of acetate, vinyl or mylar film which has a transparent adhesive coating on one side.

Steps in Laminating

1. Find a visual suitable for laminating.

2. Mount onto cardboard with dry mount tissue.

3. Cut a sheet of Sealamin to cover visual and mounting board.

4. Place Sealamin over picture surface; be sure dull surface of Sealamin is in contact with picture surface.

5. Rub over surface of Sealamin to level it over picture surface.

6. Be sure a minimum of laminating film is extending over the edge of visual.

7. Place protective sheet of newsprint over Sealamin surface.

8. Place in preheated press (270° F). (Most presses will require a masonite board for added pressure and rigidity.)

9. Remove from press and trim edges.

Important Hints

1. Make sure all dirt and dust particles have been removed.

2. The appearance of frosty areas indicates incomplete adherence, and it must be placed back in the press for an added length of time.

3. If a bubble of air forms, prick it with a pin and then put into the press again.

4. Make sure newsprint is free of wrinkles and creases; the laminating film is very sensitive and they may form an impression on the film.

5. When laminated material must be mounted with low-temperature mounting tissue, do the high-temperature laminating process first and then do the low temperature mounting as the last step.

3M Laminating Instructions

The 3M Company manufactures a laminating film that is designed to be used in thermocopy machines.

1. Place sheet of 3M laminating film over visual. (Make sure the original to be laminated is not folded, creased or crumpled.

2. Place the above two sheets into the carrier (carrier comes in box with laminating film).

3. Set the speed control of the thermo-copy machine at the slowest speed (darkest setting).

4. Insert materials into the machine.

5. When laminating several sheets without interruption, gradually turn the dial to a slower (lighter) setting.

OPAQUE PROJECTOR

Flat pictures may be mounted singly, from magazines or books and projected on a screen so that the entire group may see and study.

Advantages:

1. Large amount of picture material available.
2. Student's work may be projected, corrected,

evaluated.
3. Color is projected.
4. Picture is seen by entire group at one time.
5. Projected picture is an attention getter.
6. Projector is easily operated at low cost.
7. Variety in type of material projected.
8. Can enlarge small pictures or diagrams.
9. Makes good teachers better teachers.

Disadvantages:

1. Good projection needs a darkened room.
2. Will not teach--needs carefully prepared materials.
3. Size limits portability.

Suggestions For Use:

1. Select materials to correlate with work.
2. Present pertinent pictures at proper time.
3. Arrange pictures in sequence when successive ideas are to be presented.
4. Pictures for art appreciation may be studied.
5. Student drawings may be projected and discussed.
6. Written papers may be corrected and criticized. (Students' names should be on the reverse side or covered when this is done.)
7. Maps and graphs for study may be projected, copied or traced on to the chalkboard.
8. Three-dimensional materials may be projected.
9. Students may participate in preparation and presentation.
10. Preparation of sequential ideas similar to travel folders:
    a. hinged
    b. stapled
    c. glued, etc.

FILMSTRIP

Filmstrip is a roll of 35mm film with sprocket holes on both sides of the film. Printed on this film is a series of pictures which are carefully prepared for use with students. Through careful editing and sequential development the lesson to be learned may be correlated with all areas of the curriculum.

Filmstrip projector needed for projection.

Advantages:

1.   Easily stored and transported.
2.   Common denominator of experience for entire class.
3.   Projected picture holds attention.
4.   Each frame may be carefully studied.
5.   May be used with individuals or groups.
6.   Materials are available on all levels.
7.   Materials are available in all curriculum areas.
8.   Quality of produced material is constantly improving.
9.   Picture may be advanced or reversed.
10. Cost is low.

Disadvantages:

1.   Does not show motion.
2.   Sequence of frames is fixed.

Suggestions For Use:

1.   Correlate filmstrip with unit of work.
2.   Use with class --prepare; present and discuss; follow up with class.
3.   Use for skill and drill subjects: reading, arithmetic.
4.   Use for sequented subjects: history, literature
5.   Knowledge of people and place.
6.   Appreciation of art, music (sound-filmstrips are correlated with record or tape).
7.   Open-end materials for use in group guidance are excellent for discussion.
8.   In selecting a filmstrip for quality, use a good check list for evaluation.

2 X 2 SLIDES

This type of slide is made in color or black and white on 35mm film.   They may be purchased from commercial sources in every area of the curriculum or may be prepared by teachers and students with a 35mm camera.

Advantages:

1. Used as individual slides or in groups of slides.
2. Is easy and inexpensive to make.
3. Can keep a record of class activities.
4. Brings to the class a picture record of a field trip.
5. Brings to the class pictures of places visited by teachers, students, lecturers.
6. Slide projector easily operated.

Disadvantages:

1. Need care in filing.
2. Individual slides are easily lost.
3. Must check carefully for true color.

Suggestions for Use:

1. Use a small group of slides effectively.
2. Combine with tape recording for prepared talk.
3. Use to introduce a unit.
4. Use for appreciation, as in art.
5. Combine with music for appreciation.
6. Provide opportunity for students to present talk.

TRANSPARENCIES

These are made on plastic sheets in varying sizes by hand or through machine duplication for use on an overhead projector.

They are very effective for teaching or for lecturing as it is possible to have excellent projection in a partially darkened room.

Advantages:

1. Has a large projection area, 7" x 7" or 10" x 10".
2. May be prepared by teacher, student or lecturer.
3. Reproduction of materials may be made with photo-copying or diazo machines and equipment.
4. Projector is in front of group so that instructor faces class.

Disadvantages:

1. Need careful preparation.
2. Little commercially produced material available.
3. Commercially produced materials very expensive.

Suggestions For Use:

1. Use as chalkboard.
2. Demonstrate on transparency with grease pencil.
3. Develop sequential ideas through overlays.
4. Use for diagrams where each step is presented in sequence.
5. Plan forms or grids for use in science, math, and other areas to be used for demonstration.
6. Use in all areas of curriculum.

TAPE RECORDING

Recordings are made when sound is converted to electrical impulses which then magnetize particles of iron oxide coated on a strip or roll of plastic tape. When played back the sound is reproduced through a speaker.

Tape Speeds: 3-3/4 - 7-1/2 - 15

The speed selected should be suited to the material being recorded. The faster the speed the higher the fidelity.

Advantages:

1. Ease with which a recording may be made.
2. Immediate playback is possible.
3. Any activity or lesson may be recorded.
4. Some commercial recordings are available.

Disadvantages:

1. Tape must be handled carefully.
2. Care must be taken not to erase material accidentally.

Suggestions For Use:

1. Use with little children for reading, speech therapy.
2. Record music and other materials to be kept as

part of school record.
3. Use with: speech; dramatics; debating groups.
4. Use with language groups with speaker; with head
    phones in language laboratory.
5. Correlate with slides for talks or lecture.
6. Correlate with other curriculum material.

DISCS

This type of recording has been used many years for
instruction.   It is often referred to as a phonograph record.

Disc Speed

1. 78 rpm disc--must be played at a speed of 78 rev-
    olutions per minute.
2. 33-1/3 rpm disc--must be played at a speed of
    33-1/3 revolutions per minute:
    a.   long-playing microgroove,
    b.   transcriptions.
3. 45 rpm disc--must be played at a speed of 45 rev-
    olutions per minute.
4. 16 rpm disc--must be played at a speed of 16 rev-
    olutions per minute, used for "talking books."

Machines for school use should be capable of playing
all speeds.

Advantages:

1. Equipment readily available.
2. Relatively inexpensive.
3. Wide variety of instructional materials available.

Disadvantages:

1. Material cannot be erased.
2. Discs become worn and scratched.

Suggestions For Use:

1. Use in all grades.
2. Use in all curriculum areas.
3. Select and listen to discs for:
    literature   government
    history   language arts

storytelling   languages
drama   speech therapy
social studies

4. Correlate disc with class work.
5. Prepare class for listening--class must listen and comprehend.
6. Suit preparation to type of disc.
7. Follow up listening exercise with discussion and follow-up activities.
8. Correlate with other teaching materials.

MOTION PICTURES

A motion picture is a series of still pictures printed in sequence on film. When these pictures are projected on a screen in rapid succession the illusion of motion is given.

Film Speeds

1. Silent--16 frames per second--2 sets of sprocket holes.
2. Sound--24 frames per second--1 set of sprocket holes opposite sound trace.
   (A frame is a single picture in the series).

Film Sizes

1. 8mm--for home use.
2. 16mm--for educational use.
3. 35mm--for commercial use.

Advantages:

1. Holds attention of group.
2. Combines use of two senses--seeing and hearing.
3. Overcomes language barriers.
4. Makes it possible to cover periods of time in areas such as history.
5. Makes people and events real.
6. Corrects mistaken ideas held by viewers.
7. Shows continuity or sequented development.
8. Gives an opportunity to bring the people and places of the world to the classroom.

Disadvantages:

1. Needs expensive equipment.
2. Cannot be stopped readily for discussion.
3. Narration may be too difficult.
4. Narrator may be hard to understand.
5. Needs a darkened room for good viewing.

Suggestions For Use:

1. Select proper film--preview--check equipment--arrange room for best viewing--have all in readiness when class is prepared for film.
2. Prepare class for best use of film.
   a. questions
   b. statement of main points
   c. new words.
3. Present film under best possible conditions.
4. Follow up showing with discussion.
5. Plan for a second showing, if necessary.
6. Present class with topics for further study or research.
7. Evaluate through discussing, projects or tests, the advantage of using that film.
8. Keep a file of manuals so that the content may be checked when selecting films or when preview is not possible.
9. Use films in all areas of curriculum.
10. Use films for motivation--for information--for recreation.
11. Integrate film with other instructional materials.

EXAMPLE (5)

COOPERATIVE TRAINING

Cooperative training programs developed by local school districts and institutions of higher education can prove to be of great benefit to teachers, students, aides, and to the ongoing programs of the institutions themselves. The program developed by the Edgefield County (S. C.) Department of Education is presented as an excellent example of cooperative training.

TEACHER AIDE NARRATIVE

The Teacher Aide Program for the Edgefield Public Schools evolved from a Federal Grant received by the Upper Savannah Development District titled Public Service Careers, Plan "B". Piedmont Technical Education Center in Greenwood, South Carolina, was contracted to provide all necessary training for this program. The program was initiated in October, 1970. The topics covered and course description follow as Article 1.

Edgefield Public Schools contacted Piedmont Technical Education Center about a similar training program for their volunteer teacher aides. The program design and schedule follow under Article 2. The Edgefield Public School Program was a tremendous success and of great benefit to the aides.

These two programs encouraged the development of the Teacher Aide Certificate Program and the Human Services Associate of Applied Science Degree Program at Piedmont Technical Education Center. These two programs now allow a teacher aide to move up the ladder of education to possibly a teaching degree.

The Program Coordinator of the Edgefield County (South Carolina) Department of Education is John H. Cely, Jr.

139

Article 1

COURSE DESCRIPTIONS FOR THE TEACHER AIDE PROGRAM

The Paraprofessional Movement in Education - Started
publicly in medicine with the development of efficient technicians and similar kinds of people in special groups to re-
lieve doctors for the more important operations of medicine.
These practices have been tried in many places in the United
States in schools with teacher aides to take care of the clerical and non-teaching duties of the classroom so that the
teacher may be free for teaching duties and the planning and
preparation of teaching material.   Teacher aides were first
suggested in the Trump Report several years ago.   These
have been made available through various federal programs
such as Title 1 and 3 and many school systems now find
teacher aides an important part of our education program.

Research and Collection of Educational Materials -
This would be designed to develop familiarity with teaching
materials and their location and collection.   The student
would develop skill in using library resources, catalogs and
materials from local sources in putting together appropriate
materials to be used in the instructional program.

Media in Education - This course is designed to give
the student an understanding of the importance of various
aids available to the teacher in her instructional duties, and
to prepare the student in techniques of using various instructional media.

Inter-Personal Relations--Seminar - The group of sessions devoted to increase the self-confidence and personal
confidence of the teacher aide role is relatively new in
careers designed with these duties and responsibilities.
This is the concern of those about to become teacher aides
as well as those with whom they are to be working.   Teacher aides must be able to work efficiently with a variety of
people--teachers, pupils, administrators, parents, and other
teacher aides.   Thus, there is a concrete need for the teacher aide to gain an understanding of those with whom they
will be working.

Media in Education - This is designed to familiarize
the student with the operation, care, and simple maintenance
of various equipment used in schools as aids to the instructional process, and to give the student an understanding of

his responsibilities in relation to other personnel such as librarians, A-V directors and others who also have responsibilities in this area.

The Organization of the School System - This is designed to give the student an understanding of the framework of functional organization of public schools, and some appreciation of the division of responsibilities between the various levels and departments of government. The specific emphasis would be on South Carolina, with incidental comparisons with neighboring states.

The Legal Aspects of the Teacher's Work - This course is designed to give the student an understanding of the legal rights and limitations of each element in the school situation: teachers, students, parents, administrators, and non-professional personnel.

Media in Education - This is designed to give the student an understanding of the close relationship between the school and its supporting community and an appreciation of the responsibilities of the teacher aide, as a member of the school staff, for preserving and promoting good relations with the community.

The Role of the School in the Community - This is designed to give the student understanding of, and skill in, the preparation of various kinds of media materials from the research and collection of materials to the final presentation of the lesson. This is a summary and expansion of the activities of the two previous courses in "Use of Educational Aids." Since the students also lie engaged in their Practicum during the quarter, the content of their work in Development is based on the work done in the Practicum. The instructor in Development will help students plan, prepare, and evaluate projects for actual use in their Practicum situation.

Communications in the School Setting - This is designed to (a) remedy communications handicaps of the students and (b) give them an understanding of an ability to use communication skills in the school setting.

Financial and Accounting Aspects of Classroom Work - A study of record and financial forms and procedures encountered in the classroom setting in the entire year. This will encompass attendance reports, recording of test grades

and computation and recording of final averages. Included
also will be financial responsibilities, accounting, and collection procedures for the school annual, school paper, lunch,
book and special project fees.

Working with Community Members - Duties and responsibilities of the teacher aide pertaining to P. T. A.,
parent conferences, and maintaining public image of the
school. Methods and techniques of communication reflect
educational professionalism when working with the general
public.

American Education and Democracy - This is designed
to give the student an understanding of the trends in American life which produced the American school system. The
treatment is largely, although not entirely, historical.

Personal Improvement - This is designed to assess
and remedy any characteristics of the students which tend to
reduce their effectiveness as teacher aides.

Special Programs--State and Federal - Since 1958
when the federal government inaugurated the national defence
education program, the federal government has financed and
encouraged innovation in a great many areas of educational
activity. The National Defence Education Act was followed
by Elementary and Secondary Education Act, the Education
Profession Act and many others. The federal government
has made funds and equipment available for teacher trainees
and children in deprived areas, for children with special
needs such as physical handicaps. The student programs in
many classes have paralleled the program for the physically
handicapped with the programs for the mentally handicapped.
Many special schools and home education programs, including adult education, vocational education, and many others,
have been established.

Article 2

PROGRAM DESIGN FOR
EDGEFIELD PUBLIC SCHOOL
VOLUNTEER AIDE PROGRAM

I.   Organization of the School System--4 hours--Dr. James
     Matthews
           This is designed to give the student an understand-

ing of the trends in American life which have produced
the American school system. The treatment will be
largely, although not entirely, historical. Key ideas to
be stressed are:

1. The various purposes for which schools have been
   organized: Religious, vocational, democratic citizenship, Americanization of immigrants, personal
   growth, etc.
2. Basic American ideals which have shaped our
   schools: democracy, Christianity, basic support
   by taxes, education as a channel for personal improvement, education as an instrument of social
   growth and change, children and youth as a national resource, etc.
3. Relationships between schools and other institutions of American society: the church, the home,
   the business world, the courts and legislatures,
   etc.

II. Audio-Visual Aids in Education--20 hours--Dr. Arthur
Jensen
    This course is designed to give the student an un-
derstanding of the importance of various aids available
to the teacher in her instructional duties, and to prepare the student in techniques of using various instructional media. Key ideas to be stressed are:

1. The importance of sensory, (and multi-sensory)
   impact upon the student in developing and clarifying concepts, attitudes and skills in the classroom.
2. The various types of media which are available:
   records, tapes (both audio and video), transparencies, films and filmstrips, etc.
3. Ability to prepare and use the simpler types of
   media: transparencies, charts, posters, etc.
4. Ability to locate and evaluate more sophisticated
   types of media: films, filmstrips, etc.

III. a. Research and Collection of Educational Materials--8
        hours--Mrs. Elizabeth Galloway
     b. Programmed Material--8 hours--Mrs. Elizabeth
        Galloway
        This is designed to develop familiarity with teach-
ing materials and their location and collection. The student would develop skill in using library resources, catalogs and materials from local sources in putting together appropriate materials to be used in the instructional

program. Key ideas to be stressed are:
1. Familiarity with library organization and typical
   holdings.
2. Familiarity with sources of materials outside the
   library--commercial offerings, local brochures,
   maps, samples, etc.
3. Familiarity with magazines like Grade Teacher,
   Instructor, Music Journal, etc.
4. Development of system of organization so that
   materials will be available when needed.
5. Adaptation and proper use of programmed materials.

SCHEDULE FOR
EDGEFIELD PUBLIC SCHOOL
VOLUNTEER AIDE PROGRAM

Group I   Group II
18 Students   18 Students
8:30 a. m. -12:30 p. m.   1:00 p. m. -5:00 p. m.

September 10 -- Dr. Matthews
Organization of the School System

September 13 -- Dr. Jensen
Audio-Visual Aids in Education

September 17 -- Mrs. Galloway
Research and Collection of Educational Materials

September 20 -- Dr. Jensen
Audio-Visual Aids in Education

September 24 -- Mrs. Galloway
Research and Collection of Educational Materials

September 27 -- Dr. Jensen
Audio-Visual Aids in Education

October 4 -- Dr. Jensen
Audio-Visual Aids in Education

October 8 -- Mrs. Galloway
Programmed Instruction

October 11 -- Dr. Jensen
Audio-Visual Aids in Education

October 15 -- Mrs. Galloway
Programmed Instruction

TEACHER AIDE CERTIFICATE PROGRAM

The Teacher Aide curriculum is designed to prepare the student to participate in a vital role in the educational system. Emphasis is placed on assisting the teacher in his regular duties.

The student will acquire fundamental knowledge of the use of audio-visual aids, research and collection of educational materials and typing. The necessary background obtained through the Teacher Aide curriculum will prepare the student to assume responsibilities in public and private educational institutions.

First Quarter		C	L	CR
TSY 111	Typing I	2	4	3
EDU 101	Educational Aids I	3	6	5
		5	10	8

Second Quarter				
TSY 121	Typing II	2	3	3
ENG 101	Reading Improvement	0	2	0
EDU 211	Educational Aids II	3	6	5
		5	11	8

Third Quarter				
EDU 201	Communications in the School Setting	3	3	4
SOC 115	Personal Improvement	3	0	3
EDU 321	Educational Aids III	3	3	4
		9	6	11

Fourth Quarter				
EDU 202	Research and collection of Educational Materials	3	3	4
TSY 113	Filing and Record Control	2	3	3
EDU 301	Child Development	5	0	5
		10	6	12

TEACHER AIDE COURSE DESCRIPTION

EDU 101 Educational Aids I (3-6-5)
This course would be designed to give the student an
understanding of the importance of various aids available to
the teacher in her instructional duties, and to prepare the
student in techniques of using various instructional media.
Key ideas to be stressed would be: (1) The importance of
sensory, (and multi-sensory) impact upon the student in developing and clarifying concepts, attitudes and sills in the
classroom.   (2) The various types of media which are available: records, tapes (both audio and video), transparencies,
films and filmstrips, etc.   (3) Ability to prepare and use the
simpler types of media: transparencies, charts, posters,
etc.   (4) Ability to locate and evaluate more sophisticated
types of media: films, filmstrips, etc.

EDU 211 Educational Aids II (3-6-5)
This is designed to familiarize the student with the
operation, care, and simple maintenance of various equipment used in schools as aids to the instructional process,
and to give the student an understanding of his responsibilities
in relation to other personnel such as librarians, A-V directors and others who also have responsibilities in this area.
Key ideas to be stressed are: (1) General understanding of
operation of electrical and electric motor driver devices, including safety precautions.   (2) Characteristics of typical
equipment such as tape recorders, film and filmstrip projectors, overhead and opaque projectors, etc.   (3) Facility
in setting up, operating, and adjusting typical equipment including an understanding of the uses and limitations of each
type.   (4) Areas of responsibility for maintenance and repair.

EDU 201 Communications in the School Setting (3-3-4)
This would be designed to (a) remedy communications
handicaps of the students and (b) give them an understanding
of an ability to use communication skills in the school setting.
Key ideas to be stressed would be: (1) Remedial work, as
needed, in spelling, punctuation, sentence structure, writing
of letters and reports, etc.   (2) Understanding and implementation of school policy statements, school regulations, etc.
(3) Understanding and use of school forms, such as textbook
inventories, filing systems, census sheets, attendance regis-
ters, etc.   (4) Clear, concise, and appropriate language in
preparing media methods ...

EDU 202 Research and Collection of Educational Materials
(3-3-4)
This is designed to develop familiarity with teaching
materials and their location and collection.   The student will
develop skill in using library resources, catalogs and materials from local sources in putting together appropriate materials to be used in the instructional program.   Key ideas
to be stressed are: (1) Familiarity with library organization
and typical holdings.   (2) Familiarity with sources of materials outside the library--commercial offerings, local brochures, maps, samples, etc.   (3) Familiarity with magazines
like GRADE TEACHER, INSTRUCTOR, MUSIC JOURNAL,
etc.   (4) Development of system of organization so that materials will be available when needed.

EDU 301 Child Development (5-0-5)
This would be designed to familiarize the student with
the development of a child from age five (5) through age
thirteen (13).   The periods of growth, change in stature,
maturity, learning abilities, habits and characteristics of the
child will be introduced.   Key ideas to be stressed are: (1)
General understanding of the problems of a child.   (2) De-
tection of various childhood diseases.   (3) Learning levels
of a child.   (4) Special techniques for the development of
the "problem" child.

EDU 321 Educational Aids III (3-3-4)
This is designed to give the student understanding of,
and skill in, the preparation of various kinds of media materials from the research and collection of materials to the
final presentation of the lesson.   This would be a summary
and expansion of the activities of the two previous courses
in "Use of Educational Aids."
Since the students would also lie engaged in their
Practicum during the quarter, the content of their work in
development would be based on the work done in the Practicum.   The instructor in development would help students
plan, prepare, and evaluate projects for actual use in their
Practicum situation.

RELATED COURSES

ENG 101 Reading Improvement (0-2-0)
A 24 hour course designed to increase the eye span
reading speed.   Emphasis will be placed on comprehension,
understanding and vocabulary improvement.

SOC 115 Personal Improvement (3-0-3)
This is designed to assess and remedy the characteristics of the students which would tend to reduce their effectiveness as teacher aides.   Some of the factors to be considered are: (1) Speech habits--voice, grammar, pitch, ar-
ticulation, etc.   (2) Grooming--dress, hair, shoes, etc.
(3) Psychology of relations with other members of the staff,
and with students, parents, etc.

TSY 111 Typing I (2-4-3)
The practical side of typewriting is stressed, providing an opportunity for rapid and accurate typists to work on
problems comparable to those found in actual office work;
letter styles, invoices, statements, rough drafts, tabulation,
and duplication.

TSY 113 Filing and Record Control (2-3-3)
Lecture and laboratory work; modern filing systems
and equipment, with extensive practice in applying indexing
rules and filing correspondence.

TSY 121 Typing II (2-3-3)
This course requires students to type business forms,
special reports, production reports, tables, charts, graphs,
reports that are used in Accounting Offices, Medical Offices,
and Technical Offices.

HUMAN SERVICES CERTIFICATE PROGRAM

This program is designed to prepare students for em-
ployment as a paraprofessional in a wide range of services,
agencies and organizations.   Skills such as observing and
recording behavior, interviewing and leading group discussions are important aspects of this program.   The student
will be given the opportunity to choose between the Education
Aide and Child Care Aide options in selecting his major field
of concentration.   Length--4 quarters.

HUM 111 Human Services I
HUM 121 Human Services II
HUM 131 Human Services III
ENG 112 Communications I
ENG 131 Technical Writing
HST 222 Education Aids
HST 223 Research and Col-
       lection of Educa-

       tional Materials
HST 233 Principles of Child
       Care
HST 234 Nutrition and Health
HST 235 Observing and Re-
       cording Child Be-
       havior
SOC 113 Introduction to So-

ciology   SOC 135 Social Problems
SOC 117 General Psychology   TSY 111 Typing I
SOC 127 Human Growth and   TSY 121 Typing II
        Development I

HUMAN SERVICES COURSE DESCRIPTIONS

HUM 111 Human Services I (3-3-4)
Students are acquainted with major human service agencies and institutions in this region with emphasis on the roles and functions of paraprofessionals in the various types of human service work. Students are required to participate in scheduled field visits to these agencies.

HUM 121 Human Services II (3-3-4)
A study of the major client groups with which the paraprofessional may work. Emphasis is placed on characteristics of individual and situational problems. A developmental study of client training and assistance is also included. Students are required to participate in an internship training program.

HUM 131 Human Services III (3-3-4)
This course is a study in interpersonal relationships, including the development of social behavior and self-awareness through levels of communications. Emphasis is placed on personal development and openness in interpersonal relationships. A correlative analysis of classroom work and internship training is required of the student.

RELATED COURSES

ENG 112 Communications I (5-0-5)
This course is designed to aid the student in the improvement of writing and self-expression with emphasis on practical application of grammar and sentence structure. Vocabulary building, as well as functional approach to writing, is stressed by use of projected materials with emphasis on the mechanics of construction in all areas of good English.

ENG 131 Technical Writing (3-0-3)
A study designed to develop ability in using research tools and techniques, to increase proficiency in the principles of good writing including those unique to technical fields, to explore all types of technical writings, to give practice in

150

In-Service

basic formats for technical reports, and to give experience
in oral reporting.

HST 222 Education Aids (3-6-5)
    This course is designed to give the student an under-
standing of the importance of various aids available to the
teacher in her instructional duties, and to prepare the student in techniques of using various instructional media. Key
ideas to be stressed are: (1) the importance of sensory and
multi-sensory impact upon the student in developing and clarifying concepts, attitudes and skills in the classroom. (2)
the various types of media which are available: records,
tapes (both audio and video), transparencies, films and filmstrips, etc. (3) ability to prepare and use the simpler types
of media: transparencies, charts, posters, etc. (4) ability
to locate and evaluate more sophisticated types of media:
films, filmstrips, etc. (5) facility in setting up, operating,
and adjusting typical equipment.

HST 223 Research and Collection of Educational Materials
    (3-3-4)
    This course is designed to develop familiarity with
teaching materials and their location and collection. The student will develop skill in using library resources, catalogs
and materials from local sources in putting together appropriate materials to be used in the instructional program.
Key ideas to be stressed are: (1) familiarity with library
organizational and typical holdings, (2) familiarity with
sources of materials outside the library--commercial offerings, local brochures, maps, samples, etc., (3) familiarity
with magazines like Grade Teacher, Instructor, Music Journal, etc., (4) development of systems of organization so
that materials will be available when needed.

HST 233 Principles of Child Care (5-3-6)
    The study of the history, philosophy, and the ethics
of child care, types of child care institutions, laws and
standards governing institution management, and the functions
of persons employed in various staff positions. Emphasis is
placed on the duties of the child care worker.

HST 234 Nutrition and Health (3-0-3)
    This course will introduce the students to the basic
law of nutrition and health. Appropriate menues for child
care centers will be developed. Laws governing food preparation and service will be studied.

HST 235 Observing and Recording Child Behavior (1-3-2)
The student will apply the principles of early childhood development by observing and recording patterns of behavior characteristics of pre-school children.

SOC 113 Introduction to Sociology (5-0-5)
An analysis of the society and culture dealing with social organization, control, institutions, stratification and social change.

SOC 117 General Psychology (5-0-5)
A survey of psychology, including organic structure, perception, motivation, learning, principles of behavior, measurements and theories of psychology.

SOC 127 Human Growth and Development I (5-0-5)
Development of the normal child through childhood, with consideration of the social, biological and cultural influences upon growth.

SOC 135 Social Problems (5-0-5)
A study of the major social problems of modern society, including family disorganization, minority groups and problems associated with industrial and urban development.

TSY 111 Typing I (2-3-3)
The practical side of typewriting is stressed, providing an opportunity for rapid and accurate typists to work on problems comparable to those found in actual office work; letter styles, invoices, statements, rough drafts, tabulation, and duplication.

TSY 121 Typing II (2-3-3)
This course requires students to type business forms, special reports, production reports, tables, charts, and graphs, reports that are used in accounting offices, medical offices, and technical offices.

PART III

TRAINING FOR PROFESSIONAL
LIBRARY/MEDIA PERSONNEL

5. THE RACE BETWEEN MAN AND MEDIA: IN-SERVICE TRAINING FOR MEDIA PERSONNEL

If it is understood that each child learns as an individual (and learning is always an individual matter), then the school must provide a wide range of services, facilities and materials to satisfy the requirements of each student within the school. If we do indeed live in an ever-changing society where the total accumulated knowledge of the world doubles every generation, then learning how to learn should be the primary goal of education. But this is costly, in time, in money and in the retraining of instructional personnel who share responsibility for the education of today's youth. For just as the world is changing at an unprecedented pace, methods and materials must also undergo constant change if the educative process is to be relevant to the learner. We can no longer confine instruction to a single classroom nor even to a single building, for students must be given the opportunity to inquire, discover and explore a large mass of knowledge, both inside and outside of the school, and select from this mass of knowledge what is most pertinent to the problem at hand. We must help the student to locate information; acquire it through a determination of the accuracy and authenticity of the material; separate fact from opinion, the significant from the less significant; determine cause and effect; evaluate his findings and reach a conclusion based on his research. In performing each of these tasks, and in guiding this performance, both pupils and teachers seek from media personnel the best available in research methods and materials.

The task of keeping up with the information explosion is a formidable one and requires ever changing competencies on the part of librarians and media specialists. It encompasses not only the problem of making new knowledge available to students and teachers as rapidly as possible, but an expertise in the evaluation and use of new carriers of knowledge.

154

A brief comparison of the equipment and materials available in most school libraries thirty years ago with the equipment and materials in use today should demonstrate the rapid changes in communication which have taken place in that short period of time.

A School Library Materials and Equipment List

1942

Books	Maps	Pictures	Radio
Periodicals	Globes	Museum Pieces	Records (mono)
Pamphlets	Charts	Models	Record Player

1972

All of the preceding plus:

16mm films and projectors
8mm films & loop projectors
Filmstrips & filmstrip
  projectors
Slides and slide projectors
Short strips and viewers
Individual filmstrip viewers
Slides and microprojectors
Microfiche or microfilm and
  readers
Reader-printers
Photographic equipment
Transparencies and overhead
  projector

Reel to reel tapes and re-
  corders
Cassette tapes and recorders
Stereo phonograph & recordings
8-track tape players
Listening centers
Dial access information re-
  trieval systems
Videotape equipment
Copy machines
Hot press
Thermofax secretary
Programmed learning materi-
  als

Problems of New Media

Along with the introduction of each new carrier of knowledge to the educational program must come problems involving selection, evaluation and utilization of the new media; the development of new skills on the part of media personnel, teachers and students in media use; the difficulties which occur until some form of standardization of the media has taken place; and the determination of the place of the new media in the educational program. Any one of these problems can prove to be time-consuming to the usually overworked library/media director. Taken en masse and

compounded by the addition of ever new forms of communications carriers, such problems could become overwhelming.

Media personnel in many school districts and in State
Departments of Education have attempted to meet the crisis
of the information explosion through ongoing in-service training. Recognizing that new methods and materials will be
pouring into media centers at an ever increasing rate, planning for continuous, ongoing in-service training is an essential part of every library/media director's job.

Forms of In-Service Training

The forms of in-service training for media personnel
can be as varied as the types of media with which they work.
Successful programs have been planned on a continuous year-
round basis with district or county wide media personnel
meeting, usually monthly, to explore problems of mutual interest. Other programs have been planned cooperatively
with neighboring colleges or universities to provide intensive
short-term training in specific competencies. In still other
training models, new methods and materials are gradually
introduced into the media centers of the district and training
takes place through supervised use. Educational television
has played an important role in the training of media personnel, as have Educational Telephone Networks which provide
for conference calls to higher education institutions. A number of school districts provide released time for in-service
training of media personnel for one or more specific training sessions, including visitations to other media centers.
State Departments of Education are playing an increasingly
important role in disseminating information on new methods
and materials through both written communication to individual media personnel and in-service training workshops held
throughout the state by trained state media supervisors.
Both national and state organizations play a vital part in
helping media personnel to bridge the information gap, again
through written communications and through national and
state conferences. One often unmentioned but important
source of new information for media directors is the publisher's or company representative whose job it is to bring
new materials and products to the library/media director's
attention and to point out the possibilities for use in the educational program.

Applying the Basic Principles of In-Service Training

Once again, the basic principles of in-service training must apply if such training is to be successful in upgrading the competencies of media personnel. Cooperative
planning by those involved is essential. Training should be
based on need and requires direct involvement of participants. Released time from routine duties is a basic requirement and provision should be made for evaluation of
the in-service program. The in-service training models
which follow cover six basic types of training:

1.   Monthly in-service training meetings undertaken
     throughout the entire school year.

2.   The single session in-service workshop planned to
     develop one or more specific competencies.

3.   Multi-session training meetings co-sponsored by
     the school district and local college or university.

4.   Series workshops planned and produced by local
     school districts.

5.   In-service training through ETN (Educational Tele-
     phone Network).

6.   In-service training sponsored by State Departments
     of Education.

The models selected are those considered to be highly
successful and easily adaptable to local school district situations. Each is presented as closely as possible to the form
in which it was developed to better provide media personnel
with working models for adaptation.

6. IN-SERVICE PROGRAMS FOR PROFESSIONALS

EXAMPLE (1)

Monthly Meetings Throughout
the School Year

School District: Bay County School District, Panama City,
Florida: Arabelle Grant, Director, Educa-
tional Media

The following are summaries of the in-service activities of the Bay County media specialists from the 1969-70
school year through the 1972-73 year. In-service consists
of two types: first, entire days--county or area-wide days
set aside for in-service; and second, monthly workshops
held in the afternoon after school hours. The workshop
summaries are preceded by a form used by Bay County
Media Personnel in determining cooperatively the selection
of topics for exploration and discussion.

Dear

The following are topics suggested by Bay County
media specialists for discussion at future Panhandle
area meetings of media specialists. I think the
suggestions are excellent! Please indicate your
preference by placing the numbers 1-11 (or 12) in
the blanks before each topic, number 1 indicating
your first choice, number 2 your second choice,
etc. Please return this sheet as soon as possible
because the results must be tabulated by Thursday,
October 16. Thanks!

158

Arabelle Grant
Director, Educational Media

Suggested Topics for Area Meetings

____ The changing role of the media specialist as a result of
newer organizational patterns in schools--team, block,
non-graded, etc.

____ Updating knowledge of newer materials, equipment,
trends

____ Censorship

____ "New and exciting" ways of teaching media skills

____ Methods of getting teachers to use a variety of media

____ How to evaluate the usefulness of the media center to
teachers and students

____ Planning and actually producing a video tape recording

____ Planning for expansion of the media center into additional space

____ Planning for more effective use of the space presently
occupied by the media center

____ Programmed material

____ Job analysis--What does the position of media specialist
entail?

____ Other

        Selecting topics for in-service is a cooperative ven-
ture.   This sheet is one example.

Title: MEDIA SPECIALISTS WORKSHOP:
              WRITING INDIVIDUALIZED LEARNING UNITS

                     Monthly 1972-73

General Objective:
        Participants shall be provided opportunity to develop
        individual learning units to implement a Bay County
        continuum of media skills.

Specific Objective:
        Participants shall gain knowledge necessary to suc-
        cessfully write sequential units of work to be used by
        individual students in acquiring skills in the use of
        materials and equipment, K-12.

Description:
        From the Bay County scope and sequence of media
        skills, K-12, media specialists will select skills and
        develop units of work which can be used by the indi-
        vidual student to acquire the skills.   Each unit will
        also contain directions and materials for the media
        specialist/teacher.   Each participant will write units
        in specific areas for specific levels of achievement;
        participants writing in the same area will coordinate
        the sequential broadening of the concept and the in-
        creasing level of achievement of the units.

        Participants will work on the common inservice day
        in November and at monthly meetings throughout the
        year.   As needed, the Florida Department of Educa-
        tional personnel and the PAEC staff will serve as
        consultants.   The literature in the area will be sur-
        veyed and examples of individualized units produced
        elsewhere will be studied.   Tentative drafts of the
        units will be field-tested and revised before being
        reproduced for inclusion in Bay County Schools:
        Media Skills Units which will be a companion volume
        to Bay County Schools: Media Skills, K-12.

Evaluation:
        The long range success of the component will be de-
        termined by the degree to which participants imple-
        ment the continuum of media skills.

        The physical inventory of field-tested units produced
        during the year will constitute the year's evaluation.

Title: MEDIA SPECIALISTS WORKSHOP:
GUIDE FOR DEVELOPING SKILLS IN THE USE OF MEDIA

Monthly 1970-71; 1971-72

General Objective:
Opportunities will be provided for media specialists
to write a guide for developing skills in the use of
media K-12.

Specific Objective:
Media specialists will write a guide for developing
skills in the use of media K-12.

Description:
Media specialists will work in small committees.
Each committee will select skills and write sequential
guides for the development of the skills selected.

They will select types of printed materials, audio
visual software and hardware requiring specific skills
for student use. Participants will write a sequential
guide, K-12, for the development of skills required
in the use of prepared materials. Participants will
also include in the guide techniques for the development of skills in gathering information and in the
production of written, graphic and auditory presentations of information.

Consultants will be Eloise Jones, James Harbin,
Dorothy Heald and Robert Smith.

Evaluation:
The committees will make program reports to the entire group for evaluation and suggested revision.
The tentative guides will be field-tested before final
revision and publication.

Title: WORKSHOP ON
INSTRUCTIONAL POSSIBILITIES WITH NEW MEDIA

April 27, 1973

Place:
Mowat Junior High School.

General Objective:
    The participants shall be given an opportunity to learn
    the variety of instructional techniques made possible
    through new hard and software media.

Specific Objective:
    The participants shall be given instruction on and un-
    derstand instructional possibilities of new hard and
    soft media.

Description:
    The participants will meet as a group for introduction
    and discussion on how to use hard and soft ware
    media such as:
        second generation VTR equipment, super 8mm
        cameras and projectors with and without sound
        synchronization, "do-it-yourself" filmstrip kits,
        synchronized slide tape presentations, speech com-
        pression tape recorders, and 3M sound on slide
        projector.

    The participants will divide into small discussion
    groups for indepth study of the new media.

    The consultant(s) are urged to present any other new
    equipment and materials that could be potentially use-
    ful to the group.

Evaluation:
    Each participant will complete evaluative instrument
    #1 and #2.

    Each participant will be able to demonstrate an under-
    standing of the possibilities of the new "hard and soft"
    media to the satisfaction of the consultant(s).

Title: WORKSHOP ON THE PRODUCTION OF
    STUDENT-MADE MATERIALS AND TECHNIQUES FOR
              TEACHING MEDIA SKILLS

              February 16, 1973

Place:
        Hiland Park Elementary School.

General Objectives:
> Participants shall be provided opportunities to understand the techniques involved in the production of student-made media.
>
> Participants shall be provided opportunities to gain knowledge in obtaining or producing materials for teaching media skills.

Specific Objectives:
> Participants shall improve techniques to be used in developing student-produced media.
>
> Participants shall become more knowledgeable of ways to obtain and produce material for teaching media skills.

Description:
> The participants will meet as a general group for organization, announcements, and introduction of the consultant(s). After that the participants will divide into two (2) groups. The groups will see examples of student-produced media and receive instruction on techniques to be employed in developing student produced media.
>
> There will be a group presentation on (a) isolated or integrated media skills, (b) commercially available materials for teaching media skills, and (c) the development of materials for teaching media skills.
>
> The two groups will change consultants after lunch.

Evaluation:
> The participants will list four (4) ways to involve students in media production, to the satisfaction of the consultants.
>
> The participants will outline one technique (for teaching media skills) they will attempt to implement at their school media centers. This outline will be to the satisfaction of the consultants.
>
> The participants will complete Evaluative Instrument #1 and #2.

Title: EDUCATIONAL MEDIA WORKSHOP ON
          COMPREHENSIVE UTILIZATION OF PERSONNEL
                    AND FACILITIES

                    August 22, 1972

Place:
          Callaway Elementary School.

General Objectives:
          Participants shall be provided opportunities to gain a
          better understanding of the factors involved in adapt-
          ing old facilities for better utilization.

          Participants shall be given an opportunity to learn
          proper techniques of personnel utilization.

          Participants shall be given an opportunity to learn
          how to better administer a school media center.

Specific Objectives:
          The participants shall demonstrate an understanding
          of facilities renovation.

          The participants shall demonstrate an understanding
          of personnel utilization.

          The participants shall develop techniques for effective
          administration of a school media center.

Description:
          Morning Session: The participants will meet as one
          group for a presentation and discussion on adapting
          old facilities for better utilization.

          Afternoon Session: The participants will divide by
          choice to either (group 1) personnel utilization or
          (group 2) school media center administration

Evaluation:
          Participants will:

          list at least four (4) factors to be considered in adapt-
          ing old facilities for better utilization (i. e. , writing
          specifications, consideration of all media services
          rendered).   The evaluation of these factors will be
          to the satisfaction of the consultant(s);

develop a job description of each of the following:
a) media specialist, b) paraprofessional, c) aide or
clerk, d) student aide, to the satisfaction of the con-
sultant(s);

list at least three techniques to be employed in administering a school media center to the satisfaction
of the consultant(s).

Title: ROLE OF THE MEDIA CENTER
          IN INDIVIDUALIZED INSTRUCTION

April 28, 1972

General Objective:
     Participants shall be provided opportunity to identify
     the role of the media center in individualized instruc-
     tion.

Specific Objective:
     Participants shall update knowledge and gain skills
     needed for individualized instruction in the media
     center.

Description:
     Presentation: participants will be divided into two
     groups determined by pre-registration at the February
     18, 1972 meeting.   Consultants will lecture on the
     role of the media center in individualized instruction,
     demonstrate use of language masters, film loops,
     Hoffman reader, System 80, Talking book, micro-
     film, microfiche; other equipment and materials
     recommended by media specialists at the meeting
     February 18, 1972, and commercially prepared indi-
     vidualized instructional programs not covered above.

     The afternoon session will be devoted to the UNIPAC,
     LAP, and contract, and how media specialists can
     best help teachers develop and use them in their
     classroom, also ways multi-media materials can re-
     inforce the UNIPAC, LAPS, and contracts.   Consul-
     tant will make available to participants sample copies
     of UNIPACS, LAPS, and contracts.

     Practice feedback: each participant will list at least
     one way the equipment demonstrated can be used to

individualized instruction and develop basic steps in developing a UNIPAC, LAP, or a contract.

Evaluation:
Each participant will:

complete Evaluative Instrument #1 and complete other evaluative instruments as provided by the consultant;

list at least one way equipment demonstrated can be used to individualized instruction;

list the basic steps involved in developing a UNIPAC, LAP, or contract.

Title: WORKSHOP: CURRENT TRENDS AND IMPROVEMENTS IN ADMINISTRATION OF AN EFFECTIVE MEDIA CENTER

February 18, 1972

Place:
Bay County Educational Media Center, Panama City.

General Objective:
Participants shall be given opportunities to gain a better understanding of the factors involved in the development of an effective media center.

Specific Objectives:
Participants shall:

develop a job description for media specialists, paraprofessionals, aides or clerks and student aides;

update knowledge in selecting, processing, storage and circulation of new materials for a multi-media center;

gain skill in the development and arrangement of physical facilities in his particular media center that will make it more effective and usable;

make more effective use of multi-media in curriculum improvement.

Description:
  Presentation: participants will meet as a large group for a lecture and discussion on an effective multi-media center.

  Practice and feedback: after attending two small group discussions the participants will be able to-- list at least one (1) new idea concerning selection, processing, storage and circulation of multi-media; list at least one (1) new idea concerning a change in arrangement of his particular media center that will make it more effective and usable; list at least three (3) new ways the multi-media approach can be used for curriculum improvement.

Evaluation:
  Each participant will complete Evaluative Instrument #1.

  The degree to which the information gained in the workshops is utilized in school media centers will determine the success of the component.

Title: WORKSHOP: EDUCATIONAL MEDIA ON INSTRUCTIONAL POSSIBILITIES AND USES OF CASSETTES IN CURRICULUM

August 20, 1971

Place:
  Bay County Educational Media Center, Panama City.

General Objective:
  Participants shall be provided opportunities to gain more knowledge of the curriculum possibilities in the production of cassette tapes.

Specific Objective:
  Participants shall gain knowledge as to the instructional possibilities of cassette tapes to reinforce the curriculum.

Description:
  Presentation: participants will be divided into four production groups as follows--cassette recorder-player operation and production of language arts cassette

tapes; cassette recorder-player operation and production of science cassette tapes; and cassette recorder-player operation and production of social studies cassette tapes.

Each media specialist will bring a cassette recorder-player and two blank cassettes with ideas for production.

Practice and feedback: after organization of the four groups, instruction will be given in the utilization of cassette tapes to reinforce the curriculum areas of language arts, mathematics, science, and social studies for the less able reader.

Groups will then meet in designated rooms where each participant will produce one cassette for an able reader and one for a less able reader.

Evaluation:
Each participant will complete Evaluative Instrument #1 and other evaluative instruments as provided by the consultants.

Title: WORKSHOP FOR MEDIA SPECIALISTS
       APPRAISAL TECHNIQUES/TECHNOLOGY AND
       FACILITIES OF THE '70'S

April 13, 1971

General Objectives:
Opportunities will be provided for participants to:

learn how to design an instrument of evaluation for their library/media center;

learn how the facilities and technology of the future will affect their roles in education.

Specific Objectives:
Given instruction on how to construct an instrument of evaluation, the participants will compose evaluation forms, of at least fifteen questions, for the following types of library/media centers: elementary, junior high, senior high and county level.

After hearing a lecture on facilities and technology of the '70's, the participants will list at least three innovations that could be carried out in their present facilities--with or without major renovation.

Description:
Presentation: Lecture and interest area discussion groups will be held with the consultant acting as moderator of each group and using as many visual aids as possible. The consultant will also distribute a bibliography on facilities, technology and innovations of the future.

Practice: Each library/media center level--elementary, junior high, senior high and county will spend the morning developing an evaluation instrument.

Feedback: The various evaluation instruments will be reviewed by the entire group. A question and answer session will be followed by the participants listing three innovations that could be carried out in their centers.

Evaluation:
The participant will complete an evaluation form (see attached sample in exhibit section under the area of Media).

The participants will list the most useful information presented and explain how they plan to use it in their program.

Title: WORKSHOP ON PRODUCTION OF AND
          PRACTICAL APPLICATION OF MEDIA

Workshop was repeated three days; participants
    selected a different area each workshop.
August 21, 1970; October 23, 1970; February 22, 1971

General Objectives:
Participants will be given opportunities to:

gain experience, knowledge and production skills in three of the following four areas--the video-tape recorder/teaching tapes; a slide/tape presentation; teaching units employing dry mounting and laminating;

transparency production.

Specific Objectives:
   Given instruction on the operation of the video-tape
   recorder and instruction on production techniques of
   making a teaching tape, the participants, working in
   three teams of not more than six people per team,
   will create a fifteen minute informative/education
   video-tape on a topic determined by the consultant.

   Given instruction on the operation of the Kodak slide
   maker and given instruction on how to make an audio
   tape the participants, working in four teams of not
   more than five people per team, will create a slide/
   tape story, composed of at least fifteen slides.

   Given instruction on the operation of the dry mount
   press and given instruction on how to laminate with
   the dry mount press, the participants, working in
   four teams of not more than five people per team,
   will create a presentation on a topic to be determined
   by the instructor.

   Given instruction on the various types of transparencies; i. e., thermal, diazo and hand, and given instruction on the production of various types of transparencies, the participants, working in four teams of
   not more than five people per team, will create a
   cartoon presentation depicting the various roles of the
   media specialist.

Evaluation:
   The participants will complete form on component
   evaluation (see attached exhibit).

Title: CONFERENCE ON ACCREDITATION
              STANDARDS FOR THE MEDIA CENTER

                    April 13, 1970

General Objectives:
   Media specialists will study the state accreditation
   standards related to media.

   Media specialists will tour the new Port St. Joe High
   School to observe evidences of application of accredi-

tation standards.

Specific Objectives:
Plans will be formulated as to the best means of
working toward implementation of the new accreditation standards.

Participants will study the extent to which the new
facility at Port St. Joe meets state accreditation
standards.

Description:
Media specialists will meet in the new Port St. Joe
High School media center.

State Department of Education personnel in the area
of Educational Media will serve as consultants and
will lead the discussion of the accreditation standards.

Media specialists will participate in guided tours of
the school plant.

Evaluation:
A questionnaire based on the day's activities will be
given each participant. Results will be tabulated, recorded and reported.

Title: VISITATION TO A DEMONSTRATION
                MEDIA CENTER

                February 16, 1970

General Objectives:
Media Specialists will be afforded an opportunity to
improve their understanding of the operation of a
demonstration media center.

Specific Objectives:
To visit a model media center program for the evaluation of a model program as it relates to individual
school media centers.

To permit media specialists the opportunity to determine effective procedures used for interaction between
the media center and the classroom.

Description:
   The media specialists of the area will visit the demonstration media center at the Marianna High School,
   Marianna.   This center will present its usual program.
   After this presentation there will be group reaction to
   this program as it concerns the area schools.   Time
   will be available for some indepth evaluation of the
   materials at this center.

Evaluation:
   Subjective comments as to the feasibility of using observations of the demonstration center program in individual schools of the area will serve as the evaluative instrument for this activity.   Positive and negative comments will be given equal consideration.

Title: WORKSHOP FOR MOTIVATION OF
          TEACHERS AND PUPILS IN UTILIZATION
                   OF MEDIA CENTERS

                  December 1, 1969

General Objectives:
   Media Specialists will be given the opportunity to explore new ideas and techniques in order to motivate
   teachers and pupils to utilize the media center for
   more effective educational programs.

Specific Objectives:
   Media Specialists will be able to adapt new techniques
   for group interaction.

   Media Specialists will be able to improve individualization of services to both students and teachers.

   Media Specialists will be able to evaluate their present program and techniques to ascertain how ideas
   presented can strengthen the media program in their
   particular school.

Description:
   Media Specialists will meet where facilities will afford space for the group to have a luncheon.   A university consultant will lead the discussions followed
   by small group interaction and reactions.   A summary
   will be presented.

Evaluation:
Pre- and post-evaluation forms will be distributed, filled out, tabulated, and recorded on items pertinent to the workshop theme and program.

Observation of:

increased utilization of Media Centers for more effective educational programs.

Title: WORKSHOP FOR COORDINATION OF SCHOOL MEDIA CENTER WITH THE TOTAL PROGRAM

October 20, 1969

General Objectives:
Media Specialists will gain information, knowledge, and skills in order to coordinate more effectively the school media with the total educational program.

Specific Objectives:
Media Specialists will become aware of their role as a member of the instructional team.

Media Specialists will explore ways to provide pertinent services to the classroom teachers.

Description:
Media Specialists will meet at the Media Center in Bay County, Panama City. Group discussions will be led by noted consultants in educational media. Following large group meetings, specialists will divide into small groups to study and react to the consultant's presentation. A panel discussion will be presented by a representative from each group. The consultant will clarify and summarize the total presentation and discussion.

Evaluation:
Pre- and post-evaluation forms will be distributed, filled out, tabulated, and recorded on items pertinent to the workshop theme and program.

Observations will be made by supervisory and administrative personnel to determine the effectiveness of the coordination of the School Media Center with the total school program.

Title: EDUCATIONAL MEDIA WORKSHOP ON
INNOVATIVE IDEAS IN MATERIALS AND EQUIPMENT

August 25-26, 1969

General Objectives:
Media Specialists will become acquainted with the innovations in materials and equipment available.

Specific Objectives:
Participants will be able to:

preview and evaluate the newest equipment such as--
VTR, Diazo, Slidemaker, Microfilm Reader, Retrieval
Systems;

investigate the inter-relationships that exist between
new approaches of instruction used in the various
schools and the media center such as--individualized
instruction and prescribed instruction.

Description:
All Media Specialists in the PAEC Area will be afforded the opportunity to attend this two day workshop
at the Media Center in Bay County, Panama City,
concerning innovative materials and equipment.   Consultant services will be obtained from various materials and equipment companies.   The workshop will
include demonstrations and individual participation by
the Media Specialists.

Evaluation:
Pre- and post-evaluation forms will be distributed,
filled out, tabulated and recorded on items pertinent
to workshop theme and program.

EXAMPLE (2)

Cooperative in-service training programs have been
undertaken by media personnel who represent a number of
independent school districts. The St. Louis Suburban Media
Directors' Association lists members from 29 separate
school districts. Members of the association meet monthly
to discuss problems of mutual interest and to develop competencies through planned in-service training. The planning
rationale and outline of meetings for one full school year
follow:

Rationale

The St. Louis Suburban Media Directors' Association
has in the past served largely a liaison function between individual school districts and the AV Center. This has been
valuable to both districts and the Department and should be
retained. However, the organization can and should serve
a larger function, that being one of expertise and leadership
in media programs for schools. School administrators, curriculum consultants and teachers are looking for guidance
and leadership in developing sound, efficient and economic
media programs regardless of the budget capability and
space availability of that district. Therefore, a thrust
should be made this school year to bring all Media Directors
up-to-date on current programs, issues, research and directions in instructional media through in-depth presentations
by personnel in our field in this area.

Topical Outline of Monthly Meetings

September   The Role of the Media Director in a Public
             School System

             A brief introduction of the "textbook" definition
             of Media Director as well as a realistic descrip-
             tion of the job as reported by county districts
             followed by the views of a panel of discussants--

instructor, principal, curriculum director, and
superintendent. The program is designed to be
informal providing opportunities for questions
and exchange of ideas.

October   In-Service and Communications Programs

Guidelines for planning and implementing effective media in-service programs--building and/or
district level for teachers, supportive staff, and
students. Includes newsletter editing and production ideas.

November   Local Production of Instructional Materials

Design and organization of production facilities
necessary for a district or building media program. Existing programs will demonstrate how
a few districts handle this opportunity. Includes
discussion of copyright status and new developments.

December   Visual Literacy and It's Implications

What is "Visual Literacy"? What is the Visual
Literacy Movement? When is a person considered visually literate? What makes visual
literacy a new and useful idea? These and
other questions will be posed to an expert with
opportunities for questions and exchange of ideas.

January   Sequential Graphics

The basic theory and purpose behind the kind of
work sequential graphics can accomplish as a
time saving device providing background material
for the study of any discipline using a series of
topics which are presented in visual-comic book
format.

February   Hardware Maintenance and Repair

An introductory presentation will outline the
topic in general. One or two district maintenance programs will be described and analyzed.
The viewpoint of commercial repair firms and
equipment dealers will be presented and the

feasibility of selective co-op repair service will be explored.

March   Computer Education

April   Television and Its Implications

Video Tape production, cataloging, maintenance, and distribution ... cassette video--state of the art ... Cable TV development and status. Possible representatives available from local television stations making contributions to the topic.

May   Luncheon Meeting (Review of the year)

Single-Session Workshops
To Develop Specific Competencies

The effective single-session workshop for media personnel requires all of the planning steps detailed in Part I, In-Service Training for Teachers. A review of that section would be helpful for anyone charged with the responsibility for workshop or conference development for media personnel.

Implementing the effective single-session workshop is perhaps more difficult than planning multi-session meetings because of time limitations. Among the pitfalls to be avoided in planning the "one-shot" training session are the following:

1. The goals of many one session workshops are too broad. Concentration on too many goals within a short time span results in meeting none of the goals.

   Major goals for in-service training fall into three categories: a) the transmission of information, b) the upgrading or introduction of specific competencies, c) the alteration of existing attitudes or development of new attitudes. Only one of these goals should be considered for the single workshop.

2. The content is too inclusive. The attempt to cover too much ground in a single workshop is related to the development of goals which are too broad. The result is often "touching on a little bit of everything and not much of anything."

3. Workshop participants are not prepared for the information to be received.

   A receptive mind is one that has gained some background knowledge of new material to be presented. Only with such background knowledge can one compare, contrast, select and integrate new knowledge. Workshop planning should include the development of pre-conference materials and reading lists.

178

The workshop example which follows, "Bringing Children and Folktales Together through Media," was held for elementary media specialists at Lindenwood College, St. Charles County, Missouri. It demonstrates a successful attempt to bring related knowledge and competencies together into a unified whole.

EXAMPLE (3)

Bringing Children and Folktales Together Through Media

Sponsor: Lindenwood College, St. Charles County, Mo.

Sessions/Place: One-half day (3-1/2 hours), Library Tower Room.

Basic Theme: Children can be led toward an appreciation of literature through active participation in the development and study of folktales.

Training   1) To examine the origin and content of
Objectives: well-known folktales.
                    2) To discover the basic motifs of the folktale.
                    3) To examine the basic criteria for developing a folktale: plot, theme action, setting, characterization, language patterns.
                    4) To produce an original folktale on U film to be demonstrated to the group and retained for use with children.
                    5) To evaluate original folktales produced in light of the basic criteria examined.

Pre-conference Reading:

Huck, Charlotte S. Children's Literature in the Elementary School. 2nd edition. Holt, Rinehart & Winston, 1968. Chapter four.

Arbuthnot, May Hill. Children and Books. Third edition. Scott Foresman, 1964. Chapter ten.

Arbuthnot, May Hill. Time for Fairy Tales, Old and
New. Scott Foresman, 1954.

Outline of Content

I.   Origin of Folktales
      A.   Narrative forms handed down orally from one gene-
           ration to another
      B.   Placed in written form by well-known collectors of
           tales
           1.   Grimm Brothers - Germany
           2.   Charles Perrault - France
           3.   Original tales of Hans Christian Andersen -
                Denmark

II.   Basic Motifs of the Folktale
      A.   Enchanted objects and people
      B.   Legendary heroes or events
      C.   The wise vs the foolish
      D.   The granting of wishes
      E.   Personification of good vs evil

III. Criteria for Developing a Folktale
      A.   Uncomplicated plot
      B.   Rapid action
      C.   Simple setting established early in the tale
      D.   Characters--all good or all evil
      E.   Theme--usually moralistic
      F.   Language patterns--unique to the country of origin

IV.   Group Work--Producing an Original Folktale
      A.   Group writing of the tale
      B.   Determination of simple illustrations (one figure)
      C.   Recording of the tale
      D.   Illustrations placed on U film
      E.   Presentations of original tales

V.   Evaluation
      A.   Application of criteria as applied to original tales.
      B.   Comparison of criteria for judging folktales with
           criteria for judging children's fiction.
      C.   Adapting knowledge and techniques acquired for use
           with children.

Activities

1.   Presentation to general group on origin, content and

motifs of folktales.
Use of sound filmstrip--<u>Fairy Tales</u>.   Pied Piper Productions.

2. Large group divided into small groups of four or five.
    a. Small group discussions on criteria for developing
        folktales.
    b. Reports to whole group from small groups.

3. Small groups write, illustrate and record original folk-
    tales.
    Presentation and critique by whole group.

4. Evaluation-discussion with whole group of criteria for
    judging folktales vs criteria for judging children's fiction.
    Suggestions from group members for adapting knowledge
    and techniques acquired for use with children.

Equipment Needed

1. six blank cassette tapes and recorders
2. 18 feet U film--colored pencils
3. one filmstrip projector
4. one record player

Commercial Materials Used

1. Sound filmstrip--<u>Fairy Tales</u>.   Pied Piper Productions.
2. U film--(write-on filmstrip material).   Miller Brody
    Productions.

Local Materials Produced

1. Invitations to the workshop--duplicated sheet sent to all
    media personnel giving the title of the workshop, basic
    theme, objectives, time, date, place, and suggested pre-
    conference reading.
2. Workshop outline for participants.
3. Stories and filmstrips produced during the workshop
    which were taken back to individual schools by partici-
    pants.

        The sample story which follows was developed, writ-
ten, narrated and illustrated in a one hour period during the
workshop.

The Mushroom Crisis

by Martin J. Hente; Linda Coleman;
Sharon Bogard; Jackie Dillon

Frame #	Narration
1--Opening picture	Once upon a time there was a small kingdom of mushrooms. This tiny village minded its own business and was never disturbed by outsiders, except when the dreaded seven year's blight happened. Now, it only came once every seven years but had the power to completely destroy their village.
2--King Og throne	The king of the village was named Og. As you can see, Og was a kind, gentle man. All the mushroom people in the village depended greatly on Og for his wisdom and advice in times of peace and times of trouble, such as the occurrence of the Blight!
3--Tig walking through forest	In the village there also lived a young orphan mushroom named Tig. Tig served King Og in any way he could for he felt Og was a great and wonderful man. On this particular day, Tig was walking through the forest. Og had always told him that walking in the fresh air was good for his health. Tig was enjoying
4--Blight at distance	his walk, until!! he looked up at the sky. "Oh no! It's the blight! Something must be done right away! I must tell the king!"
5--Tig running to castle	Tig was sorry he had walked so far from the village. He needed to warn the king and it had to be soon! Tig ran and ran until he tought he could run no more. He finally reached the castle. The warning signal in King Og's village for extreme danger was the firing of a cannon. Tig knew that the king was

6--Tig firing
the cannon

usually the only one allowed to fire the cannon. But ... he realized the need to warn the village right now! So he loaded the cannon and Boom!

"Now everyone will know. I must find the king now!"

7--Tig search-
ing for king

Tig climbed each and every long staircase in the entire castle looking for the king. He was getting very worried. Where could he be? Why didn't he come when the cannon was fired? Could he be in danger?

8--Everyone
looking out
window reaching
in castle

By this time, everyone in the village had gathered at the castle. They were ready to work together to defend their home. All the mushrooms crowded around a large window to look at the frightening approach of the horrible blight.

9--King sleep-
ing; blight
over him

Meanwhile the king had also taken a walk that day. Perhaps he, too, had walked too far away from the castle; for he had become very tired and had laid down to rest for a few minutes. However, he fell into a deep sleep and even the cannon had not awoke him. No one knew where he was except the Blight!

10--Tig comes
back; he can't
find him

Tig completed his search of the entire castle, and a quite worried and disappointed little mushroom returned to tell the others that their king was nowhere to be found.

"I can't find him," he said sadly, "Oh what will we do?"

11--Varg sees
king out
window

"Wait, wait," said Varg, another of the mushroom citizens, "I think I see him. Look--out there. The blight is so close to him. Why doesn't he move? He's in danger!"

The king was sleeping so peacefully

12--Blight
engulfing king

that he did not notice the blight getting closer and closer. All at once...! The blight completely surrounded King Og and picked him up. King Og was trapped in the middle of this huge blob.

13--Tig &
soldiers get
together to
plot

Tig began to realize he must take action quickly. Their lives and the king's were in danger. Tig called together all the mushroom soldiers of the village and they began to plan a way to destroy the blight, without hurting the king.

14--Rubber
darts

"What about our rubber darts? What do you think, would they work, Varg?" asked Tig. King Og had made rubber darts many years for the mushrooms to use for games. They were completely harmless for the mushroom people, BUT, they had a magic power that protected them against evil things. They had never used them against the blight before, but without the king to advise them, Tig made the decision to go ahead and use the darts.

15--Mushrooms
firing darts

16--Blight gets
hit

The soldiers got their darts as the blight came closer. Boing! Boing! The darts came from all directions out of the castle windows. The blight didn't have a chance against these mushrooms.

17--Blight
opening up

All at once, the huge blob opened up and the king fell to the ground.

18--King
unconscious

King Og was stunned as he hit the ground, but quite unharmed, thanks to the brave mushrooms.

19--Blight
going away
20--People
rushing out
21--King
awakes

As the blight began to disappear, all the little mushrooms rushed out to carry the king back to his place in the castle.

As the king woke up, he was quite confused. "What has happened?" he asked. All at once the group of mushrooms began telling him the events of the day. After they had told him he asked, "And who is responsible for taking charge and being so brave?"

22--Picture
of Tig

"Tig is the hero," said Varg, "he knew what to do."

23--Tig is
adopted

"Tig, my boy," said the king, "it's about time you had a real home. As of this moment I adopt you as my son."

24--Tig
with smile

Nothing could have made Tig happier. The mushroom he admired most in all the kingdom was now his father.

EXAMPLE (4)

In-Service Training of Media Specialists of the School District
of Volusia County, Florida

Leatha Garrison, Director, Educational Materials & Related
Services

Title: IMPROVING MEDIA PROGRAMS

Participants:
    Media Specialists and Teacher Committee Chairmen--
    South Volusia Area.   2-hour workshop.

Goal:
    Improvement of the school media program with em-
    phasis on meeting the individual needs of teachers and
    students.

Specific Objective(s):
    To provide school media specialist information with
    regard to the planning and assessment of school media
    programs.

    To emphasize the media programs responsibility of
    meeting the individual needs of both students and teach-
    ers through cooperative planning.

    To involve participants in the process of planning (of-
    fering in-put) for the improvement of school media
    programs.

Procedures--including activities and materials:
    Presentation of a pictorial (sequential) sample planning
    units (slide presentation) with emphasis on meeting the
    needs of the individual.

    Report on planning and assessment of school media
    programs.   (Materials acquired and prepared at media
    planning and assessment institute, F. S. U.).

186

Discussion by participants on the status of school media programs and specific plans for improvement (possibly group discussion).

Evaluation method:
   Standard form.

EXAMPLE (5)

Title: EDUCATIONAL MATERIALS DEPT.
          PRE-SCHOOL WORKSHOP ON IMC POLICY

Participants:
    15 Secondary Media Specialists.
    One and one-half day workshop.

Goal:
    To develop basic rationale and procedures for the dis-
    semination of information relating to the services
    available at the school level for teachers, student
    body and student assistants.

Specific objective(s):
    I.   Develop written plans for services for teachers.
    II.   Develop written plans for providing services for
          individual students.
    III. Develop handbook for student assistants including
          lesson plans for instruction.

Procedures--including activities and materials:

Select participants	Work sessions of component
Pre-meeting instructions by	preparation
mail--bring input material	Full group review of com-
Task orientation	ponents
Presentation of existing school	Rewrite components
procedures and plans	Full group review of rewrite
Presentation of county ma-	Finalize
terials	

Evaluation method:
    Product.
    Standard evaluation form for inservice component.

188

EXAMPLE (6)

Title: DEVELOPING A CATALOG
                 OF MEDIA COMPETENCIES

Participants:
     All Media Specialists.   2-hour workshop.

Goal:
     Improvement of Media Program
     Program planning
     Inservice calendar for year
     Catalog of competencies
     Media instructional program
     Professional activities
     Assessment

Specific objective(s):
     Say "HELLO"
     Adopt Inservice calendar
     Organize volunteer committee for writing Catalog of
        Competencies
     Panel presentation of instructional materials and tech-
        niques (Jr. High level)
     New methods of assessment
     Professional presentation of current concern

Procedures--including activities and materials:
     Distribution of materials for consideration
     Discussion and decision
     Panel presentation

Evaluation method:
     Standard form

Committee for Catalog of Competencies:
     8 Elementary
     6 Junior High
     6 Senior High

Co-Sponsored Multi-Session Meetings

For school districts fortunate enough to be within commuting distance of a college or university, opportunities exist for cooperative education programs of teachers, para-professionals, media aides and professional media personnel.

Programs utilizing the expertise of university personnel can be developed to meet specific training needs within a local school district. In proposing such a cooperative training program, personnel of the school district should make available to university staff members, who will be involved in the development of the program, the following information:

1. Sponsoring institution
2. Location of the workshop or training meetings
3. Title of the program
4. Outline of the program desired
5. Those responsible for initiating the request and developing the outline
6. Number of training meetings desired
7. Request for specific university staff members (if applicable)
8. Source of financing
9. Procedures to be followed
10. Participants (qualifications if applicable)
11. Arrangement for use of necessary university facilities or equipment
12. Determination of credit (if applicable)
13. Procedures for evaluation

The program which follows on The Supporting Role of the School Media Program in Curriculum and Organizational Change in the Greensboro Schools is presented as a model for developing multi-session training meetings for media personnel in cooperation with the local university. The program was developed by the staff of the Greensboro, North Carolina Public Schools, Leonard L. Johnson, Director of Libraries, in cooperation with staff members of the University of North Carolina-Greensboro.

190

EXAMPLE (7)

In-Service Education Workshop for Greensboro
School Media Specialists
October 18-December 13, 1971

The workshop is designed to help practicing school
librarians/media specialists in the Greensboro public schools
gain a better understanding of the role of the school media
center in supporting curriculum and organizational change in
the Greensboro schools. Participation in the workshop is
voluntary. On satisfactory completion of the workshop each
participant will receive two units of credit toward State certificate renewal. The workshop sessions, except for two
field trips, will be held in the Center for Instructional Media,
McNutt Building, University of North Carolina at Greensboro.
Miss Cora Paul Bomar, UNC-G Assistant Professor in Library Education, will serve as the director of the workshop.

General format for the workshop will consist of 1)
general session presentations, 2) small group discussions,
3) work by individuals/small groups in previewing, examining,
and selecting media for acquisitions to be added to particular
school media collections, 4) review and development of audio-
visual equipment operation skills. One field trip will be attendance at the biennial conference of the North Carolina Library Association Conference in Winston-Salem and one field
trip will be made to Salem, Virginia to visit and observe the
demonstration school media program in the East Salem Elementary School.

Each participant will be expected to determine an
area in the media collection in his school that needs strength-
ening and to identify, examine, preview and select media to
be ordered and added to that collection. In addition participants will work in small groups on problems and projects of
mutual concern.

Consultants and speakers from the Greensboro administrative staff, UNC-G faculty in the School of Education,
and from the Division of Educational Media of the State Department of Public Instruction will participate in workshop
general sessions. Mr. Leonard L. Johnson will work closely with Miss Bomar in planning and conducting the workshop.
The resources of the Center for Instructional Media will be
used extensively by workshop and staff participants.

CALENDAR

October 18	Overview and Planning

October 25   Curriculum Trends in Greensboro Public
Schools
Jerry Byrum, Science Consultant, Greens-
boro Public Schools
Mrs. Frances Crimm, Art Consultant,
Greensboro Public Schools
Mrs. May Parrish, Social Studies Consul-
tant, Greensboro Public Schools

November 1   Role of All Media in Instruction
Dr. Michael Molenda, School of Education,
UNC-G
Audiovisual Equipment Lab
Arnold R. Medlin, Director of Audiovisual
Education, Greensboro Public Schools

November 4   NCLA Conference, Winston-Salem
10 a.m. -Dr. Daniel Fader, Associate Professor of English, University of Michigan
and author of Hooked on Books

November 15   Building Media Collections
Mrs. Frances K. Johnson, Associate Professor, School of Education, UNC-G

November 17   All day field trip to Salem, Virginia--visit
and observe school media services program
in the East Salem Elementary School, a
Virginia demonstration school

November 22   Program of Media Services

November 29   Operation of the Media Center
Mrs. Judith Garitano, Chief Consultant, Division of Educational Media, N.C. Department of Public Instruction

December 6   Services to Teachers

December 13   Humanizing the Media Program and Services
Evaluation of Individual and Group Projects

Outline of Content

I.   Overview and planning
     School organization change
       Individualization
       Teaming
       Open-concept
       Student directed learning
     Implication of school organization change on the
     media center

II. Curriculum trends in Greensboro Public Schools
     Identification of needs and specific projects for
     individual participants

III. Role of all media in instruction
     Characteristics of media
     Multi-media approach
     Techniques of media examination

IV. Building media collections
     Principles
     Selection aids

V.   Observation of Media Program (field trip)

VI. Program of Media Services
     Learning centers
     Independent study station
     Research and study skills
     Instruction in use .of media center
     Guidance in listening and viewing

VII. Operation of the Media Center
     Organization
     Accessibility
     Scheduling
     Circulation
     Media staff

VIII. Services to Teachers
     Techniques of working
     Teaming
     In-service

IX. Humanizing the Media Program and Services

X.   Evaluation of Individual and Group Projects

Basic reason(s) for developing this particular program:

To become more familiar with the concepts, current
trends and approaches to curriculum and organizational
change

To become aware and develop an appreciation of the role
of all media in instruction

To become more knowledgeable in the selection and use
of all media

To better understand their role in curriculum change and
new organizational patterns

To look at and improve their inter-personal relationship
with pupils and teachers.

Name(s) of proposed consultant(s) and qualifications:

Dr. Michael Molenda, School of Education, UNC-G
Mrs. Frances K. Johnson, Associate Professor, School
of Education, UNC-G
Mrs. Judith Garitano, Chief consultant, Division of Edu-
cational Media, N. C. Department of Public Instruction
Mrs. May Parrish, Social Studies Consultant, Greens-
boro Public Schools
Mrs. Frances Crimm, Art Consultant, Greensboro Pub-
lic Schools
Jerry Byrum, Science Consultant, Greensboro Public
Schools

Participant's Evaluation

I.   To what extent did you gain new insights or informa-
        tion in the following areas?

        1. Knowledge of new school organization and implica-
            tions for the media center.
        2. Presentation of Greensboro supervisors on curri-
            culum trends in the Greensboro School System.
        3. Role of all media in instruction, including the
            characteristics of various types of media.
        4. Dr. Daniel Fader's presentation, "The Naked
            Children. "

     5.   Field trip to Salem, Virginia.
     6.   Selection and evaluation of media.
     7.   Program of media services.
     8.   Mrs. Garitano's presentation.
     9.   Ways of working with teachers.
    10.   Time spent in previewing, evaluating and selecting media.

II.   What do you consider strengths of the workshop?

III.   What do you consider weaknesses of the workshop?

IV.   What would you have liked for the workshop to include that wasn't covered?

V.   Did you learn anything new in the workshop?

VI.   Were any ideas promoted in the workshop that are in conflict with yours?
If the answer is yes, would you identify one?

VII.   Has the workshop caused you to question any practice in your library?

VIII. As a result of the workshop have you made or do you anticipate making any change in media services in your school?

IX.   Mr. Johnson and Mrs. Townsend would like you to answer the following two questions.

     1.   How do you suggest that we utilize our regular staff meetings for the remainder of the school year?

     2.   What topics would you like to have incorporated in the between semester inservice program for media specialists?

DO NOT SIGN YOUR NAME

Series Workshops Planned and
Produced by Local School Districts

In addition to regularly scheduled monthly in-service
meetings of media personnel within a school district, it is
often desirable to initiate special workshop programs to develop specific competencies in the acquisition, utilization
and evaluation of the newer media. Such a series of workshops conducted by the Library and Media Specialists of the
Unified School District No. 1 of Racine County, Wisconsin
for district librarians is described in the article "Media In-
Service Education for School Librarians." It is reprinted
here in its entirety from the Wisconsin Library Bulletin,
May-June 1971, with the permission of its author, William
D. Grindeland.

EXAMPLE (8)

Media Inservice Education for School Librarians

William D. Grindeland
Carl Helmle
John Hempstead

"Mr. Grindeland is Director, Instructional Materials Center;
Carl Helmle, Media Specialist; and John Hempstead, Library
Specialist, in the Unified School District No. 1 of Racine."

To the harried school librarian, it might seem that
she is being bombarded with endless demands for a variety
of new media, methods and equipment. Teachers are no
longer complacently asking for assistance, but are demanding
that librarians and media specialists provide for the independent study and curriculum needs of their students NOW!

The Unified School District No. 1 of Racine County,
formed in 1961, has a student enrollment of approximately

32, 000 and is increasing by more than 1000 students each
year.   The District now has three senior high school libraries, six junior high libraries and 30 elementary libraries.
A major problem is providing adequate instructional materials services, especially since the advent of the newer media
of communication and the rapidly increasing volume of ideas
and activities that students must experience if the best
learning is to occur.

    We have placed as much library staff as possible in
the individual school buildings, rather than at the district
level; and we have also implemented a retraining program
for school librarians with the emphasis on all types of media,
materials and services.

    The situation is complicated by the fact that the great
majority of school librarians have had only a minimum amount
of training in the media or audiovisual area.   Only recently
have a few university library science departments moved in
the direction of a joint library and media degree program.

    The first of a series of planned workshops was con-
ducted this past spring at the District instructional materials
center for all school librarians.   It was decided that rather
than using the shotgun approach of trying to cover all types
and varieties of media in one workshop, it would be better
to give one in-depth experience on one type of material and
have other topics covered in the same manner in subsequent
workshops.

    At the first workshop meeting, librarians were given
two narrated slide production projects as a requirement for
the workshop.   The first project was to produce a series of
slides of their own individual library.   This series could be
used as an orientation to the library for students and also
for informative programs such as open house, P. T. A. and
other visiting groups.   Some of the topics or pictures that
were taken for the individual library project included the
main desk, circulation area, reserve desk, date card system, Readers' Guide, card catalog, study carrels, conference
rooms and various types of audiovisual equipment.   The District library specialist provided a list of suggested slide
shots that could be adapted to fit each individual library.

    The second assignment was a cooperative project by
groups of three or four on some area of the Library Skills
Program.   Topics were suggested from a list drawn up by

the entire library group, and librarians were given the opportunity to select from these.   Some of the topics selected
were publishing unit, card catalog, care of books, use and
care of audiovisual equipment and materials, the Readers'
Guide, and reference materials.   After a topic was chosen,
the group selected a project team leader to coordinate the
work.

Each group project was arranged first in discussion
and planning sessions, and then put into storyboard form before the actual shooting took place.   The three instructors
were the library specialist, the media specialist and the
IMC director at the District level.   They worked with the
groups to prepare scripts and tapes that would be used with
the slide series.   The outlines for the group projects were
typed and presented to the entire group of librarians for suggestions.   After receiving suggestions, groups again assembled and made final revisions and plans for their projects.

Each participant received a carousel projector, several slide trays, a cassette tape recorder and tapes for the
library--on the premise that, if the training was to be most
effective, every librarian who received it would need proper
equipment available at all times.

The District media specialist gave small-group training in equipment utilization.   The training included the operation of the projector and the remote control system, and minor maintenance of the projector such as changing the bulbs
and solving minor problems.   Having the participants become
familiar with their equipment was one of the prime objectives of the training sessions.

The Ektographic copy camera was introduced as an
easy and inexpensive menas of producing slides in the library.
Following the production of the slides for the two projects,
the total group was assembled for the last session of the
workshop to view the various presentations.

The real test of the value of the workshop will come
with the utilization of the projects and the skills that were
learned during the workshop.   It is anticipated that these
materials will make library skills classes more interesting
for students, and will aid in the retention of the ideas presented.   One of the most stimulating benefits of the workshop
came from the opportunity librarians had to meet with their

peers and exchange ideas regarding materials and the Library Skills Program.

As an outgrowth of the workshop, a library media preview committee was established which previews and selects 16mm films and other media materials for general use by the total library system. Through the preview committee, librarians are being exposed to a wide variety of materials and consequently should be able to make better selections and use of existing funds.

With the success of this workshop, another workshop will be arranged this coming year for in-depth training on transparencies and laminated materials. With such a great spirit of cooperation and sharing of ideas, an effort such as this will benefit all the students and teachers of the Unified School District No. 1 of Racine.

EXAMPLE (9)

A Five Year Master Plan for In-Service Education

Sponsor: The School Board of Pinellas County, Florida, Clearwater, Florida. Elizabeth M. Stephens, Dir. Library Services.

Introduction: The School Board of Pinellas County (Florida) has devised a 5-year master plan for in-service teacher education. Through this program teachers may renew their certificates by earning credit in the program. Credit points earned are from participation in basic courses, updating or exploratory courses.

                The five courses which follow are those of particular interest to librarians and audio-visual specialists. Objectives, descriptions and evaluations are given for each.

Component: Production and Utilization of Audio-Visual Materials

General Objective:
  Increase the competencies of the professional staff in their respective disciplines.

Specific Objective:
  Each participant will produce non-print materials for use in specific instructional programs.

Description:
  Participants will be instructed in the use of reel-to-reel tape recorders and cassette tape recorders in order to produce teacher made tapes for instruction.

  Participants will be instructed in the transparency and 35mm slide production for classroom instruction.

  Participants will be taught the operation, the application, and the limitations of the video tape recorder.

  Participants will spend eight three-hour sessions receiving instruction at the Pinellas County Materials Center.   They will also be required to spend 18 hours in laboratory work.   This instruction will extend over an eight-week period.

Evaluation:
  1. Each participant will produce:
      a. An audio tape and a series of slides combined into a sound slide presentation, for use with his students.
      b. A series of diazo transparencies demonstrating various techniques of production and utilization, for use with his students.
      c. A short video tape demonstrating an appreciation and understanding of television techniques, for use with his students.
      This component will be Updating for librarians and audio-visual specialists and people who have had prior professional audio-visual training in college.   It will be Basic for all others.

  2. The component itself will be evaluated by each participant and by the instructor on an objective check list.

Group Activity Hours   42

Component: Care, Use, and Repair of Audio-Visual Equipment

General Objective:
Increase the competencies of the professional staff in
their respective disciplines.

Specific Objective:
Participants will learn the use, care, and minor repair of equipment used in the classroom.

Description:
The workshop will be conducted by a consultant familiar with all audio-visual equipment. Participants will
be shown how to use correctly such audio-visual equipment as the controlled reader, overhead projector,
filmstrip projector, 16mm projector and tape recorder. The participants will be trained in minor repair,
bulb replacement, and timer regulation.

This component is particularly suited for giving in a
school for the faculty of that school. It will be
scheduled at the request of the principal.

Evaluation:
1. Each participant will make minor repairs on 90%
of equipment demonstrated.
2. An objective check-out test will be taken by each
participant. All participants should answer 90%
of the items correctly.
3. Each participant will demonstrate the operation of
each machine.
4. The component itself will be evaluated by each
participant and by the instructor on an objective
check list.

Group Activity Hours   6

Component: Use of Video in Foreign Language Instruction

General Objective:
Increase the competencies of the professional staff in
their respective disciplines.

Specific Objective:
Each participant will produce a fifteen-minute video

tape program of his own design.

Description:
This will be a workshop conducted by a County TV specialist.

The workshop will consist of four class sessions of three hours each plus three lab sessions of three hours each.

The workshop will train Foreign Language teachers in developing materials for closed circuit TV.

The instructor will demonstrate and explain camera techniques and the use of the video tape recorder.

Each participant will write a script and produce an original fifteen-minute video tape program which he could use in Foreign Language instruction in his own classroom.

Evaluation:
1. Each participant will produce an original fifteen-minute video tape program which must be acceptable to the instructor when judged for audial and visual qualities, plus relevancy of material.
2. The component itself will be evaluated by each participant and by the instructor on an objective check list.

Group Activity Hours   21

Component: Use of Video Tape in Classroom Instruction

General Objective:
Introduce the professional staff to innovative techniques of teaching and develop their skills in utilizing them.

Specific Objectives:
Participants will learn the techniques of video taping necessary for implementing innovative approaches to the teacher situation.

Participants will learn how to operate television equipment.

Description:

The workshop, conducted by a County television specialist, will consist of five class sessions of lecture and demonstration of three hours each. During these sessions, participants will learn techniques and procedures dealing with writing of script, production and direction, lighting and microphone placement. Using County-owned equipment, participants will learn to operate video tape recorders, cameras, receiver-monitor and sound equipment.

Participants will be required to spend an additional nine hours of laboratory work during which participants will write scripts, produce, direct, and videotape short television lessons designed to implement a classroom learning situation.

Sections of this component will be offered upon request, to any grade level or subject group. Text: Goodwin--Closed-Circuit Television Production Techniques--Howard W. Sams & Company, Inc.

Evaluation:

1. Given a list of utilization techniques, each participant will identify those appropriate for use in short classes.
2. Each participant will state, in order, the steps for producing a video tape.
3. Given items of equipment, each participant will demonstrate proficiency in operating television equipment.
4. The component itself will be evaluated by each participant and by the instructor on an objective check list.

Group Activity Hours   24

Component: The Use of Audio-Visual Aids in Social Work

General Objectives:

Assist the professional staff in developing curricula which are relevant to the needs of students.

Broaden and deepen the knowledge of individuals in their respective areas of responsibility.

Specific Objectives:
    Participants will become familiar with the various
    types of audio-visual aids such as filmstrips, slides,
    movies, and puppets.

    Participants will learn what specific aids are current-
    ly available within the Pinellas County School system
    which are applicable to social work.

    Participants will learn what additional relevant audio-
    visual aids are available for purchase.

Description:
    There will be two two-hour meetings with staff mem-
    bers within the school system serving as consultants
    during lecture, demonstration, and discussion periods.

    Participants will do directed individual study in con-
    sultation with media specialists and others, for an
    additional two hours.

Evaluation:
    1. Participants will describe at least three audio-
        visual aids.
    2. Participants will develop a bibliography of avail-
        able aids around a topic or topics of their own
        choosing.
    3. Participants will develop a list of audio-visual
        aids desirable for future purchase.
    4. The component itself will be evaluated by each
        participant and by the instructor on an objective
        check list.

Group Activity Hours   6

In-Service Training Through ETN
(Educational Telephone Network)

Just as in-service training programs are vital in helping media personnel keep abreast of new innovations in the
communications media, these same innovations are playing a
vital role in many in-service programs. The following
speech delivered at the Detroit ALA Conference in July,
1970 by Bernard Franckowiak, defines clearly the role
played by the Educational Telephone Network of the University of Wisconsin in in-service training of media personnel.

EXAMPLE (10)

ETN In-Service in Wisconsin
by
Bernard Franckowiak
School Library Supervisor
Department of Public Instruction
Madison, Wisconsin

(Reprinted with permission of the author)

Upon coming to the Department of Public Instruction
in February, 1968, I realized the great change taking place
in developing school libraries into Instructional Materials
Centers. It was also apparent that many librarians and A-V
personnel did not have training in operating a modern media
center. There are 1, 070 school librarians and 225 A-V
coordinators and directors working in Wisconsin schools.
Training programs available include 13 undergraduate and
three graduate library programs and three graduate audio-
visual programs. The problem was, how to reach the
people in the state, up-date their training, and interest
them in continuing their education.

In discussing the problem with Muriel Fuller at the

205

University of Wisconsin Extension, she suggested that I consider the Educational Telephone Network of the University
Extension. For over 50 years the Extension has worked at
the "Wisconsin Idea, " that is, making the "boundaries of the
University of Wisconsin Campus the boundaries of the state. "
After discussion of the system, it was decided that an ex-
perimental series of programs would be designed. Planning
for the series began early in the spring of 1968 with an attempt to determine topics and meeting locations.

A survey was sent to all school librarians asking for
subjects of interest and ETN outlets preferred. An interest
poll was also taken at the 5th Annual School Library Institute
at the U of W, Madison, in June, 1968. This information
was compiled and it was clear that interest revolved around
the IMC concept and the handling of A-V materials.

The ETN network is a huge party line which is used
to transmit educational material throughout the State. It
was originally designed to meet the needs of doctors for in-
service training which could be accomplished without going
away for extended periods of time. Later, nurses, veteri-
narians, pharmacists, etc., used the system. Over 120
stations are located at courthouses, U W campus centers
and hospitals in over 100 Wisconsin communities.

ETN is a two-way communication system. Each station has a telephone and a loudspeaker. The system enables
a person at any ETN station to hear anything transmitted on
the system as well as participate in discussion with other
points in the network. The loudspeaker is used for listening
purposes. It has an OFF-ON switch and volume control.
When a participant wants to contribute to the discussion he
picks up the phone and speaks into it. Picking up the phone
disconnects the loudspeaker from the network, but every location can hear what is said. Programs originated from
WHA radio at UW, Madison, and used commercial telephone
lines.

It was decided to have five one-hour and 15-minute
programs each evening on consecutive Tuesdays from 6:30
until 7:45 on the network. The dates were November 19,
26, December 3, 10 and 17, 1968. Planning meetings were
held to determine topics, program format, speakers, procedures for handling arrangements, etc. It was recommended
that each lecturer tape his presentation and use visuals extensively to illustrate points. Because of availability of

equipment at the location, it was decided that 35mm colored slides would be the visual media. Most programs used hand-outs to present objective, bibliographies, floor plans, people and sources to contact, and additional information.

Twenty-nine (29) outlets were selected for the 1968-69 programs to blanket the state with program sources. Ahead of time, slides and handouts had to be duplicated and sent out to the local convener who acted as the contact person. They were responsible for setting up the equipment, taking roll, handing out materials and handling the telephone. In order to familiarize conveners with locations, equipment and procedure, a training session was held during the same time period one week before the first program.

The overall subject of the series was "Non-Print Materials in School Libraries." The first session, on the "Concept of the Instructional Materials Center" with Dr. Carolyn Whitenack, opened with an enrollment of 435. Carolyn was on leave from Purdue at the time, so she did her presentation "live" from Normal, Alabama, to the 29 stations in Wisconsin. She used 56 slides to visualize the various components of a modern IMC program, stressing the role of the librarian as a curriculum materials specialist. (Problem: Carolyn's projector jammed half way through and she played it blind.) (Produced 1, 680 slides for the program.)

The second program covered "Selecting Non-Print Materials" and featured a librarian and an A-V man team from an excellent Junior High School program in Madison, Wisconsin. They covered selection sources, and reviewing media, and discussed problems in evaluating and selecting non-book material. They produced their own SELECTORAID which listed criteria for selection, selection sources and re-viewing media. Each participant received a copy of the Se-lectoraid.

Program 3 dealt with "Organizing Non-Print Materi-als," covered considerations in cataloging audiovisual ma-terials, sources of bibliographic information, and commer-cial cataloging available. Frankly, though the program was helpful, it did not meet the needs of the audience.

Ken Taylor, Assistant Director of Instructional Ser-vices for the Madison Public Schools, presented the fourth program, on "Administering the Instructional Materials Cen-

ter. " He stressed the importance of relating theory to IMC
program objective. The four basic functions of the IMC of
providing space for: individual study, small group discussion, student production, and large group instruction were
covered. Consideration was given to the role and function
of the IMC staff and job descriptions.

The final program was the then forthcoming "Standards
for Media Programs. " It was a joint presentation by Mr.
Robert Wheeler, Supervisor of Audiovisual Instruction for the
Department of Public Instruction, and myself. A portion of
the program featured slides on "What is Happening in IMC
Development in Wisconsin, " with a slide series. This portion showed trends in media center program developments.

The last 25 minutes were used to have participants
fill out an evaluation instrument consisting of 64 items. Dr.
Harry Zimmerman of U. W. Extension prepared the independent evaluation and used the program as a model for developing evaluation techniques for all ETN programs. The
questions were grouped into clusters. The areas which participants gave the highest ratings were: Program Process,
which consisted of 15 items with a maximum rating of 60.
The format of the program and involvement of individuals in
the program was the main concern here. The participants
gave it a rating of 46. 6, which indicated the format of the
program was generally good. The evaluation of Program Influence involved 17 items. Participants gave the program a
rating of 53. 3, which the evaluation concluded "left little
doubt that the program's content influenced the participants. "
The participants were asked to evaluate the program as a
complete unit on a 9-point scale. The average rating was
6. 1, which indicated it was above average.

The clusters were also evaluated based on Mean and
Standard Deviation. Analysis of the clusters indicated that
areas dealing with Program Process, Program Influence and
Environment showed the strongest response. A closer study
of data gathered on individual items indicated that in future
programming, thought should be given to ways of involving
groups and their moderators in the actual lesson process.
There was indication that too much material was covered in
too short a time. Participants wanted to see more redun-
dancy, more summarizing of material. They wanted to see
the program paced a little slower; also, there was indication
that more visuals and illustrations would have been appreciated. The evaluation concluded that the program was "ob-

viously a good one. " It recommended that the conclusions
be used to improve future programs.

After the series was completed, five sets of slides,
handouts and a tape of each program were assembled into
multimedia kits. These kits were made available on free
loan to anyone interested.

A slightly different group of 35 stations was selected
for the 1969-70 series. It was decided that we would program for two hours on the air. Three consecutive Thursdays
in December and two near the end of January were reserved.
Five programs were planned with the topic, "Developing Effective School Media Programs. " The first session was on
"New Media: Its Role in Instituting Educational Change. " It
featured a tape of a presentation by Dr. Henry Brickell,
which was given at the Institute for State Media Personnel at
Western Michigan University, Kalamazoo, in May, 1969.
The presentation covered considerations in dissemination and
adoption of innovation in schools and was focused on the new
Standards. The text of this presentation has been published
in School Libraries (Summer, 1970). Dr. Brickell was
picked up "live" from New York for the question and answer
session.

The second program, titled "Integration of Materials
Into Instructional Programs, " led off with a team of librarian
and A-V man from an exciting open-concept middle school
program in Madison, Wisconsin. They discussed the changing role and relationship of librarians and A-V specialists
in developing utilization of materials. They covered ways of
involving the librarian and the A-V specialist in curriculum
planning. After a question session, a high school librarian,
an elementary librarian and a system A-V director discussed
techniques of working with teachers, students and the community in developing greater support for strong media programs and integration of materials into the curriculum of the
school. Participants were enthusiastic about the ideas
covered in this session.

The third session used three people to cover "New
Developments in Social Studies and Implications for Media
Use. " A university professor, Dr. Glen Kinzie, who had
been active in developing Wisconsin's Social Studies Curriculum Guide, Knowledge, Processes and Values in the Social
Studies, gave a presentation on "Trends and Developments"
in the field. He discussed the new emphasis on the con-

ceptual approach and on helping the student to develop values
and value systems. A curriculum consultant for an elementary school district covered new Social Studies material and
implications for multi-media use. A district-level social
studies coordinator completed the evening by discussing
"Problems" in using new materials in Social Studies.

The fourth program attempted to introduce "Local
Production" as an important part of the media program. A
District A-V Director led off, developing the rationale for
local production of media. Emphasis was placed on the part
it can play in improving the teacher's communication of ideas.
A high school media consultant who has developed a very interesting program told "Where to Start and How to Get Involvement." He makes extensive use of trained students in
his work. He also works closely with students and teachers
in producing materials to suit their needs. The final portion
of the program consisted of the Director of an ESEA Title
II project on local production of media. She discussed procedures for developing programs and each location viewed one
program which was produced.

The final program of the series took up the subject
of "Educational TV as a Learning Tool." Mr. Bob Suchy,
Director of Instructional Resources for the city of Milwaukee,
led off by developing the rationale for using educational TV.
He was followed by the Director of Instructional Services
for WHA-TV at UW, Nancy McNamara, who discussed "Utilization of Educational TV" and the development of programs
at WHA-TV. The media coordinator from another large
system discussed the program of local production of television programs and the centralized distribution of programs
and films in the district. A Department of Public Instruction guidance consultant gave a presentation on the "Newist"
project which uses a commercial TV station for programming vocational materials to the schools in northeastern Wisconsin. The wrap-up featured Mr. Lee Franks, Executive
Director of the State Educational Communications Division,
discussing the potential of educational TV in long range planning in Wisconsin. The end of the program was used to fill
out a modified evaluation instrument.

For the first time the results were put on a computer
and analyzed. The print-out gives frequency distribution and
percentage for the answer to each question. The evaluation
showed that 86 per cent felt the whole series had fulfilled
participants' expectations as a learning experience "somewhat"

to "very well." The same percentage (86) indicated that the series had provided information and concepts applicable in their job situations. Participants overwhelmingly (95 per cent) stated that the ETN network is an effective tool for communicating the types of subject matter presented. When asked if an ETN series should be offered in 1970-71, 72 per cent said "Yes."

Specific topics and suggestions were:

More on cataloging and processing of non-print materials,
More emphasis on elementary schools,
More "How to" and less theory,
Library instruction,
Working with teachers and public relations,
New developments in other disciplines and implications for media use,
Make subjects smaller in scope,
Evaluate after each program, not at the end of the series,
More specific things geared to smaller schools--(and at the same time, some wanted more ETV, information retrieval and computer application),
Classes at less busy time of the year.

One librarian commented, "Where do we get the money to carry out these programs?" Another said, "Any subject, I need information in all subject areas." The final comment I will quite stated, "For those of us who have not had the opportunity of spending time in a functioning IMC, the two years have given me a better conception of the idea. It has provided suggestions as to what can be done in the school I am now serving."

In-Service Training Sponsored
by State Departments of Education

The library/media services divisions of State Department-
ments of Education have, in many instances, played an important role in the in-service training of library/media personnel. Through the leadership provided at the state level,
needs throughout the state can be ascertained and provision
made for meeting them.

In 1971, a series of workshops was held throughout
the State of Missouri by personnel of the library/media division of the Missouri State Department of Education. Effort was made to reach all librarians and media personnel
throughout the state. The major purpose of the workshops
was to assist library/media personnel in evaluation of and
planning for growth in their respective libraries or instructional materials centers. Each workshop was a full day in
length and provided opportunity not only for instruction in
the evaluative process but for an interchange of ideas among
those attending.

The rationale for the workshop series and a copy of
the evaluative instrument follow. Both were provided by
Carl Sitze, State School Library Supervisor, State of Missouri.

EXAMPLE (11)

Workshop on School Library Evaluation

Rationale:

Through the years many school districts have failed
to provide the quality of library service needed to meet effectively the needs and interests of their students and teachers. This has been especially true in elementary schools,

212

one reason being that libraries are not required for classification and accreditation at this level. This has resulted in
wide disparity in school library services to boys and girls
throughout the state. In some cases, there has also been a
disparity of library service within individual districts, because emphasis on library service is sometimes higher for
one school in the district than another.

We have also found that many of the small and some
medium-sized districts in Missouri have not been able to
employ trained professional personnel to organize and direct
their libraries effectively. This has resulted in many schools
having a library in name only, one that is so poorly organized
as to be ineffective. Many of the medium-sized districts,
while able to organize a program of acceptable quality and
service, have many questions concerning the operation and
various divisions of work that go together to make up the library. While we have not worked directly with many large
districts, we know from conversations with them that they
also have many questions concerning their library programs,
such as planning for district-wide service on the elementary
level, improved methods of service to students and teachers--
especially to the exceptional child, etc.

These facts came to us through our work with librarians and administrators during school visitations, workshops, professional meetings, etc. As a result of such
meetings, it became apparent to us that a common evaluation instrument was needed, which school districts throughout the state could use in evaluating their own programs of
library service.

In considering this need we at the SDE also realized
that we needed to know a great deal more about the school
libraries throughout the state if we were to plan and put into
operation a program of quality and leadership that the schools
deserve. In preparing the evaluation instrument, we felt it
important to research what had been done in the past. In
doing so, we found that data concerning the quality and status
of school library programs in our state were almost non-
existent. There had never been an in-depth evaluation of
our school libraries on a state-wide basis. In fact, unless
the school was a member of the North Central Association
the chances are that its library program had never been
formally evaluated. Many had just evolved through the years.

In planning the evaluation we definitely wanted an

evaluation instrument that would be of value to the school and that would provide us with the information about the school's program which we felt we needed. At the same time we wanted to cover, so far as possible, the total library program that should be in operation.

On the evaluation instrument we attempted to word the questions in such a way as to provide the school with information as to what they should be doing or have going on in their library. In other words, the evaluation was designed not only to gather information but also to instruct and provide the schools with ideas for better service to boys and girls and their teachers. We hoped it would act as a catalyst for the local school in providing services that heretofore had been non-existent. We feel that the evaluation will enable individual schools and school districts to: 1) examine the district's total library program, 2) recognize and assess accomplishments, 3) plan for the future, and 4) compare the program with others.

State Department of Education
Division of Public Schools
Jefferson City, Missouri

EVALUATION OF CENTRAL SCHOOL LIBRARY
(or Instructional Media Center)

School Year 19___-19___

DIRECTIONS: Please complete one of these evaluations for each central library in the school system. It is recommended that the librarian or certificated teacher in charge of the library complete the form, and that it be reviewed and approved by the appropriate administrative official.

Return the white and blue copies to Director, Title II, ESEA, State Department of Education, Jefferson Building, Jefferson City, Missouri 65101. The yellow copy is for the school's file. The pink copy is provided for a work copy.

School District Name & Number_____

County_____Grade Span_____

Classification (AAA, AA, A, or U)_____

Mailing Address_____
                        Street   City

_____
            State   Zip Code

==

                                    Librarian's School
Name of Librarian_____Phone No._____
                                            (Area Code)

Name of Library (Instructional Media Center)_____

Name of Library Supervisor serving this library_____

Mailing address of Library_____
                                    Street   City

_____
            State   Zip Code

Name of school(s) served by this Central Library_____

_____

Grade span served_____Enrollment served_____

No. of Teachers served_____

PERSONNEL

1. For librarian(s) and other certificated personnel serving this library, please complete the following:

Name	Degree: BS, MA, or MLS	Sem. Hrs. Credit in Library and/or Media Courses	No. of Hours Per School Day		
			In This Library	Other Library	Providing Dis. Wide Service
1. _____ (Head Librarian)					
2. _____					
3. _____					
4. _____					
5. _____					

2. For non-certificated personnel serving this library, please complete the following.

	Number of Paid	Total Hours Per Week	Number of Volunteers	Total Hours Per Week
Adult Library Aids				
Adult Library Clerks				
Other_____				
Student Workers				

EXPENDITURES

1. What is the annual per pupil expenditure for this school library (budget for current school year) for books, periodicals, and audiovisual materials?

   NOTE: Do not include expenditures for textbooks, supplementary materials, reference materials, supplies, and audiovisual equipment. $_____

                                                              YES   NO
                                                         (check applicable
                                                              column)

2. This amount meets Missouri School Media Standards for a school of this classification and enrollment.   ____   ____

   NOTE: See p. 11 of MSMS, especially the opening statement.

3. Are additional funds in sufficient amount budgeted for the purchase of:
   a. textbooks   ____   ____
   b. supplementary materials   ____   ____
   c. reference materials   ____   ____
   d. supplies   ____   ____
   e. library furnishings and equipment   ____   ____
   f. audiovisual equipment   ____   ____

4. Are adequate funds provided for the repair or rebinding of damaged or worn materials?   ____   ____

MEDIA CIRCULATION

(If records of this type are not maintained, indicate by NA)

1. Media circulation (report number circulated last school year) - library books_____periodicals_____other printed materials _____audiovisual materials_____

2. Average monthly, per pupil circulation of all media_____

3. Estimated number of student and faculty visits to the library per week_____

4. Based on the number of students and teachers, do you feel that
    adequate use is being made of the materials in this school li-
    brary? yes_____ no_____
    If no, briefly state reason:

5. This library ( ) does, ( ) does not, maintain a fine system for
    overdue materials.

PHYSICAL FACILITIES

YES   NO
(check applicable
column)

1. Does the library have adequate seating for the
    average size class?   ____ ____

2. Will the library seat at least;
    a. 10 percent of the school enrollment   ____ ____
    b. 15 percent of the school enrollment   ____ ____
    c. 20 percent of the school enrollment   ____ ____
    d. 25 percent of the school enrollment   ____ ____

3. Is the library reading room kept free from regu-
    larly scheduled study halls?   ____ ____

4. If the answer to question number 3, above, is
    "no," is some staff member other than the li-
    brarian responsible for study hall supervision
    in the library.   ____ ____

5. If the answer to question number 3, above, is
    "no," is additional library seating available for
    the average size class, when study hall students
    meet in the library?   ____ ____

ORGANIZATION AND SERVICE

YES   NO
(check applicable
column)

1. Does the school have cooperatively developed
    written statements of library philosophy and
    objectives, which have been approved by the
    Board of Education?   ____ ____

2. Are cooperatively developed written policies,
    which have been approved by the Board of Edu-
    cation, maintained and practiced in the follow-
    ing areas:
    a. media selection   ____ ____

    b. weeding
    c. censorship

3. Are written policies and/or procedures maintained and practiced in the following areas:
    a. overdues
    b. repair and rebinding
    c. accession records
    d. acquisition of materials
    e. requisitions (supplies)
    f. circulation of materials
    g. materials arrangement
    h. evaluation of materials
    i. book talks and/or storytelling
    j. annual inventory
    k. class use of library
    l. responsibilities of professional staff
    m. responsibilities of non-professional staff
    n. student assistants
    o. library clubs
    p. cataloging and processing materials
    q. treatment of materials purchased with Fede-
ral funds

4. Is the library organized as a media center where
all types of media, necessary equipment, and
services are available to students and teachers?

5. If the answer to 4 above is no, is the library
working toward a media center concept of service and organization?

6. Does the library have extended hours for student and teacher use:
    a. before school
    b. after school
    c. noon hour
    d. nights
    e. Saturday
    f. summer

7. Do students have free access to the media collection at all times during the day:
    a. books
    b. reference books
    c. other printed materials
    d. audiovisuals

8. Does school policy generally permit students to
check out the following media for home usage:
    a. books
    b. reference books

    c.   other printed materials   _____ ____
    d.   audiovisual materials   _____ ____

9.   Has a sequential program of instruction in work/study skills been developed for the grade span served by this library?   _____ ____

10.   Does the librarian teach the library work/ study skills?   _____ ____

11.   Do the teachers teach the library work/ study skills?   _____ ____

12.   Are faculty members adequately involved in selecting and/or recommending instructional materials for purchase?   _____ ____

13.   Does the librarian keep lines of communication open with faculty members in planning library services to meet curriculum needs?   _____ ____

14.   Does the librarian keep faculty members informed of new materials added to the library?   _____ ____

15.   Does the librarian keep faculty members informed of new materials available for purchase in their grade or subject areas?   _____ ____

16.   Does the librarian serve on or advise with curriculum planning committees?   _____ ____

17.   Does the librarian introduce materials to students for units of work?   _____ ____

18.   Does the librarian work with students and teachers in independent study programs?   _____ ____

19.   Is an adequate in-service program in use of educational media provided for teachers?   _____ ____

20.   Does the librarian confer with faculty members concerning reading problems of students?   _____ ____

21.   Does the librarian make:
    a.   frequent informal reports to the administrator   _____ ____
    b.   monthly or quarterly reports   _____ ____
    c.   annual report   _____ ____

22.   Is there a written plan or list of goals for li-
      brary improvement and upgrading?   _____ ____
      If yes, are they:
          short range (within the next school year)   _____ ____
          long range (within the next 3 to 5 years)   _____ ____

23.   Please write a brief summary of the plan(s)
      for future improvement of this library.

This evaluation was:

Completed by_____
                   Name   Position   Date
Reviewed and
Approved by_____
                   Name   Position   Date

PART IV

STATE AND NATIONAL
LIBRARY MEDIA CONFERENCES

7. THE STATE LIBRARY/MEDIA CONFERENCE

Keeping in mind the earlier definition given of the li-
brary/media specialist as a master teacher, one might easily
apply the following quote to the library/media director's situation:

> Method grows out of a basic concept of aim.
> Knowing what he wants to accomplish generally,
> the teacher may then consider specific purposes,
> and finally decide how best to do what he decides.
> At this point he can adequately evaluate his mo-
> tives. A basic understanding of where one is
> going in teaching is essential to the establishment
> of a method which is really workable for any
> given teacher. [1]

The busy daily schedule followed by most library/me-
dia specialists leaves little time for the evaluation of present
aims and objectives and the development of new concepts.
Yet, a well developed library/media program must be based
on clearly stated behavioral objectives as they relate to
student-teacher use of the instructional materials center. It
is not difficult to lose sight of goals and objectives in a mire
of routine duties and processes. The materials and services
found in many of the nation's library/media centers exist
simply because of tradition. Outdated materials and outmoded routines provide little inspiration for those involved
in center operation and use. The development of clear and
positive behavioral objectives, along with concrete models
for action, must be an on-going process, flexible and ever-
changing as the educational needs of teachers and students
change.

The great value of the state or national library/media
conference lies in the opportunity it affords those attending
to see their individual programs in a different perspective.

222

Opportunity is provided to examine new methods and materials and to exchange views and information with others in the library/media field. Thinking is, of necessity, redirected toward a changing or expanding concept of aim and an upgrading or updating of materials, methods or routines. The successful conference sends its participants back to their respective schools refreshed, more knowledgeable, inspired, and either more confident about their present methods and procedures or ready to initiate changes that will improve and upgrade their programs.

Both state and national professional organizations for library/media personnel play important roles in upgrading services to students. In working closely with State Departments of Education these organizations assist in preparing standards for media programs, developing and disseminating current information in the library/media field, working with state and national governments to secure funding for improved media services, and providing consultant services upon request. The year-round activities of the state or national organization are summarized at the annual conference and new plans for action are developed.

Planning the Conference

Careful state conference planning can help to avoid or minimize many of the problems usually connected with the large two- or three-day meeting. Many volunteers are needed to accept committee chairmanships and committee assignments. Back-up personnel are needed in emergencies and alternate plans are kept ready for use if all does not go as planned. Planning must begin at least one year prior to the conference to provide for problems of distance between personnel responsible for the conference, location of a suitable site, budget development and approval, and attention to the hundreds of small details necessary to a successful conference. Many of these details are noted in a description of the duties of state conference planning personnel.

1. Conference Chairman

The conference chairman is responsible for:

Overall conference planning and implementation

The appointment of and constant communication with

committee chairmen

The approval of committee plans (usually in conjunction with the Executive Board of the Organization)

Preparation of the budget

Preparation of alternate plans of action for use in
emergencies

Coordination of all program plans and activities

At the close of the conference, preparation and submission to the Executive Board of an evaluation of
the work of the committee with suggestions for next
year's chairman

2. Program Chairman

Develops and schedules main program events

Schedules special programs and events (field trips,
library school reunions, etc.)

Selection and notification of speakers or consultants

Development of needed equipment and materials lists

Notifies local arrangements chairman of required facilities

Notifies audio visual chairman of needed equipment
and personnel

Works with the chairman on conference materials to
develop programs, handouts and other needed materials

Prepares and submits program budget to conference
chairman

At the close of the conference, prepares and submits
to the Executive Board an evaluation of the work of
your committee with suggestions for next year's committee chairman

3. Local Arrangements Chairman

Receives space and facility requirements from program chairman

Makes personal visitation to proposed conference sites

Recommends selection of site (usually one year in advance of conference)

Checks on space for large and small meeting groups and exhibitors

Ascertains charges by hotel for space

Reserves a block of rooms for estimated number of conference attendees

Secures and distributes information on room rates and reservations

Develops maps, if necessary, to direct participants to parking, conference site, special meetings, etc.

Makes sure facilities are adequate for needed equipment and materials: sufficient outlets, speaker's stand with microphone, screens, other special equipment

Determines number and cost of meals; selects menus for meals

Develops seating and meeting arrangements for conferees including placement of registration desk, space to sell author's books

Makes hotel reservations for speakers

Arranges for speakers' and officers' seating arrangements at meals and events

Works with speakers on travel arrangements; arranges to meet speakers' planes and return to airport

Checks on need for union personnel and cost if needed

Surveys facilities for adequate heating, ventilation,

telephone service, first aid facilities, suitable viewing rooms

Arranges for serving of coffee, cocktail hour, cash bar, if required

Prepares local arrangements budget for submission to Executive Board for approval

At the close of the conference, prepares and submits an evaluative report on the work of your committee to the Executive Board with suggestions for next year's chairman

4. Audio Visual Chairman

Determines facilities needed for use of AV equipment; refers to local arrangements chairman

Determines audio visual equipment needs

Determines cost for renting equipment if necessary

Secures union help if necessary

Secures equipment including standby equipment

Arranges for security of equipment when not in use

Secures extra bulbs, extension cords, adaptors and minor equipment parts

Arranges for equipment operators and alternates; develops schedules and informs operators of the time and place they are to work

Arranges for the return of the equipment

Determines responsibility for damage

Prepares audio visual budget for submission to chairman for approval

At the close of the conference, prepares and submits an evaluative report on the work of your committee to the Executive Board with suggestions for next year's chairman

5. Exhibits Chairman

Works with local arrangements chairman on securing needed space requirements

Works with program chairman to determine desired exhibits

Contacts exhibitors. Informs exhibitors of space available, type of exhibit desired, availability of outlets if needed, cost to exhibitors, time and place of the conference, arrangements for exhibits, time exhibits can be set up and removed

Provides exhibitors with a map of available spaces. (Schedules space on a first come/first served basis.)

Sets a deadline for space reservations

Informs exhibitors to whom any fee charged is to be sent

Is on hand to greet exhibitors and to solve any problems that may arise during the conference concerning exhibitors

Submits exhibit budget to conference chairman for approval

At the close of the conference, prepares and submits an evaluative report on the work of your committee to the Executive Board with suggestions for next year's chairman

6. Registration Chairman

Prior to the conference:

Prepares registration materials

Sets registration fees

Sets deadlines (if necessary) for registration

Arranges for personnel to take charge of registration desk

Works with chairman on conference materials in developing registration forms and conference packet for participants

Accepts conference reservations by mail

Keeps a careful record of monies received and reserves meal tickets or tickets for special events to be picked up at the registration desk

Prepares budget for registration materials and personnel.

During the conference:

Supervises the registration desk

Is prepared to handle problems which arise

Collects money from the desk periodically and turns over to financial chairman

Keeps a careful record of overall attendance, attendance at meals, special events, etc.

At the close of the conference, prepares and submits an evaluative report on the work of your committee to the Executive Board with suggestions for next year's chairman.

7. Chairman on Conference Materials

Checks with the conference chairman and with the chairman of each committee to determine number of printed materials needed (programs, tickets, badges, maps, information on registration or reservations, duplicated materials of all types)

Develops each type of material with each chairman

Obtains estimate of costs of printed materials

Submits materials budget to program chairman for approval

Arranges for printing of materials

Arranges for distribution of each type of material

At the close of the conference, prepares and submits
an evaluative report on the work of your committee to
the Executive Board with suggestions for next year's
chairman

8. Publicity Chairman

Confers with conference chairman and committee
chairman on publicity needs

Prepares general conference flyer to be mailed to all
prospective participants. Include in the flyer: conference theme, sponsor, time, date, place, general
program, major speakers, cost, how registration
should be done, to whom fees are sent. Also included
with the flyer might be information on travel and hotel
arrangements.

Determines journals or news media to be used in pub-
licizing the conference

Determines cost of publicity in these journals or news
media

Prepares publicity releases in the format of the journal or news media and arranges for publication

Determines publicity budget for submission to conference chairman

Prepares summary of concluded conference for distribution to news media, members of the organization
and other interested parties. Arranges for distribution as necessary.

At the close of the conference, prepares and submits
an evaluative report on the work of your committee
to the Executive Board with suggestions for next
year's chairman

9. Hospitality Chairman

Works closely with the local arrangements chairman
to acquire thorough understanding of conference facilities and arrangements

Appoints committee members to greet arrivals,

answer questions, direct participants to meetings. (Arrange for hospitality or information booth.)

Arranges for a hospitality room where participants may rest, have coffee, chat. (Determines cost of room, if any.)

Prepares identification badges for conferees and distributes

Arranges for lost and found department and volunteers to work there

Arranges for postage and mailing facilities for conferees if needed

Prepares budget for hospitality committee work and submits to chairman for approval

At the close of the conference, prepares and submits an evaluative report on the work of your committee to the Executive Board with suggestions for next year's chairman

10. Evaluation Chairman

Secures complete program plans from conference chairman

Determines and devises necessary evaluation procedures including recording of comments, forms, and reports from committee chairmen

Distributes evaluative forms

Receives and compiles evaluative data

Duplicates summaries of data for submission to Executive Board and to those responsible for planning future conferences

11. Financial Chairman

The financial chairman is usually the treasurer of the organization.

The chairman receives all estimates of expenses.

Compiles the total conference budget

Receives all monies collected before, during and after the conference

Receives all invoices

Has invoices approved by the President or Executive Board of the organization

Pays all bills

Keeps all records and accounts concerning the conference

Prepares the final conference financial report of receipts and expenditures

Budgeting for the Conference

Careful planning in financial matters can avoid many of the financial headaches which often arise in the planning and implementing of the state conference. Most state conferences are self-supporting and some are even designed to add funds to the organization's treasury. The following breakdown of receipts and expenditures can serve as a guide in planning the state conference.

Receipts

Organizational Dues
Registration Fees
Exhibitor's Fees
Receipts for selling of authors' books

Payment for Meals (Housing arrangements and fees are usually handled between the hotel and the conference participant)

Expenditures

Renting of conference facilities (usually no charge if banquets, luncheons, etc., are scheduled)
Renting of exhibit space
Renting of equipment and replacement parts
Payment of union personnel for setting up equipment, etc.
Expenses and honorarium for speakers and consultants
Transportation expenses for field trips
Pre-conference travel for committee chairmen

Payment to publisher for author's books sold during con-
ference
Payment for meals, coffees, cocktail parties
Payment of union personnel if needed
Telephone
Conference badges
Publicity releases
Postage
Printing (tickets, forms, programs, handout materials,
publicity flyers, maps, notices, announcements, etc.)
Payment of any hired personnel--example: workers at
the registration desk, registered nurse on duty if neces-
sary, security guards if necessary
Payment for transportation of equipment or materials
Contingency fund

Approximately one year prior to conference time, each
committee chairman should draw up and submit a budget to
the Executive Board or to the conference chairman. Overall
budget decisions are made by the Executive Board upon recommendation of the conference chairman. Committee chairmen are informed by the conference chairman of their budget
allocations and the manner in which funds can be secured or
payments made for budgeted services and materials. All
receipts and expenditures are handled by the financial chairman. Invoices for payment should be initialed by the committee chairman who incurred the expense and approved for
payment by the Executive Board. The financial chairman
should be bonded and an audit of conference receipts and expenditures should be included in the annual audit of the organization's books.

The Program--Something for Everyone

The state school library/media conference will draw
as its participants librarians, media specialists, and educators from school libraries and materials centers of all
types: public or private schools on the elementary, secondary, or college level. They may work with students from
the inner city, suburbia, small towns or rural areas. The
libraries or media centers they represent may be among the
most modern and sophisticated, the most innovative, the
most traditional, or be yet unborn (as in the case of conference attendees interested in starting a library/media program). Provision must be made, as far as possible, to
offer a program of value to every participant. Thus, variety

in planning is essential.   Speakers in general sessions should
touch as much as possible upon universal needs.   Small
group sessions should be arranged to cover specific needs.
Provision should be made whenever possible for direct participation of conferees, and exhibits should cover a broad
range of materials and services.   Meetings should not be so
tightly scheduled that conferees are left without time to meet
with others and to exchange ideas.   Time should be set
aside for visiting exhibits and for discussions with exhibitors.
Program planning to meet the needs of such a variety of participants is a challenge.   The examples which follow are of
programs which have met this challenge.

Each of the program models to be presented was selected because of one or more strong points.   They range
from the planning of a "no-budget" state conference for the
beginning organization to the two- to three-day "high budget"
conference.   Some of the conferences were planned in cooperation with universities or State Departments of Education,
others by the dedicated individuals of single organizations.
They are presented here to serve as blueprints for those interested in successful conference planning.

Two conferences of the Michigan Association of School
Librarians were selected as excellent examples of the attempt to "provide something for everyone."   Examination of
the conference programs for 1971, "Materials Based on Educational Diagnosis and Individual Achievement," and for 1972,
"Accountability and Public Relations," will reveal the offering of from thirty-five to fifty separate sessions designed to
interest specific groups.   The choice of speakers and the
variety of topics offered is excellent.   In addition, the evaluative procedure employed by the Michigan Association of
School Librarians is thorough and complete and tabulated results from the evaluative questionnaire are utilized by conference planning personnel in developing future successful
conferences.   This material was made available by Maxine
Larson Hough, Executive Secretary, Michigan Association of
School Librarians.   Summaries of both conferences follow.

EXAMPLE (1)

ORGANIZATION: Michigan Association of School
                         Librarians.

CONFERENCE TITLE: Materials Based on Educational Di-
                   agnosis for Individual Achievement
                   (1971 Spring Conference).

LENGTH OF
CONFERENCE: Two Days.

CO-SPONSOR: The University of Michigan Extension
                         Service and the Bureau of School
                         Services.

Basic Topics Covered:

Accountability
Best of the 1970s for Small Frys (Children's Books)
Creative Dramatics
Current Books for High School Students
Differential Education
Kiva Kollage
Building Librarian-Administrator Cooperation
The Librarian's Role in Negotiations
Locally Produced Materials
The Instructional Media Center
Manpower
Media Philosophy
Performance Contracting
Student-Made Films

Methods of Presentation:

Large group meetings
Small group meetings
Single speakers
Panel Presentations
Demonstrations
Discussion Groups
Film Potpourri
Multi-media Presentations

The Conference Program

On the opening morning of the two-day conference,

attendees chose from six full morning sessions. Major topics covered in the sessions were Accountability, Negotiations,
Manpower Policy Statements, Current Books for High School
Students, Best Books of the '70s for the Small Fry, and a
Demonstration of Multi-Media Techniques for Reading Guidance. Morning meetings were followed by a luncheon with
keynote speaker, Stanford Ericksen, Director, Center for
Research on Learning and Teaching, the University of Michigan. His topic was "Academic Freedom--For Third Graders
for Example."

The day continued with small group discussions in the
afternoon, an evening banquet centered around the topic,
"Media and the Medium," with Roberta Young of the Colorado Dept. of Education as speaker, and a late evening film
potpourri.

The second day of the conference began with a business meeting of the organization followed by full morning
group meetings. Again, conferees were able to choose from
six major topics presented, including: Guaranteed Performance Contracting; The Librarian and Administrator Cooperate
to Build a Good School Library Program; Differential Education: A Resource Team Approach to Prescriptive Programming; Facilities; Student Made Films; and Creative Dramatics:
Use or Misuse. Luncheon speakers on the second day were
H. A. and Margaret Rey, creators of the Curious George
books.

Afternoon activities for the second day included "hands
on" experiences with instructional materials. Conferees were
able to choose from five separate sessions, including: Locally Produced Materials; "Take to the River," a sound filmstrip produced by MASL/MAVA Standards Committee; Graphic Production; Materials from Neighborhood Education Projects; and Special Materials for Special Reading Problems.

Each conference participant received a copy of the
evaluative questionnaire and throughout the conference period
was encouraged to evaluate individual meetings and the conference as a whole. Comments from the questionnaire are
valuable not only to future planners of the Michigan Association of School Librarians Conferences but to all conference
planners. A number of the major positive and negative comments are listed below:

Positive Comments

1. A refreshing and reinforcing event for librarians to attend each year.
2. Small sessions were valuable.
3. Resource people were good.
4. Group meetings with student involvement were most informative and enjoyable.
5. Well known authors are always a joy to see and hear.
6. Both sessions and exhibits were very informative.
7. Film presentations were excellent.
8. It was nice not to have to stand in line for meals.
9. It was helpful hearing of other school districts' programs and problems.
10. Enjoyed the reviews of new books.
11. The promptness of all meetings was appreciated.

Suggestions for Improvement

1. The food could have been better.
2. Topics and speakers should be more specific, less generalities and theories.
3. Sessions should be specifically geared to elementary, junior high and senior high.
4. Needed maps or guides to find the way around the center.
5. Room arrangement was poor in some cases.
6. The program should indicate the topics and grade levels for all groups.
7. Not enough time to attend all the sessions one might have wished to attend.
8. Have a booklet containing most of the main speakers and ideas presented at the conference.
9. Too many evaluation sheets. One should do it.

Suggestions of Interest Areas to be Covered in Future Conferences

1. Evaluation of IMC Programs and Services
2. Repeats of Performance Contracting, Negotiations and Accountability
3. More book review sessions
4. Always have an author and/or illustrator
5. Concrete ideas and examples of media centers and their activities
6. Budget--how to get the most for your money in a

budget squeeze era
7. Parent Power--Use of Parents to Develop and Foster Library Programs
8. Production of Materials
9. Involving Teachers in Library Use
10. Audio Visual Reference Materials
11. Afro-American History
12. Effective Political Action for Librarians

EXAMPLE (2)

The 1972 Conference of the Michigan Association of School Librarians had as its theme Accountability and Public Relations. The theme was chosen in response to the desires of members of the Association as indicated in the evaluations of the 1971 conference. Basic format was similar to the 1971 conference with three conference general sessions and numerous small group sessions, including concurrent small group presentations and discussion meetings.

Rationale for the 1972 conference was stated as follows:

One of the most pressing needs of the media community today is to tell our story, stress our worth and value, to teachers and administrators, boards of education, state and federal agencies, and the community. We who are in the media business should do this routinely--but we don't. The result is that audiovisual and library personnel and services are cut when budgets get tight, that we are perceived according to obsolete rules, and that our services are underutilized. The responsibility is ours to prove our worth and to tell our story. If we don't, who will? This conference is intended to help provide the tools for successful accounting of our value and communication of our story.

Major topics covered in this conference were:

Accountability and the Media Professional
How Others See Us: Feedback From the School and Commu-

nity
Public Relations Clinic
Media Surveys
Public Relations with Administration, Staff and Students
Michigan Accountability Model
Effective Legislative Relations
Accountability Systems--Management by Objectives
Accountability Case Study
Selection of Media by Specific Objectives
Toward Media Competency
Instructional Design and Accountability
Production of Public Relations Materials
External Relations at the District Level
Federal and State Funds for Media Programs
Accountability Systems--Program Planning Budgeting System
Public Relations Survey Techniques
Performance Contracting
Individually Guided Instruction

The Evaluative Instrument. Note has been made previously of the need for an evaluative instrument for almost
any type of workshop or conference held. This holds especially true for the large state meeting where the aim is
to provide enough diversification to meet the needs of all
conferees. If annual meetings by state library/media organizations are to justify the time and expense of those
traveling to such meetings, they must be relevant to participant's needs. The evaluative instrument used at the
MASL/MAVA 1972 conference is reproduced here in its entirety to serve as a guide for other organizations who plan
to develop such an instrument.

Evaluation Form

Accountability and Public Relations
Conference Evaluation (1972)

Total Forms Returned_____

1.   What is your responsibility in the media field?

   A.   Local Building Librarian
   B.   Local Building AV Coordinator
   C.   Local Building Library/Media Specialist
   D.   Central Media Administrator
   E.   Higher Education

F. Other:

> Teacher
> State Level
> El. Lit. Coordinator
> District Librarian
> Media Specialist
> Oakland Community College (Pres.)
> Consultant
> Speech Correctionist
> County Region
> Regional Media Director
> Intermediate (IMC)
> College Student (EMU)
> District Supervisor
> Central Processing and Cataloging
> School Administrator
> Public Relations
> College Instructor
> Retired Librarian Supervisor

2. Check the organization you belong to:

MAVA_____ Years_____ MASL_____ Years_____
Other_____

3. What is your major reason for selecting this conference?

A. Organizational affiliation____
B. Conference program____
C. Exhibits____
D. Other:____
> Representative from Local District
> Professional Growth
> Support of Elementary Media Program
> Presentation
> Invited Speaker
> Training Experience
> Did an Exhibit
> Panel Participant

4. Rate the overall value of this conference
> Extremely useful____
> Some use____
> No use____

5. Rate each of the following components of the conference,

using the following scale:

3 - Most Useful   2 - Some Use   1 - No Use

A. General Session on Accountability: 3___ 2___ 1___

B. General Session on Public Relations: 3___ 2___ 1___

C. Small Group Sessions on Accountability: 3___ 2___
    1___

D. Small Group Sessions on Public Relations: 3___
    2___ 1___

    Name the small groups you selected:
        How Others See Us--Feedback from School and
            Community___
        Accountability Case Study--Harry Hill High
            School___
        Selection of Media by Specific Objectives___
        Instructional Design and Accountability--Instruc-
            tional Development Institute Approach___
        Accountability Systems--PPBS___
        Public Relations Clinic___
        Public Relations/Administration, Staff & Students
            ___
        Michigan Accountability Model___
        Michigan Assessment Program & Media___
        Federal and State Funds for Media Programs___
        Take to the River___
        Production of Public Relations Material___
        Effective Legislative Relations___
        Toward Media Competency___
        Media Surveys___
        Public Relations Case Study___
        Custer___

E. Exhibits--Audio Visual: 3___ 2___ 1___

F. Exhibits--Books, Print Materials: 3___ 2___ 1___

G. Multi-Image Themes: 3___ 2___ 1___

H. Instructional Film Preview Arena: 3___ 2___ 1___

I. Graphics Workshops: 3___ 2___ 1___

J. Materials Organization Exhibits: 3___ 2___ 1___

K. Film Festival: 3___ 2___ 1___

6. What recommendations can you make to improve a similar conference?

7. What concerns or purposes should a future combined conference of MAVA and MASL be directed toward?

EXAMPLE (3)

1971 Conference for Pennsylvania School Librarians

The 1971 Annual Conference for Pennsylvania School Librarians was the 26th annual conference of that organization. The conferences are sponsored and financed by the library science programs at the State Colleges in Clarion, Kutztown, Millersville and Shippensburg, Pennsylvania. The conferences are noteworthy both for the careful planning of the two-day meetings and for the excellent materials prepared for use by conferees both before and during the meeting.

Materials sent to the participants prior to the meeting include:

Registration Form
Motel and Hotel Accommodations Directory
Conference Program
Special Meal Registration Forms
Registration Forms for school library visitations with directions and descriptions of programs to be seen
Map of the Conference Area
Complete Parking Directions

Materials prepared for use during the meeting include:

Complete Conference Program in booklet form
Conference Directory which includes information on Library and Related Associations, Exhibitors, and Educational Films shown during the Conference
Evaluation Form

The program, directory and evaluation form are reproduced as follows with the permission of Charles Economous, Dean, Division of Library Science, Clarion State College.

LIBRARY
NEEDS...

Relating to
and
Responding to
                                        student
                        teacher
      curriculum
                        administrator

26th Annual Conference for
Pennsylvania School Librarians

Sponsored by
Division of Library Science
Clarion State College
April 23-24, 1971

Badges Must Be Worn
For Admission
to All Meetings And to The Exhibits.

Your Selections of Group Meetings
Have Been Indicated on Your Name Badges.

Uri Shulevitz Books on Sale

The Fool of the World and The Flying Ship and Rain Rain
Rivers published by Farrar, Straus & Giroux will be available for purchase at the registration desk.

The first day of the conference featured educational
films including: At the Center, The Library Is, Make a
Mighty Reach, Reaching Out: The Library and the Excep-

tional Child, There's Something About a Story. Showing of
films was continuous throughout the morning. Also featured
on this first day were tours of the college library, school
library visitations and large and small group meetings centered around the following topics:

Relating and Responding to Library Needs
Revitalizing Elementary School Libraries
Storytelling and the Library Program
Science and Culture: A Multi-Media Effort Involving
   Team Preparation
The District IMC: Support Services for the School Cur-
   riculum
Design and Re-Design of School Library-Media Facilities
The Library Supervisor--Catalyst for Change
Illustrating Children's Books, an Address by Uri Shule-
   vitz

The program for the second day began with a business
meeting followed by group meeting and discussion sessions
centered around such topics as:

Re-assessing Library and Educational Goals
Administrative Support for Library Programs and Ser-
   vices
The Disadvantaged Reader and the Library
Relating Media to the Social Studies Program
Innovative Uses of the Library with Students and Teach-
   ers
Developing a Library Program to Meet Standards
Oral Interpretation of Literature
Designing Programs for Change

An interesting feature of this conference was the
wealth of material produced for those attending. Conferees
received a Directory of Library Associations for the School
Librarian including a complete list of publications of these
associations, a Directory of Commercial Exhibitors, a Directory of Publishers, an evaluation instrument, and a complete annotated list of Educational Films shown at the conference. The film list is reproduced here for those seeking
excellent films for conference use. Also reproduced is the
evaluative instrument as a second example of what might be
used in the evaluation of a state conference.

EDUCATIONAL FILMS

Shown at the 26th Annual Conference of the
Pennsylvania School Librarians

AT THE CENTER
School Library Manpower Project (AASL), American Library
Assn., 1970. 28 min. color. Sale price: $175.
"Presents the role of the school library media spe-
cialist as a changing, exciting and dynamic force in our na-
tion's total educational system."

THE LIBRARY IS ...
Bro-Dart, Inc. 1968. 13 min. color. Sale price: $150.
"History of the library; its purpose; what it is to be
a librarian; place of the library in the media explosion. Selection, organization and categorizing of materials housed in
a library."

MAKE A MIGHTY REACH
Charles F. Kettering Foundation. 1967. 45 min. color.
Sale price: $300.
"Review of the changes taking place in American education; technological, plant, staffing and curriculum innovations designed to deal with the knowledge explosion and to
make learning more enjoyable and effective."

REACHING OUT: THE LIBRARY AND THE EXCEPTIONAL
CHILD Connecticut Films, Inc. 1968. 25 min. color.
Sale price: $225.
"Shows in spontaneous sequences how children with
various handicaps respond to books and other materials. It
shows how a child's use and enjoyment of them can contribute to his development. Children who are blind, deaf, hos-
pitalized, homebound because of physical handicaps, the edu-
cable mentally retarded, and the socially maladjusted in a
correctional school are among those served in the Demonstration of Library Services to Exceptional Children conducted
by the Public Library of Cincinnati and Hamilton County."

THERE'S SOMETHING ABOUT A STORY
Connecticut Films, Inc. 1969. 27 min. color. Sale price:
$240.
"... was made by the Dayton and Montgomery County
Public Library to share one community's experiences with
storytelling. It was done in the hope that it would stimulate
others to find a similar joy in sharing this folk art with
children."

EVALUATION OF THE
26th ANNUAL CONFERENCE FOR SCHOOL LIBRARIANS

Your reactions to the following items will assist future conference planners in providing programs of interest and relevance. Please deposit your evaluation sheet at the registration desk in the Marwick-Boyd Fine Arts Building or in the Division of Library Science Office on the second floor of the Administration Building.

1. The library (or library system) with which I am affiliated is:
_____ a. in Pennsylvania
_____ b. outside Pennsylvania

2. Indicate your current responsibilities:
_____ Elementary School Librarian
_____ Jr. High School Librarian
_____ Sr. High School Librarian
_____ Teacher-Librarian (Please indicate grade levels: _____)
_____ School Administrator
_____ Coordinator of Library Programs
_____ Library Science Student
_____ Library Educator
_____ Audio-Visual Specialist
_____ Other (Specify): _____

3. Years of experience as a school librarian:
___0-5 ___6-10 ___11-15 ___16-20 ___20+

4. Approximately how many students do you serve in your present position? _____

5. How many annual conferences for school librarians have you attended?
___1 ___3 ___5 ___11-15
___2 ___4 ___6 ___16 or more

6. Please check those items which best express your personal reasons for attending this conference:
_____ a. To keep up to date with new ideas and products in the field.
_____ b. To meet professional obligations.
_____ c. To gain new insights for solution of old problems.
_____ d. To stimulate intellectual growth and profession-

al advancement.
_____ e. To meet professional colleagues.
_____ f. To look for a job.
_____ g. Other (Specify):_____

7. My objectives were:
    _____ fully satisfied   Comments:_____
    _____ partially satisfied
    _____ unsatisfied   _____

                                   _____

8. The conference has provided:
    _____ theoretical insight
    _____ practical insight

9. Which segments of the conference did you find most
    interesting and of greatest personal value? (e.g., ex-
    hibits, banquet speakers, group meetings, general ses-
    sions)_____

    _____

10. Was there a particular session which you would have
    liked to attend but could not because of a program con-
    flict? If so, please indicate:_____

    _____

11. Do you feel that the conference topics were appropriate
    to your needs and interests?_____

    _____

12. If not, please indicate those which you felt to be irrele-
    vant:_____

13. Do you prefer the small discussion group sessions to
    the large group lecture sessions? Explain.

    _____

    _____

14. In my opinion, the conference program materials were:
    _____ readable   Suggested improvements:_____
    _____ well arranged
    _____ comprehensive   _____
    _____ attractive

                                   _____

                                   _____

15. Overall, I would rate the conference:
    _____outstanding
    _____above average
    _____average
    _____not worth my time and expense
    Comments: _____

    _____

16. Suggested topics and speakers for next year's confer-
    ence: _____

    _____

EXAMPLE (4)

The Massachusetts School Library Association
1972 Conference

     An interesting approach for a one-day state confer-
ence was initiated by the Massachusetts School Library Association in cooperation with the Massachusetts Department of
Education, Bureau of Library Extension. The conference
theme centered around projects throughout the state which
were funded under special purpose grants (Title II ESEA).
The day provided an opportunity for schools receiving special purpose grants in the field of library or media development to share the results of those grants with librarians
throughout the state. Little expense was involved in the implementation of the program since local districts donated
their services to discuss their programs. However, the
ideas generated proved extremely helpful to those attending.
A summary of the conference program follows:

CREATIVE LEARNING EXPERIENCES

ESEA TITLE 2

A Special Purpose Grant Workshop

presented by
Mass. School Library Association
in cooperation with
Mass. Dept. of Education
Bureau of Library Extension

Wednesday   April 12, 1972
Lexington, Massachusetts
9:30 a. m. to 4:00 p. m.

Program reprinted with permission of: Lynn Simpson, Dept.
of Education, Boston, Massachusetts

9:30-10:00   REGISTRATION AND COFFEE

10:00-11:00   Seminar:
repeated   VISUAL LITERACY PROJECTS
11:00-12:00

        An open-ended discussion of programs in film study
and visual literacy including determination of objectives, selection of materials, realities of implementation.   Participating in the panel will be representatives from projects in
Brookline, Haverhill, Quincy, Winchendon, and Woburn.

10:00-11:00   Presentation:
repeated   A CRASH PROGRAM IN TOTAL
11:00-12:00   PERCEPTUAL AWARENESS FOR
                  HUMANITIES STUDENTS

        Presented by the teachers and students of Framing-
ham South High School.   Student projects on creativity.

10:00-11:00   Presentation:
repeated   ACTIVISM AND THE LAW
11:00-12:00

        A multi-media commentary on war, by the students
and teachers of Mary Immaculate Jr. -Sr. High School, Marlboro.

10:00-11:00   Seminar:
repeated   MATHEMATICS PROJECTS
11:00-12:00

        How media services can assist the development of in-
dividualized math programs.   Participating in the panel will
be representatives from projects in Brookline, Granby, and
Wayland.

12:00-12:30   COCKTAILS AND SOCIAL HOUR

12:30-2:00   LUNCHEON AND BUSINESS MEETING

2:00-3:00   Presentation:
repeated   ZERO REJECT MATH LEARNING LABORA-
3:00-4:00   TORY

A participating experience with manipulative materials created by media specialists and administrators in Granby.

2:00-3:00   Seminar:
repeated   WORKSHOP IN PROPOSAL WRITING
3:00-4:00

Designed to acquaint school librarians with techniques of developing curriculum related projects. Topics covered will be needs assessment, development of objectives and learning activities, selection of materials, and evaluation. Discussion leaders will include staff from the Bureau of Library Extension. Interested participants should come to this seminar with an idea for a potential project.

2:00-3:00   Presentation:
repeated   CONTINUING STUDY IN OCEANOGRAPHY
3:00-4:00

A hands on demonstration involving the preparation of materials for ecology and marine life conducted by students and staff from Nahant Junior High School.

2:00-3:00   Seminar:
repeated   SOCIAL STUDIES PROJECT
3:00-4:00

An open-ended discussion of programs in youth activism and social concerns including determination of objectives, selection of materials; realities of implementation. Participants in the panel will be representatives from projects in Attleboro, Marlboro, Worcester, and Walpole.

EXAMPLE (5)

The Missouri Association of School Librarians

Three conferences held by the Missouri Association

of School Librarians show the growth which can take place
in a state organization through working cooperatively toward
common goals.   The first conference, held in 1969, was a
"no budget" conference.   The major goal of the conference
was to locate and share, through demonstration and through
the compilation of a booklet, innovative programs in school
library/media services throughout the state.   The conference
description follows:

TITLE: INNOVATIVE PRACTICES IN
                                MISSOURI SCHOOL LIBRARIES

SPONSOR: Missouri Association of School Li-
                                brarians.

LENGTH OF
CONFERENCE: One-half day.

MAJOR   To bring Missouri librarians closer
OBJECTIVE: together through both direct and writ-
                                ten communication concerning innova-
                                tive programs in library/media ser-
                                vices throughout the state.

PROCEDURE: Prior to the conference, officers of
                                the association contacted by letter and
                                phone calls, school librarians through-
                                out the state requesting written pro-
                                gram descriptions which would contain
                                material helpful to other librarians.
                                Consultations with members of the
                                State Department of Education also re-
                                vealed innovative programs.   Librari-
                                ans in charge of these programs were
                                asked to present them orally at the
                                conference.

DETERMINATION OF   The date chosen for the conference
CONFERENCE DATE: was one morning of the annual three-
                                day conference of the Missouri State
                                Teacher's Association.   Since most li-
                                brarians would be in attendance at the
                                State Teacher's meeting it was felt
                                that they would welcome a program
                                geared specifically to their needs.

SELECTION OF SITE --PUBLICITY:

A hotel near the main conference site was selected. Notices of the conference were mailed to all members of the association and were published in the MSTA monthly magazine, School and Community, two months prior to the conference.

SELECTION OF MATERIALS FOR THE CONFERENCE BOOKLET:

One member of the executive committee of the organization acted as editor for the innovative practices booklet to be compiled and distributed to each conferee. Program descriptions selected for inclusion ranged from descriptions of large school programs to small rural area library programs. Other descriptions included those of computer services, junior review boards, book fairs, departmental resource centers, and variable modular scheduling.

PROGRAM:

In a short conference it is difficult to provide "something for everyone" but the attempt was made even here. The morning program included visual presentations on "Individualizing Instruction Through Media, " "School-Public Library Cooperation, " "Secondary Library Practices, " and "Organizing the Elementary Library." The morning's activities were concluded with the introduction and distribution of the handbook, Innovative Practices in School Library Services.

EVALUATION:

No formal evaluative instrument was used. However, those responsible for planning the conference visited with librarians who attended to gauge the general reaction. Response was so favorable that plans were laid for an independent conference in the spring, two days in length to further expand the goal of helping Missouri Librarians to share ideas.

Thus, the success of the 1969 M. A. S. L. conference
led to a more ambitious undertaking in 1970. A two-day
conference was planned on "The Instructional Materials Center and Independent Study. " In this and all future conferences, provision was made for direct participation of conferees. One portion of the conference entitled "Creative
Problem Solving" presented participants with problems which
arise in many school instructional materials centers. Small
groups worked together on solutions and a group spokesman
presented the solutions to the entire group. The program,
problems and a summary of the solutions follow.

Missouri Association of School Librarians
and
Missouri Library Association

Present

THE INSTRUCTIONAL MATERIALS CENTER
AND
INDEPENDENT STUDY

Annual Spring Conference
April 24-25, 1970
Ramada Inn (Stratford Room)
Jefferson City, Missouri

Program

FRIDAY, APRIL 24, 1970

7:50 p. m.   Special M. A. S. L. Premiere: "A Fairy Tale
              for Librarians"

8:00 p. m.   Opening of the First General Session Confer-
              ence Moderator: Dr. Frederick Mundt, De-
              partment of Instructional Resources, Southern
              Illinois University

8:15 p. m.   The Administrator and the Librarian: Keys to
              Successful Independent Study Activities
                  Mr. Nelson Smith, Principal, St. Ann
              School, Pattonville School District, St.
              Louis County, Missouri

9:00 p. m.   Questions, Comments, Introductions

NOTE: Questions and comments from conference participants are welcomed and encouraged following all conference presentations.
Direct questions and comments to Dr. Mundt, Conference Moderator.

EXHIBITS: Stratford Room: Display of juvenile non-fiction by Missouri State Library
Main Lobby and Mezzanine: Displays of new materials available in the work/study skills area.

SATURDAY, APRIL 25

8:50 a. m. Opening of the Second General Session: Dr. Mundt

9:00 a. m. Skills for Successful Independent Study Activities Dr. John Voth, Associate Professor of Education, University of Missouri
The Place of Media in Independent Study Activities Dr. Eldon Madison, Chairman, Department of Instructional Resources, Southern Illinois University

10:20 a. m. Coffee Break

10:30 a. m. Creative Problem Solving-Conference Participants Followed by Panel Evaluations of Problem Solutions - Mr. Smith, Dr. Voth, Dr. Madison, Miss Banks, Dr. Mundt.

11:50 a. m. Break before lunch

12:15 p. m. M. A. S. L. Luncheon

1:30 p. m. The Pursuit of Learning, an International Endeavor Miss Marjorie Banks, Associate Professor of Education, Lindenwood College

2:15 p. m. Questions and Comments: Conference Summary Dr. Mundt

2:45 p. m. Conference Adjournment

PROBLEMS PRESENTED ON SATURDAY, APRIL 25
SECOND GENERAL SESSION

The eight problems that follow were distributed among
the round table groups, each table working on a solution to
one problem. Since several tables received the same problem diverse solutions were presented. Panel members evaluated the solutions for feasibility and soundness of approach.
This is recommended as an excellent activity for any library/
media conference.

Problem One
Miss X has been teaching in Blank School for ten
years. The IMC is in its second year of development and
contains a fair collection of materials, adequate space for
independent study activities, and is staffed by a full time librarian and library aide serving 600 students. Miss X's
students are never seen in the IMC. "I don't have time for
my students to use the IMC," says Miss X. "After all, I
hardly have time to teach the basic skills, let alone anything
extra."

Question: How can you as librarian or media specialist get
            Miss X and her students on the way to independent
            study activities in the IMC?

Problem Two
Mr. Y is a secondary school administrator who believes in the "slots and bells" system of education. "A
place for everything and everything in its place, especially
students," says Mr. Y. You are a librarian or media
specialist who sees great potential in the IMC program for
independent study activities. However, in this school students may not come to the IMC as the need arises. When
and if a teacher schedules a class to use the IMC, that
class must leave at a specified time to move on to the next
"slot" in the educational day.

Question: How can you foster greater flexibility and use of
            IMC facilities in this school?

Problem Three
In Blank High School study halls are regularly
scheduled in the IMC. Because of overcrowded conditions
resulting from this scheduling there is little room for students who might want to come during the day to do research
projects and seek solutions to problems. Those who do

come receive little help from the librarian who is busy keeping order.

Question: How can you secure the release of IMC facilities
             for the use to which they should properly be put?

Problem Four
The new Missouri School Library Standards call for
one elementary librarian for 1, 500 students.   Clerical help
requirements are so vague that they have been ignored by
your school district.   You serve two schools whose libraries
consist of book collections housed in large broom closets.

Question: What positive steps can you take to secure IMC
             facilities for these schools that will serve stu-
             dents and teachers in the manner in which they
             should?

Problem Five
You have taken a new job in Blank School as librarian
or media specialist.   You have replaced Miss Z, the librarian at this school for the past 30 years.   Miss Z has, over
the years, "trained" the students and teachers to: a) allow
students to use the library only with two to three days prior
notice, b) submit requests for materials three weeks in advance, and c) avoid immediate requests of any type.   As a
result of this "training" students and teachers avoid the library as much as possible.

Question: What steps can you take to "retrain" students and
             teachers to accept the library or IMC as an inte-
             gral part of the teaching-learning experience?

Problem Six
Miss W, an elementary teacher, believes in her students using the IMC.   At least one-half to three-fourths of
her students are spending an hour or more in the IMC each
day.   However, when you ask these students if there are
areas in which they need help, or what subject they have in
mind when they request recordings or filmstrips for use they
reply, "Oh, Miss W says we can do anything we want in the
IMC just so we don't bother other kids. "

Question: How can you correct this misuse of IMC facili-
             ties without "turning Miss W off" completely?

Problem Seven
        As librarian or media specialist in Blank School you
have been an enthusiastic proponent of independent study.
You feel it is important for students to seek their own answers to problems rather than being given the solution by
their teacher.   You have finally gotten this idea through to
Mr. L, a traditionalist teacher.   He has just sent 30 of his
students to the IMC, each student to research and report on
the same subject.   Obviously, there are not enough materials
available.

Question: How can you handle this problem without discourag-
            ing Mr. L from attempting the IMC approach to
            learning with his students?

Problem Eight
        As librarian or media specialist in Blank School you
have, at the beginning of the school year, held a series of
work/study skills or library orientation sessions with every
class.   These lessons stressed the skills of location, acquisition, organization, recording and evaluation.   However,
most students coming to the IMC still show difficulty in locating materials, do not use an index as a key to specific
material located, and seem to have little knowledge of basic
reference sources even though you have presented them in
class sessions.

Question: How can you develop a skills program that will
            be more meaningful and relevant to these stu-
            dents?

Suggested Solutions

1.   How can the librarian encourage reluctant teachers
     toward greater use of IMC facilities?

     Suggested Approaches:
        The librarian should be helpful and enthusiastic in her
     approach to the teacher.   Offer to introduce IMC ma-
     terials to students beginning a new unit of work.   Take
     materials to the teacher; ask the teacher to help in eval-
     uating new materials; have displays of new materials;
     offer to take part of the class for research activities
     while the teacher works with others; place book carts
     with a variety of materials near the classroom for stu-
     dent use; offer to produce materials to meet specific

needs if necessary; encourage flexibility in IMC use; en-
list the aid of the department chairman.

2. & 3.   How can the librarian foster flexibility in the use
of IMC facilities that have previously been used on a
scheduled basis?

Suggested Approaches:
   Use questionnaire with teachers to determine their
IMC needs; form a teacher committee to study needs and
make recommendations; arrange for librarian and administrator to visit successful flexible scheduling programs
in other schools; approach through students who will
pressure administration for allowing greater IMC use;
explain need for flexibility to CTA with a request for
CTA help in bringing about greater flexibility in IMC
use; work with parents and community to bring about
greater understanding of the role of the IMC.
   Submit written plans to the administration suggesting
solutions to those specific problems which prevent IMC
use.   (1) Suggest use of cafeteria or stage for scheduled
study halls.   (2) Seek volunteer help.   (3) Promote workshops for teachers on independent study.   (4) Press for
more professional help.

4.   What positive steps can be taken to secure improvement
of IMC facilities?

Suggested Approaches:
   Educate school board, administration, faculty and
parents concerning the vital educational role the IMC in
the school can play; form a committee with representatives from each group to study the problem and suggest
concrete solutions; push for stricter enforcement by the
Missouri State Department of Education of the required
standards for Missouri school libraries.   Actively seek
the hiring of a Missouri School Library Supervisor to
enforce standards.   Work through state library groups,
MASL-MLA, for higher standards for Missouri school
libraries and strict enforcement of these standards.

5., 6. & 7.   These problems dealt with abuse rather than
use of IMC facilities.   Specifically, students sent to the
IMC for no purpose; 30 students sent at one time to research the same topic; a new librarian coming into a
previously highly structured and restrictive library situation.

Suggested Approaches:
Orient faculty as to the purpose, use, and materials
available in the IMC through workshops, grade level or
department meetings, and informed individual discussion;
orient pupils toward purposeful use of facilities; give
extra time and assistance to new teachers; make IMC
facilities flexible and inviting; advertise new material;
know the curriculum and be ready to suggest purposeful
IMC activities to the teacher; set up an "interest box"
in the IMC for independent activities; prepare bibliographies with written suggestions for use of materials to be
sent to appropriate departments; broaden topics to be
researched through a variety of media approaches.

8.   How can you develop a work/study skills (or library ori-
     entation program) that will be meaningful and relevant to
     students?

Suggested Approaches:
Give skills instruction at a time when the teacher indicates a specific need and relate instruction directly to
classroom work.   Begin instruction in the elementary
school and coordinate skills instruction with secondary
schools to assure sequential skills development.   Always
coordinate instruction with the teacher's program.   Consult skills charts to become aware of what skills need
to be learned at what grade levels.   When introducing
materials to a class for units of work, give each student a bibliography of pertinent materials and instruction
on how to locate them.   Give direct and understanding
help to individual students showing difficulty in IMC use.
Place materials for a specific study in one area of the
IMC.   Allow free access to all materials--students
should be allowed to borrow anything in the library (except the librarian!).

After moving slowly into conference planning during
1969 and 1970, the M.A.S.L. butterfly emerged from its
cocoon and held a highly successful two-day conference in
1971, entitled "Books for the New Breed." The conference
was sponsored jointly by M.A.S.L. and the Children's Services Round Table of the Missouri Library Association.   Although it was a "high budget" conference, due to the expenses involved in securing speakers who had to travel some
distance, the conference paid for itself through registration
fees.   The quality of the program and of the speakers made

it a sell-out conference with standing room only.   Again,
participants became involved through round table discussions.
A pre-conference reading list was sent to prospective conferees, along with registration materials.   It included the
following suggested reading:

Suggested Pre-Conference Reading:

Neufeld, John   Edgar Allen. S. G. Phillips, 1968.
Neufeld, John   Lisa, Bright and Dark. S. G. Phillips,
                    1969.
Neville, Emily   Berries Goodman (65), It's Like This Cat
                    (63), Seventeenth Street Gang (66), Traveler
                    from a Small Kingdom (68).   Harper & Row.
Neville, Emily   "Social Values in Children's Literature, "
                    from A Critical Approach to Children's Lit-
                    erature, ed. by Sara Fenwick.   University
                    of Chicago Graduate Library School, 1967.
Karl, Jean   "A Children's Editor Looks at Excellence in
                    Children's Literature," Horn Book, February,
                    1967.

In addition: Conference participants are asked to bring
                   along a book which has been purchased but
                   which the participant is adverse to placing
                   on the shelves.   These books will serve as
                   a basis for the Saturday morning session.

The actual conference program included contrasting
reviews of books of yesterday and today by two Missouri librarians: Helen Smith of the Ladue School District talked
on "The New Breed and Realism, " and Alice Vinyard of the
Festus Public Library spoke of "The New Breed and Romanticism. "   "The New Breed" itself was defined by Dr.
Howard Barnett, Vice President of Lindenwood College, St.
Charles, Missouri.   Challenging speakers and their topics
throughout the two-day session included:

        John Neufeld, author of Edgar Allen, Lisa Bright and
        Dark, and Sleep, Two Three Four;
        Emily Neville, author of the Newbery Award Winner,
        It's Like This Cat; and
        Jean Karl, Children's Book Editor, Atheneum Press.

Questions, round table discussions and all conference
moderation was done by Dr. Frederick Mundt, Dept. of Instructional Technology, Southern Illinois University, Edwardsville.

In summary, the successful state conference can provide for the acquisition of knowledge, exchange of views, renewal of enthusiasm, and improvement of existing library/
media programs. It can also give impetus to the start of
new programs and, most important, can bring library/media
personnel closer together in working cooperatively toward
common goals. The conference does not have to be costly
to be successful, but it does have to be carefully planned,
well-thought-out as to major goals and purposes, and smooth-
ly implemented. Provision should always be made for evaluation in order to plan with greater ease and achieve future
conferences that will truly meet the needs of participants.

Promotional Materials and Methods

If one were to construct a mathematical formula for
a successful state library/media conference, it might read:
SC = HM = LA, or, a Successful Conference equals a
Healthy Membership, equals a Large Attendance. The circle
is continuous, with stimulating, thought-provoking conferences leading to an increase in membership in the organization and, conversely, a poorly planned, disorganized conference leading to a drop in membership and in attendance at
future conferences. While the major goal of the state conference is not to attract membership, neither is it to lose
members from the organization. Since a strong and unified
membership leads to the attainment of higher goals for all
in the library/media profession, it is to be nurtured and
encouraged. A well-planned conference is a major step in
moving the organization in this direction and this planning
should include creative approaches in the development of promotional materials. Three basic areas of promotional materials and methods that might be considered are 1) personal
contact, 2) written communication, and 3) visual communication.

1) Personal Contact

Personal contact with prospective members is vitally
important. Attracting and keeping members should be a primary goal of the hospitality committee as well as of the
membership committee. A hospitality booth or information
booth can be set up and manned by knowledgeable members
who have a sincere interest in people and who can make new
arrivals feel welcome and at home. Members of the hospitality committee should be scheduled also to circulate

throughout the conference to talk with those who seem "lost" or "confused" in the crowd. Registration fees should be lower for members than for non-members and a membership booth can be a prominent part of the exhibit area. Students should be attracted to the conference through special rates and made to feel welcome from the moment of arrival.

2) Written Communication

While membership promotion should be a year-round activity with frequent communications from the organization to prospective members, extra effort should be made to develop and distribute promotional materials at the conference. Enthusiastic attendees should not lack for membership materials to take back to their communities when, in the first flush of post-conference enthusiasm, they discuss the conference and the organization with colleagues. Written membership materials might include flyers on: past conferences or activities or accomplishments of the organization; the basic aims or goals of the organization; present activities undertaken by the association to improve library services throughout the state; examples and statements concerning the combined effectiveness of library/media personnel working together toward common goals.

3) Audiovisual Communication

While personal contact and written communication are important in membership promotion a new approach is always welcome. When conference participants leave a conference talking about the membership promotion activities, the membership committee has, indeed, scored a victory (and hopefully, acquired a number of new members). The aims and objectives of the association can be promoted effectively through synchronized slide-tape presentations, locally produced films or filmstrips or even through puppet shows. A little creative thought (and the tighter the budget, the more creative the thought must be) can produce a credible audiovisual presentation. A good example of this type of promotional activity was cited earlier in the 1970 conference program of The Missouri Association of School Librarians. Used as a program opener and billed as a "Special M. A. S. L. Premiere: A Fairy Tale for Librarians, " this tape/transparency presentation was amusing, different, to the point, and long remembered. Two members of the association collaborated on the script and artwork for the transparencies, and background music on the tape was provided by a local

high school "rock" group. The fairy tale was printed and
illustrated in booklet form (with membership application
blanks attached) and given to each participant after the
"Premiere" presentation. In adapting for your organization
the fairy tale which is reproduced here it is necessary only
to change the name of the prince to match the initials of
your association. The point made in the tale should be universal to all library/media organizations.

THE PITIFUL PLIGHT OF PRINCESS PERSEVERANCE

(A fairy tale for (your state) librarians)

by
Miss Ima True Crusader

Long ago and far away in the LAND OF PENURY
there existed the tiny KINGDOM OF MEDIA. And in this
kingdom lived a most beautiful princess. She was known to
all for her multitude of good works and kind acts. She was
called Princess Perseverance.

Her father, King Emptycoffers, was a truly beloved
monarch, caring only for the welfare of his subjects and
possessing full knowledge of the myriad difficulties involved
in providing for their individual differences to assure their
continued well-being.

In truth, King Emptycoffers had, during his long
reign, held a most particular concern for the development
of his subjects' minds and to this end had provided in the
palace a most wondrous ROOM OF LEARNING.

To this room came all who would partake of the
knowledge thus gathered (in both print and nonprint form)
and the multitude marveled at the wondrous audiovisual machines contained therein.

But alas, came the sad day when King Emptycoffers
passed to his reward and being true to his name left both
the kingdom and Princess Perseverance with empty coffers.
Not a penny, not a sou, not a drachma, not a single coin
remained to provide for the good people of MEDIA.

The palace ROOM OF LEARNING fell quickly into
disrepair. No longer did its walls echo with the joyous

sounds of those who had known the pleasures of seeking and discovering knowledge. With no funds for repairs, the projectors soon ceased to project and the recorders refused to record. In due time, the study prints faded, the transparencies became transparent, the globes collapsed, the models molded, and the books, oh dear children, the books became sustenance for the mice of MEDIA, who, in time became quite obese from devouring such weighty thoughts.

And in this desolate and dreary time sweet Princess Perseverance grew more and more unhappy as she viewed with dismay the citizens of the KINGDOM OF MEDIA wringing their hands in despair (in individually different ways, of course).

Again and again she appealed to King Slackwell of THE LAND OF PENURY for aid for THE KINGDOM OF MEDIA, but being a truly miserly monarch, and never having partaken of the joys of learning, he dismissed her request as "not necessary at this time."

However, being true to her name and not ready to abandon her noble cause to save the ROOM OF LEARNING, Princess Perseverance summoned to the palace the wisest man in all the Kingdom, Sir Davi.

And thus she spoke, saying, "Oh, Sir Davi, truly a great darkness has descended upon the KINGDOM OF MEDIA. No longer can the ROOM OF LEARNING exist with empty coffers. Please, kind Sir Davi, in all your wisdom tell me what can be done to once again restore the ROOM OF LEARNING to its full glory."

And Sir Davi thought mightily and spoke many phrases, for indeed having gained much wisdom at a recent media convention he was much learned and could quote from memory the number of sprockets and wheels in every projector in the land. But alas, he could not tell the Princess how to restore the ROOM OF LEARNING.

And so, the once happy and gay Princess dwelt in the depths of gloom and the people of the KINGDOM OF MEDIA did much crying and sighing and knew great sorrow (in individually different ways, of course).

And this was the sad scene beheld by Prince [Masl] (spelled M. A. S. L.) as he entered the KINGDOM OF MEDIA

much wearied from his travels throughout the LAND OF
PENURY in search of a maiden of both beauty and learning.
In truth, these qualities seemed sadly lacking in the female
half of the LAND OF PENURY, for King Slackwell, having
no need for knowledge of his own, had not encouraged its
development in others.

Beholding the fair Princess Perseverance in the depths
of the doldrums Prince [Masl] immediately inquired of her
difficulty.   Upon hearing of the plight of the KINGDOM OF
MEDIA he spoke to the Princess thusly:

"Fear not, dear princess, for together we shall save
the kingdom.   I bring thee the long awaited and joyous news
that King Slackwell has of recent days been deposed.   Thus
together you and I shall approach the gates of the LAND OF
PENURY and shall hold council with the ruling body (for are
they not in essence, reasonable men?) and they shall see
the need for the ROOM OF LEARNING and the coffers shall
be opened and knowledge found in full measure throughout
the kingdom once again. "

And that, dear librarians, is exactly what they did,
for the members of the ruling council of the LAND OF
PENURY had also individual differences which needed caring
for, and so established most wondrous ROOMS OF LEARN-
ING in every kingdom in the land.   And thus is the LAND
OF PENURY known in this day by its new name, THE LAND
OF IMCAWC, which translated means, THE LAND OF IN-
STRUCTIONAL MATERIALS CENTERS ALL WITH CLERKS.

And as for Princess Perseverance and Prince [Masl]
it is predicted throughout the land that their marriage shall
be a long and happy one, and that their children shall be as
individually different as royal progeny can be.   THE END.

DO YOU NOT ALSO WISH TO IMPROVE YOUR
ROOMS OF LEARNING??? IF SO, JOIN M. A. S. L.
AND TOGETHER WE CAN PRESENT OUR NEEDS
TO THE RULING BODY OF OUR STATE AND
PERHAPS BECOME THE LAND OF IMCAWC!

8. THE NATIONAL LIBRARY/MEDIA CONFERENCE

Planning for a library or media conference on the national level encompasses many problems not found in local, regional or state conference planning. Not the least of these is the problem of communication. The national conference must, of necessity, be broader in scope than the state or regional conference in order to provide for the wide diversity of interests and programs served by the national organization. Thus, members of a planning committee serving at the national level are widely separated geographically and keeping lines of communication open between them is no easy task.

For the purpose of illustrating the problems and rewards involved in national conference planning, the case study which follows describes the planning and implementation of a portion of the national conference in the American Library Association which was held in Chicago, Illinois in June 1972. Information on the conference planning activities is taken from the notes and working papers of Jean Coleman, Director of Educational Media, Hammond Public Schools, Hammond, Indiana and Chairman of the American Library Association Committee on Instruction in the Use of Libraries.[1]

Planning the National Conference Theme

The selection of a theme or program for a total conference or for any portion of that conference must be more than an exercise in semantics if it is to be of real value to conference participants. The basic criteria for conference planning hold true for the national conference just as for the

---

[1]With permission of Jean Coleman and Andrew Hansen, Reference and Adult Services Division, American Library Association.

local and state conference.   Conference activities must be
designed to meet the felt or expressed needs of participants.

The ALA Committee on Instruction in the Use of Libraries responded to the needs expressed by participants at
earlier conferences for demonstrations of the use of media
in library instruction.   While specific goals and details of
the proposed clinic on the use of media in such instruction
remained to be worked out in the first planning committee
meeting, the committee as a whole developed the following
basic conference objective:

Show and Tell, A Clinic on Using Media in Library
Instruction Conference Objective: To bring the media and the
problems ALA members have on library instruction together
in one room with opportunity for members to have "hands
on" experience with the media developed on instruction.
Members will thus have the opportunity to try out the media
in their area of concern and at the same time have access
to consultants from the library field for advice.

Planning for the "Show and Tell" clinic began one full
year before the actual conference.   During the initial planning meeting committee members discussed at length the
basic goals of the clinic.   It is important in any planning
committee, and particularly in a committee whose members
are widely separated geographically, that goals be set and
understood at the outset, so that all efforts are channeled in
the same direction.   A planning committee of eight members
was established, a number considered not too large to present massive communication problems, and yet large enough
to represent diverse interests.

During the initial planning meeting, responsibilities
were assigned to each committee member.   These responsibilities were as follows:

1.   Conference Chairman - Jean Coleman

    Set up arrangements with the American Library Associa-
        tion
    Handle all arrangements for local conference facilities
    Contact firms for loan of equipment
    Handle publicity
    Coordinate all conference planning
    Supervise actual conference activities during the two-day
        conference.

2. Commercial Exhibits - Mrs. Vergie Cox, Department of
                          Public Instruction, Raleigh,
                          North Carolina

    Contact commercial companies producing materials in
       the area of instruction in the use of libraries.
    Screen commercial media in the field.
    Select commercial media to be included in the clinic.

3. Consultants - Mrs. Hannelore Rader, Eastern Michigan
                  Univ.

    Identify and contact consultants in the field of instruction
       and in the use of libraries at the elementary, second-
       ary and college level.
    Make initial contact with consultants.
    Set up a schedule for consultant activities.

4. Floor Manager - John Lubans, Jr., University of Colo-
                    rado Library

    Assist the chairman with general conference arrange-
       ments.
    Be on hand during the two day conference to assist ex-
       hibitors in setting up and dismantling exhibits, assign-
       ing space, directing visitors and acting as general
       trouble shooter during the conference.

5. Exhibit contacts and catalogs - Mary Jo Lynch, Univer-
                                    sity of Michigan Libraries

    Identify and contact educational institutions wishing to
       exhibit.
    Develop an annotated catalog of exhibitors, consultants,
       and conference activities.
    Develop a feedback sheet for information.

6. Planning Assistant - Fr. Jovian Lang, liaison with the
                         Catholic Library Association

    On hand to assist wherever needed during the conference.

7. Floor assistant - Tom Kirk, Chairman of ACRL

    Assist in setting up and tearing down the clinic.

8. Warehouse Manager - Roy Marks, Chairman JCLS

    Work on warehouse items during the conference.

        Following the setting of goals and assignment of re-
sponsibilities to committee members, the chairman next explored the problems and implications for budget needs with
staff members of the American Library Association.   During
these meetings the actual requirements of such a clinic were
explored in depth.   Because a clinic with hands-on experience with the media in all formats (film, transparencies,
slide-tape, video, computer), would require considerable
equipment, space and time, an adequate working budget had
to be established.   It was determined that a large block of
time would need to be set aside in the total conference program so that librarians and media personnel could drop in
to the clinic at any time and stay for as long as they liked.
It would be necessary to run programs continuously for those
in attendance and to provide consultant service during all
open hours of the clinic.   By February, 1972 a complete
program description and list of educational exhibitors was
developed and submitted to the American Library Association.   Copies of this material follow.

TENTATIVE PROGRAM   Return two (2) copies to:
COPY FOR MAY 1972   Mary Cilluffo
"AMERICAN LIBRARIES"   ALA Conference Arrange-
                                     ments Office
Copy due: 50 E. Huron Street
BY FEBRUARY 23   Chicago, Illinois 60611

Name of group(s) presenting program: ALA Committee on
    Instruction in Use of Libraries. Joint sponsorship:
    JCLS AND ACRL.

Day, date, hour of meeting: Wednesday, June 28, 8:30pm -
    10:30pm; Thurs., June 29, 8:30am - 11:30am.

Name & professional address of chairman of group: Jean A.
    Coleman, Director Educational Media Center, Hammond
    Public Schools, 3750 E. 169th St., Hammond, Indiana
    46323.

Name & professional address of presiding officer of meeting

if different than chairman_____

Overall program theme (if any): Media can solve problems
in how to use a library and it can stimulate use.

Program objective(s): To bring the media & the problems
   ALA members have on library instruction together in one
   room with opportunity for members to have 'hands on' experience with the media developed on instruction. Members will thus have opportunity to try out the media in
   their area of concern & at the same time to have access
   to consultants from the library field for advice.

Give details of program below and continue on other side, if
necessary. If individual speakers, give full names and professional addresses and titles of papers. If panel discussion,
give full names and professional addresses of moderator and
panel members, also topic for discussion; if panel members
will present individual papers, give titles. In the case of
meal meetings where tickets will be required, be sure to indicate if tickets will be sold by advance reservation (usually
required for events on Monday and earlier) or from the ALA
Central Ticket Desk; if by advance reservation specify who
shall receive requests and/or ticket payment.

"Show & Tell" - A clinic on the media in library instruction for public, school & academic librarians to upgrade
the quality of instruction.

If you believe nothing turns off your library user more
than the frustration of seeking & not locating information,
then this clinic is for you. See how other librarians
have improved their communication through the tapes,
slides, etc. we've brought together. Can you squeeze
only 20 minutes for some practical help? We'll have
continuous showing Wednesday night & Thursday morning.
Pick up a catalog listing of the media. Stay as long as
you like. We'll run the program for you, or better yet,
get 'hands on' experience by trying them yourself. Compare one with the other.

Every hour we'll have nationally known librarians from every
field there to talk with you about your problems. How do
you structure information for the disadvantaged? How difficult is it really to shoot an 8mm film? To do a video tape?
Where do I start? Do you have to have a studio? What's
the best way to explain a handbook? Ask about costs.

Sharp & sustained interest in this subject has been shown by the profession throughout the year & at the '70 & '71 conferences. We've talked about goals, how to improve instruction, and had innovative position papers presented. With the conference theme as media this year we are no longer talking, but going all the way with media. The clinic is designed to give librarians from all fields an opportunity to diagnose their problems with library leaders and examine media in instruction. The clinic will therefore:

be easily accessible   stimulate libraries to use
                                     media in all formats for
afford comparison of   instruction
media

enable librarians to
evaluate media

Determining Budget Needs

Budget requests must be based on the basic goals of the conference. Those charged with the responsibility for determining budget allocations to numerous planning committees within a national organization must be given as much information as possible. A budget request should include the following:

1) Basic objectives or goals of the conference

2) Documentation of the need for such a conference

3) The specific audience for whom the conference is intended

4) The estimated size of the audience

5) Estimated expenses to be incurred including rental of conference facilities, equipment, union operators if needed, electricity and/or other utilities, publicity and other printing costs, security if needed, supplies, transportation, fees for consultants, speakers, etc.

The budget statement and request submitted to the ALA Budget Committee by Jean Coleman is reproduced here in its entirety. A study of the statement will reveal the myriad

ALA - Committee on Library Use Instruction Exhibit
June 28, 29 - Hilton, Chicago

Name of School & Program & Contact	Form	Equipment	Screen	Wall Plug	Telephone
1) Univ. of Denver (CALUI) Patricia Culkin	CAI+(Paper)	Burroughs to supply	--	Yes	Yes
2) Brigham Young University (not verified) Marvin E. Wiggins, tour + catalog use handbook	Cassette- program inst.	Cassette player	--	Yes	--
3) Western New Mexico Univ. Edward C. Werner (video) (not prep'd yet)	Video tape	Video player	--	Yes	--
4) Univ. of Alaska. Lib. skills Program - (self paced program) Millicent B. Hering	Paper	--	--	--	--
5) Univ. of Calif. Irvine (cassette) tape tour) Margaret Kahn (not verified)	Cassette	Cassette player	--	Yes	--
6) Univ. of Colo., Boulder film loop on Readers' Guide. J. Lubans. also programmed lib. use instr. Carol Cushman	Film loop paper	Rear view projector (or will bring one)	--	Yes	--
7) Univ. of Oregon. Slide/tape how to R. R. McCready, (not verified)	Slide/tape	Carousel-tape player	Yes	Yes Yes	--

Name of School & Program & Contact	Form	Equipment	Screen	Wall Plug	Telephone
8) Ohio State Univ. (CALUI) Alice S. Clark - to be contacted by Jean Coleman	CAI	they furnish terminal	--	Yes	Yes
9) MIT (point of interest) Charles Stevens (contact re definite)	Tape/slide (Pathfinders)	Enclosed unit compact	--	Yes	--
10) Brown Univ. guides, Connie Evrard (not definite)	Guides to collection (paper)	--	--	--	--
11) Colo. State Univ. (tape slide point of use) Dick Stevens (verified)	Tape slide video?	Enclosed unit/ compact video player	No	Yes Yes	--
12) Earlham College (bibs & trans) Tom Kirk (not verified but confirmed to Jean Coleman)	Paper transper	Overhead projector	Yes	Yes	--
13) Hofstra Univ. sound & color film ? of avail. may show through commercial outfit	Motion pic. film	Projector 16mm? with sound	Yes	Yes	--
14) Univ. of Western Ontario - Video-Tape on the library business (30 min.)	Video-tape	Video player	--	Yes	--
15) Miami-Dade Junior College slide/tape on research paper	Slide/tape	Slide Projector & cassettes ?	Yes	Yes	--

Name of School & Program & Contact	Form	Equipment	Screen	Wall Plug	Telephone
16) Prince George's Community College. Tape slide workbook tape/slide library tour, super 8 film loop program for periodical literature & microfilm.	Slide/tape super 8 loop	Kodak Carousel slide projector Wollensak Model 2550 cassette player, Super 8 projector for loop	Yes Yes Yes	Yes Yes Yes	--
17) University of Missouri slide tape orientation program	Slide/tape	3M-Manufacter projector/recorder	Yes	Yes Yes	--
18) SUNY-Plattsburgh Cassettes for indexes, etc.	Cassettes	Bring own	--	Yes	--
19) Penn State - slide-tape orientation	Slide/tape	Kodak Carousel slide projector Wollensak 2550 AV slide sync. Cassette player	Yes	Yes Yes	--
20) Tarrent County Junior College tape & programmed text for library instruction	Sound tape player - paper	Can bring own	--	Yes	--
21) Greenwich Public School Media Center - video tapes (Mrs. McCauley) ? of transp. + super 8 loop	Video tape	Video player	--	Yes	--

Name of School & Program & Contact	Form	Equipment	Screen	Wall Plug	Telephone
22) UCLA - minority library skills package. Mimi Dudley	Paper	--	--	--	--
23) Portland Public Schools (Media?) Ms. Sayles	Slide/tape	Slide projector and cassette player	Yes	Yes / Yes	--
24) William Rainey Harper College video tape on library (Ms. Rupar)	Video tape	Ampex - 1 player	--	Yes	--
25) Elmira College, 2 tape/slide of personnel, etc. programs Mr. Fenton	Slide/tape	Slide projector and tape player	Yes	Yes / Yes	--
26) Pattonville R-3 School District - St. Louis County, Mo. Mrs. Pollette (variety)	Hand puppet, recorder, transper.	Cassette over head	-- / Yes	Yes / Yes	--
27) North Dakota State Univ. (Mr. Miller)	tape/slide film strip cassette tour	Slide projector film strip proj. cassette player	Yes / Yes	Yes / Yes / Yes	--
28) Mrs. Murrey (transp. on monthly cat.)	Transp.	Overhead proj.	Yes	Yes	--
29) Mrs. Kay Brown Purdue Univ.	?				
30) Ms. Palmer - tape/slide	Tape/slide	Slide proj.	Yes	Yes	--

Name of School & Program & Contact	Form	Equipment	Screen	Wall Plug	Telephone
transp.	Transp.	tape player, overhead proj.	Yes Yes	Yes Yes	- -
31) Ms. Melum	Tape slide/film	Bring own?	Yes Yes	- -	- -
32) Mr. Sellmer, Nora Element. School	Prog. text	Paper	- -	- -	- -
33) Mrs. Gilmore, Michigan State Library, slide/tape	Slide/tape	Slide proj./tape player	Yes	Yes Yes	- -
34) Dartmouth College Library, sound on slide presen. (3M) cassette tour	Sound on slide Cassette tour	3M sound on slide proj. cassette player	Yes	Yes Yes	- -
35) Dept. of School Libs. (Mich) Ms. Nickel, 8mm film, transp.	8mm Trans.	8mm projector overhead proj.	Yes Yes	Yes Yes	- -
36) Glen Ellyn Jr. High School Mrs. Rife. Video tape, slide tape	Video tape/slide tape	Video player Ampex 1", slide projector, tape player	- -	Yes	- -
37) David Lipscomb College Mr. Ward slide/tape	Tape/slide	Slide projector Cassette player	Yes	Yes Yes	- -
			25	51	

details involved in conference planning.

TO: Warncke, Ruth   FROM: Coleman, Jean.   Chairman

Estimated budget--ALA Committee Instruction in the use of
            libraries Clinic on the media (on the basic
            schedule of program meetings for 72 con-
            ference)

            Hours: Wednesday - 8:30-10:30 PM
                     Thursday - 8:30-11:30 AM

Objective: To bring the media and the problems ALA mem-
            bers have on library instruction together in one
            room with opportunity for members to have "hands
            on" experience with the media developed on in-
            struction and access to experienced consultants.

This meeting builds on the experience of the committee at
the '70 and '71 conference under the chairmanship of Helen
Brown, Wellesley, Mass.   Feedback from the presentation
and panel discussion of '70 and the ten round tables of '71
definitely pinpointed the need for a major showing of the
media in order to acquaint the membership and upgrade instruction.   In '70 and '71 the meetings were limited for attendance and were always oversubscribed.   The large block
of time will allow greater attendance and accommodates the
unstructured format of the meeting.

Attendance: ACRL and AASL are the major audience, with
             some from public library field and some from
             special.   Frances Hatfield of AASL and Tom
             Kirk of ACRL estimate a total of 500.

Budget total: Mary Cilluffo believes the cost of the SRRT
               presentation at COBO Hall in '70 was $1400.00.
               25 machines were rented for a multi-media
               presentation, electrical cost for the machines
               she thinks was $400 of the total.

               This cost may be compared with the tentative
               information that follows for implications for
               cost for the media clinic.

Breakdown of tentative cost items for the clinic:

EQUIPMENT

> 75 exhibits are confirmed (in various formats)
>> 25 are commercial - ALA will not have to provide equipment for these
>> 6 are print - no equipment needed
>> 2 computor exhibits will be provided by Ohio State University and U. of Denver - no equipment from ALA

Need for equipment breaks down as follows:

Program	Minimum Equipment to Handle	Real Need
19 slide-tape; 5 tape only; 1 slide only	3 programs per 1 machine would be: 8 slide proj. (carousel & cartridge, not single)	12
	plus 4 reel to reel tape recorders capable of synchronizing with slide projector for automatic showing	6
	plus 4 cassette battery operated recorders or playback units	6
5 transparency sets	2 overheads	3 overheads
4 video tape	1 Amplex 1" monitor plus recorder 1 IVC 1" monitor plus recorder	if necessary we will contact AMPEX and IVC about this equipment on loan for clinic
1 super 8mm loop (Technicolor)	1 super 8mm loop (Technicolor) projector	
1 super 8mm film	1 super 8mm film projector	

2 phone lines in room to accommodate the 2 computor terminals (cost of installation and line time to be paid by exhibitor)

3-5 tripod screens, with ordinary poster board (see supplies) utilized on wall for the numerous slide-tape presentations.

ELECTRICITY

A separate outlet needed for each of the machines rented by
ALA requiring power, (only battery op. cassettes will not
need outlet) plus 1 outlet each for the 2 computor terminals,
plus a minimum of ten additional outlets to accommodate the
25 commercial exhibitors bringing their own equipment.

Wiring and outlets need to be over rather than under mini-
mun if participants are not to be frustrated waiting for machines.

UNION MEN

To cover ALA obligations for equipment ALA provides.
        Wed. night   8:30-10:30
        Thurs. AM   8:30-11:30
        to plug in the above equipment initially and unplug
        after the clinic
It is our understanding that ALA has a rule of thumb with
the Union on % of manpower needed.

CATALOG - offset press at ALA.   Typed in machine ready
            format by Committee (Mary Jo Lynch)

        Approx. 30 pages 8-1/2 X 11 stapled together
        # of copies - 500

Turn in to Delores Vaughn at headquarters by May 8 (our
liason)

Cost-Committee has been unable to find out at Mid-winter
who specific approx. cost of this.   Or who determines exact
format (which affects cost).

        #Includes exhibits with annotation, indexed by subject,
        list of consultants, feedback sheet for ALA.

SECURITY

Cilluffo recommends change of locks before and during the
        clinic on the room assigned to increase security for
        all the equipment.   It will be locked up overnight.

Committee members will have only keys (?).

Insurance - does the regular ALA coverage on equipment
    cover the added expense to cover possible loss of
    equipment rented - equipment loaned by exhibitors.
    ALA must be sufficiently covered for this large amount
    of equipment.

Security Guard - The committee, ACRL members assigned
    and others from ALA will circulate during the clinic--
    but only ALA knows if a guard in this case is neces-
    sary.

SUPPLIES

This ALA committee has no budget at all this year.   We
have absorbed all our considerable expense from August to
Mid-winter.

For the conference we will need:
    ordinary white posterboard to serve as temporary
        viewing screens plus masking tape to attach to wall.
        Posterboard needs to be approx. 3 ft. wide.
    pencils - 50 at least for participants to mark feed-
        back
    postage - 150 8 cent postal cards to mimeograph to
        send to exhibitors and consultants just before con-
        ference.
    phone calls - committee on arrangements for confer-
        ence.

Will $25.00 do the above?   All exhibitors (ALA members
and commercial people) will be responsible for getting media
to the clinic and picking it up so there will be no charge on
that.

However, Charles Stevens of Project Intrex at MIT has asked
for special consideration on shipping some innovative items
in point of use to the clinic.   We have asked but not received an answer to the advisability of making an exception
in his case--Apparently we will not have them if the shipping
is not covered.   He has submitted no budget amount for an
estimate.

The above is as definite as we can make at present.   May
we notify Cilluffo of a change in equipment up to March 1 if
further correspondence with exhibitor reveals need to do so

(for example, a specific brand name required or need for 2
loop projectors instead of 1 loop and 1 regular 8mm proj.).

SIZE OF ROOM - a room for 500?

> Tables cannot be placed too close together, there
> must be plenty of room to gather around a viewing
> area.

> Tables needed - 40 to handle 75 items, plus ALA
> Committee staff, consultants, ACRL committee.

> Chairs - 100

Set up - Committee and ACRL committee on instruction will
work in room 3 hours before clinic and 3 hours after. 2
computers will have to be installed and taken down in that
time.

The arrangements of this clinic in the room and the use of
the room for Wed. night and Thurs. AM should be likened
to the ALA exhibitors' hall--on a smaller scale with consultants available.

We have contacted all library associations, all state
dept.'s of education, all innovators known to us, previous
participants in the '70 and '71 conference for exhibits in
order to have as much variety in format as possible for
ALA members.

Locating Conference Participants

The task of locating a wide range of media programs
centering around the area of instruction in the use of libraries was not an easy one. Not only was it desirable in
a national conference to have all levels of library instruction
represented, but programs from a wide geographic area
were desired. In order to identify such programs the following steps were taken:

1. Publicity releases were prepared for American Libraries,
    Library Journal, Wilson Library Bulletin, The Catholic
    Library Association, Top of the News, School Libraries,
    and College and Research Libraries News. The an-
    nouncement asked for media programs developed by
    members in their respective educational or academic

areas and gave full information concerning the procedure
to be followed to present an exhibit.

2. The committee also contacted all state library associa-
    tions, all state departments of education, previous par-
    ticipants in the committee's '70 and '71 conference
    meetings, and all innovative projects referred to the
    committee in order to give as broad a coverage in for-
    mat as possible.

3. Additional exhibits, consultants and assistance during the
    conference were forthcoming from other divisions of
    ALA, (AASL, JCLS, and ACRL) who agreed to joint
    sponsorship of the clinic.

Preparation of the Clinic Catalog and Evaluative Forms

It was determined by the committee that each visitor
to the clinic should receive a catalog describing each exhibit
in detail. The catalog would be annotated and indexed to
provide a valuable reference source for some time to come
concerning programs on the use of media in library instruction. Compiled by Mary Jo Lynch, the catalog was entitled:
Show and Tell, Exhibits and Consultants for the Show and
Tell Clinic on the Use of Media in Library Instruction.
Components of the catalog were as follows:

1. Materials Prepared by School Librarians
    Including the name and mailing address of the in-
    stitution and a full description of five programs.

2. Materials Prepared by Academic Librarians
    Including the name and address of the institution
    and a full description of 28 programs.

3. Materials Prepared by Other Librarians and by
    State Departments of Education
    Including the name and address of the institution
    and a full description of 4 programs.

4. Materials Prepared by Commercial Firms
    Including a full description of the type and cost of
    the material and name of producer.

5. A List on Consultants
    Including the name and address of each consultant,
    present position and accomplishments in the field

of library science.

6. Consultants on Video Tape
    Including name, address and qualifications of con-
    sultants specializing in this area.

7. Appendixes
    Members of the ACRL Junior College Library
    Section Instruction and Use Committee

    Members of the ACRL Ad Hoc Committee on Bib-
    liographic Instruction

    Firms loaning equipment to the clinic

    Academic Libraries, not listed in the body of the
    catalog, which use nonprint materials in orienta-
    tion programs.

Publicity

Publicity for the clinic began early in the fall of 1971
with the notice in all standard library periodicals calling for
media programs. Additional publicity releases including a
full description of the clinic were prepared in the style and
format of individual library periodicals and submitted for
publication in the spring.

The importance of early submission of publicity releases to the news media cannot be overemphasized. Professional journals and news media for the general public
have deadlines which must be met. The early submission
of news releases will often determine whether or not the
news item appears by a desired date. The following news
release was developed by the committee:

"Show & Tell" - A clinic on the media in library
instruction for public, school & academic libraries
to upgrade the quality of instruction.

If you believe nothing turns off your library user
more than the frustration of seeking & not locating
information, then this clinic is for you. See how
other librarians have improved their communication
through the tapes, slides, etc. we've brought together. Can you squeeze only 20 minutes for some
practical help? We'll have continuous showing

Wednesday night & Thursday morning. Pick up a
catalog listing of the media. Stay as long as you
like. We'll run the program for you, or better
yet, get 'hands on' experience by trying them
yourself. Compare one with the other.

Every hour we'll have nationally known librarians
from every field there to talk with you about your
problems. How do you structure information for
the disadvantaged? How difficult is it really to
shoot an 8mm film? To do a video tape? Where
do I start? Do you have to have a studio? What's
the best way to explain a handbook? Ask about
costs.

Sharp & sustained interest in this subject has been
shown by the profession throughout the year & at
the '70 & '71 conferences. We've talked about
goals, how to improve instruction, and had innovative position papers presented. With the conference theme as media this year we are no longer
talking, but going all the way with media. The
clinic is designed to give librarians from all fields
an opportunity to diagnose their problems with consultants qualified in the field.

Handling the Mechanics of the Conference

The conference chairman, most members of the committee, and willing personnel from other divisions of ALA
were on hand throughout the conference to assure a smooth-
running operation. In order to avoid last minute confusion,
instruction sheets giving full procedures for display of materials and full directions to commercial firms and educational consultants were mailed to each participant six weeks
before the conference. This six-week time span allowed participants who had any question about procedure to contact
Floor Manager Lubens with their questions and problems.

Special tags were printed and were attached immediately to arriving exhibits. Each exhibitor was given a
claim check for materials in his exhibit and at the close of
the conference materials could be removed only when the
claim check was produced or proof of ownership made available.

While exhibitors were assisted by the floor manager

and his assistants in setting up exhibits, consultants were greeted by Ms. Rader and given full instructions concerning their role in the conference. Specific times for consultants to be on hand were assigned well in advance of the conference. Many of the consultant sessions were taped for future listening by students of library science.

PART V

THE COLLEGE OR UNIVERSITY
LIBRARY/MEDIA PROGRAM

9. COLLEGE AND UNIVERSITY PROGRAMS

The In-Service Role of Higher Education

In planning in-service training programs for teachers, administrators, and library-media personnel, staff members of colleges and universities must wear two hats. They must be both leaders and followers. The role of leader in educational innovation has long been recognized as a basic function of the college community. The role of follower is one which has more recently emerged in this era of relevance and responsiveness to both the stated and implied needs of educators.

The demands placed on the college or university through the exercise of this dual role are great. The stereotyped image of the professor in the ivory tower is no longer valid (if, indeed, it ever was). Higher education has opened its doors and expanded its campuses to the nation, the state, and the community, to determine and meet existing needs and to assist educational leaders in acquiring a growing awareness of future needs. In this age of McLuhan's "Information Implosion" and Toffler's "Future Shock" the transmission of new methods and materials to those working in the library/media field must be a prime responsibility of higher education. At the same time, helping educators to gain expertise in the use of more standard methods and materials must not be overlooked. What was once the slow process of transmitting research into practical applicability has now become a rapid transmission of theory into practice. The quandary of educators grows daily as they are besieged with new programs and materials. It is, therefore, the responsibility of those in higher education to assist teachers, administrators and library/media personnel to make choices based on specific needs within a school system or community, and to point the way toward practical, economical and successful educational innovation.

College and university programs in library/media in-service training generally fall into three categories: 1) programs which respond to new legislation within a state, 2) programs which respond to new theories or materials in educational innovation, and 3) programs to assist educators in more meaningful utilization of current materials and services. The length, type and format of in-service programs within these three major areas can vary greatly, but regardless of the specific type of in-service activity, a basic model for the planning of such programs can be followed.

In-Service: A Basic Model for Effective Programs

1. Determination of the general school or community educational need:

    A. By state legislation
    B. Through communication from educators
    C. From examination of deficiencies in the educational field
    D. From the emergence of innovative plans in education
    E. From requirements of community action programs

2. Establishment of the in-service committee

    A. Members of the college/university staff
    B. Members of the State Department of Education
    C. Local educators
    D. Community leaders
    E. Prospective students

3. Development of survey instruments to determine specific needs

    A. Questionnaires
    B. Letters
    C. Small group discussion meetings

4. Development of Basic Goals and Objectives

    A. Basic goal of the workshop, course or conference
    B. Specific objectives
    C. Behavioral objectives

5. Planning program details

    A. For whom is the activity planned?   How many?
    B. Length of the program
    C. Date(s) and time
    D. Place
    E. Type of credit to be given
    F. Equipment needed
    G. Printed materials needed
    H. Staff members needed
    I. Amount of clerical assistance required
    J. Publicity for the program
    K. Cost of the program
        1. To the college or university
        2. To the participant

6. The In-Service Program

    A. Organization
        1. Large group meetings
        2. Small group meetings
        3. Workshops
        4. Laboratories
        5. Self instruction

    B. Instructional techniques
        1. Lectures
        2. Media demonstrations
        3. Student materials production
        4. Seminars
        5. Independent study
        6. Other

7. Evaluation

    A. Formal tests
    B. Questionnaires
    C. Student/teacher self evaluation
    D. Reports

     To illustrate the manner in which both large univer-
sities and small colleges are responding to educational needs
in the library-media field (both nationally and locally), several program models have been selected.   Each model included
is noteworthy for the careful planning involved in its implementation and the subsequent success of the programs in
meeting basic goals and objectives.

Programs Which Respond to New Legislation

EXAMPLE (1)

Workshop Title: LIBRARY AND INFORMATION SERVICES
FOR PRISON POPULATIONS

Sponsor: University of California, Santa Cruz.

Date(s):   2-day workshop - Summer, 1972.

Participants: All persons concerned about this area--leg-
                  islators, legislative staff, prison adminis-
                  trators, institution librarians and others in
                  the state or county governments whose con-
                  cerns include prisons.

Basic Need: Recent California legislation requiring that
                  inmates have access to law libraries makes
                  more urgent a problem already recognized
                  as important to our institutions and our so-
                  ciety.

Outline of the Program:

1. The Prison Library
    A. Its mission
    B. Its position in the prison system

2. Access of Inmates to the Library
    A. The problem
    B. Realistic access methods

3. Acquisitions
    A. Positive and negative aspects
    B. Other special problems

4. Multi-media Possibilities
    A. In general
    B. As an approach to language and literacy problems

5. Legal Reference Materials
   A. Need
   B. Legislation
   C. What materials

6. The "Post-release" Problem
   A. Its nature and scope
   B. Relation to the library's potential for assistance to the inmate

7. The Librarians
   A. Need for capable, mature, understanding people
   B. Types of suitable training
   C. Recruitment

8. Sources of Funding
   A. Public
   B. Private

EXAMPLE (2)

Program Title: INSTITUTE ON CABLE COMMUNICATIONS FOR LIBRARIANS

Sponsor: Drexel University, Philadelphia, Pennsylvania.

Dates: Three days--Fall, 1972.

Participants: Librarians from large cities where cablecasting can be utilized for outreach and special community programs and to state library personnel interested in conducting their own institute on cable communications.

Basic Need: In response to the expressed interest of many librarians in cable communications and to the growing need for local legislative decision making in granting cable communications franchises.

Content of the Program:

1. An address by a member of the Federal Communications Commission on the status and future of cable communications for the people.

2. A mini-workshop providing "hands on" experience with equipment.

3. A summary and practical consideration of recent FCC regulations and their effect on local franchising activities.

4. A panel of active cable-casters who shared their experiences.

5. A demonstration of a 2-way interactive cable system operational in Virginia.

6. A "how-to-do-it" presentation on local involvement in franchising activities.

7. A viewing of videotapes made for cable casting to local community rooms.

8. Small group discussions with experienced resource people on topics of interest to participants.

9. An information packet containing a cable primer, model ordinances and franchises, sample testimony and plans by communities for use of public access cable channels, and an annotated bibliography.

10. A videotape simulation of a "real" situation involving a city council negotiating with a cable operator and community groups.

Programs Which Respond to Emerging Needs

Emerging needs in the library/media field are numerous and ever-changing, and colleges and universities must be alert to them if they are to be met. One of the most pressing needs which media supervisors are attempting to meet within their own educational communities is the development of managerial skills. Robert Foley, Director of Media and Materials for the Cedar Rapids Community Schools (Iowa), defines the need and his District's attempts to meet the need in this manner:[1]

> Currently, we are concentrating on developing district managerial skills in our media staff. Since a manager is, by definition, any person who makes decisions which affect the allocation of resources, and who can be held accountable for results, we feel our people need the skills to function effectively in a managerial capacity. Our program this year consists of nine major sessions, each with pre-work, assigned readings, and tasks related to the subject at hand. These sessions are: Opportunities versus Non-Productive Activities, Effective Decisions, Managing Time, What is My Contribution, Staffing for Strength, Control and Coordination, Analyzing Performance Problems, Goal Setting and Priorities and Communications.

Realizing that the need for development of managerial skills on the part of library/media personnel is not a problem unique to any one educational community, numerous colleges are now responding by developing institutes, short courses or workshops in this area. Two such programs are described here.

---

[1] Foley, Robert. "Staff Development & Utilization in Cedar Rapids Community Schools." District Bulletin. n.d.

EXAMPLE (3)

Program Title: DESIGN AND MANAGEMENT OF LEARNING
RESOURCES PROGRAMS

Sponsor: Indiana University, Bloomington, Indiana.

Dates: 2-day conference - Summer 1972.

Participants: Library/media supervisors, all levels of education.

Basic Need: To emphasize the design and management of
learning resources programs as an important
aspect of the audiovisual communications
area.

Content of the Program:

1. Management in Education
2. Management by Objectives - A Case Study Approach
3. Learning Resource Management - What and Why
4. An Architect's Perspective on Designing Innovative
   Instructional Spaces
5. Sound-Slide Reports of Learning Resource Centers
6. What Research Says About Facilities Design for Implementing Instruction and Promoting Learner Comfort
7. Focus on Materials, Resource, and Learning Centers
8. Cost, Benefits and Effectiveness: The Presumptive
   Ratio Problem.

EXAMPLE (4)

Program Title: CONTEMPORARY MANAGEMENT ISSUES
IN ACADEMIC LIBRARIES

Sponsor: University of California - Santa Cruz.

Dates: 2 days. Summer 1972.

Participants: Persons concerned with the planning and

operating of academic libraries. Administrators, department heads, and branch librarians with university, college and community college libraries.

Basic Need: In response to stated needs of academic librarians concerning the development of managerial skills.

Content of the Program:

1. Program Planning and Forecasting
    A. The institutional framework
    B. How to plan
    C. Who is involved
    D. What studies for what purposes

2. Student Relations with the Library
    A. Policies on access
    B. Security of collections
    C. Handling of disruptions
    D. Fees for use by outsiders

3. Branch Libraries
    A. Rationale
    B. Types of branches
    C. Geographic dispersions
    D. Service designs
    E. Financial support

4. Recent Personnel Developments
    A. Affirmative-action programs
    B. Unions
    C. Status of librarians
    D. Professional staff development
    E. Staff participation in decision making

5. Automation of Technical Operations: Why, Where,
    How, When, With Whom

6. Data Base Services
    A. Justification
    B. How to integrate them into the academic insti-
        tution
    C. Who is responsible for what
    D. Achieving the service fiscally and administra-
        tively

7. Cooperatives and Consortia
   A. Purposes and types
   B. Organizations, financing

8. Reduced Budgets and Austerity
   A. Methods of judging
   B. Staff participation
   C. "Selling" to the community

Other Emerging Issues in Education

      Foremost among emerging issues in education in the 1970s is increased emphasis on instructional design systems, mechanization and computerization of library technical processes, and the changing role of the librarian to that of media specialist. College and university training in these areas ranges from full degree programs to the short conference or workshop. The brief program descriptions which follow include samples of each type of training.

EXAMPLE (5)

Short Term Workshops on Instructional Design Systems

Workshop Title: MECHANIZATION OF LIBRARY/TECHNICAL PROCESSES

Sponsor: University of California - Santa Cruz.

Dates: 2-day workshop. Summer 1972.

Participants: Library administrators and system analysts with libraries of all types.

Basic Content: An overview of system analysis (what makes up a system) and system synthesis (putting it together) applied to libraries, and where and how mechanization is and may be applicable.

Topics: 1. Data Processing
    A. Hardware and software

B.   General considerations
C.   Formal and record structures
D.   Data files
E.   File management systems

2.   Acquisitions
A.   State of the art
B.   Case studies

3.   Book Catalogs
A.   State of the art
B.   Case studies of some major systems

4.   Cataloging
A.   Case studies
B.   Local and central card production
processing methods

5.   Circulation: State of the Art

6.   Serials: State of the Art, Selected
Case Studies

7.   On-Line Library Systems: State of the
Art

8.   Cost Analysis
A.   Techniques
B.   Forms
C.   Goal directed time-value-of-money
studies

EXAMPLE (6)

Instructional Design Short Courses

For more than a quarter of a century the Audio-
Visual Center of Indiana University at Bloomington has held
a series of annual conferences emphasizing an important aspect of the audiovisual communications area.   Each conference is approximately three days in length and major topics
stressed in recent years have centered around problems
arising in the field of instructional design.   The brief con-

ference descriptions which follow should provide some insight into the direction of change which is to come in library/media centers throughout the nation.

1968 Educational Media Conference

Topic: DESIGN FOR INSTRUCTIONAL DEVELOPMENT

Subtopics: 1. Conditions for successful development
            2. Case studies for instructional development
            3. Preparation for planners of instructional development
            4. Behavioral objectives and task analysis
            5. The use of network based management systems in curriculum project development

1969 Educational Media Conference

Topic: THE DIFFUSION AND ADOPTION OF TECHNOLOGICAL INNOVATION IN EDUCATION

Subtopics: 1. Strategies for innovation
            2. Processes of diffusion-paradigms and models
            3. Diffusion technology related to individually prescribed instruction
            4. The evaluation of diffusion strategies

1970 Educational Media Conference

Topic: EVALUATION IN INSTRUCTIONAL SYSTEMS TECHNOLOGY

Subtopics: 1. Overview of educational evaluation
            2. Empirical development of instructional materials
            3. Systems evaluation
            4. Case study reports on national evaluation projects
            5. Evaluation toward the future

1971 Educational Media Conference

Topic: THE DESIGN OF INSTRUCTION FOR THE DISADVANTAGED

Subtopics: 1. The role of the university in the education

of the disadvantaged
2. The disadvantaged learner in his cultural
   setting
3. Content and instructional strategies for the
   disadvantaged learner
4. Design of media for the disadvantaged
5. Accountability
6. Mississippi Headstart Program
7. Research on instruction for the disadvantaged

EXAMPLE (7)

Changing Programs in the Training of Library/Media Personnel

The 1969 Standards for School Media Programs helped
focus the attention of educators and library/media personnel
on the need for a new type of library/media person, one
trained in the selection, evaluation, organization and utilization of both print and nonprint materials. Higher education
has moved to meet the need for the training of new sources
of manpower and for retraining those in the field. The ra
tionale for the development of new graduate programs in li-
brary/media is stated in the University of Colorado media
program bulletin. It is reprinted here with the permission
of Otis McBride, Professor of Education.

> The library/media center program is designed to
> meet the needs of people in operating and super-
> vising the library-media service and in becoming
> a library-media director or specialist. This
> seems to be the field of fastest growth and most
> rapid development. With the demand for faster,
> greater teaching efforts at a time when schools
> are overflowing with too many eager young people,
> we are called on for such things as dial access,
> special disc recordings, tapes, films, computer-
> assisted instruction, ungraded classrooms, large
> group instruction, individualized instruction, pro-
> grammed learning, individual use of the library
> while the student directs his own program of study,
> and educational television in all its aspects. The
> person whose training equips him to develop and

direct this type of program is now being sought.
That person who can organize and operate a library-
media center which includes wet carrels (those
which have in them various types of electronic
equipment-dial access, recorders and recordings,
film, television, filmstrips and slides) is in constant demand; and greater need develops daily.

Among courses offered in the graduate library/media
center program at the University of Colorado are:

Requirements - 30 hour M. A. program

1. Field of Specialization: Librarianship and Educational
    Media.   Required courses:
    Educational Media: Theory and Practice
    Children's Literature
    Cataloging and Organization of School Library and
        Media Materials
    Literature for the Adolescent
    Production of Educational Materials
    Book and Other Media Selection for School Libraries
    School Reference Service
    Administration of Educational Media Programs

2. Suggestions for Electives:
    Reading in the Elementary School
    Television in Education
    Improving Reading Skills in Junior and Senior High
        School
    Elementary Statistics
    Advanced Psychological Foundations of Education
    Advanced Social Foundations of Education
    Programmed Learning
    Curriculum Construction
    Remedial Techniques in Reading
    Current Literature for Children
    Problems in Processing, Retrieval, and Handling of
        Materials in Today's Library
    Methods of Educational Research
    Seminar: Educational Media
    Internship in Educational Media
    Seminar in Children's Literature

The foregoing course listings are presented as an
example of the many new programs available in colleges and
universities throughout the country.   A check with one's lo-

cal college or university will probably reveal the initiation
or establishment of new programs in the training of library/
media personnel which offer many of the course areas listed.

Programs in Effective Utilization
of Current Materials and Services

Since school districts are continually seeking ways to
improve existing services or programs without expanding the
instructional budget, colleges and universities can play an
important role in helping educators to make the most of the
staff, programs, materials and services currently included
in school budgets. Increased knowledge on the part of li-
brary/media personnel can result in greater use of existing
facilities and materials by students and teachers. Summer
courses and conferences offered by institutions of higher
education, aimed at improving the current state of the art,
can be most valuable for those in attendance. The annual
Children's Literature Conference af Fort Hays Kansas State
College and a three-week workshop on "Nonprint Materials
as Learning Resources," sponsored by the Millersville
(Pennsylvania) State College, are good examples of this type
of training.

EXAMPLE (8)

Conference Title: CONFERENCE ON CHILDREN'S LITERA-
                    TURE

Sponsor: Fort Hays Kansas State College.

Dates: One week annually each summer.

Summary of the 1972 Conference:

        Donna Harsh, Conference Director, describes the con-
ference design in this manner:

        The conference is designed to acquaint teachers
        and librarians with recent trends in literature for
        children. Rather than choosing one theme and

301

structuring the whole conference around that topic,
I attempt to 'balance' the presentations by inviting
a picture book author, an author of realistic
stories, one who writes fantasy, someone involved
in poetry, a person who writes books for special
interests (i. e., sports), a folklore specialist,
someone well known in the curriculum area of
Reading and Literature, and some speakers outstanding in the field of media. One of the high-
lights of this year's (1972) conference was the
'strand' on new films for children. Don Freeman
added to this by bringing new films he had made.
Lee Bennett Hopkins brought new filmstrips he had
helped develop.

The Conference Program:

Monday   - Eleanor Cameron "The Power of High Fantasy"
             Gene Walsh "The Library on Sesame Street:
                Children's Literature and the Expanded
                Cinema"
             Marilyn Sachs "From Little Women to Synanon"
             Small group discussions with authors
             Films

Tuesday   - Marilyn Sachs "Does It Always Have to Hurt"
             James Giblin "Choosing Manuscripts and Work-
                ing with Authors and Illustrators"
             Eleanor Cameron "McLuhan, Youth and Litera-
                ture"
             Small group discussions with authors
             Films

Wednesday - Loula Erdman "On Writing"
             James Giblin "Genuine Trends or 'Trendy'
                Fads"
             Helen Francis "Producing Books on the High
                Plains"
             Group discussions with authors
             Films

Thursday   - Lee Bennett Hopkins "Pass the Poetry"
             Loula Erdman "An Added Bonus"
             Don Freeman "Windows of the Night"
             Small group discussions
             Films

Friday   - Lee Bennett Hopkins "The Seed is Growing
                Deep Inside"
              Don Freeman "The Storyteller"
              Evaluation of the Institute

EXAMPLE (9)

Workshop Title: WORKSHOP ON NON-PRINT MATERIALS
                  AS LEARNING RESOURCES

Sponsor: Millersville (Pennsylvania) State College.

Dates: Three weeks - Summer 1972.

Participants: Teachers, media specialists, A-V Directors,
                  librarians.

Purpose: To provide participants with an opportunity
                  to achieve familiarity with non-print ma-
                  terials and the appropriate equipment
                  needed to use them, in order to develop the
                  same expertise in this area as has been
                  achieved in the field of print materials.

Workshop Activities:

Participants were required to:

1. Do extensive reading and reporting in the area of
   non-print materials.

2. Evaluate at least 5 standard or super 8mm single
   concept loops and/or 8mm sound cartridges; 5 disc
   or tape recordings not connected with a filmstrip;
   10 filmstrips, sound or silent; 2 transparencies; 3
   from other media such as study prints, microforms,
   slides, kits, simulation games.

3. Prepare a cross media bibliography stating basis
   for selection or rejection of materials, scope of this
   subject, intended audience and special problems.

4. Complete a local production project which might be:
    mounting of a visual, lamination, lettering, poster,
    transparency, enlargement from microfilm, duplica-
    tion of slides, tape cassette.

The workshop was a three-credit graduate course with instructional sessions held each morning of the three-week
period and laboratory sessions in the afternoons. In addition to the workshop director, Minda M. Sanders, consultants
for local production, dial access and data processing were
available.

A Final Note on the Contributions of Higher Education
to Library/Media Training

        Staff members of colleges and universities assist in
ongoing in-service education of teachers, administrators and
library/media personnel in many ways in addition to direct
teaching activities. Through providing consultant services
to local districts, through published research, and through
many hours of service on state and national committees of
library/media organizations, members of library and education faculties serve as consultants independent of their academic commitment. An example in point is William Quinly,
Director of the Media Center, Florida State University, who,
as President of the Information Systems Division of AECT,
is concerned with information storage and retrieval, com-
puterized booking and cataloging, and the instructional program for those entering the media field. Wearing another
hat, as chairman of the AECT Nonbook Cataloging Committee, he helped to develop the much needed Standards for
Cataloging Nonprint Materials (AECT 1972). Mr. Quinly's
commitment to the field is duplicated by staff members in
universities and colleges throughout the nation. Through
their work and through the work of all dedicated library/med-
ia personnel, in-service activities will continue to be a vital
part of the educational scene. In-service training brings to
education new methods, materials and services to be discussed, examined, developed, and adapted toward the ever-
present goal of improving education for all who seek it.

APPENDIX ONE

Diagram of Media Terminology

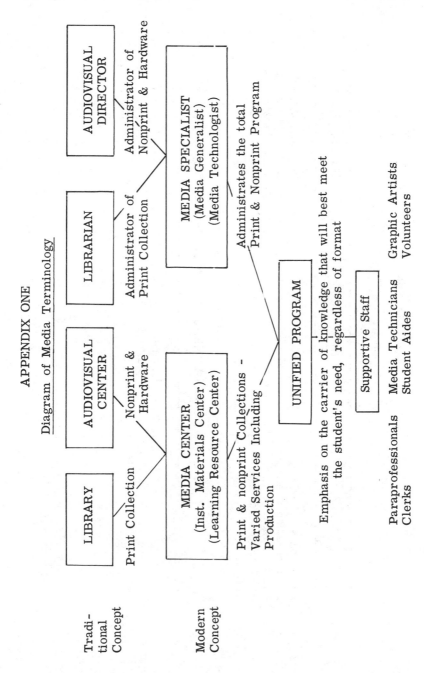

Traditional Concept

LIBRARY	AUDIOVISUAL CENTER	LIBRARIAN	AUDIOVISUAL DIRECTOR

Print Collection — Nonprint & Hardware

Administrator of Print Collection — Administrator of Nonprint & Hardware

Modern Concept

MEDIA CENTER
(Inst. Materials Center)
(Learning Resource Center)

Print & nonprint Collections –
Varied Services Including
Production

MEDIA SPECIALIST
(Media Generalist)
(Media Technologist)

Administrates the total
Print & Nonprint Program

UNIFIED PROGRAM

Emphasis on the carrier of knowledge that will best meet
the student's need, regardless of format

Supportive Staff

Paraprofessionals   Media Technicians   Graphic Artists
Clerks   Student Aides   Volunteers

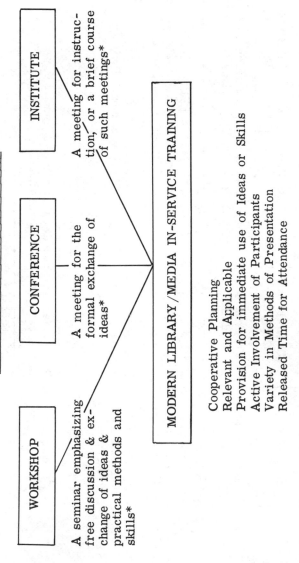

APPENDIX TWO

Diagram of In-Service Terminology

| WORKSHOP | CONFERENCE | INSTITUTE |

A seminar emphasizing free discussion & exchange of ideas & practical methods and skills*

A meeting for the formal exchange of ideas*

A meeting for instruction, or a brief course of such meetings*

MODERN LIBRARY/MEDIA IN-SERVICE TRAINING

Cooperative Planning
Relevant and Applicable
Provision for immediate use of Ideas or Skills
Active Involvement of Participants
Variety in Methods of Presentation
Released Time for Attendance

*Webster's Seventh New Collegiate Dictionary, G&C Merriam, 1970.

INDEX